Veiled Desire

VEILED DESIRE
Augustine on Women

KIM POWER

CONTINUUM • NEW YORK

1996

The Continuum Publishing Company
370 Lexington Avenue
New York, NY 10017

Printed in the United States of America

ISBN: 0-8264-0934-2

Library of Congress Catalog Card Number: 96-85678

Patrick Cyril Monaghan
12 May 1910–18 October 1994

This one was for you, Dad.

Contents

PREFACE

THIS book had its genesis in postgraduate research on woman as the image of God. I discovered that the contemporary debates were dependent on the patristic texts which cast the moulds of stereotypical gender roles in western anthropology.

A deeper pastoral question underlies the historical study; a question that our era has in common with Augustine's. What is the source of the distortion in relationships between men and women, which makes the search for loving intimacy such a hazardous quest? What led western culture to believe in the inferior status of women, and the virtual impossibility of non-genital friendships between men and women? What role has theology played in creating and/or maintaining asymmetrical power relations within our societies and institutions? How was one of the most influential theologians in Christian history influenced by his experience and culture, and where was he able to transcend it in developing his anthropology?

It is my hope that this study will be helpful not only to historical theologians working in patristics or early medieval studies, but to scholars in other theological and feminist arenas who wish to be informed about the Christian influence on cultural interpretations of sex and gender, and the manner in which these are encoded in gendered symbols and sexual meanings to express and inculcate religio-cultural ideals. Thus I have aimed to make the material as accessible as possible to readers who will not have specialist training in the field. As a scholar, I have desired to make access to the primary sources as easy as possible, for that is where the evidence lies. So I have provided references for the texts in both Latin and Greek as well as the English translations. The exceptions are the Greek classical sources, Canons from Synods and Councils, and Philo. These I have principally used in English translations.

I am conscious that to some readers use of Latin terms, or some technical jargon can seem intimidating and I take seriously the feminist critique of those who control information by the use of language codes to which few have access. I would wish to crack some of those more technical codes, so I have given Latin terms in parentheses. However, where Augustine has used certain words in a technical sense, it is more helpful to keep the Latin term and explain what it meant to him, than simply to use the English equivalent. Since Augustine's time there have been many shifts in meaning; the use of an unfamiliar term like *Scientia*, rather than Knowledge or Skill, suggests the affinities between Latin and English, yet prevents us slipping into the assumption that Augustine's concept of 'Knowledge' and ours are identical.

Since the original research was written up, the new translations of St Augustine's texts, *The Works of Saint Augustine: a translation for the 21st century*, have begun to appear. The translations of all Augustine's sermons for the first time is a real boon, and the text is eminently readable. I have been able to incorporate some of this new material, but I regret that it was not possible to alter all the original references which are scattered through various collections in the Nicene and Post-Nicene Fathers and Fathers of the Church series.

I am under obligation to my supervisors, mentors and friends Dr Michael Casey and Dr Maryanne Confoy for their help and support over the four years of my studies with them. They challenged me to strive for the best that was in me. Where I have achieved that, I am indebted to them. Where I have not, it is entirely my responsibility.

I would also like to acknowledge the help of Dr Denis Minns who not only taught me Latin, but became my friend. I thank Denis for his generosity and his encouragement. Dr Constant Mews is another to whom I am in arrears for his close reading and detailed comments on the original text and his encouragement and friendship since. I also wish to acknowledge the help of Dr Laurence McIntosh. To Father John McCristal OFM who first taught me church history I owe a debt of friendship and scholarship. John's command of his field, his delight and joy in discovery, and his merry integrity opened my eyes to what history was about, even while he believed that, 'The study of history hasn't often made us wiser, only sadder.' Vale, John.

In the interim, I have had the opportunity to spend a semester as Visiting Scholar at the University of St Thomas in St Paul, Minnesota. I thank La Trobe University for the Grant-in-aid which made this possible, and Dr David Hunter, who facilitated my visit and gave generously of his time and encouragement both professionally and personally. My thanks also to those friends who read parts of the manuscript and helped me 'debug it' for the non specialist reader. I also wish to thank my editor, Jane Williams, for her gracious patience in initiating me into the processes of publication and editing a manuscript which grew to alarming proportions in the revision.

My family and friends had much to bear with in the final stages of my research. This last rewrite was easier for them, mainly because they had almost all left home. To those who couldn't, my husband, Paul and my son, Daniel, my heartfelt gratitude. To all of them, I thank you for your love and your support.

Finally I would like to thank all those who believed in me whenever I stopped believing in myself. My sisters, my friends, and my colleagues belonging to La Trobe Post-graduate Religious Studies group. And I thank too the women I have met whose friendship and encouragement kept me persevering through some difficult times. Special thanks to my mother for her support and encouragement. Her faith in me has been a precious gift. My deepest regret is that my father, who encouraged my scholarship from my earliest years, did not live to see this book come to fruition.

PART I
Introductory

1

THEORETICAL CONCERNS AND SCHOLARLY INFLUENCES

'LATE have I loved you, Beauty so old and so new: late have I loved you.'[1] Augustine's cry has echoed down the ages, palpable with yearning and regret for the lost years. Yet, when the passage is taken out of context, the object of his love and desire remains a mystery. Does he yearn for a beloved? Is he paying a Keatsian homage to personified Beauty? In context, it is clear that he cries to God, but the text serves as an example of the ambiguity of the language of desire. Augustine's passionate desire for God expresses itself in the same language another might use to a lover, yet within the Christian tradition the latter desire has been suspect at best. Such desire directed to God is good, such desire between human partners is a far more questionable emotion. One cannot desire God too much, but all other desires, especially sexual desire, run the risk of becoming inordinate.

To complicate matters, the interpretation of desire is intricately interwoven with gender issues and values. It has become a truism of feminist scholarship that woman is not only the object of desire but equated with it; but in the Christian domain God, too, is the object of desire. The Christian discourse of desire sets up a choice between woman and God, wherein the sexually desirable woman is represented as being in direct conflict with God for the hearts of men. The other side of the coin is that properly ordered desire for God will eradicate disorderly desire for women. Thus the actual experience of desire is judged by its object and by its orderliness.

The papal document *Inter insigniores* established another criterion for the judgement of desire. Desire is judged not only by its order and its object, but by the gender of the subject. In *Pacem in terris*, Pope John XXIII had discerned that one of the three signs of the times that demonstrated the action of the Holy Spirit within the world was women's desire for an increasingly active and participative life in both church and world. Yet *Inter insigniores* judged that the yearning in the hearts of men which is discerned as the first sign of the vocation to priesthood is in women not a sign of a

vocation but the wish to use the ministerial priesthood as a means
of social advancement – a judgement that may say more about the
authors of the document than about women themselves. Thus
desire is gendered in its subject and object. The female as both
subject and object of desire is equivocal at best and dangerous at
worst.

Woman's symbolic status as dangerous desire reinforces her
uncertain standing within the Christian community and impinges
directly on the way in which she is perceived as the image of
God. In recent decades, religious attitudes to women, encoded in
canonical texts, have been made more conscious and overt in the
debates over the liturgical participation and ordination of women.
From these it has become clear that although the Catechisms might
proclaim that all human beings are made in the image and likeness
of God, this is not necessarily interpreted as applying to men and
women in the same way. Viewed through the Incarnation, maleness
is religiously legitimated as the normative human condition.

The magisterial position is a product of traditional Christian
anthropology which is itself premised on the assumptions, first,
that biological sex essentially determines the broad parameters of
gendered behaviour in social roles and relations, and second, that
sexual difference implies inequality. So any discussion of woman in
the Vatican documents, and any affirmation of her public place, is
always with the caveat that this not be at the expense of her feminine
nature and role. *Mulieris dignitatem* has proclaimed that woman's
fulfilment is found solely in loving others, and fulfilment is dependent on a spouse to find its full flowering.[2]

Papal texts are an intriguing blend of patristic anthropology and
Victorian sentimentalism. The ontological inferiority of women
found in the ancient texts has been supplanted by the argument
from complementarity. Woman is now equal but different, and the
difference determines her destiny and her subordination. Particularly significant is the manner in which the argument from complementarity has been used to maintain the power relationships
established in the patristic texts.

Both ancient and modern writings appeal to a biological determinism to legitimate the structures of power in heterosexual social
relations. In both, the explanation of woman's nature is totally
male-defined, that is, androcentric. Androcentrism is any mode
of thinking, understanding or expression which is formed almost
exclusively by male experience and understanding and which identifies male experience with 'human' experience.[3] In a document in
which the Pope explains a mother's feelings when she gives birth,
and defines the source of her fulfilment and the nature of her social
role, he does not draw once on women's experience as evidenced

by his sources. Not one of his citations is from women's writings, but eight are from Augustine's. In both anthropologies the differences between men and women are so great that women do not share in the *imago Dei* in the same way that men do. Hence they cannot represent the Christ. The thorny questions that this raises about women's salvation are never directly addressed. The contemporary assumption seems to be that although women cannot represent the Christ, Christ as the fullness of humanity can represent women. But if the magisterium were true to their sources, then they would acknowledge that, in the Augustinian texts, Christ does not and cannot represent women.

It is hoped that this study will enable a critical examination of Christian anthropology through an analysis of Augustine's writings on women. The goal of this book is to demonstrate how introducing the question of attitudes to women reveals that sexual meanings and the interpretation of gender are not peripheral to 'mainstream' theology but central to questions of church identity, anthropology, power and relationship.

It is virtually a truism that Augustine was one of the men who made the West. So any historical theologian struggling to understand why Christianity in general and Catholicism in particular has such difficulty in affirming the full human dignity of women as the image of God must turn to Augustine's system of thought, which was the distillation of the fourth-century debates over the place of sexed and gendered being in creation. His anthropology became one of the platforms of orthodoxy and his concepts of order and holiness have shaped western thinking for sixteen hundred years.[4] It has been suggested that he devoted more sustained reflection to sexuality than any Christian writer before or probably after him.[5] Certainly, his resolution of the fourth-century debates about the significance of sexual difference and its place in creation has been perceived as the dominant voice in the Christian discourse of sexuality.

Theoretical concerns

One of the dangers in attempting to understand the writings of a man so distant in time, belonging to a culture which informs ours still, yet which is in many ways so alien, is that the differences are elided. This may happen particularly if 'sexuality' is the topic. Since the eighteenth century, western culture has developed the discourse of sexuality. Yet very often modern commentators on 'sexuality' use it as a global term without acknowledgment of the differences between modernity and antiquity. Often sexuality is the term employed to discuss attitudes to the body and sexual intercourse, but gender analysis may often be absent, and the power dynamics of social relations ignored.[6] In modern sexuality theory, sexuality is far more complex. It connotes personal identity, and is seen as central to the individual's sense of authentic selfhood. Sexuality is defined by the object of sexual desire, as heterosexual, homosexual, bi-sexual, transsexual, and to a greater or lesser degree is perceived as culturally constructed in the interests of those in power who control the discourses which frame it. Since the eighteenth century, medicine and psychoanalysis have been seen as the definitive discourses, and it is an act of personal liberation to seize back control of one's sexuality.

The ancients did not think in these categories. Theirs was the discourse of desire. Certain objects and expressions of desire were appropriate, others were not. Cultures differed in their judgements, but the object of desire did not define the individual. The Greeks exalted homosexual love between male peers, because they were spiritual, intellectual and emotional equals, but they did not perceive themselves as homosexual in modern terms. The Romans denigrated the man who engaged in homosexual practices, not because he was 'homosexual' but because one partner was passive, a role which was not in keeping with the active subjectivity of Roman men, as passivity was considered a feminine trait. Thus whilst it might have been acceptable for a free man to take the active role with youths or slaves, it was not acceptable to be the passive partner to one's peer. This difference in itself illustrates the manner in which cultures construct 'sexuality' by interpreting sexual behaviour and responses according to the dominant cultural values.

For the Greeks, sexual love was at its best when celebrated by equals; women were not men's equals, so mutual male relationships were exalted over asymmetrical heterosexual ones. However, the Roman ideal posited a superior active partner and an inferior passive partner; as women were not men's equals and were defined as passive complements to men's activity, heterosexual unions were to be preferred. The ancients believed in biological determinism, despite the different ways in which desire was expected to express itself, while modern theorists argue for the cultural construction of gendered behaviours; some even go so far as to say that the biological sex, usually considered a given, is itself subject to cultural inscriptions on the body. So how is the gap to be bridged in a way that respects the otherness of the text and yet reveals its significance for theology and cultural studies today?

In 1981, the influential studies published by Sherry Ortner and Harriet Whitehead found it more useful to speak of sexual meanings and symbol systems rather than 'sexuality', and they pointed to sexual symbolism as a transhistorical nexus of political, economic and kinship symbol systems, congregating around the concepts of honour, shame and power.[7] Hence, I would argue that the contemporary discourse of sexuality and the ancient discourse of desire find their common interpretive horizon in concerns about the meaning of sexual difference and its significance for social structures and power relations. Such concerns are a part of the attempt to answer the fundamental question, 'What does it mean to be human?', when humanity is a sexed species. Therefore sexuality must be studied as a central aspect of cultural systems.

Applied to Christianity in late antiquity, this translates to the role of theological discourses in fostering an ascetic consciousness, the sexual meanings and symbols which they employed to explain Christian understandings of the cosmos, and the social roles which they prescribed for each gender. Culturally determined gender roles defined the division of labour, the hierarchy of social or ecclesial relations, and access to power, resources and decision making. Different forms of Christianity, with different visions of an unfallen world and differing beliefs about the degree to which eschatology was realised, developed different structures. The fourth century was the time when 'orthodoxy' was forged from the polemical debates about Christologies and their concomitant anthropologies and ecclesiologies.[8]

The interdependence of intellectual discourses, political power and behavioural disciplines in forging orthodoxy reminds us that they are interrelated in complex webs of meanings and symbols that sometimes resist being isolated for independent scrutiny. For example, those who dominate the discourse stand in certain relationships of power to others; discourse influences the practices which form the community and the individual subject; yet new experience through new disciplines can initiate new discourse.

The most influential cultural theorist for my purposes has been Mary Douglas.[9] Douglas has demonstrated in her studies on organisational belief systems that societies and organisations are not structured according to what they believe, but that they believe in systems which are congruent with their lives and experience. This is a development of her earlier research on body symbolism, which showed how the structure and order attributed to the body are those most valued in the society itself. The perceived naturalness of the body serves to establish the social structures that it embodies as 'natural' and providential.

Thus Douglas inverts our normal understanding of body symbolism. The body is not used as a symbol because it is essentially 'like' the community it symbolises; rather the powers and dangers credited to the social structure are reproduced in the microcosm of the human body.[10] If the society is hierarchical, the structure of the body will be seen as hierarchical; if male power is the rule, then what are perceived as the properly 'ruling' parts of the body will be masculinised. Hence body symbolism expresses and legitimates the dominant values of the community. But because the body is the symbolic tool, the construction of the symbol is hidden and 'seems to be more natural than language'.[11] Because the body on which culture inscribes meaning is a gendered body, sexual symbolism can be expected to play a dominant role in expressing cultural values. In this way, the biological differences between male and female bodies become symbolic of other cultural boundaries and categories. As a boundary between the categories of man and woman is a human universal, and as male leadership in its varying forms is common to almost all cultures, it is not surprising that the use of sexual symbols to encode status and prestige is transcultural and transhistorical.[12]

Thus in classical and Christian thought, God is to creation as man is to woman, God is to church as man is to woman, heaven is to earth as man is to woman, public is to private as man is to woman, night is to day as man is to woman, spirit/soul is to flesh as man is to woman. This is not just another way of pointing out that dualistic thinking has been imposed on anthropology. It is saying that two sexes which are experienced as the primary categories of existence are therefore especially appropriate to define other cultural boundaries. If humanity is gendered, then the cosmos must be so also. Because male and female are perceived as natural categories, their symbolic use helps to construe other categories and boundaries as eminently natural also. Where gender difference is used to ascribe different status, power and value, the beliefs about gender are then read onto cosmos and into philosophical systems through the gendered symbolism they employ.[13] The structure of the cosmos will mirror the structures of the society.

Douglas's work has been supported by recent anthropological studies which have demonstrated how sexual symbols and religiously legitimated taboos and rituals are used to enhance men's honour and constrain women's power in contexts where women have the ability to subvert male authority and to impinge on male honour.

This is consistent with Douglas's argument that societies distinguish between 'clean' and 'unclean' power to define the proper order of society. Those holding office in the explicit, religiously legitimated social structures are credited with consciously controlled powers. In contrast, those whose roles are less explicit tend to be credited with unconscious, uncontrollable powers, that menace those in better defined positions. Douglas found cross-cultural evidence that impurity, formlessness, inarticulateness and disorder coalesce to symbolise dangerous power.[14] Conversely, purity, form and order become synonymous, and identified with orthodox power. To control the subversion of masculinised holiness and integrity, the explicit structures are endowed with punitive power that maintains them in being.[15] In this way, 'natural' symbols and cultural structures are correlated to maintain those structures and explain why they must be thus and no other.

One gap identified in anthropological studies has been the extent to which gender relations within Christian thought can be subsumed under the category of the prestige system.[16] Therefore the analysis of the Augustinian texts will pay particular attention to body symbolism, to language about honour and shame, and its use to legitimate access to power and status. The emphasis will be placed on the manner in which Augustine took the cultural values of his time and through his manipulation of sexual meanings and gendered symbols helped construct the face of Christian patriarchy.

One great advantage for the Augustinian scholar is that Augustine left primary sources which permit insight not only into his intellectual processes, but also into his personal dynamics and development. These sources allow the historian to pursue the connections between his experience and his theology, his experience embracing both the dominant beliefs and attitudes of his cultural and social milieux and the unique quality of his life within those milieux.

Scholarly influences

This project builds on the work of other scholars in a variety of disciplines. Research in feminist and historical theology on women or sexuality has tended to focus on broad surveys of the Christian tradition, or has attempted to cover the wide spectrum of patristic thought in articles and essay collections.[17] There has been a great deal accomplished in the last few decades. First there are the Augustinian and patristic scholars. If it is true, as Augustine's biographer once said, that Augustine wrote so much that no one could read it all in a lifetime, then the wealth of secondary material would occupy several lifetimes.[18]

In interpreting the texts, the insights of anthropologists and historians concerning culture and social groupings have been amplified by those of psychology concerning individual personality dynamics. The result of a misspent youth as a psychologist is that questions about psychological dynamics are virtually a given part of my approach to the texts. The school to which I owe most is that of the developmental psychologists influenced by Erik Erikson. Erikson's initial work on early life stages has been complemented by that of Roger Gould. Gould sets forth a perceptive and insightful developmental model of adult growth which highlights the need for individuals to develop the characteristics of the opposite sex stereotype if they are to become fully mature human beings.[19] However, my use of psychological theory tends to the eclectic. The work of Melanie Klein and Dorothy Dinnerstein has sharpened my awareness of the significance of the very early mother–child dynamics which, they have argued, do so much to perpetuate gender stereotypes. Klein wrote the seminal text on the psychosexual development of the child, and the introjection of the 'good/bad' mother within the psyche.[20] Her theories were grounded in therapeutic work with children, and she is less culture-bound than Freud because she places the roots of psychosexual dynamics in the child's first year, when in most cultures the child's primary carer is a woman, who both nurtures and controls the child, attracting both love and anger.[21] Building on Klein's work, Dinnerstein explains the social perception of woman as resulting from child-rearing practices in patriarchal society, again emphasising the role of the primary carer in the child's infancy.[22]

Another fertile stimulus was the Jungian theory of archetypes, especially the work of Neumann on the 'Great Mother' in religious thought. Neumann's work offers an understanding of how feminine nature is consistently understood and symbolised by humanity, across cultures and across time.[23] More recently, analyses of the archetype of the Virgin in western culture have provided further food for thought.[24] It has been argued that Jung is vulnerable to critique on the point of the transhistorical and transcultural nature of his archetypes.[25] He is most vulnerable on the question of archetypal manifestation as an expression of instinct. Jung declared that specific images and motifs are representations which link historical consciousness with ancient symbols expressing the instinctual. However, it is arguable that the spontaneous and compelling nature of the archetypal symbol is not the result of instinct, but intuitive perception of significant meaning 'handed down' from time immemorial.[26] So Jungian insights may adapt to theories of the cultural construction of identity. In European thought, the sexual stereotyping found from Plato, to whom Jung is indebted, to the present is enough to account for the transhistorical similarities. The commonality of maternal care and the predominance of male leadership in most cultures is enough to account for many transcultural parallels. As Jungian scholars have noted, the differences indicate to us the particular historical context which helps to illuminate the meaning of the archetype for any particular age. The Augustinian material on Mary indicates how cultures and even individuals at crucial times shape and develop aspects of the archetypal figure, highlighting one aspect, erasing another.

These psychological tools do not dominate the analysis, but are utilised where they may prove helpful – to illuminate some aspects of Augustine's relationship with Monica, the dynamics of grief resolution in his dismissal of his concubine, the comparison of Marian imagery with other images of a divine virgin-mother.

As an interpreter, I take the text and the author's intention seriously, but I believe that the text can convey more meaning than the author consciously intended. The analysis will allow for levels of meaning in the texts, and will take into account both the author's personality and biography, and the possibility of inconsistencies arising not so much from lack of logic but from the differing contexts within which the issue of women arises.

2

INTERPRETING AUGUSTINE

IN the previous chapter, reference was made to the danger of eliding the differences between Augustine's era and our own with regard to the discourse which controls gender issues. If these differences are not kept in mind, there is a danger not only that Augustine will be misread, but that he will be misjudged. Our modern consciousness will receive the text differently because what we take for granted, our horizon of belief, differs greatly from his. It is one thing to judge whether Augustine's theology is still appropriate for our own era, and another thing altogether to condemn him for thinking like a man of his own time. So it is worth while to make explicit the similarities and differences in our concerns and our assumptions. His era and ours have in common enormous social and cultural changes. As a result, both are confronted with shifting national borders and cultural identities. In both, Christianity faced and still faces a major identity crisis, provoking questions about women's roles and access to power, information and decision-making in religious contexts; the restructuring of the church; the question of charismatic or institutionalised power; and the chance to be open to the revelation of the Spirit in doing a new thing on earth. In the guises of Gnosticism and New Age spirituality, both eras too have been permeated by a 'free-floating spirituality' which has affected all religious traditions and philosophical endeavours in subtle ways. In both ancient and modern times they have brought sharply into focus questions of mediation between the spiritual and the material world, be that expressed in images of hypostases, protective deities, patronal saints, guardian angels or spirit guides.

But the differences run deep: not only the different discourses which convey sexual meanings, but attitudes to the body and the material, biological paradigms, and the relation of the individual to the group. It is the very things which are taken for granted and so never articulated that can be of prime importance. One extremely important factor is that the dominant biological model of late antiquity assumed that only men held procreative power. This assumption legitimated men's power, prestige and authority over women, and led to a belief in the ontological inferiority of women both physically and morally. The twentieth century assumes that both partners contribute to procreation, and whilst the issue of gender roles is still being renegotiated, it is arguable that the modern women's movement can be traced back to women's claim to greater power when medicine rediscovered their ovaries.[1] Certainly it would be a brave theologian who argued for the intrinsic inferiority of women either physically or morally today.

Although both periods share a 'free-floating spirituality' their attitudes to the material world are often radically opposed. In antiquity Gnosticism expressed the belief that élite knowledge was the prerogative of the few, to whom it had been personally entrusted through religious revelation, and it had a deep distrust of the material world.[2] Gnostics believed that the spirit was trapped in matter and must reject the material world to be free. In these tenets, albeit taken to extremes, their religious formulae reflected the spirit of their age. Today's 'New Age' spirituality has heard more rumours of angels than the desert Fathers, but believes deeply in the goodness of the interpenetration of spirit and matter.

A third significant variable is the concept of the individual. Although it is sometimes said that Augustine was instrumental in shifting the focus onto the individual and his or her internal dynamics, within his own era this must be balanced by the fact that public, communal life was what mattered. This life might be built on the *familia* as a social unit, but the gaze of powerful men was directed outward. The personal was the private, and it had limited meaning in antiquity. Whether in state or church, major social investment was in the community. Today, individualism reigns supreme to such an extent that individual rights and privileges are hotly defended, but individual obligation to the community often has the same limited meaning as the private had in antiquity. If, in antiquity, people knew where they belonged but perhaps felt constrained individually, today individual constraints are dissolving while people seek for somewhere to belong.

The great disjuncture between Augustine's world and my own interpretive horizon lies between the assumptions we hold on the ontological nature of women, and the divinely given 'natural law' which prescribes a hierarchically ordered cosmos with social and ecclesial leadership a male prerogative. My own assumptions have been formed not only by intellectual issues and scholarship, but by life experience as a Christian woman which provokes questions and the search for the answers. Thus no more than Augustine's can my research be entirely value-free. In all my research I am informed by a feminist perspective, and in the theological arena would align

myself with those who understand feminist theology as a critical
theology of liberation.[3] Sexism, racism and classism are interdependent and inherent in any ideology that posits hierarchies of
human being as constituent of the natural order. Fundamentally, I
am concerned with critiquing structures which constrain both
women and men to remain half-human, and demonstrating how
interpretations of sexual difference are central to Christian anthropology.

Researching women's history

Sources and the scholarship prior to twentieth-century feminism
are androcentric. The thinking and self-understanding of women
is also androcentric when formed by male-dominated institutions
which do not take female experience into account in their definitions of what is valuable. Conservative and progressive writers
concur that theology is androcentric,[4] but the conservative position
asserts that this is because 'women are less interested in theological
discussion'.[5] That this type of assertion is made without regard to
the manifest behaviour or felt experience of women is odd, and
itself exemplifies androcentric thinking.

Androcentrism also affects the translation of sources. English
translations use the generic man for the Latin *homo*, meaning human
being, and the feminist scholar must be wary of working from
translations which give no indications as to whether the original
language is inclusive or not. At times it masks the intent of the
author, as when 'man' is used for 'anyone' in categories which
included women in antiquity, but might not include them today.
When Augustine is concerned to articulate very clearly on issues
involving social relations, he picks his way carefully through the
argument and is careful in his use of language.[6] He uses inclusive
language in most doctrinal treatises. However, his language is often
illuminating when the reference is in passing. He slips into 'the
little woman', *muliercula*,[7] and speaks of the 'torpid effeminacy of
inaction'.[8] Although when speaking of the 'just man', he usually
employs *homo*, occasionally he slides between *homo* and *vir* (man)
as if the two are interchangeable, not surprising when maleness
expressed the form of humanity closest to God.[9] But it means that
the interpreter must be careful in taking *homo* to include women in
all contexts and in all authors.[10]

The under-representation of women in the primary sources
themselves is related to ancient androcentrism, and to constraints
placed on women. Many women did not receive the education that
might have enabled them to leave literary sources, nor did most
women have the leisure to pursue philosophical reflection. Further-

more, epigraphic evidence tends to use stock language, giving little insight into relationships, especially between women and children. Finally, most of the anecdotal evidence about women in social history relates to the nobility and thus must be applied circumspectly to other classes of women.[11]

Christian sources, even within the milieu of powerful ascetic women such as Melania the Elder and Macrina, are similarly problematic. Even though these women corresponded with bishops who sought their opinion and patronage, none of their letters has been preserved.[12] Despite the bond between Monica and Augustine, nothing she wrote is extant, nor is the epistle from the influential women he says he used as evidence in church disputes. It is uncertain just how much effect the legislation of church synods had, especially outside their own jurisdiction, but the Synod of Elvira legislated early in the fourth century that women should not receive any mail addressed to them personally. All correspondence should be conducted through the male head of the household. It is known that women did study and write, but obedient women handed their work over to their clerical mentors or clients to be approved and published under the cleric's name.[13]

In evaluating writing about women there is the need to distinguish between what is descriptive and what is prescriptive. For example, Augustine writes that ascetic women are to withdraw from the world into a life of prayer.[14] But one of the few fourth-century sources by a woman reveals that she travelled on a long biblical pilgrimage for which she was honoured and respected.[15] So what is received in sources about women is not objective reality, but one vision of how reality ought to be. The focus is usually on the male writers and their concerns about women rather than on the women themselves.

Methodological issues in interpreting Augustine

More specific methodological issues arise with respect to the interpretation of Augustine's work. When considering how a text was received in the past and how it might be received in the present, the audience of the text can be as much a key to its correct interpretation as its content.[16]

Where Augustine is writing on difficult and often abstract theological questions which he addressed in all their complexity, it is most probable that his intended audience was not the wider Christian community but the spiritual ones (*spirituales*), those whose reflection about God had moved away from the more anthropomorphic imagery of popular Catholicism under the influence of Neoplatonism.[17] Mature works such as *De Genesi ad litteram* and *De*

Trinitate fall into this category and it will be assumed that the teachings in such works can be regarded as accurate reflections of his thought. However, not all his work was directed solely towards this élite group. The sermons were directed to the whole congregation of the church at Hippo; his epistles were written to a wide range of individuals from his peers to his students, and the *Confessiones* were written for the widest possible audience.

In the sermons, Augustine was attempting to reach a heterogeneous congregation composed of men and women, free and slave, rich and poor. His concerns were pastoral and his rhetoric often colourful. It is in the sermons that we find a great deal of his Marian imagery, which suggests that it was a vehicle for presenting his ascetic agenda and his ideology of male headship to popular Christianity. As a general principle, it is considered that a trained rhetor, to whom words were 'choice and costly glasses', truly valuable only if they contain the wine of truth, is likely to be precise in conveying his meaning as fully as possible, whatever he writes.[18] Augustine consistently strove to proclaim the Word, and at the most fundamental level to speak the truth as he understood it. However, in the sermons, designed to engage the emotions and enthusiasm of his congregation, and in his polemical works written to demolish his opponents, the role of rhetoric must be considered in evaluating content.

There is a school of scholarly opinion which argues that symbolic gendering of universal order into 'male' and 'female' elements is simply a rhetorical device which has no real implications for social relations and is, in fact, in tension with the 'true' beliefs of patristic authors about women.[19] This argument tries to distance ideas and rhetorical devices from the 'real' world.[20] In doing so, it neglects the fact that these arguments and devices were attempts to portray the divinely regulated real world, albeit in a highly coloured manner, and that the function of rhetoric is to persuade through the imagination what one might not be able to convey through dialectics – a fact that Augustine himself used to justify his use of rhetoric in sermons and treatises to teach the 'unwise'.[21]

He also commented on the use of hyperbole, which clearly exaggerates or extenuates without 'real departure from the part of truth', and there is little doubt that where he uses stock images such as 'chains' for sexual ties, or 'beastliness' or 'festering sores' for sexual desire, his audience would receive them as such.[22] Nevertheless, the impact of constantly reiterated imagery of wounding, bestiality or imprisonment for sexual love should not be underestimated. It is the way in which rhetorical images are caught up in the cultural imagination, replicated in images and art, that impresses them into the individual psyche and integrates them into the system of cultural symbols which will ensure these meanings are passed on to the next generation.

What is most powerful about Augustine's own literary style is the way he weaves scriptural verses and allusions into his writing so intimately that his own writing shares in the authority of the divine Word.[23]

In his epistles Augustine was addressing the theological, pastoral or personal problems of his correspondents; he was responding to problems important enough for people to write to him, sometimes over considerable distances. This applies especially to the letters' theological content, but also to matters of his daily life. The fact that they were usually directed to specific situations means that care should be taken in generalising from statements in individual letters. Only if the same advice or principle is found consistently in other epistles or treatises can it be considered a general principle. It is an interesting point that Augustine was well aware that no matter how carefully he wrote, his words would be open to multiple readings. Not only did this not worry him, he welcomed the fact that his hearers and readers could find levels of meaning in his work. In heaven, Augustine assumed, truth is one, but on earth, like light refracted, truth has many colours and, likewise, many levels of truth are to be found in Scripture. He emphasised that truth was never his alone, but hoped that his writing would carry all meanings to all readers, rather than one truth, one particularity.[24] Augustine has often been called the first psychologist. Perhaps in this he was the first postmodernist. Certainly this book hopes to offer one colour of the spectrum of 'truth' about Augustine's work.

Interpreting the Confessiones

The major interpretive problem arises with the *Confessiones*. Why were they written and why did Augustine invent a new genre? Ostensibly the *Confessiones* are addressed to God. Augustine's primary intention was to explicate and develop all the permutations of the word *confessio* in relation to God. He intended confession of praise to God, confession of faith in God, and confession of sin against God. The three aspects are intimately intertwined. But why such a public confession and why use autobiography?[25]

The first clue is found in Book 1.1 where Augustine states the dependence of conversion upon those who preach the faith, and affirms his own debt to such preachers.[26] In Book 2.3 Augustine testified that his goals were to bring others to faith in God, and to deepen and clarify his own understanding of God working in his life.[27] He was further motivated by a need to justify himself in the light of personal criticism directed against his ambition and his unorthodox election to the See of Hippo,[28] and to legitimate his authority as God-given in battles with doctrines and churches he perceived as heretical.[29]

If Augustine desired to inspire conversion to the Catholic faith, why use autobiographical narrative? Part of the answer is in the form itself. Like that of biblical narrative, the form of the *Confessiones* is integral to the content it conveys. It reveals that salvation is experienced as God's deliverance of the individual within history.[30] The *Confessiones* recount Augustine's own salvation history. They serve as a theological review of the past and also create a new world for the future shaped by his ascetic vision.[31]

Also, conversion stories had had a powerful impact on Augustine, and he was convinced of their power to touch the heart. Immediately before recounting his own conversion he places a multiple conversion story, which confronted him with his own sordidness.[32] In revealing to his fellow human beings his drivenness, his yearnings and his redemptive relationship with God, he exposed the matters closest to their hearts, and invited them to a similar conversion.[33]

Can the *Confessiones* be considered objective history? Scholars agree that what we have in the *Confessiones* is Augustine's later reconstruction of events as he makes sense of his life in the context of God's grace.[34] This becomes clearer when Augustine's conversion story is read in the Cassiciacum dialogues. The difference between the two accounts is a measure of the degree to which theological reflection developed and changed his thought in the ten-year period between the two texts.[35] Thus, the pertinent question is not, 'Did this event really happen like this?' but, 'What significance did this hold for Augustine?'[36] How did it colour the issues that he perceived as integral to a Christian world-view?[37] So interrelated are the proclamation and the narrative of his 'gospel', that we cannot understand his ideas without reference to his own estimation of his experience.[38] The narrative is as much a disguised account of where he stands in the present as it is an ostensible description of what occurred in the past.[39]

So what kind of world does Augustine create from his reflection?[40] It is a world where life is lived under the hand of a God who is committed to the gracious and graced redemption of the sinner: a world that makes sense out of the call to live heroically in the face of inevitable death, because it asserts the reality of life beyond death.[41] Therefore, although the *Confessiones* undoubtedly has its roots in Augustine's experience, the text may be considered as indicative of significant events and attitudes at the time of writing, rather than as a strictly objective, historical account of Augustine's life.

Chronology and theological development

In the following chapters the themes and concerns emerging from Augustine's broader social and ecclesial context will be discussed and related to Augustine's own writings to reveal his distinctive approach to these issues.

Part III will examine his relationships with women to determine not only their influence on his later theology, but also the ideology of Christian womanhood that is present in his *Soliloquia*, his *Confessiones* and his *Epistles* to women. Part IV will treat the systematisation of his gender ideology in the theology of the *imago Dei* found in the *De Trinitate*, the symbolic use of marital imagery, and his discourse of the veil. Part V takes for its subject his Marian writings, which construct an ideal woman to serve his anthropology. These writings are found in his sermons, and in two groups of polemical texts. The earlier texts, circa 400 CE, are directed against Jovinianism and ascetic extremists, and the later against the Pelagians, circa 419 CE and after.

Although texts will be treated in roughly chronological order, since Augustine's thoughts on gender issues developed during his lifetime, inevitably there will be some overlap in the dates of texts in each chapter. But it is possible to see his anthropological system taking shape – to see how his understanding of sex and gender informs not only social relations but his imagery of the church and his definition of ecclesial order to create a consistently gendered cosmos wherein masculine and feminine express spiritual values and the hierarchy of holiness.

PART II
Women, church and Graeco-Roman culture

3

WOMEN AND SOCIAL RELATIONS

THE fourth century was a period when Christianity was in flux, groping towards new institutional and liturgical forms. The conversion of Constantine had brought about the cessation of persecution and a Christian mandate. The clash of ecclesial and cultural values in the post-Constantinian Church as converts flooded in meant that issues of proper ecclesial order had to be renegotiated. Order is by definition about boundaries and limits. The attempt to establish clear Christian boundaries and categories manifested itself in the conflicts over orthodoxy in the Manichaean, Arian, Jovinianist, Donatist, Pelagian and Origenist controversies – to name just some major battlegrounds. Emperors legislated for the church, and bishops confronted emperors. With the rise of asceticism, new forms of spirituality emerged, which affected the nature of social relations and the most significant concerns of the state. Thus the dominant discourses of religion and culture interacted to create a church in a new relationship to the state, and very different from the apostolic church.

Part II offers a very brief sketch of the late classical world-view, then highlights crucial facets of ancient cultural tradition and social practice. It will be argued that the melding of Christianity and late classical culture fostered a climate of thought which prescribed constraints on women's access to public roles. Therefore, the spotlight will be on the aspects of ancient thought particularly pertinent to the exploration of Augustine's writings on women: the prescribed order of social relations, and especially cultural attitudes towards the maternal role; the perception of women and sexuality in philosophic thinking; the interconnections between women and the sacred in more popular tradition; and the effects of the Constantinian revolution on women in the fourth-century church.

Late antique cosmology

Classical and Christian culture shared an understanding of an ordered hierarchical cosmos, under the control of a divine being, although Christianity differed from classical thought on matters such as creation *ex nihilo*, and the closeness of God to his (*sic*) creatures.[1] In both philosophic and Christian discourse this Being was defined in terms of fatherhood, although incorporeal and spiritual. As the source of creation God was its head, the one to whom worship was due. The cosmos God created was integrated, ordered and hierarchical, with its structures replicated in each order of existence, physical and social. Thus each human being and each social relationship had its own heaven and its own earth, its own spirit and matter, its own soul and body – from heaven to earth, man to woman, soul to body, master to slave. Each union was ideally ordered by the control of the material by the spiritual.[2] Thus the 'natural' cosmic order appeared to prescribe the right ordering of society, and obscured its social origins.[3] Therefore, the social structures will be explored before considering the philosophic treatment of sexual relations.

Women and social relations:[4] honour and shame

In late antiquity, men (theoretically) controlled women as they controlled children and slaves. Indeed, legally, a wife stood in the same relation to her husband as she did to her father.[5] A man was considered woman's head, both in the sense of dominance and in the sense of source. The dominant biological model in late antiquity held that only men had procreative power. So men, generically speaking, were the human 'source' of all life.[6] When proper order was maintained in both home (*domus*) and state, due honour was paid to those responsible. Where a man failed to keep proper order, he was shamed before his peers (cf. 1 Tim. 2.11–14; 3.4–13). Women's behaviour could render their men vulnerable to shame, and so they were tightly constrained by legal and religious mores.[7] Hence Graeco-Roman woman's most precious attribute was her modesty. Usually modesty is thought of in terms of sexual chastity, but one of the ancient definitions makes it clear that chastity was tied to female withdrawal from public affairs. Ulpian, in *Digests* III. 1.5, defined modesty as withdrawal from male roles and duties so that, by implication, a woman without modesty was one who intruded where she did not belong, and who could only have sexual motives for doing so.[8] It is significant that the Latin word *pudor* means both modesty and shame. The modest woman is the one who is aware of her shameful potential and so guards well against it. Late antiquity saw a nostalgia for the more restrictive mores of the Republic, and indeed Constantine introduced legislation to control respectable women's appearances in public.[9] Christianity would invoke this attitude to women's behaviour to exclude women from public ministry in the emerging institutional church from the second century on.[10]

The lives of non-reputable women are barely accessible because Constantine deemed that their vile origins 'put them beneath the consideration of the law'.[11] Indeed noble women and women below the law altogether mark the two extremes symbolised in Roman ethical and moral systems as Virtue and Vice. As will become evident throughout this chapter, the virtuous woman is marked by her modesty, the vicious woman by her sexuality: her other name is Pleasure.[12] Therefore the material in this section about maternal roles and expectations applies mainly to women who fall into the category of *materfamilias*. However, even the most privileged of women was not unaffected by the weight of cultural beliefs about woman's inferior nature, and whilst prescriptive writings may be a long way from social practice in particular situations, they do show us the 'default' settings from which women had to manoeuvre.

Roman motherhood

Susanne Dixon's research on Roman motherhood found remarkable stability in the views of the maternal ideal over several centuries, although two movements did become apparent:[13] the first defined the legal rights of women, generally giving them more legal power to act for their children,[14] the second emphasised the sentimental ideal of the conjugal and parental bond.[15]

Typically, the Roman child had access to a more extended family than the modern child, if the notion of 'family' is enlarged to embrace at least personal slaves and pedagogues.[16] Few Roman women took responsibility for their infants' daily physical care, and wet-nursing was the norm. In fact, breast-feeding was regarded as an important child-rearing function because the child was assumed to imbibe the moral qualities of the wet-nurse through her milk; hence some philosophers objected to wet-nurses on the grounds that servants were immoral, and the mother–child bond was lessened.[17]

Such beliefs were an aspect of the ancient medicine, where the capacity for virtue was tightly tied to the gendered body. Men's physical and moral superiority was based on their optimal formation in the womb, which conferred on them strength, vitality and the power to procreate.[18] Women were the weaker sex (*sexus infirmitas*) and given to levity (*levitas animi*) in both Roman law and Christian literature.[19] Hence the importance of women's education to alleviate their moral fragility, which could be passed on to children through their breast-milk.

Augustine certainly speaks of his nurses in a way that includes wet-nursing, although he states that Monica herself also fed him. Augustine recollects fondly his nurses' love for him, which he perceived as God-ordained,[20] recalling how easily he learnt Latin as a babe, and he contrasts this experience with the fear and discipline, 'subject to violent threats and cruel punishments', with which he learnt Greek at school.[21]

Both marriage and motherhood enhanced a woman's status. Roman marriages in earlier times had seen the wife handed over from father to husband in a fictive 'sale'. She was legally and literally in her husband's hands, for under the Republican law the power of the head of the household (*patria potestas*), meant the power of life and death over members of the household. Over time, such stringent rights were ameliorated or fell into disuse, and a less restrictive form of marriage became the norm. Known as *sine manu*, or 'free' marriage, the woman remained in the hand of her father or of his household head (*paterfamilias*).[22] To establish this, she had to spend three nights per year in her father's house. This form of marriage increased female economic independence and limited her husband's authority, over her,[23] by allowing her to bring her family's influence to bear on her spouse where necessary, assuming she had male support for her case. As the wife remained, legally, under her father's authority, her husband had no right to beat her. Her financial resources remained her own, and her independence could be further enhanced, for an upper-class woman who bore three living children (*ius trium liberorum*), or a freedwoman who bore four, was granted lifelong freedom from male guardianship (tutelage),[24] and may have had some distinction in dress conferred on her.[25]

However, even within a *sine manu* marriage, the husband retained full rights over his own children. A child was not legally part of the family until acknowledged by its father, and exposure of unwanted infants continued until well into the Christian era before it was made illegal in 374 CE. Given the preference for sons, and the expense of rearing children, scholars speculate that girls may have been exposed more than boys, as is the custom in other societies practising infanticide, but there is little extant evidence to substantiate this.[26] Despite the Augustan legislation encouraging second marriages to increase the birth rate, the Roman ideal of womanhood remained the one-man woman, the *univira*.[27] The likelihood of widowhood was very high if a woman survived childbirth, given the relatively early marriage age for girls, and the late marriage age for men.[28] This ideal was further supported by the legislation of

390 CE, which increased a mother's legal rights if she did not remarry.

The respect in which a mother was held was related to a complex interaction of factors. Although she might be learned, influential behind the political scenes, or even actively acting as a patron as did Livia, the wife of Augustus, her public praise would focus on the domestic virtues, modesty and chastity.[29] There were several significant factors which operated to increase feminine honour. First, her moral reputation and her personal distinction, which in turn conferred status on her children; second, her personal wealth and her power to bequeath legacies, so that those desirous of becoming heirs had constraints on their behaviour;[30] third, her responsibility for rearing her children in the absence of her husband, whether through public office, military duty or death,[31] as Monica educated Augustine.[32]

As she had few legal rights, and yet was expected by society both to be responsible for the education of her children and to be the moral arbiter of their lives, her ability to fulfil her role demanded great strength of character, creating a 'formidable stereotype' of the 'unbending moral mentor, guardian of traditional virtue and object of lifelong respect comparable with, though not equal with, that accorded a *paterfamilias*'.[33] Where fathers could command, mothers must entreat, threaten or shame their children into compliance with their wishes.[34]

Thus the Roman mother was concerned with the same issues as the Roman father. Both were concerned with the continuance of the family through grandchildren, both were ambitious for their children and so fostered a thorough education, and both were concerned with their children's moral reputations.[35] Both also bore responsibility for arranging suitable marriages for their children and contributing to their daughters' dowries.[36] In Augustine's *Confessiones* we find Monica and Patricius sharing these common interests. Both wish to see him settled and producing grandchildren, both are ambitious for him in terms of his career and make sacrifices for him to this end.[37] A mother's role did not end with a child's legal majority.

However, whilst women were expected to do everything possible to further their son's careers in the public arena, it was to be from behind the scenes. Women were not permitted a public role on their own account. The exceptions were the Vestal Virgins, whose status as idealised women created a tension with the ideal of fecundity.[38] It has been argued that to men who had a vivid sense of the power of the orator over his audience, and the superiority of the teacher over his disciple, it would have been extremely inappropriate for women to take such public roles, because of women's essential inferiority to men.[39] Certainly, this reasoning is explicit in the Christian texts from the fourth century.

The role of divorce in Roman society constituted a further factor affecting parent–child relationships.[40] Where divorce occurred, children continued to reside with their fathers, although mothers were expected to maintain contact with the child(ren) and work in their interests.[41] But this only applied where both parents were Roman citizens enjoying the right to marriage (*ius connubii*) who were joined in legal marriage (*iustum matrimonium*).[42] Otherwise, children took the mother's status and name, and remained with her.

Motherhood and sentiment

It is important to note that Romans shared the stereotype of women as more emotional in general than men, and more timid altogether.[43] Mothers were expected to feel deeply for their children, and to mourn their early deaths intensely, although noble women were expected to show restraint. Indeed, mourning itself was considered a womanly (*muliebris*) activity.[44] Interestingly, in the light of the *Confessiones*, sea voyages of sons were an occasion of special anxiety and worry.[45]

Concerns for daughters, especially in childbirth, do not figure in the stereotype of the anxious mother (*anxia mater*). Whether this is because such anxiety is taken for granted because of the high maternal death rate, or whether it is because male writers were more sensitive to the relationships of mothers and sons, is impossible to determine, although Dixon inclines to the latter point of view. Nor were a mother's emotions restricted to concern. With young children, mothers were perceived as being more indulgent and less demanding than fathers, and as enjoying their children's company. Adult sons were expected to visit their mothers regularly, bringing pleasure to both parties. It appears that 'these women, who could be suitably intimidating on occasion, were meant to be charmed by their adult sons'.[46]

Control of youthful sexuality

Roman parents were not held personally responsible for their children's lapses or sexual reputations. Both Christian and pagan circles expected some youthful excesses and sexual dalliances from their sons. In fact, it was seen as virtually unavoidable.[47] Where some responsibility was imputed, fathers were perceived as more influential than mothers.[48] This may be why Augustine is more severe with Patricius when recounting his attitude to Augustine's sexual maturation.[49]

Parents did concern themselves with the sexuality of girls.[50] As we have seen, Roman society stressed female chastity and moreover, only women could be charged with adultery under classical law. Even a betrothed girl could be charged with adultery.[51] Christian law later changed this double standard. Until then, a Christian man who forgave an adulterous wife could be legally at risk, because he could be charged with pandering.[52] This pagan structure arose from the concern about paternity and descent through the male line.[53] As illegitimate children did not have citizen status, a man's offspring by slaves and concubines were not a focus of political concern. But his acknowledged children by his legal wife were. Consequently there was great concern that young women should not feel desire before marriage. As young women were considered to be sexually motivated from puberty onwards, they were married young to control their desire.[54] Apart from the social constraints of Roman life, intercourse and pregnancy were seen as both controlling desire and preventing the *hysteria* often attributed to a celibate life.[55] Young brides were often forced to a marriage bed which only reinforced their fears about sexual behaviour.[56] They were expected to bear children regularly, in the knowledge that they might not rear even a healthy child if their husband decided otherwise. Abortion was morally neutral, but only at a husband's discretion. Women who aborted would be considered as infringing the rights of the *paterfamilias*, and be perceived as motivated by adultery or greed for wealth.[57] These latter attitudes were fostered by the belief that women were essentially passive in child-bearing, being simply a vessel for the male seed.[58]

Beryl Rawson has suggested that this ideal of women's role as limited to the domestic arena, and defined by modesty, fecundity and service, was derived from early Roman origins, and fostered by the (male) leaders of society out of self-interest and self-protection.[59] Her argument is supported directly by the research of Thomas Laqueur on ancient medicine,[60] and indirectly by Peter Brown who asserts that 'the exquisite ideal of marital concord deliberately stared past the grief, pain and illness associated with childbirth. It aimed to absorb marriage into the greater order of the city.'[61] The darker side of the maternal role only emerged with the Christian ascetics who delighted in highlighting the disadvantages of marriage *vis-à-vis* virginity. Death hovered over pregnancy and childbirth.

It must always be borne in mind that this maternal stereotype was the ideal. In real life, Roman women were extremely influential within their own homes.[62] They could sit in family councils, and in late antiquity could travel with their husbands appointed to foreign service. They dined in mixed company, and could move freely in public with unveiled faces, though always appropriately attended of course.

4

PHILOSOPHY: ATTITUDES TO WOMEN AND SEXUALITY

THE cultural mores concerning women found their intellectual legitimation in the philosophic texts which, from the second century on, began to be assimilated into the thought of Christian apologists like Justin Martyr.[1] This process of assimilation was powerfully influenced by Philo of Alexandria, whose exegesis of Scripture was so informed by Platonic concepts that Jerome called him the Jewish Plato.[2]

To the new breed of Latin bishops like the urbane and intellectual Ambrose, and his would-be urbane disciple Augustine, a philosophic perspective on their scriptural exegesis was as natural as breathing. Even though Scripture might challenge some particular theory, such as the co-existence of God and matter, philosophy had shaped the categories and the very processes of their thought.[3]

Long an influence on the Roman nobility and upper classes, philosophy, especially the resurgence of Platonism, as interpreted by Plotinus, not only shaped Christian thought, but filtered through sermons and theological treatises to a wider audience.[4] Scholars agree that it was not the pure metal of Neoplatonism which had the greatest influence on Augustine, but rather an alloy of Neoplatonism and Stoic philosophy, in which the principles of the Stoa were heavily conditioned both in formulation and resolution of questions by both Christianity and Neoplatonism.[5]

After his conversion, Scripture became the criterion by which Augustine evaluated the truth of philosophy.[6] In the *Confessiones* he distinguished carefully between the wisdom of the Platonists and the full truth of the Gospel.[7] Yet often he used Platonic concepts to interpret Scripture;[8] he identified the Christian Word with the Platonic Λόγος, and believed that Platonic philosophy was the instrument used to lead him to self-knowledge and to bring him to the light of God.[9]

The social function of the philosopher

Just as significant as the maxims of the philosopher was his social role. Within the hierarchy of Roman society, the philosopher filled the role of the Christian holy man in the East or the bishop in the West. He was the man who, by rigorous discipline or denial, ascended to the highest plane of the self.[10] Standing closer to the supernatural than other men, he has been described as the 'saint of the classical culture', whilst the holy man was the *vir sapiens* of Christianity. Both administered clean power because their hearts were pure. Both stood outside of patronage systems and could judge without fear or favour.[11]

> As a consequence of this, they were allowed to wield an authority over other human beings which was frequently all the more effective for being intangible: What they taught was more true, what they commanded was more readily obeyed, and the life style was held to represent the life of a human being at its best.[12]

However, although philosophers and ascetics superficially appeared to share many characteristics, such as spiritual authority, a conversion experience, and renunciation of material desires and bodily indulgence in the service of a common goal, their fundamental ideologies differed and each group perceived the other as somehow missing the mark.[13] The earliest, and especially the Eastern Christian ascetic was a counter-cultural agent who rejected the values of the predominant culture, whereas, in Brown's assessment, the philosopher was the refined distillation of the 'idyllic essence' of that same culture.[14] Augustine's own early dream as he sought to retire from teaching and explore philosophy at Cassiciacum arose from this cultural ideal.[15] But both philosophers and ascetics could be seen as models by the groups for which they maintained the central values.[16]

The philosopher-bishop in the West

The role of the post-Constantinian Christian bishops, acting as ecclesiastical patrons, was more ambiguous. With the sacralizing of social systems, the functions of the bishop and philosopher converged. The early confrontation between ascetic and dominant culture gave way in the West to a synthesis of the self-disciplinary ideals of the philosopher and the spiritual ideals of the celibate episcopacy. This was not a surprising development given that this was the period during which the episcopacy became a goal for ambitious men.[17] Augustine himself believed that the unity of the Catholic church was dependent on the validation of social order. The social structures 'must be made to serve the Christian cause'.[18]

Augustine, order and the natural law

Fundamental to Augustine's thinking on any issue was his acceptance of the philosophical assumptions about the nature of the
created world. One such assumption crucial for Augustine was that
of order (*ordo*). At the pinnacle of the hierarchical order is the One,
who is as superior to the mind as the mind is superior to the soul.
It is in his image that spirit controls matter and soul controls body.
Likewise, creatures are ranked according to nature and species,
which leads to a natural harmony.[19] In their commentaries on
Genesis, the patristic authors conflated natural and divine law, for
the 'natural' law as perceived in creation had been mandated by the
Word of God.[20] Eric Osborn has explored the manner in which
Augustine used this concept of *ordo* to give ethical structure to
Christian love.[21] He needed such a framework to avoid an individu-
alistic mysticism in conflict with church law and order[22] but, as
Osborn notes, he worked out the *ordo amoris* so badly that it was
possible for him to legitimate persecution if motivated by love.[23]
Augustine developed order and love so thoroughly that order, not
love, became the dominant motif in a relationship.[24]

Everyone and everything in Augustine's universe had an appropriate place in the structure, and each one should desire to be ruled
according to its nature, 'namely under him to whom it ought to be
subject, and above those things to which it is to be preferred: under
him by whom it ought to be ruled, above those things which it
must govern'.[25] Built into this statement is the assumption that
those at one level of the structure are to be preferred and are
superior to others. In this he is very close to Aristotle's arguments
in *Politics*: men rule wives, parents rule children and masters slaves.[26]
Christian leadership is characterised by the primary importance of
neighbourly love, so the proper 'order of concord' requires that, in
the first place, a man injure no one and do good to everyone he
can reach, and that his subordinates obey him. Male dominance is
part of the natural order of the universe, not the result of social
organisation or of sin, although this may exacerbate the situation.
For example, the rational must rule the irrational, so man must
rule beast; as men are not beasts, slavery is the result of sin, not of
an intrinsic inferiority in the slave, as Aristotle taught.[27] But Augustine never attacks the institution of slavery *per se*. Rather he argues
that the lowly position of the servant does the slave as much good
as the master's prideful position does him harm.[28] But as men must
rule over women, the implication, at least, is that women are less
rational than all men. If the proper movement from subordinate to
superior is achieved, *ordo* is realised. Corruption of any kind leads
to disorder.[29]

When it came to gender relations, Augustine perceived women as inferior and subservient to men, even before the Fall, but he argued that then this subordination would have been a bond of love, a kind of benevolent despotism where men would lead in love and women would love to obey. Since the Fall, this inherent concord is problematic. Spouses may still serve each other with love, but male domination is mandatory to prevent the increase of corruption and sin.[30] Given his overriding assumptions concerning order, the implication here is that female autonomy, as well as female leadership, has a corrupting effect and would inevitably lead to disorder.[31] The propinquity of sin and disorder in the text collapses the categories, so that she who threatens one, threatens the other.

Ordo also structures Augustine's theology of the mystical ascent or return to God,[32] which is integral to his understanding of the mind's masculine and feminine dimensions and their relationship to one another.[33] Platonism opposed the sense world of flux and change to the unchanging reality of the world of ideas.[34] The inmost part of the soul, the mind (*nous*), exists beyond the tensions of the material world, protected in the head, and separated from the passions of the body by the neck.[35] Translated into Augustinian terms, the person who grows in the knowledge of God, in true holiness, transfers love from 'things temporal to things eternal, from things visible to things intelligible, from things carnal to things spiritual, and diligently perseveres in bridling and lessening his desire [*cupiditas*] for the former and in binding himself by love to the latter'.[36] In the context of the mystical ascent, the Forms of Plato correspond to the perfection of God as ultimate reality. 'The God who is' is the 'Being of Truth' towards which the Christian yearns and moves.[37] For Augustine, this movement is through the Feminine to the Masculine dimensions of the mind, symbolised as a movement away from the body towards the soul, a movement that will be fully documented in Part IV.

To illuminate the order of Christian love, Augustine draws parallels between three bonds which structure Christian life. They exist between Christ and the Church, husband and wife, and spirit and flesh. In all relationships the former rules and cares for the latter, and the latter obeys the former. All are good: the former 'excellently' as superiors, the latter 'fittingly' as subjects. 'Thus is the beauty of order preserved.'[38] These structures are consciously modelled on the analogy in Ephesians 5.21ff but there is evidence that they are related as much to the inculturation of patriarchal assumptions as to foundational theological principles.

For the underlying assumptions of Augustine are not theological but natural. He states that 'on natural principles it is more feasible

for one to have dominion over the many, than for many to have
dominion over one', and further concludes that 'it cannot be
doubted that it is more consonant with the order of nature that
men should bear rule over women than women over men'. He cites
1 Corinthians 11.3 and 11.18 in support of his argument. But 1
Corinthians theologically legitimates, rather than proves, his
reasoning. It does not form the basis of the argument: that is taken
from the order of nature. Although human beings must normally
rise above the natural temporal elements in themselves to become
more spiritual, it is paradoxically appropriate for men and women
to base their relationships on examples from the animal world.
He insists that 'nature loves singleness in her dominations' whilst
plurality 'exists more readily in the subordinate portion of our
race'.[39] The theological argument here assumes the philosophical
criterion of the totally self-sufficient individual as the human ideal
of integrity,[40] an ideal somewhat at odds with the Pauline concept of
the church as interdependent body (1 Cor. 12.12–31). In *De bono
conjugali* he writes: 'By a secret law of nature things that stand chief
love to be singular; but what are subject are set under, not only
one under one, but if the system of nature or society allow, even
several under one, not without becoming beauty.'[41] It is an example
of an endearing, almost naïve honesty, which emerges in Augustine's
rhetoric occasionally, that he freely acknowledges the obscure
nature of this natural law. His argument was not without its problems, one of which was logical consistency. During the later Pelagian debates with Julian of Eclanum, Augustine rejected Julian's
argument that nature demonstrates that intercourse is a natural
good. Augustine's response was that animal representation is inappropriate to our understanding of human marriage, and therefore
Julian's examples demonstrated pagan rather than Christian attitudes to marriage.[42] However, audiences socialised into male
headship, many of whom had a personal interest in the structures
being maintained, would not have been over-critical of his self-
contradictions.

Secondly, his caveat, 'if natural or social systems allow', was
necessary, as some Christians, resistant to asceticism, asserted that
patriarchal marriage set a precedent for Christian marriage, and
Augustine's reasoning could be used to support a case for polygamy.[43] Augustine developed an elaborate argument: the marriage of
Adam and Eve demonstrated that monogamy best promoted the
good of marriage,[44] but that as it was necessary that the descendants
of Abraham increase and multiply, to found the nation which would
produce the Messiah, 'the patriarchs had possessed wives for the
work of creation, not in the disease of desire like the nations who
do not know God'.[45] That their polygamy was for fecundity, not

lust, is established by the fact that the holy women had only one husband. As a woman cannot increase her offspring by increasing her number of husbands, polyandry could only be motivated by lust and such a woman would not be a wife but harlot.[46] But because a man with several wives can beget many children, the patriarchs were motivated solely by desire to do God's will and never by carnal desire. Even in this context, women are responsible for male sexual behaviour. Joseph, who fathered twelve sons and one daughter by four women, would really have preferred one wife and procreative sex only, but his wives had conjugal rights, a legitimate power over his body, and so they urged him to sexual intercourse.[47] Augustine concluded that owing to changed historical circumstances, the nature of patriarchal marriage could not be used to change or enhance the status of marriage in the fourth century.[48]

Although Augustine was convinced that it is man's nature to lead, he was also well aware that it was men, not women, who had the greater problems with lust and adultery, and he seems to have had difficulty in understanding why. He was aware that one argument the men put forward was that, if they too were subject to penalties for sexual offences, they were being relegated to the rank of women. This argument defines the problem as one of status. It would be effeminate to be subject to controls on one's sexuality. Perhaps here there is a glimpse of a less élitist attitude, for the philosopher revered the man who was in control of his appetites and desires. Similarly, within Augustine's ideal order, men should be able to control themselves; they ought to be exemplars, and their wives should follow them.[49] In reality, however, it was men who were so strongly 'inclined to this malady'[50] whilst 'continence has usually been pleasing to the woman'.[51]

One way out of this dilemma would have been to question the underlying assumption that women are weaker and more carnal than men. Augustine's solution was to blame the women and diminish the achievements of their self-discipline. If husbands strayed, then wives have given them cause.[52] This is also implicit in his comments on incontinent men 'wishing to cast off wives who are quarrelsome, insulting, domineering, finicky and ill-disposed to rendering the marriage debt'.[53] He trivialised the virtue of women by attributing chaste behaviour to the fact that they were supervised, that they feared harsh social sanctions and the loss of their reputations. But a chaste man demonstrated 'manly discipline'.[54] In this he differed greatly from Ambrose's arguments in the *De institutione virginis*, books 3–4. There Ambrose had challenged men to stop blaming women for sin, especially sexual sin. If they were attracted to women because of their beauty, they were looking for the wrong thing in a wife. In the ascetic women of Milan, Eve is rehabilitated, for she has done her penance and been redeemed.

Plato, procreation and the Christian dispensation

Given the emphasis on both asceticism and women's natural inferiority, it is quite understandable that, in Christian homes, women who embraced continence had little sympathy for the men who did not. Augustine himself had taught these women that men were their superiors and that the new era was a time to refrain from embracing. In a passage that resonates with echoes of Plato's argument that the truly spiritual man transcended physical procreation to create children of the spirit – wisdom and virtue, temperance and justice[55] – Augustine asserted that there was no longer the same necessity to create a nation for God, but instead a need to provide spiritual regeneration for all.[56]

Therefore, a continent marriage was truer, because endearment and concord there derive from the 'voluntary affections of souls'.[57] He was adamant that the chastity of marriage is inferior to the chastity of celibacy, and that, in fact, married people cannot have continence of soul for, if they did, they would not have to marry.[58] Given these comments on lust and desire, and his outright statement that a concubine who endures the marriage bed without pleasure for the sake of offspring is more virtuous than a wife who seeks it with desire, a particularly invidious situation existed for the married.[59]

Particularly important to this study are Platonic attitudes to sex and gender. William Alexander has argued that such was Plato's attitude to sexuality that he could not perceive it as the proper object of philosophy.[60] But this is to use the term sexuality in an undefined and unhelpful manner. There is no doubt that the way of the sexually indulgent man was opposed to the way of philosophy,[61] but Plato was well aware of the significance of marriage and sexual relationships for the concerns of the state, and he argues forcefully in the *Laws* that one of the most important tasks of the guardians of the ideal city-state was the regulation of sexual behaviour.[62]

Yet unquestionably the philosophic journey was essentially the transformation from the sexual man to the wise man.[63] The fundamental association between masculinity and wisdom is revealed in the language itself, for the purpose of the journey is not to become *homo sapiens*, but *vir sapiens*. Women, by definition, were excluded from this category.[64] Certainly Augustine acclaimed women who participated in the philosophic enterprise as 'manly'.

Sex and reason

For the philosopher, sexual desire offered a threat to rationality. Because the body was not under the control of the will, it was in rebellion against reason. Within the temporal conditions of existence, sexual activity was a necessity, and even good, when employed in the service of procreation, but any sexual activity beyond this was rationally unjustifiable.[65] It has been asserted that 'the pagan civilisation had so fouled the very notion of sex that it would seem [to Christian ascetics] psychologically easier to renounce it entirely than to impregnate the daily practice of married life with the Christian spirit'.[66] If this assertion is correct, it would provide an additional pressure on all men who aspired to the life of the *vir sapiens* to focus on the negative aspects of sexuality, and consequently to view women more and more as temptresses, and objects of sexual desire, and hence a threat to rationality.

However, this understanding of Roman sexual mores has been strongly challenged. The thesis is that Roman customs regarding marriage, divorce and remarriage were not necessarily dissolute, especially in the light of modern practices, but that from the perspective of the nineteenth-century standards held by the original researchers, the data on divorce and serial marriages in the imperial families was interpreted as indicating absolutely immoral behaviour. The strategic use of divorces and marriages to promote political alliances and to regulate the circulation of women and their property may seem calculating and exploitative by modern standards, but these ends were also served by medieval marriage, which tradition has not regarded as licentious. Also, the philosophic ideal clearly held to continence in the exercise of even conjugal rights.[67]

William Alexander asserts that Augustine synthesised the Platonic evaluation of sex and the Hebrew-Christian view of humanity's sin and fall. If so, Augustine accomplished this by employing Platonic perceptions of sexuality to reconcile biblical texts he understood as antithetical.[68] There is ample evidence of the significance of Scripture to Augustine, so the question is to what extent he interpreted biblical texts through the filters of Platonism. One specific conflict he perceived between his philosophically informed understanding of human sexual nature and Scripture was the biblical evaluation of creation and gendered humanity as good. The Platonic distinctions he assumed provided him with the means to reconcile the two. Thus, he can affirm with both Scripture and Plato that biological sex for reproduction is good and, with Plato, that any sex beyond that is totally unjustifiable.[69] His understanding of sexuality after the Fall as being inextricably entwined with lust (*concupiscentia*), reinforces the negative evaluation of sexual desire, and permits him to retain the philosophic rejection of any action not totally under rational control. And so the transitional equation from philosophy to theology for Augustine may be presented thus:

non-procreative sexual behaviour = rebellion against reason/wisdom (Plato)
God = eternal reason/wisdom
ergo
non-procreative sexual behaviour = rebellion against God

rebellion against God = sin (Judaeo-Christian)
ergo
non-procreative sexual activity = sin against God

There are important consequences from this stance. Augustine can maintain the Scripture's endorsement of sexual difference as essentially good, because it concurs with the Platonic endorsement of sexuality as good for the purpose of procreation. But sexual activity that is motivated to any extent by passionate desire is evil. As we shall see later, his theologising of original sin as a sexually transmitted spiritual disease was essential to split sexual desire from the goodness of marriage. It allows for a pre-Fall idyllic bonding, under total control of the will, to be opposed to the corruption of passionate desire introduced by sin, through which the body overthrows reason.[70] His ideal marriage is an asexual Platonic relationship,[71] which reflects the sexless God who corresponds to the sexless Platonic Forms.[72] In *De civitate Dei* Augustine puts this rhetorical question:

> What friend of wisdom and holy joys, who, being married, but knowing as the apostle says, 'how to possess his vessel in sanctification and honour, not in the disease of desire, as the Gentiles who know not God', would not prefer, if this were possible, to beget children without this lust, so that in this function of begetting offspring the members created for this purpose should not be stimulated by the heat of lust, but should be actuated by his volition in the same way his other members serve him for their respective ends?[73]

One can only wonder with bemusement how many men amongst his readership could respond with a fervent 'Yes!' But the argument is clear. Desire for intercourse beyond what is required for procreation is no longer controlled by reason but passion and therefore defilement, although within marriage such defilement is pardonable.[74]

Ἀπάθεια[75] and the passion of Christ

The Stoic concept of ἀπάθεια raised serious problems for Augustine regarding the nature of God.[76] Because passionate emotion (*pathos*) possesses the individual, it was considered incompatible with masculine dignity and action. It impeded reason and revealed the imperfections of men who become passive – read effeminate – under the influence of joys and sorrows.[77] *Pathos* which was experienced as an emotion rather than as a strong moral imperative, and which was felt towards anything less than God, was understood as antithetical to eternal wisdom. This was especially the case when *pathos* manifested itself as sexual desire, which could control a person more completely than any other emotion.[78] Therefore the philosophers' God was an immutable and impassible deity, the fulfilment of ἀπάθεια. It has been argued by Joseph Hallman that Augustine himself solidly established immutability and impassibility as attributes of God, but, as Hallman acknowledges elsewhere, the assumption of impassibility is found in other Christian texts.[79] Augustine could not uncritically appropriate Stoic principles, because of the biblical texts attributing emotions to God. But these texts created problems for him, because he equated emotions with change and weakness.[80]

He had three ways of dealing with this problem. His most frequent choice was to reduce the language to idiomatic, metaphorical and possibly improper terms for actions of God rather than feelings.[81] Thus, God does not change and feel angry in response to men's actions. God may take vengeance, which the Bible calls anger, but God acts without what would be the concomitant emotional response in a human person.[82] Such actions God eternally foreknows and immutably wills.[83] A second option for Augustine was to interpret the language as referring to the differing ways the individual experiences God, and he sometimes employed rather slippery exegesis to do this. From this perspective, although God does not change, the individual experiences God's vengeance as anger. Occasionally, Augustine exercises a third option, rejecting the biblical imagery altogether as irredeemably wrong.[84]

Biblical attribution of love to God therefore also posed a problem. Augustine resolved it in either of two ways, both of which fall under the rubric of *ordo*. One solution was that emotions become moral states. Love is then understood by Augustine as ordered will:

> The right will then is, therefore, well directed love, and the wrong will is ill directed love. Love, then, yearning to have what is loved, is desire; and having and enjoying it is joy; fleeing what is opposed to it, it is fear: and feeling what is opposed to it, it is sadness. Now if these motions are evil, then the love is evil; if good, the love is good.[85]

As God's will is always rightly ordered, then God loves. In this Augustine echoes Origen, who argued that it is not only appropriate to have a passion for God, but that it was quite licit for Ignatius of Antioch to call God 'passionate Love' (*Amor*) because God-willed love is always willed to the holy.[86]

The alternative solution was to determine the moral character of emotion by the quality of its object. This solution was used to interpret texts attributing emotion to Jesus. Because of Jesus' suffering, ἀπάθεια had become an ambiguous virtue for Christians.[87] And as Jesus was the perfect image of God, did this mean that God experienced *pathos*? If he did, then the emotions of human beings were an aspect of the image of God. Augustine argued that Jesus did have human emotional responses, but they were never the result of infirmity as they are with other humans, but the result of his judgement as to where they should be exercised. Where emotions were directed by a right will, as they were in Jesus, then they are a force for good. Therefore Augustine argued, 'Because their love is rightly placed, all these affections of theirs are right. They fear eternal punishment, they desire eternal life; they grieve because they themselves groan within themselves, waiting for the adoption, the redemption of their body, they rejoice in hope...'[88] Hence Augustine differed from the Stoa in that he did not believe that ἀπάθεια was an attainable or an unequivocal asset, during this life. He further differed from them in seeing the acquisition of heavenly ἀπάθεια as the result of grace, not human self-discipline. Emotions such as compassion are appropriate for the Christian, because they are subject to reason. To be utterly impassive is to be less than human or humane.[89] In this he comes closer to Irenaeus, who also accepted the impassibility of God, but who did not believe that human beings should be too quick to deny their emotional responses. Irenaeus accused men who railed against human emotion of wanting to be like God before they had become fully human. Irenaeus' gentle acceptance of human *pathos* and his understanding of detachment as a developmental process stand in contrast to the harsh judgements which Augustine imposed on himself in the *Confessiones* for being what he was created – a man subject to passion.[90]

Ἀπάθεια therefore is appropriately reserved for irrational emotions which are controlled by the classical virtues.[91] The saints in the resurrection are the only ones who enjoy true ἀπάθεια which has been attained through their dependence on God, not through their own efforts.[92]

Here again the language is significant for the philosophic perception of womanhood. The Latin *virtus* is a masculine concept and the attributes of moral excellence that it connotes are culturally male-oriented: manliness, the sum of the corporeal or mental excellences of man – strength, vigour, bravery, courage, gallantry, military talents.[93] Although the concept of *virtus* was applied to women, the implication in the very root of the word is that they have acquired manliness, rather than displayed human characteristics available to all individuals. Probably it is these a priori assumptions about the nature of manliness that informed the Platonic doctrine that women were the reincarnations of men who had failed in their first incarnation. Those who failed as women came back as beasts.[94]

Even in this brief introductory overview, it is clear that there were certain common assumptions concurrent in society and philosophy that would have been 'natural' for Augustine. The basic philosophical assumptions about *ordo*, ἀπάθεια, and *virtus*, so dear to the male social and philosophical élite, undergirded the social structures of society, and contributed to the impetus towards classical *ordo* in the fourth-century church.[95] Those who did not even have a nodding acquaintance with the philosophic concept of *ordo* nevertheless lived with its consequences in the juridical nature of the *familia*, the hierarchical rankings of patronage, the actual physical organisation of people at games, theatres or banquets, and legislation concerning marriage, citizenship, dress and trade. When faced with inconsistencies and paradoxes, those same assumptions would provide the resolution for problems. The subordination of women is so obvious a 'natural law' in strongly patriarchal societies, that to move beyond this even to a spiritual equality was a step that many Christian leaders could not make.[96] Because such assumptions are accepted uncritically by the majority, they are rarely even recognised as biases.

5

WOMEN, THE NUMINOUS AND THE SACRED

Gods and *daemones*

SOME access to the less conscious world of antiquity, particularly in its perceptions of womanly power, may be found in its beliefs about the supernatural. Pagans, Jews and Christians shared a supernatural world that was vital and immediate. Occupied by spiritual powers both godly and demonic, it represented a realm which mediated between the highest gods and humanity.[1] However, pagan and Judaeo-Christian traditions took different trajectories.[2] For the pagans, *daemones* or spiritual entities could be good, evil or indifferent, and sometimes the word was used simply for a god whose name was unknown. They were held responsible for fate, divine protection, miracles, oracles, astrology and healing; or, conversely, illness, evil and demonic possession.[3]

Judaeo-Christianity, on the other hand, demonised the *daemones*.[4] Non-angelic spirits in the Gospels are all evil, often possessing the human soul.[5] In late antique Christian writing, angels and demons-*daemones* are clearly defined categories of good and evil which permit no neutral beings. In the stories of the desert Fathers, wrestling with the devil becomes typical of the genre, as did the presence of guardian angels.[6] With the emphasis on the creation narratives in late antiquity, the seductive, deceptive serpent of Genesis becomes the prince of demons, the prince of this world, who enticed Eve to sin. Christ's death and triumphant resurrection had overcome evil, and believers could conquer demons in his name.

But the church would have found it more difficult to change the beliefs of the new Christians pouring into the churches for instruction. It is quite conceivable that, to a convert, maintaining belief in a protective or malevolent deity was little different to maintaining belief in a guardian angel or a satanic one, or a patronal saint.[7] In fact there is evidence that Christians invoked spirits and blessed amulets or talismans for protective magic in the name of

Jesus or the angels, just as pagans would invoke their own gods.[8] This caused problems for the bishops, who were already concerned about syncretism and the proper understanding of God. The war against the daemonic was the war against polytheism.

Augustine also took the presence of *daemones* for granted,[9] but found it necessary to argue emphatically for their malevolent character, against both popular piety and philosophers. In *Epistle*, 245.2 to Possidius, Augustine forbade the wearing of amulets by both women and men who sometimes wore them as ear-rings. Yet he reports a fascinating story, which clearly indicates that Christian and Jewish practice had incorporated the same types of popular piety as their pagan neighbours. A noble woman, Petronia, on her way to seek healing at the shrine of Stephen, was given a charm by a Jewish friend – a hair girdle and a ring with an ox's kidney stone in it. When the complete ring fell off the knotted girdle during the pilgrimage, Petronia took it as a pledge of healing, and threw away the charm. The healing is attributed to Stephen, not the girdle and ring, but Augustine did not criticise the wearing of the talisman. Indeed, he likened the miraculous removal of the ring to Jesus' leaving the womb without rupturing his mother's hymen. Even more, he exhorted Petronia to publish an account of her healing to be read in public, which he indicates is becoming a standard procedure. Petronia's nobility provides support for the authenticity of the miracle and the veracity of the recipient of grace.[10] Clearly, popular practice did not make the same fine discriminations between *daemones* and angels that the theologians did. It is important to highlight four characteristics of this story: it involves the nobility, a woman, a martyr cult, and the social influence of the woman in bringing others to faith.

In *De civitate Dei*, Augustine castigated philosophers for believing that *daemones* could ever be benevolent. Such men are pitiable, he asserted confidently, because 'any Christian old woman would . . . most unreservedly detest' the malicious and deceitful *daemones* which facilitate wickedness and delude the souls of men. His argument employs a rhetorical strategy used very frequently by Christian polemicists, and indicative of popular attitudes to women. The opposition is sillier than the silliest old woman. Yet note that not only does he not dispute the reality of other heavenly powers, he actively argues for their reality, which is proved by the occurrence of 'predictions and operations, which seem to be miraculous and divine, yet form no part of the worship of the one God, in adherence to whom, as the Platonists themselves abundantly testify, all blessedness consists'.

That these occurrences must be 'the work of wicked spirits, who thus seek to seduce and hinder the truly godly', is a revealing statement also.[11] Theologically, this shifts any responsibility for pain and evil in the world from God, its creator, to demonic enemies, and so what is at stake is not simply a question of syncretism, or Christian praxis, but a significant aspect of ancient theodicy.

Within this framework, temptation is not so much from within as it is the work of *daemones* from without, and sin is no longer error, but the experience of being vanquished.[12] Psychologically this allows the disowning of temptation and the projection of appetites onto *daemones*, who sought to satiate their lusts through the bodies of human beings. Christians did bear responsibility for trying to control the demons. The ideal mode of control was fasting, so that there was little or no excess food to fuel desire. As sexual desire was lust, *par excellence*, it was inevitable that a synthesis of the temptation offered by women and that offered by *daemones* would take place.[13]

Under Graeco-Roman patriarchy, the original numinous power of women's fertile sexuality was controlled by reducing it to the idea that women were vulnerable to, or under the influence of, a destructive supernatural power.[14] As the 'godly' was pre-eminently the masculine and the male, *daemones* were expected to tempt them to incontinence via women and the appetites hitherto projected onto *daemones* were now projected onto women. Women become the 'hunters of souls'.[15] The logical answer was for holy men to distance themselves from women as far as possible.[16] Thus to reject woman was to reject the demonic, at least in one of its aspects.

Women and reproduction

That women's child-bearing was another area especially vulnerable to the demonic indicates that, at some level of consciousness, giving birth held numinous power. There is archaeological evidence that the womb itself was considered a deity in some areas.[17] This power is linked to the importance of reproduction for the individual, the *familia* and the state. Its political significance also meant that birth processes could be subject to the magic of enemies or the power of hostile spirits. Such numinous power rendered female sexuality suspect in all its aspects.[18]

In the patristic era all the physical sexual processes of women were associated with corruption.[19] Defloration corrupted the body initially and childbirth even more. Ideally, in the minds of many early Christian writers and communities, if the Fall had not occurred, sexual intercourse would not have taken place at all.[20] The *corruptio* associated with sexuality is one of the imperatives behind the development of the doctrine of the virgin birth, and Mary's virginity *ante partum*, *in partu* and *post partum*. Women's reproductive organs were considered foul,[21] and menstruation was perceived not only as ritually impure, but having magical properties. Indeed, it was so powerful it was indestructible. Pliny himself believed that menstrual blood had the power to protect a home from magical spells if smeared on the doorposts.[22]

Whilst taboos surrounding women's reproductive capacity originally expressed the holy powers of fertility and birthing, these powers were feared as well as celebrated and, in patriarchal cultures where women were denied procreative power, the numinous aspects were lost whilst the peril remained.[23] Anthropology offers one perspective on this. In antiquity, women were simply the vessels of reproduction. In a culture predicated on the power of the father, the inability to reproduce would be a source of shame. Yet men were dependent on women for their heirs. The fact that the blood of the womb was considered to have both abortifacient and contraceptive power indicates why its power was so feared. It holds the power to subvert male procreativity and hence the patriarchal lineage.[24]

It is not surprising then that birth-giving was considered polluting, and potentially dangerous, spiritually and physically. What contemporary science would see as purely physical risks were understood in antiquity as vulnerabilities to supernatural powers and magic. Therefore, about a week after giving birth, mother and household were purified with the rite of *lustratio*, and the child was protected with an amulet, known as the *bulla*, which would be worn until adulthood.[25] Augustine describes such a pagan ritual in *De civitate Dei*:

> Three gods are assigned as guardians to a woman after she has been delivered, lest the god Silvanus come in and molest her; and . . . in order to signify the presence of these protectors three men go round the house during the night . . . Thus the guardianship of kindly disposed gods would not avail against the malice of a mischievous god, unless they were three to one.[26]

Such rites have their basis in the dependence of the community on safe births and healthy children in a culture which attributes illness and death to malevolent gods or spirits. Christian women also were purified after childbirth, and ascetic Christian culture in late antiquity increased the ambivalent attitude to female sexuality and birthing. The celebration of childbirth in earlier Roman art is rarely found in Christian art, song or culture from this period.[27] Religious rites such as the churching of women did not consecrate motherhood, but cleansed women of the impurity deriving from it. Augustine taught that Mary did not need purification after childbirth, precisely because Jesus was conceived virginally.[28] In the context of his developing doctrine of original sin, the baptism of the children was understood as a sacrament which cleansed them of the taint of their birth.[29]

The churching of women, which did not take place until after the cessation of post-partum bleeding, was related to attitudes to menstruation. Despite numerous attempts, the church never definitively eradicated the attitude that menstruating women were ritually polluted and could not attend mass and receive communion. Some authors castigated women for receiving, and other bishops prohibited them from doing so. Dionysius of Alexandria was one of the latter in the third century.[30] It is possibly significant that his canon is preserved in vastly different forms. One version tersely instructs:

> Menstruous women ought not come to the Holy table, or touch the Holy of Holies [Gk: body and blood of Christ], nor to churches, but to pray elsewhere.[31]

Another version explains less dogmatically and at some length:

> The question touching women at the time of their separation, whether it is proper for them when in such a condition to enter the house of God, I consider a superfluous enquiry. For I do not think that if they are believing and pious women, they will be rash enough in such a condition to approach the holy table or to touch the body and blood of the Lord ... the individual who is not perfectly pure in soul and body, shall be interdicted from approaching the Holy of Holies.[32]

The latter may have been the result of softening the absolute prohibition whilst trying to preserve the practice by manipulating women's desire to perceive themselves as devout. Priests also were discouraged from celebrating Eucharist, and men from receiving communion, after nocturnal emissions. However, men were not purified after sexual emissions as women were after childbirth and, in some cases, menstruation.

Augustine himself wrote on the issue in 401. He did not consider menstruation was a sin, but it symbolised the mind unformed by discipline, 'flowing and loose in unseemly matter'. Likewise semen signified life 'formless and untaught'.[33] The necessity for such a statement is illuminating, and Augustine's concept of formlessness is a more sophisticated manner of dealing with the anxieties aroused by sexual fluids crossing bodily boundaries. What is formless cannot be categorised; if it cannot be categorised, it is dangerous. As representative of all that is lacking discipline, it has no place in the Christian community, and especially not at the eucharistic table.[34] In the human body, the formless then becomes a source of ritual pollution, while the formlessness of God is taken as an indication of his transcendence of human categories.[35]

Note too his gendered symbolism. Menstrual blood symbolises the mind, but unformed, or unordered, that is (potentially) sinful. Semen symbolises life itself, albeit unformed and unordered life. The creation of life is a godly property. In this text, Augustine describes menstruation as merely 'unseemly'; however, in another text he follows those Jewish and Christian writers who moved from the concept of ritual pollution to using menstruation as a symbol for irrational or worldly passion, thus adding another symbol to the systems which categorised womanliness as sexual and worldly being.[36]

The Levitical taboo is never given as a reason against the ordination of women in official church documents. Yet, if menstruating women were forbidden to touch the bread and wine, it would have made priestly ministry impossible, and menstruation very public as women withdrew from service each month. As the documents testify, concern about ritual pollution was certainly continuously present. Undoubtedly the re-culturation of Christianity in the fourth century, with the huge influx of catechumens, would reinforce the weight of popular opinion and prejudice because the fear that woman would defile the holy was pervasive.[37]

It was during this period also that the church councils began to legislate the compulsory celibacy of the clergy. Scholars have perceived this trend not only as an aspect of asceticism, but as part of the growing sacralisation of the clergy.[38] If clerical celibacy had been simply motivated by the freedom from the necessity of the body, or the desire for the angelic life, then there would have been no need for it to be imposed on clerics by law.[39] Certainly, the honour accruing to ascetics, with its imputation of élite spiritual standards, would have been one factor, when holiness was one of the criteria for election. However, married chastity had not been incompatible with priesthood in the early church communities (1 Tim. 2.11–14), so it cannot be argued that celibacy was necessary to free the cleric from familial responsibilities to tend to his flock.

Brown has argued that in late antiquity, precise taboos concerning bodily fluids became more diffuse and attached to intercourse in general, so that a sexually active man could be rendered ineligible for leadership of the Christian community, thereby being 'demoted' to the position of women.[40] However, other, perhaps more fundamental fears were also at work. In late antiquity, semen was held to contain something of man's divine essence, even to conveying the human soul, a tenet of Christian Traducianism, which Tertullian propounded. Too great a loss of the divine essence rendered a man incapable of communicating with the divine.[41] This is another perspective on the ancient belief that intercourse caused a 'rift in the soul' which could be damaging to the community.[42] The individual had to choose whether to expend semen in sexual intercourse or to conserve it to energise relationship with God.[43] In the Eastern monastic tradition we also find the fear that nocturnal emissions give demons access to the body. Indeed, they may even cause them, to prevent the monk communicating.[44] As increasing emphasis was placed on the threat sex posed to sanctity and the efficacy of appropriate liturgical celebration, sexual abstinence was required of Christians on holy days and church festivals.[45] Gradually the church adopted Roman attitudes to ritual purity until by the sixth century the church surrounded marital relations with a maze of taboos and restrictions.[46] Married men were eventually excluded from priesthood, although men as a class were not, despite sexual emissions.

Clerical celibacy was first legislated in the Synod of Elvira, which forbade bishops to continue physical relations with their wives.[47] Such canons were in direct contradiction of the Apostolic canons which forbade a cleric to put away his wife, and to the mind of the Nicaean Council which refused to endorse the Synod of Elvira, Canon 33.[48]

As nearly all known third-century clerics whose marital status is known were married,[49] these canons must have created enormous problems within the Christian communities. The fact that both Theodosius and Honorius had to order clerics not to abandon their wives suggests that social problems were caused by these women lacking the means of livelihood.[50] As the church moved away from offices defined by function, its leadership model regressed to that of a sacralised, sacrificial priesthood, surrounded by the constraints of ritual purity. Whoever served the sacred in Rome must be set apart, and it is significant that under pressure from the papacy, the Western church developed a far more rigorous attitude to celibacy than did the Eastern church.[51]

As clerical celibacy also underlined the moral superiority of the clerical caste, this development can be seen as an aspect of the struggle for a new Christian self-understanding.[52] Barriers are being erected between the sacred and the profane, so that the parameters of the holy are clearly delineated in a culture where Christian and Roman are increasingly overlapping categories. However, this strategy had a subversive effect that operated against its own direct intent. It enabled ascetic women to 'edge closer to the clergy' through their acquisition of holy power.[53] However, for the majority of women, the combined effect of such attitudes to sexuality fed men's fear of women as a source of disorder and encouraged enforcement of more restrictive measures even for religious women, so that men's sexual honour might remain intact.

Given the ambiguous attitudes to maternity in both pagan and Christian circles, it is interesting that in the classical Roman hierarchy of values, virginal women, the Vestal Virgins, and married men, the *Flamines* of Jupiter, were 'the joint pillars of the sexual ideal'.[54] Within this symbolic structure, both virginity and marriage are reflections of the sacred, for the Vestals, under the control of the *Pontifex Maximus*, guard the hearth of Vesta, the spirit of the *domus*, the foundation of the *patria*. The structure symbolises the family under the *paterfamilias*.[55] With the full flowering of asceticism, the feminine dimension of the symbolism is lost as Christianity presented female virginity as a virile virtue.

Theological anthropology

The church's self-understanding is intimately connected to questions about the nature of God. In a spiritual universe where humanity is created in the image of God, where God incarnate reveals the image of God, theology and anthropology are intimately and reciprocally connected. The theological axis where the world of angelic and demonic spirits interconnected with Christianity was the changing image of God. The immediacy of God's presence in Jesus and his Spirit characteristic of the apostolic era, and the gentle Father/God of the second-century *Martyrdom of Perpetua*, who cupped her face in his hands, was replaced by the emperor God of the imperial religion who rules his empire from afar through subordinates both clerical and secular.[56]

Similarly, there were developments in the interpretation of the Christ as the incarnate Word of God. The interpretation of the Johannine Λόγος in terms of the Greek seminal Word (σπερματικὸς Λόγος), facilitated by Philo's platonic exegesis, had assimilated the Christian Word to the classical Λόγος. From being understood and experienced as a Redeemer who was set against the oppressive powers of the world, the Word came to be perceived as the foundation of the world order, hallowing all cultural systems.[57] The Arian debates over the relation of Jesus to the Father led to the Nicaean emphasis on Jesus' nature as Incarnate Word, and despite every intention to the contrary, Jesus was distanced from his humanity. Christological language becomes Λόγος language. The emergence of the church as the official religion of the Empire was interpreted as the earthly triumph of the Λόγος.[58] In iconography, images of the Pantokrator, Christ Almighty, governing all creation, replace those of the Good Shepherd. With the change in imagery, cultic dread becomes part of the liturgy.[59]

There were social and individual consequences in these redefinitions of identity. If the image of Christ begins to change, the theology of the *imago Dei* should become a focus of theological attention. And indeed, this is what occurs, especially with regard to women. Theology began to legitimate the social order, with the holy man standing 'in the shadow of the rapprochement of religion and political authority'.[60] Thus socially accepted patterns of relationship and order were seen as divinely ordained (*ordinatus*).[61] Conversely, Constantine felt an overwhelming responsibility for the church, provided almost unlimited financial help, and believed his decisions regarding it were acts of divine providence.[62] In the words of Robert Markus, 'they were almost lured into believing that a new messianic age had dawned with Constantine's conversion'.[63] Yet within a century Rome would fall. The world that had appeared so recently to be the Kingdom-of-God-on-earth appeared to be returning to chaos, as manifested in the barbarian invasions.[64] The church's need to account for the apparent failure of the Kingdom motivated Augustine to write the *De civitate Dei*. It also accounted for the need to create order and meaning from the experience of disintegration.

A spiritual vacuum was created as God was distanced from the ordinary Christian. To fill this vacuum a spiritual hierarchy emerged. Angels, the patronal saints and their earthly representatives, the bishops and holy ascetics, mediate between God and God's people. This awareness of the omnipresence of the spiritual world in human life permeated the cult of the saints. The patronal saints, often martyrs and ascetics, conferred power to exorcise *daemones* on their earthly representatives. It must have seemed incomprehensible to Christian men that women, the tools of the devil himself, should hold positions of authority in the very cult which was the Church's bulwark against him.[65]

However, not all Christians held a positive view of the patron saint. The enthusiastic celebrations at the grave-shrines were perceived as akin to ancestor worship, or deification of the martyr. Where this happened, the martyr did indeed take over the role of the pagan god or *daemon*.[66] This troubled Augustine on two counts, particularly after the fall of Rome. The first was that the spiritual powers, pagan and Christian, were expected to protect humanity from physical danger and hardship. When this did not happen, people lost faith. Addressing such questions was a major concern in *De civitate Dei*. The second was his anxiety about recidivism into a Christianised polytheism. He consistently emphasised that saints are not mediators, and 'they are not our gods, but their God is our God'.[67] What is to be learned from the martyrs is hope and humility in adversity. This perception of the dangers of the martyr cults would have added another dimension to women's prominence in the cult. Where bishops like Augustine saw it as more dangerous than orthodox, then women were simply perceived as being in the forefront of another (potential) heresy. That even devout bishops like Paulinus of Nola and Ambrose supported the cult indicates that it was a grey area in late antiquity. A practice which appealed so greatly to popular piety that it persisted through almost two millennia, it had to be approached with tact and diplomacy.

Asceticism and the demonic

Women's enmeshment with the demonic was further facilitated by the patristic perception of woman's leading role in the Fall and women's closer connection to all that was temporal and mutable. Consistently, in both East and West, the 'holy' was that most removed from the human and, therefore, women were by nature further removed from holiness than men.[68] People were constantly reminded of their standing in the hierarchy of holiness. One example was the rigid stratification which governed the celebration of the Eucharist, the Kiss of Peace and reception of communion. In churches which observed taboos on communicating after sex, menstruation, childbirth and nocturnal emissions, those excluded stand outside the eucharistic community, defined as impure.

The fourth-century *Life of St Cyprian of Antioch* illustrates one such ascetic perspective.[69] Cyprian summons a demon, Aglardis, to 'seduce' a young woman, Justa.[70] This appears no true seduction to modern eyes, for Cyprian desires marriage, and Justa is under considerable social pressure to consent.[71] But to the ascetic girl, marriage is a temptation tantamount to sin.[72] The language is extraordinary and revealing. The demon's aim is to 'tame' Justa.[73] His proposal nevertheless, 'fans a flame in her heart dividing her against herself'. Justa reacts with prayer and exorcism.[74] The cross is the 'strong sign' which overcomes the demon and she sees clearly 'that the intelligent, scaly, huge, puffed up, mighty, terrible monster didn't have even the power of a single mosquito'. As the monster is more powerful than his master, Eudokia's implication is that against women with the power of God, men, too, are as powerless as mosquitoes. The ultimate indignity is reserved for Cyprian who is 'degraded into a woman or a flighty creature'.[75] The beauty, virtue and dignity of Justa stand in silent contrast to this indictment. That Cyprian tempted Justa does not negate the association of women, sexuality and the demonic. Cyprian, succumbing to the daemonic, becomes womanly. The story may well have functioned as a moral fable demonstrating the consequences for men who surrendered to desire, as well as demonstrating the 'virility' of continent women.

Written by a woman, the story shows how strongly devout women were socialised into the prevailing judgements on their own nature. Justa is a member of the 'degraded' sex who, through her commitment to asceticism, and the power of Jesus, is able to conquer communal pressure, her own yearnings for intimacy, and the might of the demonic. Such power is charismatic and, as such, becomes a potent threat to be controlled by the hierarchy.[76] Understandably, these women were also perceived as threatening by those who did not choose the ascetic path. Such stories explicitly condemned their choices which were at best inferior, at worst, sinful.

Hence respect for ascetic women was a two-edged sword. Such self-assertion by members of hitherto powerless and/or subordinate groups tends to surface the unconscious fears of the community.[77] Because of the tensions generated by the ascetic deal for ordinary Christians, the bishops would have had formidable allies in the community in controlling powerful women. Eventually, as we will see below, they would be tamed by the bishops, if not by the *daemones*.

Concentration of holy power in the hands of the bishops was also a rejection of the traditional pagan healers, who were often women. Healing power, including control of *daemones*, became the power of the saint whom the ascetic or the bishop represented. Loyalties sometimes collided. It was a common tactic in antiquity for men to combat their enemies, especially in insoluble conflicts, by accusations of witchcraft, magic or demon worship, and women were vulnerable to such strategies. The wise woman within the culture could so easily become the witch responsible for bad luck and illness that, for her enemies, the terms could begin to indicate overlapping categories. Thus a whole tradition of women's healing, feminine knowledge and authority was vitiated in the cause of perceived holiness and power.[78]

Women and the goddess

Worship of the goddess encountered particular virulence in Christian writings.[79] This was not discontinuous with the hostility to the pagan wise women, but an aspect of the same problem. The church was battling the fertility rites of the goddesses, and the Isis cult which worshipped wisdom as a feminine symbol.[80] M. I. Finley has suggested that the Isis cult was the most tenacious of the pagan cults because it offered women equal power with men, and blessed the marital relationship, ordaining that women be beloved by men.[81] Augustine broadsides Isis only in passing. He reserves his severest condemnations for Cybele, the Great Mother. For Augustine, the worship of Cybele was profligate and guileful, for it practised such obscenities that even the goddess would not suffer herself to be invoked and celebrated in terms so immodest. Such worship is demonic for only demons could be refreshed by obscenity. He especially condemned the cult of the *magna Mater*, because eunuchs served her. Any feminine principle which demands the mutilation of men is diabolical.[82] Thus the celebration of fertility as a dimension of the sacred was identified in the Christian mind with obscenity and evil, and women who held office in the goddess religions were anathema.

WOMEN AND THE FOURTH-CENTURY CHURCH

A changing church

The final chapter of Part II will draw together the threads of the preceding discussion of variables which affected the ecclesial communities in the heady days after Constantine's conversion. Of particular importance was the shift from house churches to public basilicas. As Karen Torjesen has demonstrated, this was one of the single most important factors in removing women from clerical office, for the influx of converts could not accept public leadership exercised by women in the church any more than in political life.[1] To some extent this indicates how far the church came to be seen as a public institution, for Rome certainly accepted priestesses in the service of the feminine goddesses. But a female priest in a public (male) cult was an impossibility, for the bishop stood *in loco Dei* as both father and bridegroom of the church.[2]

This is the wider background against which conservative church traditions concerning women came into their own. Although the fourth-century church was heir to conflicting traditions concerning women's role, Roman culture in late antiquity offered a fertile ground for the ethos of the household codes of the Pastoral Epistles. Certain traditions of the early Jesus movement, under the charism of the Spirit, were freer of the cultural conditioning of patriarchy,[3] and there is clear evidence of women in clerical office.[4] However, as communities encountered conflicts with social structures inimical to an egalitarian stance, some began to modify their position on the equality of all believers enshrined in the text of Galatians 3.28 (cf. 1 Tim. 2.11–15; 2 Tim. 3.6–7; Titus 2.3–5, 9–10; 3.1).[5] Before the fourth century, one of the acceptable religious roles had been the prophetic, but prophetesses became extremely suspect due to the prominence of women in the Montanist and Gnostic heresies. The leadership roles of women in these movements were used to justify the contention that women teachers, like Eve, led the church into error, an argument which totally ignored the fact that all heresies had male leaders too.[6]

With the inculturation of both theology and practice after Constantine, conservative theological stances were reinforced by Roman ideas of tutelage,[7] and the Graeco-Roman idealisation of male friendship.[8] Gradually, the subordination of women in the Pauline and Pastoral Epistles began to take on the nature of revealed teaching.[9] By the late fourth century, the religious climate was such that Jovinian could be condemned as a heretic for teaching that marriage was equal to virginity,[10] whilst Ambrosiaster could teach unequivocally, without harassment, that women are not made in the image of God. Ambrosiaster's teachings are important for, although his *Questions on the Old and New Testaments* were originally published anonymously, they were highly esteemed and from a very early period they were attributed to Ambrose, and were quoted as such by Augustine. Later, they were ascribed to Augustine himself.[11]

Attitudes towards women were inevitably influenced by the changes in the Christian church's self-understanding, the concomitant developments in theology, and by the shifting grounds of religious politics in the fourth and fifth centuries. The changes involving authority and ministry would have affected women, and it is clear from the patristic sources that women's role became problematic. Church councils, many of them ecumenical, passed canons excluding women from ordained office.[12] Clearly, the acceptance and religious freedom accorded women in the early church and exemplified by women such as Prisca, Thecla, Paula, Melania and Egeria was under threat. There was intense opposition among institutional churchmen to works such as the *Acts of Thecla*, which provided models of women as autonomous evangelists in their own right.[13] Aspegren has traced the shift in Christian texts which replaces the virile and independent Thecla with virginal, peripatetic heroines who will resist pressure to renounce the faith, but who reject any opportunity to teach, lead or baptise.[14]

The Councils on women

Official opposition is enshrined in the canons that were promulgated in the church Councils which increased as Christianity moved away from charismatic models of community.[15] The freedom of ascetic women was condemned by the Council of Gangra (prior to 341), which went so far as to deny the authenticity of female asceticism altogether in its condemnation of male dress and short hair for women.[16] The synodal letter accompanying the Canons is an excellent example of how church law is constructed as inherently natural law. Women's hair must remain long because long hair is natural for women.[17] The agenda of power is revealed in Canon 17, where the bishops explicitly recognise the social implications of short hair: 'If any woman from pretended asceticism, shall cut off her hair, which God gave her as the reminder of her subjection, let her be anathema.'[18]

The original canon omitted the reference to subjection, but the canon in its late form was incorporated into both the *Corpus Iuris Canonici* and Gratian's *Decretum*. Later church tradition reveals the final resolution of the question of the status of ascetic women's hair. They could cut their hair short, to assert their independence of a human spouse,[19] but hide it under a veil to indicate their subordination to a divine one.

An early prescription to place a physical boundary between women and the sacred was the requirement that women exchanging the sign of peace with a celibate man must fold their cloaks over their hands so that there should be no flesh contact at all.[20] Later a series of local and ecumenical synods moved to exclude women from the vicinity of the sacred and to restrict them to simple church membership. They were prohibited from approaching the altar because of the pollution of menstruation,[21] they were forbidden to live in mixed communities, and even later laws prescribed that they must withdraw from any locality where a bishop might desire to be present.[22] The prohibitions on sexual congress for the higher clergy were extended to forbidding wives to remain in the homes of bishops. A wife must give her permission to separate and consent to be enclosed in a monastery.[23] The legislation for celibacy of the clergy impinged directly on these women's lives, for the need for constant ritual purity could be threatened by the sexual temptation presented by wives, even the most chaste and devout.

Woman and the *imago Dei*

It is notable that the fourth century could even entertain the idea that Christian women were not made in the image of God. This position is exemplified by Ambrosiaster's exegesis of 1 Corinthians 11:

> For this reason the apostle says: 'A man ought not to cover his head since he is the image and glory of God.' On the other hand, he says, 'Let her wear a veil.' Why? Because she is not the image of God. For this reason the apostle repeats: 'I permit no woman to teach or have authority over men.'

From his writing something may also be gleaned of the wider cultural attitudes to women which were influencing the church.

When it is clear that she is subject to the power of man and that she has no authority whatsoever, how can we say that woman is the image of God? Since she may be neither a teacher, nor a witness, nor a guarantee, nor a judge, how much less can she exercise authority?[24]

Clearly, the image of God is identified with authority and this posed problems in a society where women were deemed to lack the capacity for authority. Both Diodore of Tarsus[25] and John Chrysostom[26] denied women the *imago Dei* for the same reason, privileging 1 Corinthians 11 over Genesis 1.28. This interpretation makes the Aristotelian position that only men, as fully developed reasoning beings, have the capacity for authority, an aspect of divinely sanctioned natural law. The purported inferiority of women in classical texts is now a God-given status.[27]

However, the Christian experience of the valiant woman martyr had already called this belief in question. The church Fathers had to account for the strength, fidelity, and authority of women such as Thecla, Vibia Perpetua, and Blandina.[28] The common solution was that truly Christian women had transcended their gender and become manly. Jerome was quite explicit. When a woman ceases to serve the world and serves Christ instead, 'then she will cease to be a woman and will be called man'.[29] Obviously, the prevailing and unquestioned assumption is that the male is the norm of Christian humanity from which the female deviates or is distanced in some way. This replicates the teachings of the major philosophical schools, with the exception of the Stoics.[30] Contrary to the majority opinion, Clement of Alexandria, influenced by Stoicism, considered man and woman to have a common nature, a common grace and a common salvation.[31]

Women and clerical ministry

One specific example of the controversies over women's ministry and the rhetoric they engendered is provided by Epiphanius. He denounced women's communities in Thrace and Scythia, who drew their priests from their own ranks, apparently as part of a cult of the Virgin Mary which, they claimed, authorised their ministry. Epiphanius was not sure whether these women actually worshipped Mary, or simply offered bread and wine to God in her name. What is interesting is that their practice must be eradicated, 'just like others similar to it'.[32] This suggests that he is not speaking simply of isolated cases.[33] Certainly he attacks the women with all the weapons in his armoury. They are irreverent, blasphemous, diabolical, degenerating the teachings of the Spirit, and worshippers of

the dead,[34] and above all, they are the mad, deceptive daughters
of Eve: 'It is apparent that through women the devil has vomited
this forth.'

Epiphanius' solution is to exert masculine authority, to 'put on a
manly mind' and disperse the mania of women diseased with the
deception of Eve.[35] So responsive were the clergy to his call that,
by the sixth century, church councils moved to suppress the office
of deaconess altogether.[36] It is often reported that the Council of
Mâcon in 585 affirmed by one vote that women had souls, but this
has been refuted by Uta Ranke-Heinnemann, who has clarified the
conciliar debate. The question put to the vote was whether women
could be called '*homo*', that is, human being.[37] It is not hard to see
how the confusion over the meaning of the decision arose, when
only human beings were held to possess souls, or as Ambrose put
it, *homo* means soul. For him the term unequivocally included
women.[38] It is a measure of how far the church had moved that the
question could be raised at all.

Augustine was responding to situations such as this when he
wrestled with the concept of women as the *imago Dei*. He was
familiar with women acting as priests and defined this as heresy.[39]
The denial of the *imago Dei* to women is a question he will explore,
rather than condemn as heretical. It posed very real problems
for Augustine, and he offers no condemnation of writers such as
Ambrosiaster, although he eventually disagrees with him.

The new Christian identity

The triumphalist stance of the post-Constantinian church created
new problems. If all the world was Christian, what practices were
Christian, and what were irredeemably pagan? The Christian had
lost the markers by which he or she might maintain a distinctive
Christian identity. Boundaries were blurred. The coming together
of one empire under one religious roof had certain political advan-
tages: a certain sense of unity and shared citizenship, both earthly
and heavenly. And yet there was a loud 'But . . .' Human communities need clear boundaries, for all identity is defined over against
the 'other', and Christian communities were no different. Intra-
ecclesial debates over the relation of Christ to the Father flared
into the Arian debate which reflected the tensions of differing
understandings of Christian identity. These were grounded in antithetical Christologies and their concomitant theologies of the *imago
Dei*. The question was not only what distinguishes Christian Roman
life from pagan Roman life, but what was authentic Christianity.[40]
It was a real question in that period whether the huge numbers of
converts were induced by true conversion or spiritual opportunism.

Brown, and more recently, Markus, argue that the loss of Christian identity was restored by asceticism and identification with the
martyr-saints.[41] The veneration of the martyrs provided a structure
and ideology whereby the comfortable Christianity of the fourth
century could forge links with the heroic Christian martyrs, of
whose fidelity and authenticity there could be no doubt. The veneration of the martyr helped the later Christians to join symbolically
in both the suffering and the triumph. The martyr cult also linked
the church on earth with the communion of saints with God. It
provided continuity and an access to spiritual power, through an
ideology modelled on the patronage systems of Roman society. The
saint intervened with the God-emperor, to bestow favours on his
or her constituency below, with the locus of power being the grave-
shrine.[42] The martyr cult offered personal and communal links
with unassailable faith, it bridged the past and the future.[43] Those
yearning for holiness gave their allegiance to the saints, rather than
to living men and women. Brown stated that women especially
made this choice, because 'Saints were the only in-laws a woman
was permitted to choose.'[44]

This yearning for an authentic faith, and the growth of the
martyr cult, were factors which led to the emergence of ascetic
spirituality within the great church. Holiness within Christianity
became less a result of service based on love (*agape* or *caritas*), but
of asceticism. Asceticism had been the athletic training ground of
the martyr, which facilitated the power of the Spirit and enabled the
martyr to endure.[45] In place of martyrdom, such asceticism effected
friendship with the divine and the ascetic came to be regarded as
the special friend of God (*amicus Dei*), a title which conferred
instant honour.[46] The ascetic came to be seen as the heir of the
martyrs, and it was a life to which women were increasingly drawn.[47]
It has become a commonplace of the literature that women were
motivated by the independence it offered, and certainly the spiritual
power ascribed to them was very great indeed, even when they
were exhorted to curtail their public activities.[48]

The practices of the ascetic woman marked her out sharply from
the community, especially the young woman who vowed virginity
and rejected the only role open to her in classical culture. The
Christian widow had not represented such a cataclysmic change.
She was in the mould of the *univira*. But in a world already
threatened by a falling birth rate, the continence of young people
was a threat to the existence of the state itself, and was illegal under
the Augustan marriage laws. Such was the influence of the church
that Constantine repealed the legislation by 320 CE.[49] The ascetic
was expected to fast, to pray, to give alms, and to intercede with
God for her community. The virgin came to be perceived as the

community protectress. In the Canons of Athanasius we find
the virgins fulfilling the same role as the Paschal lamb: 'In every
house of Christians, it is needful that there be a virgin, for the
salvation of the whole house is that one virgin. And when the wrath
cometh upon the whole city, it shall not come upon the house
wherein a virgin is.'[50] On the one hand, recent research has highlighted the manner in which the ascetic piety of aristocratic Roman
women during the fourth century was harnessed for the enhance-
ment of familial honour.[51] On the other hand, the church law and
practice acted to exclude them from public roles, enjoining them
to stay home and pray for the community.[52]

Christian women especially were caught in a spiritual dilemma
if their husband did not approve their asceticism. Their church
exalted the idea of renunciation of the temporal, but they were to
be obedient to their husband's decisions regarding their lifestyles,
including their sexual practice, their dress and the use of their own
property.[53] Unlike the bishop who was required to put his wife
aside, the Christian woman was forbidden to leave her husband to
practise the celibate life.[54] The conflict of obediences for such
women had the potential to become disruptive. Their asceticism
was perfectly intelligible within Christian traditions which supported the autonomy of women, and Ambrose of Milan even held
up ascetic women as exemplars to men.[55] However, in a world
where clerical ministry had become a public office, and where the
security of the church depended on the authority of male heads of
households, the pressure of female asceticism and the autonomy it
was held to confer, became intolerable.[56] The subordination of
women was becoming a major issue for the church.[57] The tension
was heightened by the fact that as asceticism developed, so did the
pressure for male clerics to be celibate, as sexual abstinence was
increasingly perceived as the criterion of holiness.[58]

This context of asceticism and concomitant clericalism led to the
redefinition of the idea of the 'people of God' (*laos*). *Laos* no longer
meant the whole people of God, the true Israel, but the lay congregation who lacked the specialist knowledge and status of the professional religious.[59] The laity were inevitably separated from the
church élite, for once access to any group becomes restricted by
criteria not equally accessible to all, most people come to accept
that the heights are not for them. Ordinary Christians became
content with a vicarious holiness derived from the superhuman feats
of holy women and men. The church was establishing structures of
rank and privilege adopted from its surrounding culture. The
ascetics were the new patricians.

To the bishops and theologians this was a desirable development.
Ambrosiaster, for example, was well aware that in the earlier church

all taught and all baptised, but he considered it progress in the church that such vile, irrational and vulgar behaviour had been abandoned.[60] This distancing of the spiritual élite from the vulgar is also found in Augustine, who did not hesitate to condemn what had been accepted as Christian behaviour in previous generations.[61] However, this view did not go unopposed and it was at the heart of two of the great theological debates of the fourth and fifth centuries. Both Jovinian and Pelagius resisted this 'double standard' of holiness,[62] and it was in the debates with these theologians and their followers that Ambrose, Jerome and Augustine would forge the Western tradition on Christian sexuality and sanctity.

The cult of the saints

Episcopal condemnation of earlier Christian devotional practices was especially severe when it related to those concerned with the cult of the saints. Wealthy Romans were buried in family mauso-leums. Their ashes were kept in funerary urns or their bodies in marble sarcophagi. On the anniversary of their deaths, the family would gather to share a memorial meal, and offer a libation to the spirits of the dead. It is not hard to see how in a Christian context this could evolve into the cult of the martyrs. Their faith communities or families would gather at the grave, offer Eucharist in memory of the saint, and ask his or her intercession. As we saw earlier, there were fears that the custom had become open to abuse, and to some, it was too close to paganism to be comfortable. Thus it became a site for distinguishing between pagan and Christian practice. Hence, in late antiquity, we find the bishops, including Ambrose and Augus-tine, acting to control the cult. In fact, there is evidence that there was a consequential hidden agenda centred on the power struggle between the two new high profile groups within the church – the bishops and the noble laity – both of whom wished to become the publicly established patrons of the Christian communities.[63] A major aspect of the dispute focused on funerary and martyr cult practices for a complex interaction of circumstances.

First, as we saw, there was a link between the cult and the ascetic, and both were aspects of church life to which women were drawn. The Christian emphasis on charity led to a situation where women came to a new prominence through building shrines and fostering the cult of the saint, and this broke down political barriers, as women became patrons of the community. In encouraging women in alms-giving, the bishops thus gave them access to the ceremonial life of the city technically denied them in the all-male definition of the city as a political unit.[64] John Chrysostom, Jerome and Rufinus all had powerful women patrons in Olympias, Paula, Eustochium and Melania the Elder. Women's control of their own finances in this regard raised such fears about the redistribution of wealth that in 370, 390, 455 and 458 CE the emperors acted to prevent them willing bequests to the church. The power that influential Christians had attained is apparent from the speed with which these ordinances were repealed.[65] By 529, donations and legacies to the church were immune from taxation, and in 530 the church was given the right to sue procrastinating heirs who withheld them.[66]

Second, far greater freedom of movement and association was accorded to women involved in cultic practices in cemeteries. The memorial banquets for the saints were occasions when the segregation of the sexes broke down, thus dismantling traditional social barriers. Being a private, rather than a public context, women's leadership was more acceptable.

Inadvertently, hitherto traditional Christian praxis was subverting the mores which were attempting to constrain women. The consequences of women's greater participation appeared to have caught the bishops unaware and they were not prepared to accept the challenge to episcopal power.[67]

The emergence of a group of autonomous and powerful women, who were both noble *patrona* and ascetic, further exacerbated the tensions. Scholars agree that celibacy was the source of the ascetics' freedom to overcome racial, social and sexual barriers.[68] When the two roles were combined in one woman, such as Melania the elder, or Paula of Jerusalem, such women had the potential to become a very real threat to the newly emerging institutional episcopate which needed to be circumspect in its dealings with powerful women. Just how circumspect is suggested by Optatus' account of the origins of the Donatist controversy. This schism was of direct relevance to the life and ministry of Augustine, who engaged in debates with the Donatists throughout his lifetime. One of the contentious aspects of Donatism was its self-proclaimed purity as the church of the martyrs. According to Optatus, the origins of the whole dispute lay in a conflict between archdeacon Caecilian, who opposed the cult of the martyrs, and Lucilla of Carthage, whom he threatened with church discipline for reverencing the relics of a saint before communion. Lucilla was extremely influential in the politics of the Carthage church, and had been instrumental in the election of the bishop Marjorinus.[69] The conflict was not resolved when the Diocletian persecution broke out. Later, when Caecilian was ordained Bishop, Lucilla, with two men, challenged the legitimacy of his authority on the grounds that he had been invalidly ordained by a bishop who apostasised under persecution, a *traditor* (traitor or betrayer of Christ). Stigmatised by Optatus as an 'influential, mischief-making woman', proclaimed as 'most illustrious woman' (*clarissima femina*) within the Donatist faction, Lucilla was clearly a force to be reckoned with.[70]

When these factors are placed within the context of a church membership that is predominantly female,[71] and which had found both in the cult of the saints and asceticism a greater role for women than that provided by classical society, it is not surprising that conflicts arose,[72] or that men like Jerome, Pelagius and Augustine would vie to become spiritual advisors of influential female ascetics.[73] If women could officiate at the cult of the saints, and there is some archaeological evidence to suggest that they did, there would be two sources of spiritual power in the church, the leader of the cult and the president of the eucharistic community.[74] What was at stake in what Brown called 'a conflict of rival systems of patronage', was nothing less than the right to mediate the power of the holy to the Christian community.[75] Giving due note to the political and social complexities of the situation, once it is recognised that the élite laity were predominantly ascetic women of noble rank, with all that implies in terms of familial influence, wealth and the capacity for patronage, piety and exemplary behaviour, then what emerges, in fact, is a power struggle between bishops and women. Inevitably, the bishops would act to avert what they perceived as a threat to order and authority, for women would have had access to enormous power if they mediated the patronage of the saint.[76] Although he ignores the gender issues, Brown perceives this whole issue as so significant that he states that the rise to the power of the church in western Europe was tied to the localisation of the holy.[77]

As it became increasingly clear that the cult of the saints was a nexus of the spiritual and temporal power that marked the Christian élite, the bishops took immediate steps to bring the cult of the saints under ecclesiastical control.[78] It became a means of suppressing charismatic authority and firmly establishing the new episcopal structures.[79] The Synod of Elvira forbade women to attend cemeteries in the evenings, on the basis that under pretext of prayer they would commit evil deeds, and no one was to burn candles during the day for fear of disturbing the spirits of the saints. In a related tactic, the authority of confessors, that is, those who had survived punishment, imprisonment or torture during the persecutions, was undermined. The faithful were no longer permitted to carry references from confessors stating their fidelity, but a letter of communion from their bishop.[80] That Augustine grasped the import of this situation is clear in the *Confessiones*. He uses a reminiscence about his mother to construct the ideal feminine response to episcopal control:

It had been my mother's custom in Africa to take meal-cakes and bread and wine to the shrines of the saints on their memorial days, but the door-keeper would not allow her to do this in Milan. When she learned the Bishop had forbidden it, she accepted his ruling with such pious submission that I was surprised to see how willingly she condemned her own practice rather than dispute his command . . . But she willingly ceased this custom when she found this great preacher, this holy bishop, had forbidden such ceremonies even to those who perform them with sobriety, both for fear that to some they might be occasions for drunkenness and also because they bore so close a resemblance to the super- stitious rites which the pagans held in honour of their dead.[81]

We may note that this underlying agenda between the bishops and the women appealed to the cultural attitudes that perceived women as intrinsically inferior, passive and dependent dangers, if not out- right possessions of the men. Augustine depicts the cultic celebra- tion as simply an excuse for headstrong drunkenness, which was always associated with sexual arousal in the Roman mind – for wine was the stimulator of passion *par excellence*.[82] Henceforth, all who do not accept the bishops' ruling are suspected of vice and morally culpable disobedience.[83] Something of the feminine perspective may be gleaned from Augustine's rueful, but honest reflection, that if Monica had not loved Ambrose so much she might not have submit- ted so readily – an observation which suggests that the rationale for the prohibition was not self-evident to her. In this case the bishops were so effective that the martyr cult was moved into the churches and under ecclesiastical control by the fifth century.[84] From now on, the Christian was identified less as one born of the Spirit, than as one united in sacramental communion with the bishop, the sole dispenser of sanctifying grace.[85]

Apparently, not all felt inclined to follow Monica's example, and Augustine demonstrates one of his later strategies employed to gain control of the cult, as he draws subtle distinctions between the efficacy and influence of the gospel miracles, and those miracles which are proclaimed by the lay faithful.

For the canon of sacred writings which behoved to be closed, causes those everywhere to be recited, and so to sink into the memory of all congregations; but these modern miracles are scarcely known even to the whole population in the midst of which they are wrought, and at best are confined to one spot . . . and when they are reported to other people in other localities, *there is no sufficient authority to give them prompt and unwavering credence, although they are reported to the faithful by the faithful.*[86]

Augustine accepted the miracles attributed to the saints, but he was concerned at the lack of ecclesiastical control of what was, from his point of view, a potentially disruptive situation.[87] By permitting only the bishop to acknowledge authentic relics and miracles, the power inherent in the experience of the miraculous is restricted to the episcopacy.[88] Thus miracles wrought at Milan are to be accepted because mandated by the prophetic dream of Ambrose.[89] The crucial issue here is the authority to discern the operation of holy power and to mediate it to the community.

Virile women raised a further question. The ascetic woman had been present in Christianity from its inception. The change in ecclesial status in the fourth century, and the repealing of laws that penalised celibates, had caused their ranks to swell with virgins who adopted the 'discipline', rejecting their familial and social roles as mothers. The reception of Ambrose's sister had been such a high profile event that Pope Liberius himself officiated. All the same, their presence in the church offered an ambiguous symbol. Such women, idealised by Ambrose as the epitome of fertile spirituality, had become virile women, not only spiritually but ecclesially and socially.[90]

Sexuality and institutionalisation

James Brundage argues that it was precisely the institutionalisation of the church which encouraged clear and explicit formulations about sexuality and sexual ethics, because imperial support protected the church and fostered a climate for the development of formal Christian law which relied heavily on the power of the state.[91] But his argument does not explain the dynamics of this process. Samuel Laeuchli's analysis of the Council of Elvira is illuminating as a specific and local example of how one synod exerted its control. Laeuchli demonstrates how the power of the clergy depended on their ability to control sexual practices and to impose sexual taboos, and to enforce their decrees with spiritual sanctions.[92] If they controlled the sexuality of the people, they controlled the cultural systems dependent on it, particularly kinship systems at the service of economic and political alliances.[93] Laeuchli argues persuasively that a people anxious about identity and spiritual security were vulnerable to such an exercise of spiritual control.[94]

Asceticism in collusion with philosophy, and Christian attitudes to the fertility cults provided the rationale for demonising the sexual. Twenty-six of the eighty-one canons of Elvira were devoted to greater control of women, and a further twelve regulate male sexual behaviour, including one (Canon 18) which rules that clergy found guilty of sexual offences shall be excluded from communion even at death.[95] As argued earlier, even prior to the fourth century, church leaders and theologians acted consistently to remove women and sex as far as possible from the sacred. Women were first removed from office and then also from the presence of the clergy. Consecrated women were placed under the authority of the bishop who presided over the taking of the veil,[96] and secluded from public life and even the intimacies of private life.[97] Many of these communities were given rules written by men, such as that written by Augustine for his sister's community.[98]

Conclusions: Purity and danger

To explore these findings more deeply, I want again to invoke Mary Douglas's work on purity and danger. As male control of public structures is a constant in late antiquity, this effectively means that women's power, in the context of their suspect sexuality, is perceived as ability to subvert male power and cultural systems through sexual attraction or ritually tabooed impurity. Therefore women's power is deemed generically 'unclean'. The consequence was that women, by their very nature, had the potential to become dangerous threats to orderly authority.

In the Judaeo-Christian context, any perceived threat to order also became a threat to holiness, and an attack on Wisdom, because it was assumed that the social order mirrored the eternal order. Disorder signalled a falling away from the divine Spirit, and as we saw above, disorderly sexuality signalled sinful rebellion. In this we see the patristic synthesis of holiness and wisdom which effected a convergence of Scripture and philosophic systems in Christian theology. Because threats to form and order were experienced as polluting, women were excluded from public and sacred spheres of life, especially those whose male headship was religiously legitimated.[99] Women's rigorous exclusion permitted little testing of the reality of women's presence and power as generic pollutants to the religious system, though there was no doubt that women could effectively impinge on male power.[100] Given the male fear of women's sexual power, this is inevitable. Those who challenged the holders of 'clean power', and that category itself was a subject of dispute in fourth century Christianity, were proclaimed heretics, idolaters, and analogically adulterers. Hence the condemnation of heresy is couched in the language of sexual desire and fidelity, which further reinforces both the implicit power of women and its dangerous nature.[101] One of the definitive accomplishments of the fourth century was that the authority to control unclean power was coming slowly but surely into the hands of the bishops and episcopal synods.[102]

Moreover, the Christian understanding of properly ordered

power was legitimated by ancient medicine, which taught that women as a sex were less formed and ordered than men, thus emphasising the irrational nature of women and the intrinsic pollution of disorderly female power *vis-à-vis* the rational explicit power of male being and order. This medical model undergirded earlier religious and political systems as it did Christianity; and conversely, those systems had a vested interest in maintaining certain emphases of the medical model.[103] In addition, within Christian writing there is a shift in the perception of female pollution. It is no longer only ritual impurity, but connotes moral and spiritual corruption. Women's blood and sinfulness are united in the Christian symbolic system, whilst the male blood of Christ is salvific.

The themes of cultic power, the nature of God and the human *imago Dei*, sexual desire, asceticism, patronage, identity and the ordering of social relations emerge repeatedly in each aspect of cultural and spiritual life, as Christian leaders redefined the boundaries between the sacred and profane, sexual purity and sexual pollution, orthodox and heretical faith, public and private domains, clergy and laity, men and women. In most cases, men belong to the former categories and women to the latter, and where categories overlap, for example orthodox and heretic, pure and polluted, the 'unclean' category is symbolised in female images. However, virile, continent women presented an anomaly. They looked like women but lived a life of masculine virtue. Therefore they are consecrated and isolated from profane women, and their very existence as an anomaly reinforces the subordinate status of ordinary wives and mothers.

'Real' Christians are defined by their religious discipline. Again, the celibate are more authentic in their spirituality than the sexually active. The 'orthodox' are those who give their obedience to their bishop. That this caused some problems at the time there is no doubt, because each tradition perceived itself as the true church and their opposition as heretical. In the course of time, the Nicene Creed came to a pre-eminent position, and the enduring criterion of orthodoxy was allegiance to this creed. In terms of social relationship, the patristic writers located true gender equality in Heaven. Although ascetic women were deemed virile, the discourse of the 'virgin bride', which dominated virginal and ecclesial imagery, allowed the social constraints on Roman matrons to be prescribed for the 'brides of Christ', although within their homes and convents such women could play extremely influential roles. However, their seclusion should be greater than other women's, for their divine Bridegroom possesses divine honour and so consequently the power to shame is likewise enhanced.

Clearly, in the changing church, women's nature and role

threatened order and clean power as church and culture understood it. In both his pastoral work and his theological undertakings Augustine was forced to clarify his thinking on the role and nature of women. The spheres of influence to which he was exposed during this enterprise were manifestly interdependent rather than independent. Scripture and philosophy, cultural prejudices and canon law, policy and praxis wove together in a passionate life lived against the backdrop of a rapidly disintegrating empire. The following chapters will explore in detail the circumstances which provoked such thought and the repercussions for Christian anthropology.

PART III
Augustine and his relations with women

AUGUSTINE THE SON

THIS Part concerns Augustine's relationships with the significant women in his life, his mother, Monica, his common-law wife and the women to whom he related as bishop. The *Confessiones*, the *Soliloquia* and Augustine's *Epistles* to women will be examined to trace the interactions between his experience and his theology. In each section, the influence of his specific relationships on his theological reflection will be noted to ascertain the connection between context, experience and influence. In the final section of this Part, conclusions will be drawn about the consequences of his 'theologised' experience for his perception of gender, desire, spirituality and his prescription for social relations.

Monica

Hidden in the shadows behind many great architects of ascetic spirituality stood a woman. Behind Gregory of Nyssa stood his sister Macrina; behind Ambrose, his sister Marcella; behind Jerome, his patron Paula, behind John Chrysostom, his patron Olympias, behind Rufinus, his patron Melania, and behind Augustine, Monica and his concubine. However, Monica stands forth from the shadows more often than most of these women. Her presence permeates the *Confessiones*, and scholars agree that her influence upon Augustine was undeniably powerful. She had been variously described as simple,[1] genuinely impressive,[2] noteworthy,[3] the flawed mother jealous of her son's lover,[4] dominating,[5] ambitious,[6] wise but uncultured,[7] harrying and tender.[8] It will be argued here that Monica's portrait in the *Confessiones* is based on the template of the ideal Roman mother, which Augustine modifies to incorporate his Christian and philosophic values.

Augustine writes about Monica from the perspective of her son, offering us a rare opportunity in the ancient literature to obtain an image of motherhood that is less mannered than usual, and more informed with the emotional content of the relationship. However, it must always be borne in mind that we are never presented with Monica's personal experience, only with her son's perception and understanding of her, after prolonged reflection. In light of the *Confessiones*' pedagogical and edifying intent, the principal focus of this chapter will be the function of Monica as a role model for Christian women. The emotional dynamics are not irrelevant, but they will not be the dominant motif in this discussion. The significant incidents from Monica's childhood, her marriage to Patricius, and their parenting of Augustine will be analysed. Then we shall examine in detail the facets of Augustine's relationship with his mother, and her influence on him. It will be argued that Monica presents an alternative model of spirituality, one which forced Augustine to revise some of his youthful beliefs about the role of philosophy, and that the character of Monica becomes a paradigm for the church as mother.

Monica and the demon drink

Monica was reared in a stable, pious Christian household.[9] A devout nurse trained her and her sisters in self-discipline with 'holy severity', and Monica attributed her strength of character and education to this nurse rather than her own mother. Monica's nurse is characterised not by the indulgence of Augustine's own nurses, but by the *severitas* which was the characteristic of the good Roman mother. Her nurse did not permit the drinking even of water between meals, for fear her charges would later drink wine – a habit dangerous for women for it stimulated the passions, and particularly dangerous for adolescent girls whose passions were in full flower without the discipline of a mature personality. What seems an incredibly harsh discipline today, Augustine would have seen as graced. In the *De doctrina christiana* written about the same time as the *Confessiones*, he writes, 'Every severity and every apparent cruelty, either in word or deed that is ascribed in holy Scripture to God or his saints, avails to the pulling down of the dominion of lust.'[10] What applies to God and the saints, applies also to his tool, the pious nurse.

Monica gained a reputation as a good and obedient child, carrying out the tasks required of her as a daughter of the house. Throughout her childhood, even in her misdemeanours, Augustine sees the ever vigilant love of God protecting her. An incident of particular import is the story of how Monica developed a taste for wine in her adolescence. As a trusted daughter, Monica was sent to draw the wine for her parents' meals. Motivated by mischief and high spirits, according to Augustine, one day Monica touched her mouth to the brim of the cup, barely taking any wine because she did not like the taste. Each day, she would steal more sips of wine, until little by little she worked her way up to a cupful. Monica's tippling was noticed by the slave who assisted her. Wanting to upset her during a quarrel one day, the girl called Monica a drunk. Monica repented immediately. Implicit in her repentance is the sense of her being saved not only from 'drunkenness', but from the heightened sexual desires which accompanied it.

This story has been taken to indicate that Monica was well on the way to alcoholism, but the ease with which she renounced her habit suggests that she was not really an alcoholic, but rather a thirsty child, because of her nurse's strict discipline. Augustine uses the story as a set piece at the start of Monica's history, matching it at the end with another story, so that her incremental slide from high-spirited mischief to destructive habit forms a mirror image to her gradual ascent towards the vision of Wisdom at the end of her life.[11] In each situation she is almost panting for what she desires in each she is limited by her capacity, in each her capacity increases incrementally. The former would lead her to sin and death, the latter to eternal bliss.

The second parallel is that between Monica's theft of wine and Augustine's famous pear-stealing escapade. Like Monica's first minute sip of distasteful wine, the motivation was youthful mischief, not hunger. However, the significant differences are that he had no companion to chide him, and he did not repent immediately. The group's complicity and the peer pressure to participate are all part of the scenario. The speed of Monica's return to virtue stands in contrast to the years which would elapse before Augustine would return to the church. And it raises the question, 'Where was the ever-vigilant eye of God which had protected Monica?' Augustine tells us that his soul was so debased, that it broke wilfully away from God.[12] Eventually, God did bring Augustine round, and he shared with Monica that profound experience of Wisdom just before her death.

In setting up these echoes of sinful thefts and grace-filled redemptions Augustine is making several points. First, something as innocent as high spirits can lead to pernicious habit and hidden disease. Adult vigilance is required to prevent sin gaining the slightest foothold in their irresponsible children. Monica, and presumably her young slave, were reared in a Christian household, and this may have been the source of the slave's disdain for Monica's self-indulgent behaviour. The possibility that Augustine is implicitly comparing his mother's strongly disciplined upbringing, which stood her in such good stead, with the indulgence and worldliness of his own early education cannot be ignored here. As we shall see in the following discussion, this was one area where Augustine felt considerable bitterness towards his parents.

Second, Augustine highlights two aspects of the need for

humility: the sinner's ability to accept correction, and humility on the part of the one correcting. Whilst Augustine is cheered on by his friends, Monica is corrected by a slave, thus demonstrating that God has the ability to use even another's flaws to convert us: the angry servant desired only to taunt, but unwittingly became the agent of God's action, and was used to cure Monica's folly. Therefore, we should never take the credit for influencing another, either through love or anger: God is simply using us as his tools.

Third, Augustine chose a story about wine, to impress on Christians, and especially women, the importance of continence. The thefts of wine and pears subtly evoke the idea of the Fall which introduced sin and especially sexual depravity into the world through the theft of food. Similarly, Augustine consistently symbolised desire as wine or food. Taking up Ambrose's image of the sober intoxication of the Holy Spirit derived from Eucharist, he juxtaposed it to the image of those 'drunk with the invisible wine of [the world's] own perverted, earthbound will'. This intoxication is ascribed to Patricius precisely when he is overjoyed to find that Augustine has reached puberty because he 'relishes' the thought of grandchildren.[13] Monica's greedy mouth gulping at the wine is juxtaposed to the three gaping mouths of Augustine, Alypius and Nebridius, as they wait for God to grant them nourishment.[14] Very early in the *Confessiones* these two desires are totally opposed: physical needs or spiritual ones, human love or God's, children of the flesh or children of the spirit. Those seeking God, the true desire of the heart, will practise continence with regard to the appetites of the body, as Monica's old nurse had instructed her. Furthermore, beginning this discipline in childhood will reap rewards when women are responsible for their own households. So women are not only exhorted to abstemious behaviour but to proper child-rearing practices. The fact that the protagonist of the story who conquers her physical desires so quickly is a female harnesses male shame lest a woman outdo them in virtue, a theme we shall see appearing throughout his writings.[15]

Monica the obedient wife

It has been suggested that Monica did not learn subordination in her early years from her parents, but during her marriage to Patricius, because Augustine states that God taught Monica to obey her parents rather than her parents being the ones to teach her to obey God.[16] However, the other evidence concerning the piety and frugality of the household and the strong Christian faith of the nurse suggests that Augustine is simply underlining his dominant theme that credit always goes to God. The probability that Monica's nurse had more intimate contact and influence than her mother would be quite consistent with the data on the mother's role in antiquity.

Monica was given in marriage to Patricius 'when she was old enough', and she 'served him as her lord' all her married life. He in return, 'respected, loved and admired her'.[17] Augustine writes as if his audience would immediately understand how old she was, an understanding not shared by modernity which is still seeking evidence to clarify the customs. It is known that Romans tended to marry their daughters younger than the Greeks around the first century CE, and in the fourth century twelve was considered too young to marry. Monica had Augustine when she was about twenty-three, but we do not know whether he was her first or last child, or how long she was married before she became pregnant. The likelihood is that she was married in mid-teens, and that Patricius was somewhat older.

Patricius was not a Christian, and so Augustine finds it difficult to praise his father, because it is only virtues grounded in that love of God which are genuine and efficacious.[18] In addition, Patricius was not a faithful husband, and was quick to anger. Monica bore patiently with his faults, hoping always that her obedience and patience would win him to the Christian faith, as indeed they did on his deathbed. At a later time Augustine would castigate Christian wives who tolerated their husband's adultery,[19] but here he portrays Monica's patience as a primary virtue, grounded in her trust in God's mercy, and her hope that chastity would come with faith.[20]

Interpretations of Patricius as a violent[21] and brutally tyrannical man[22] certainly do not resemble the more nuanced picture obtained from the evidence that Augustine himself presents. There is only one mention of him ordering a beating for anyone, and that is at the behest of his own mother, to punish gossiping servants who had been disrupting the relationship between Monica and her mother-in-law. Monica's patient and deferential conduct wins over her mother-in-law, and so the elder woman demands Patricius rectify the matter. Augustine further says that Patricius was a 'remarkably kind' man, generous to a fault, who won the admiration of all for his self-sacrifice in providing Augustine with a superior education.[23] In fact, it seems clear that Monica loved Patricius and that they lived harmoniously together, until she was widowed at around age forty, when Augustine was sixteen. So happily, in fact, that for most of her life Monica had 'great anxiety' to be buried beside him, in the tomb she had erected for him.[24]

From a very early age Augustine was probably well aware that his father was not a man to be feared.[25] Certainly he would write later that it was preferable to be quick to anger and quick to beg pardon than slow to anger and slow to pardon.[26] It is more likely that Augustine described his father's behaviour in a light that would present his mother as the ideal Christian wife, in a society where sexual double standards and violence to control subordinates were an accepted way of life. Certainly, a great deal of emphasis is given to his mother's obedience to authority, even when they are her moral inferiors, and her forbearance in the face of unreasonableness and injustice.

Still, Augustine makes much of the fact that his father never beat his mother. Apparently, wife-beating surprised neither Monica nor Augustine. He states that

> many women, whose faces were disfigured by blows from hus-
> bands far sweeter tempered than her own, used to gossip together
> and complain of the treatment of their men-folk. My mother
> would meet this complaint with another about women's tongues.
> Her manner was light but her meaning serious when she told
> them that ever since they had heard the marriage deed read
> over them, they ought to regard it as a contract which bound
> them to serve their husbands, and from that time onward they
> should remember their condition and not defy their masters.[27]

The Latin uses the language of master–slave relationships: the husband is lord, *dominus*, the wife is slave, *ancilla*. Translations such as 'handmaiden' or 'servant' deaden the impact of using master–slave language for the status of free Roman women. Furthermore, in *sine manu* marriages (see p. 26) a husband did not have the legal right to beat his wife. Beating was a way of shaming the offender, and had a symbolic power because of its association with slavery.[28]

Scholars have argued that violence towards women occurred because mothers were caught up in the tensions caused by the *paterfamilias'* violent discipline of his sons, and that that was Augustine's situation. To argue that Monica was enmeshed in violence between Augustine and his father is to read far too much into the text.[29] Patricius never raised a hand to Monica, and certainly not to Augustine in his early years. Brutality to children in the *Confessiones* is associated with school masters and school.[30] However, if Augustine is to hold up his mother as the epitome of obedient subordination, all credit for self-control must be stripped from Patricius. Augustine is clearly offering his mother as a model to other Christian wives whom he perceives as at best ill-judged, and at worst contentious and haughtily defiant of legitimate authority. Wives who followed Monica's advice thanked her for its value. The dire alternative was to be abused into submission.[31]

Monica the mother

The focus of the *Confessiones* is not on Monica's marriage but on the mother–son relationship. Augustine as son takes over centre stage to the exclusion of all Monica's other children. It is an intriguing gap in his narrative that he does not mention his brother and sister as part of his early life, or in relationship to Monica. One brother is mentioned, although not by name, as being present at Monica's deathbed. We assume on the basis of the Cassiciacum *Dialogues* that he was Navigius, who is named there.[32] If it was not for *Epistle* 211, the existence of his sister would be unknown from Augustine's own writings. Yet she was a continent, vowed woman, abbess of a convent, and must have shared his values and faith if little else.[33] Even given that the *Confessiones* are not history but the recounting of a spiritual journey, it still seems inexplicable that his siblings played so little part in his consciousness that he can virtually ignore them. All the more significant then, that when Navigius does appear, it is always in an anecdote showing his lack of understanding and faith.[34] Monica's deathbed is another scene which places Navigius outside the intimate understanding shared by Augustine and his mother. Navigius wants to reassure Monica that her wish to be buried beside Patricius will be respected. Augustine portrays the dying Monica reproaching Navigius with her eyes, before saying to Augustine, 'Look what he says.' Monica then uses her dying breath to instruct them that for the faithful, nowhere now is far from God.[35] Possibly there is more than the surface import in the words Augustine will write later: that his true brothers are those who love him whether they see in him good or evil, for they rejoice in his good and grieve for his sin.[36] Or it is possible that Augustine needed a foil to ask the 'dumb question' so that he could introduce his argument concerning the attempts to localise God or divine power in any earthly locality? The subtle strategy, which trivialises concerns over grave sites, may have been an almost automatic expression of his concerns about the cult of the martyrs. Whatever the motivations for his depiction of Navigius, given the conspicuous omission of Monica's other children, the intimacy between mother and son is all the more remarkable.

This intimacy begins with his birth, for although he clearly had wet-nurses, Augustine states that Monica fed him herself, a somewhat unusual situation.[37] From his earliest references to his childhood, Monica is the ever present and significant figure who mediates the gifts of God to Augustine. But as with Monica's own nurse, and young slave, Monica is merely the vehicle for God's bounty. It was God who fills the breasts of his mother and nurses according to his natural law in such a way that even the humblest child shares in the divine largesse.[38] God was also the source of the love they lavished on him. This love and nurturing are twice blest, because in acting in accordance with God's will, both Augustine and they themselves are blest.[39] Sadly, he discounts all examples of Patricius' love for him because Patricius loves the 'creature' not the 'creator'.[40]

It appears that Augustine shared the Roman moralists' opinion that morality and religious sensitivity could be imparted through the breast milk and that, therefore, feeding is now a maternal duty with a deeper spiritual significance. In feeding him herself, Monica not only nourished his body with God's material generosity, but his 'infant heart had been suckled dutifully on [Jesus'] name, the name of your son, my Saviour'. This he intimates was the root of his ultimate conversion, and the beginning of his spiritual journey towards the Father.[41]

There are several indications that he received a tolerant, even indulgent upbringing in early childhood; school would come as a shock to him. At home, his tantrums were accepted as childish behaviour that he would outgrow. He remembers nostalgically the happy manner in which he learned to talk, playing with his nurses, who were patient listeners and the source of cuddles and laughter.[42] This almost idyllic time re-echoes through his imagery of the mothering God who soothes his weariness and heals his spiritual blindness, caressing him to turn him to conversion, as a mother caresses a fretful child to turn its head to her breast.[43]

With the advent of school, paradise is lost. Not even his prayers can save him from beatings at school.[44] Narrating the events of these years, Augustine refers to Monica and Patricius inclusively as 'my parents'.[45] Like the traditional Roman mother, Monica shared his father's concerns for their son. Both were ambitious for him and Monica further believed that ultimately his studies would help her son in his approach to God. It is in these years that the strongest undercurrents of emotional tension emerge between Augustine and Monica. Although she is a practising Christian, she was 'still loitering in the outskirts of Babylon' even during his adolescence.[46] Augustine, needless to say, dwelt in the city centre. Thus Monica shares her husband's blindness to the dangers of a classical education and is presented as being so oblivious to the torments that he suffered as a schoolboy, that she could find the recital of his woes amusing. After Patricius' death, Monica funds Augustine's studies out of her own resources, which could not have been extensive, given the earlier struggles to educate him. Monica is therefore included in Augustine's bitter judgement on those parents who have pity on neither students nor masters, yet 'willingly allow their children to be flogged if they are distracted by [theatre and games] from the studies which are supposed to fit them to grow rich, and give the same sorts of shows themselves'.[47]

Other grievances expressed with anger and bitterness were his mother's neglect of an early baptism and parental procrastination about an early marriage.[48] Although his mother was more upset by his unchaste behaviour than his father, she was not worried enough to arrange an early marriage for him, though whether she would have done so against Patricius' wishes is debatable. Augustine goes to so much trouble to show her as appropriately subordinate that it is inconsistent of him to blame her here. As far as Augustine is concerned, her actions were determined by the fear that an early marriage might have hindered his professional advancement, and there is no doubting the emotional quality of his comments:

> Was there no one to lull my distress, to turn the fleeting beauty of these new-found attractions to good purpose and set up a goal for their charms, so that the high tide of my youth might have rolled upon the shores of marriage? . . . My family made no effort to save me from my fall by marriage. Their only concern was that I should learn how to make a good speech and how to persuade others by my words.[49]

Yet Augustine was still very young at this time. It was before his father's death, and society expected young men to sow their wild oats and then make advantageous marriages in their later twenties. In contradictory fashion, the Augustine who castigated his parents for not arranging an early marriage, wrote that marriage did not attract him greatly and he did not understand men who dutifully raised a family, and did not think that they should be emulated.[50] Augustine knew full well that his mother was worried about his sexual behaviour, and that as a youth he denigrated her concern as 'womanish advice' (*monitus muliebres*) shameful to accept. It is quite possible that Monica's own experience of an unfaithful husband may have influenced her desire not to see Augustine married until his youthful desire for sexual affairs diminished, so that he might be able to remain a faithful husband. He himself was not looking for marriage but romance.[51] From his more mature perspective he understands her warnings as the voice of God, yet the judgement on Monica's motivation still stands, for it follows directly on this passage.[52]

Augustine also knew that even Christians deemed it preferable to allow these youthful peccadilloes to be behind a young man before he was baptised. But, unusually for him, he appears to hold his parents responsible for his later struggles and he expresses resentment that they did not preserve him from temptation by placing his soul in God's keeping through an early baptism.[53]

It may be that the less positive aspects of Monica's portrait have been coloured by the negativity of Augustine's feelings towards his father. As wife, her first allegiance was to Patricius, not to Augustine, and the devoted son in him may well have resented this. Or the intensity of the mother–son relationship may have weakened that of father and son. An ambiguous reference to Monica's influence is pertinent here. Augustine makes the extraordinary statement that his mother

> did all that she could see that you, my God, should be a father to me rather than he. In this you helped her to turn the scales against her husband, whom she always obeyed because by obeying him she obeyed your law, thereby showing greater virtue than he did.[54]

This implication that Monica subverted Patricius' fatherly authority whilst at the same time maintaining the appropriate wifely submission sits oddly with his statements about his parents' marital harmony, and Monica's obedience.[55] If his portrayal of his mother's behaviour is objectively true it may explain why even his father's most positive attributes and behaviours are discounted by Augustine. But if Augustine rejected his father because he saw in Patricius the qualities he most rejected in himself – ambition,[56] lust and anger[57] – then the passage may be to provide justification for such rejection. Possibly he is implying that he patterned himself on his father in these youthful years, and later resented the model his father provided for him, yet he desires to exonerate Monica because she tried to provide the ultimate male role model, God the Father. It is also probable that this legacy of ambiguity and bitterness made it difficult for him publicly to express his grief for his father, whose death is mentioned in passing, and only in retrospect.[58]

For Augustine, he and his father had shared only a 'carnal' relationship, not redeemed by any shared Christian experience, and therefore any affection felt by father and son would remain suspect in the categories of the older Augustine.[59] Augustine habitually shows himself little mercy, so perhaps it is not surprising that he shows so little compassion or understanding of his father. This experience may underlie his episcopal insistence that fathers must 'tame' and 'domesticate' their sons, judiciously employing fear as well as love, to ensure proper order.

> Those who are *true fathers* of their households desire and endeavour that all members of their household, equally with their own children, should worship and win God ... And if any member of the family [*quis autem in domo*] interrupts the domestic peace by disobedience, they are corrected either by word or blow.[60]

Here the wheel has come full circle. Where necessary, women, children and slaves must be tamed by physical punishment, if it will redound to their spiritual salvation. Augustine's image of the 'true father' in this passage implies that God is such a 'true Father'. Moreover, it is reminiscent of Lactantius' use of the *paterfamilias'* duel role as Lord and father to explain the dynamics of the spiritual *familia*. As Father, God loves us as children, as Lord God, he chastises us as slaves.[61]

Monica the prophet

The focus on Augustine's heavenly Father underlines that from a very early age human relationships were presented to him as subordinate to spiritual values, and this appears consistently in his mature teaching. Although Augustine apparently repudiated this in his youthful relationships, this position would have been supported by the theology of the Manichees who relativised human relationships in the direction of either libertinism or asceticism.[62]

Certainly, when it came to Augustine's faith development, Monica was capable of serious opposition. When he became a Manichee, she refused him house room until reassured by God in a dream that her son would come to stand beside her on the 'wooden rule' of faith. She was sure enough of the dream's divine source to be reconciled to him, secure in the knowledge of God's presence and the irresistible nature of grace. Try as he would to resist her interpretation of her dream, Augustine was deeply moved by her conviction even at the time. How much more as bishop would he see in this episode the providential work of God, at once consoling Monica and influencing his own heart, and assuring him that God knew from all time his eventual acceptance of the gift of faith.[63] One cannot help but wonder how much such a certitude on the part of Monica would become a self-fulfilling prophecy for her son.

It does Monica less than justice to interpret this dream as a self-serving motherly ploy to maintain both her faith and her relationship with her son in a tense situation. During this same period, Monica had implored an ex-Manichaean bishop to intercede with Augustine. This wise ecclesiastic, discerning that Augustine was not yet ready for instruction, believed that Augustine's own integrity and intelligence when confronted with the content of Manichaean doctrine would lead him to perceive his own errors. It is ironic that the tag so associated with Monica as praiseworthy in the later tradition, 'The son of such tears could never be lost', was originally a rather tongue-in-cheek remark of this elderly ecclesiastic, who was sick of Monica's pleas and wanted to get rid of her. So by both human and divine means Monica was invited to accept God's timetable, however difficult it was for her to do so.[64]

This was the first of three graced revelations through which God's will was revealed to her. The second occurred on her voyage to Italy. During a fierce storm the sailors were all terrified, but she has a vision of a safe landing, and guarantees that God will get them to shore, which indeed God does.[65] The third is the significance of a non-dream. Monica was eager for Augustine's marriage because she seems to have identified two commitments, baptism and marriage. If he was legitimately married, there would be no bar to baptism. At Augustine's request, Monica prays for a dream to clarify God's will. Augustine reports that although Monica had some vague and fanciful dreams, she deemed these the result of her own preoccupations with the matter, and did not consider them to indicate the will of God. It appears that Monica had the gift of discernment of spirits, and did not use her dreams to self-serving ends. Nor could she experience such dreams at will, or even as the result of heartfelt prayer.[66]

The son of such a mother

Nevertheless, Monica's tears are legendary, and it is easy to overlook the fact that Augustine tells us that she preserved a serene demeanour to his face. It was before God she wept and pleaded. It is probable that Augustine exaggerated the tear motif to emphasise that it is Monica's spiritual motherhood and her grief over his spiritual death that is significant. Augustine himself interprets her tears as sacramental, foreshadowing his baptism. Her tearful suffering on his behalf effected his conversion and really washed him clean. They are the medium through which he encounters the maternal God who calls him to herself as a little child, and through which he is finally brought home again not only to Monica, but to the church, and to God.[67]

The weeping Monica personifies the mourning widow who meets Christ as she accompanies the bier of her son. She believes in Christ's power to raise her son, but still her humanity grieves for him whilst he lies lifeless before her.[68]

> If I had died in that state, my mother's heart would never have recovered from the blow. Words cannot describe how dearly she loved me or how much greater was the anxiety she suffered for my spiritual birth than the physical pain she had endured in bringing me into the world. I cannot see how she could ever have recovered if I had died in that condition, for my death would have pierced the very heart of her love.[69]

Part of Augustine revelled in his emotional importance to his mother, and the fact that her world revolved around him.[70] The Monica he portrays is, outside her religious duties, focused almost exclusively on himself and his salvation. She cared for him like a mother and served him like a daughter.[71] To her he owed everything that he loved.[72] Her death wounded his soul and shattered his life, and bereft him of all comfort,[73] for their lives had been one. The imagery here is almost marital, but it is wise to note that it is not uncommon in late antiquity to find texts speaking of father and son as one flesh and one blood. This is because the father is the source of procreative power. As the mother was deemed to provide the material for the body of the child, Augustine may have conceived of his relationship with Monica in this way. His father may have been the source of his human life, but his mother was the source of his spiritual life. In this, she is the church personified, who has suckled him on the Word of God, Jesus.

Later (*c.* 421), after Monica's death, he will even argue that our dreams are not inspired by the spirits of the dead, for if they were Monica would be present in his, and she is not. He accepts this as proof that dreams arise from within the individual psyche. Otherwise he would have to accept that in her experience of heavenly joy she had become so cruel that she would not come to comfort her beloved son's grief.[74] As far as Augustine could see, the twin pillars of his mother's life had been her love for her God and her love for her son.[75] Certainly her joy at his conversion shows these aspects of Monica at their most ecstatic:

> Then we went in and told my mother, who was overjoyed . . . she was jubilant with triumph and glorified you, who are powerful enough, and more than powerful enough, to carry out your purpose beyond all our hopes and dreams. For she saw that you had granted her far more than she used to ask in her tearful prayers and plaintive lamentations. You converted me to yourself, so that I no longer desired a wife or placed any hope in this world but stood firmly upon the rule of faith where you had shown me to her in a dream so many years before. And you turned her sadness into rejoicing, into joy far fuller than her dearest wish, far sweeter and more chaste than any she had hoped to find in children begotten of my flesh.[76]

This passage has been interpreted as revealing Monica's deep joy that Augustine will never marry. This does not necessarily indicate maternal possessiveness; an alternative source could have been the maternal pride that her son has chosen the Christian path. Remember that Monica was reared by an ascetic nurse. The passage certainly conveys her surprise that her prayers had accomplished more

than she had asked for. As her dearest wish had been his marriage
and grandchildren, it is hard to justify the interpretation that she
would have preferred him to remain unmarried. Indeed, as we shall
see in the following section, she is often accused of forcing him
into marriage. Sometimes it seems that Monica as archetypal
mother draws interpretations that go far beyond the content of the
texts.

Monica and Dido

None the less, the very depth and strength of familial attachments
cast the shadows of primal sin over affective relationships for Augustine. Throughout his clerical life he had a deep suspicion of natural
ties of kinship and their importance to human beings. Only spiritual
bonds are free of this shadow.[77] Thus Monica's natural maternal
affection for him, displayed to us most extravagantly in the episode
of Augustine's flight to Milan, is condemned as the legacy of Eve
within her, driving her to seek 'in sorrow what she had brought
forth in sorrow'.[78] Augustine wished to go to Milan to advance his
career, without his mother. She accompanied him to Carthage,
pleading with him to stay, or else take her with him. Presumably
he was taking his partner and their son, as both were with him in
Milan. To evade Monica's entreaties, he settled her at a shrine, on
the pretext of farewelling a friend. He set sail without saying good-
bye, leaving her weeping on the shore. Her tears on this occasion
stand in stark contrast to her prayerful tears for his spiritual health,
though even here God used them to good purpose. After his secret-
ive departure,

> She was wild with grief, pouring her sighs and sorrows in your
> ear, because she thought you had not listened to her prayer. But
> you were letting my own desires carry me away on a journey that
> was to put an end to those desires, and you used her too jealous
> love for her son as a scourge of sorrow for her just punishment.[79]

However, we should not take this passage at face value. Again the
carefully crafted nature of the narrative suggests that objective
history might have been somewhat more mundane. A comparison
with Book 4 of Virgil's *Aeneid* is illuminating.[80] There Aeneas, the
patriarch of Italy, is called by the gods to leave his beloved Dido,
queen of Carthage, to whom he is betrothed, and to set sail to find
the promised land. Lacking the courage to face her, he sets sail in
secret. Dido commits suicide with Aeneas' sword, and is burnt on
a funeral pyre whose smoke follows to haunt him. This drama had
been one of Augustine's favourite classical pieces and he had won
a prize as a youth for interpreting Juno's lament over Dido. There

is no doubt that he has modelled this passage on the classical tragedy, but where he once wept for Dido, now he almost seems to delight in his mother's pain. Here Augustine is contrasting the classical and Christian sentiment.[81] Monica is not to be revered for her intense human emotion, but scourged. But through this, she will enter more deeply into the life of grace, whilst Dido languished amongst the shades. Notably, Monica did not imitate Dido's grand gesture, but more prosaically, packed up and went home.

Less attractive is Augustine's casting of himself in the role of the dutiful Aeneas, whose sneaky departure was at least ordered by a god. However he may later construe his departure as God-inspired, at the time it was ambition, not piety, which led him to leave Carthage. His flamboyant rhetoric in this passage is rather undermined by the more down to earth statement in *Confessiones* 6.1 that his mother had joined him when her piety gave her the strength to follow him over hill and high water, 'facing all perils in the sure faith she had in [God]'.[82]

Years later his advice to the youth Laetus about the appropriate way to deal with a possessive mother perhaps rings with the authenticity of experience. 'Is it perhaps those ten months that you lay in her womb and the pangs of birth: and the burden of bringing you up? This is what you must kill with the sword of salvation. That is earthly affection and still has the ring of the "old man".'[83] The manipulative, maternal blackmail with which Augustine appears to be so familiar may have contributed to his suspicions of affectionate kinship ties. It may underlie his advice to Laetus that 'this very private and personal love for you [must] be killed in her, in case she thinks it a more important bond that your unity as Christians'. The 'relics of Eve' render all women so dangerous that Augustine feels: 'What difference does it make whether it is a wife or a mother, when a man has to guard against Eve in every woman?'[84]

The universal Eve reduces women to one category of being. As symbolic of women's domestic role, she is not dangerous sexually, but she tempts men to place the personal above the communal, the private ahead of the public, the temporal ahead of the eternal.[85] What springs to mind is the foundering of the philosophic community so desired by Augustine and his colleagues. Happily investing a great deal of intellectual and emotional energy in planning their retreat to a communal life, philosophising far from the vexations of public office, their castles in the air collapsed when they at last realised that they would have to include their wives in any plan for their households to join forces. Augustine was planing to marry, and several of the others had already done so. Their wives and marriages were seen as obstacles to the philosophic endeavour and Augustine, still bound by desire, did not feel the equal of those men who were both married and lovers of wisdom, and therefore presumably capable of chaste marriage.[86] It is interesting that Augustine does not say that the women refused to co-operate but rather that 'when we began to ask ourselves whether the women would agree to the plan, all our carefully made arrangements collapsed and broke to pieces in our hands and were discarded'.[87]

But any resentments attached to the loss of the dream are placed firmly at the feet of the women because, however legitimate the problems, they are not seen as arising from the men's concerns but from the women's. Monica, despite her service, had the leisure and interest to participate in the philosophic and theological discussions.[88] But younger women would be tied to the detailed management of the household, to child-bearing, to pleasing their husbands; and just as certainly they would expect some of their husbands' time and attention.[89] Clearly, the relics of Eve stood in the way of the idyllic Christian life as Augustine perceived it then, and as he was to systematise it in the future.[90]

Certainly Augustine's final word concerning his parents in *Confessiones* 9.13 relativises his familial ties by emphasising that Monica and Patricius were not only his 'parents in this light that fails, but were my brother and sister, subject to you, our Father, in our Catholic mother the church, and will be my fellow citizens in the eternal Jerusalem'. It does not stretch the texts to suggest that, after Monica's death, her place in his life is taken by his Catholic mother, the church.

Monica the matchmaker

It is a often taken for granted in theological writing and popular imagination that Monica was responsible for the dismissal of Augustine's concubine. Although the *Confessiones* say nothing of the sort, Monica has been cast as instigator of her dismissal. She is further castigated by some commentators for tolerating the relationship as long as she did.[91] The more general assumption is that a woman as close to her son as Monica could not, and would not, tolerate sharing him. So she destroyed the relationship for her own ends – ambition for Augustine's social advancement and a Catholic marriage.[92] However, Monica had accepted the relationship for fifteen years, a fact which is ignored and unexplained by those who believe that she acted out of personal selfishness. And they further ignore that it was entirely appropriate for a mother to arrange a marriage for her son, if he so desired. In fact, the parental duty to do so was eventually recognised in law.[93]

Monica, philosophy and Christian spirituality

Not only the ambiguities of their personal relationship troubled Augustine when it came to understanding Monica. The *Dialogues* written at Cassiciacum attest to a certain tension between Augustine's concept of the élite Christians as philosophers, and his less erudite mother who nevertheless was able to hold her own in debates with these confident rhetoricians and officers of the state.[94] Augustine's tension arose from his belief that mastering philosophy is the love of wisdom, and that to attain the liberal arts is 'very difficult except for some very gifted person who even from boyhood has earnestly and constantly applied himself'.[95] Certainly he is thinking of men like himself. Therefore, the younger Augustine drew clear distinctions between the souls of the wise who lived a better and more sublime life, and the souls of the ordinary folk who did not love wisdom, and who would be 'utterly disregarded'.[96] But how could Augustine consign the mother, to whom he felt so indebted, to that fate?

Scholars have held diametrically opposed opinions on Augustine's resolution of this tension and in their interpretation of his depiction of Monica in the *Dialogues*. Some insist that Augustine is presenting her as the ideal Christian, others that he is trying to reconcile his conflicting images of her as at once the means of his salvation, and yet unlettered and superstitious. The latter argue that her own words subvert this attempt, and that Augustine ends by relegating her to devotional practices while the men continue their pursuit of wisdom.[97]

That Monica was neither philosophically sophisticated nor used to joining the men in their discussions is suggested by her diffidence about participating.[98] That Augustine and his peers considered her ignorant and superstitious, at least relatively speaking, is clear.[99] Yet she was able to articulate clearly and convincingly a mature exposition of the Scriptures and the principles inherent in them, in a manner that Augustine believed could only come from years of study.[100] Furthermore she was no longer afraid of death, a most difficult achievement for even the most learned,[101] and she was held in high esteem by Ambrose, 'great preacher and holy bishop', who could rarely even find the time to talk to her son.[102] Clearly, she could not be 'utterly disregarded' as one whose soul was unfit to join the superior cadre of those wise in philosophy.[103] The conclusion of Peter Brown that Augustine established Monica as the oracle of *primitive* piety takes some the nuances of Augustine's attitudes into account.[104]

At this time he was groping towards the awareness that the life of faith could grant Monica insights into the soul of sacred mysteries, yet still he remarks that she must leave the 'body' of the learned disciplines to the eloquent. So he attempts to persuade her to undertake the study of philosophy, because her talents and attitudes of mind would make it easy for her. When it finally dawned on him that she did not necessarily share his opinion that philosophy would add to her spiritual insights, he can find no better way out of the impasse than to advise her to keep praying, whilst he keeps studying.[105] Slowly Augustine had to redefine his concept of wisdom to be less philosophically oriented and more Christian, until the search for wisdom becomes the search for the kingdom of the *Logos*, and humble acceptance of its 'lowly door', the Scriptures.[106]

How daunting and distressing it must have been for that circle of élite masculine minds to be presented with the possibility that a woman, Monica, might have arrived at the same capacity for wisdom through her spiritual experience and study of the Scriptures.[107] I cannot agree with O'Connell's argument that Monica's capacities were simply the result of Augustine's imagination.[108] Augustine has no need to establish her intellectual skills in a world that preferred to assume that to be woman was to be irrational. That Monica was relatively uneducated, and totally unconvinced that philosophy was essential to Christian faith does not necessarily mean that her capacity to understand and interpret the faith was limited. O'Connell seems to be holding the same assumption as Augustine that the capacity for wisdom is derived from a classical education. Uneducated and stupid are not synonyms. Monica's wisdom learnt at the knee of her God and her struggles to live within the divine will are closer to the paradigm of the desert ascetics, to whom pilgrims travelled in search of that same wisdom. It is more consistent with Augustine's praise of her insights, and the tensions in the texts, that her conclusions did impress him, and troubled his élitism and cherished assumptions about philosophic thought.

What is revealed here is a clash of models of spirituality, the intersection of two very different ways of encountering the holy. It is interesting, then, that when he does sing her praises, he does not challenge the cultural assumptions about the inherent inferiority of women, but sees her as having exceeded the limitations of her gender through faith; she had particularly astonished his male companions with her Christian *apatheia* – she had no fear of death, and her serenity was grounded in the utter confidence that wherever she was she was in God's hand.[109] And this was no trite verbalisation. Monica was in Milan when Ambrose defied the boy-emperor Valentinian, who attempted to claim a church for the Arian congregation. Pious Milanese Nicaeans then occupied the cathedral, singing psalms and praying, a potentially life-threatening action. Monica played a leading part in these vigils, when the bishop outfaced Valentinian on the steps of the basilica. It is not so surprising then that Augustine writes: 'We thought we had some great man in our midst while in the meantime I became more fully aware whence and from what divine source this flowed.'[110] Thus the problem is solved by making Monica an honorary man, or rather, perceiving her virile status as the result of grace. The perception of woman *qua* woman remains the same.

By the time he wrote the *Confessiones*, Augustine had resolved his conflict between philosophy and faith, coming to the conclusion that the life of faith and the experience of God could illuminate the mind as brightly as philosophy. Monica is the exemplar of the faith route to God, as Augustine is of the philosophic. The Ostia vision is irrefutable proof of the resolution of his conflict.[111] In this vision, both Monica and Augustine touched their souls to the fount of life, as Monica had touched her lips to the wine jar. Recapitulating their individual falls into sin, their desire for God burning brighter and brighter, they ascended little by little, passing 'beyond even their own souls' to touch, for one shining moment, 'the joy of the Lord, eternal Wisdom, life-giving and the source of all being'. This experience of joint ecstasy erases all distance between mother and son.[112] Their encounter with the fountain of life can only be fleeting, for embodied humanity has not the capacity for more. His depiction of his recently deceased friend, Nebridius, reveals the ultimate intoxication. The lips of his spirit can drink at the fountain until his thirst is slaked. His joy is never ending, and the nature of the intoxication is such that he never forgets Augustine, for his drink is the Lord who is mindful of his servants.[113] Only death stands between Augustine, Monica and eternal joy.

Although the nature of this experience is still a matter of debate amongst scholars, the fact that Monica and Augustine shared the same joy suggests he is intending to convey a Christian rather than philosophic vision. Yet we are told that even in ecstasy, Monica's rejoicing is on Augustine's account. His ecstasy confirmed his commitment as a 'Catholic Christian', where Catholic means despising earthly happiness. With her goal accomplished, she literally has no further purpose in life.[114] Her focus, and Augustine's, is firmly on Augustine himself.

Monica's death

Monica's death, and Augustine's reaction to it, gives a further insight into his attitudes towards relationships. He grieved bitterly, but he could not allow himself or Adeodatus to weep. Here we catch a glimpse of the rigorous control that Augustine applied to his emotions. Stoicism, cultural mores about expressing grief for a parent, and a Christian hope in the resurrection could permit little room for the expression of human grief. Yet there are grounds for thinking that his response indicates something of his individual internalisation of these ideals. First, he implies his friends' surprise that he had no sense of grief. Second, Ambrose had had no such scruples about weeping publicly for his brother Satyrus in 379, and the congregation mourned him with tears also. In fact, Ambrose gives examples of the human Jesus weeping with grief to justify his own sorrow. He acknowledges the hope of resurrection and therefore the somewhat irrational nature of grief for Christians, but sees it a fitting expression of love for the departed.[115]

Augustine allowed himself no such gentle acceptance of his humanity. Bereft of comfort as he was, still he could not weep.[116] He perceived his pain as human weakness and he feared mockery, or accusations of sinfulness; so he prayed that God would erase his feelings. Sadly, when this did not happen, he believed that God did not answer his prayer, in order to teach him how enslaved he was to habit, even whilst living by the word of God. As a consequence his grief was a double torment to him:

> It was misery to feel myself so weak a victim of these human emotions, although we cannot escape them, since they are the natural lot of mankind, and so I had the added sorrow of being grieved by my own feelings, so that I was tormented by a twofold agony.[117]

It is only when he finally succumbed to tears in the privacy of his room, that he experiences the answer to his prayer. The gently mothering God of his conversion neither mocks nor condemns. The release of tears marked a turning point in his grieving. More significantly, he can go on to say that the wound healed and he is able to commit Monica to her God to 'rest in peace with her husband'.[118] This simple phrase may indicate that, finally, Augustine was able to resolve his conflict concerning Monica as wife and Monica as mother.[119]

This is one of the examples where Augustine's experience of God was odds with his philosophy. Because he 'knew' grief was unacceptable, the idea that his prayer's answer might come in the release of control was unthinkable. Only after the experience did he realise that God's healing and consolation could come through his tears, not in spite of them. Still, as late as the *Confessiones* he feels the need to justify himself to God and to those who might construe his tears as sinful. He is not sure enough of his experience to proclaim it as the workings of a grace which subverts the ideology of control.[120]

Monica as model materfamilias

Monica clearly reflects the ideal of the strong Roman mother whose worth redounds on her son. Her status as *univira* (see p. 26) further underlines her admirable fit with the stereotype, as does her reluctance to enter into public life, however modestly. Monica as the moral mentor is the very stuff of myth. Her fabled tearfulness serves to underline her concern for Augustine's spiritual survivial, and her total absorption in him as the principal focus of her life.[121]

Like Augustine, Monica is portrayed as a Christian on pilgrimage. She is an exemplar rather than the ideal Christian. That is, she is not perfect from her youth, but rather exhibits continuing growth by the grace of God. As Augustine journeys from the theft of the pears, through the barren years to a graced faith, so Monica journeys from the adolescent tippler to the very model of the Roman matron in her Christian guise. Both journeys are imaged as the return to the promised land from the exile of Babylon.[122] Even after her death Augustine does not claim perfection for her, but prays for her sins. Withal she is merciful and forgiving,[123] chaste, devout and prudent,[124] always a discreet peacemaker in the community.[125] Much of his language when speaking of Monica in this vein is redolent with the imagery he uses to speak of Mary, the archetypal handmaid of the Lord.[126] The parallels he presents between them are telling:

Mary	Monica
handmaid of the Lord	handmaid of the Lord[127]
faithful of heart	faithful of heart[128]
ponders on the signs from God (Luke 2.19–25)	ponders on the signs from the Lord[129]
obedient	obedient[130]
chaste	chaste[131]
humble	humble[132]
conceived Jesus in her heart	conceived Augustine spiritually in her heart[133]
God was true Father of Jesus	God was true Father of Augustine[134]

It is hard to escape the conclusion that, albeit perhaps unconsciously, Augustine wanted to identify Monica with Mary and himself with Jesus, and to remove himself as far as possible from the taint of concupiscence and the sin transmitted through his birth.

There is little trace in this interpretation of Monica of the simple, middle-class mother, or the typical pious lady fussing over ritual questions described by some commentators.[135] This is a formidable yet feminine woman, characterised by *gravitas* and *severitas*. She is spiritually rigorous and intellectually resourceful,[136] capable of vulgarity,[137] and at times exhibiting great courage.[138] Peter Brown's description of her as 'awesome' seems a more appropriate accolade.[139] It seems fitting that the last word on Monica should be left to Augustine: 'She had the weak body of a woman but the strong faith of a man, the composure of her years, a mother's love for her son, and the devotion of a Christian.'[140]

It is not difficult to see how the mother whom he credits with his spiritual as well as physical birth would become for Augustine the model for his understanding of the church's character. Where the church for Ambrose is the virgin bride, a pure beauty trembling on the brink of consummation with her beloved, the church for Augustine is overwhelmingly maternal. Like Monica her yearning is ever for her erring children and, like Monica, she seeks them patiently but inexorably, finally being willing to justify even torture, if it is motivated by the desire to convert the prodigal.[141] No one can come to God unless reborn in this spiritual mother.[142] The church becomes the arena of authentic relationship, a new family where God is Father and church is Mother, and Monica is no longer mother but sister in Christ.[143]

His experience of both his parents helped shape this imagery. Although the image of God as Father was instilled by Monica, the yearning for an earthly father who would control his impulses and save him from himself definitively shaped Augustine's image of God the Father. Augustine's Father God is the ideal *paterfamilias*, one who loves and punishes, and punshes because he loves. He is stern, because that is the only way rebellious children will learn. As both teacher and student Augustine himself learnt that the hard way.[144] Yet in his capacity to be both angry and loving, God's nature is tinctured with Augustine's experience of Patricius, whose anger rarely led him to violence. Augustine's godly Father can love him for all the right reasons. He is impressed not by Augustine's intellectual achievements, but his spiritual ones, not by his fame but his humility.

Although it is this stern Father who predominates in his God-imagery, Augustine's first profound spiritual experience was of the presence of God as mother: a mother who taught him with love, not ruled him with fear. His own story, in both the *Confessiones* and in the *Soliloquia*, relates this experience of God-Wisdom as feminine. In the former, Wisdom suckles him on her milk, God mothers him in his sinful fretfulness until he can see truth more clearly, and Continence-church appears to him in all her beauty to welcome him in her chaste embrace.[145] He depicted Wisdom as a woman of great beauty who only allows a chosen few to see her face to face.[146] In his interpretation of his personal experience, this mothering. God had to be relinquished after spiritual infancy, and replaced by a therapeutically punitive father God, until the soul was ready to transcend all such imagery and experience the pure light of eternal Wisdom.[147] This spiritual progression parallels Augustine's own human experience.[148] An infancy of unconditional love and mothering yielded to a harshly punitive educational system which finally brought him to the calm and abstract shores of philosophy.[149]

AUGUSTINE THE LOVER[1]

ALTHOUGH scholars have always considered the influence of Monica on Augustine's writings, the influence of his concubine is rarely given a detailed examination.[2] There is no consensus of opinion about the nature of this relationship or its influence on his theology. Some scholars assert that his perceptions of the good of marriage derive to some degree from his concubinage relationship,[3] whilst others have argued that his ideal of companionate marriage stems from his debates with Julian of Eclanum over the nature of original sin and its relationship to sexual relations.[4] Some contend that he never loved his concubine at all, as opposed to those who perceive him as genuinely loving her.[5] Although philosophy and Manichaeism are usually blamed for any negative attitudes he had to sexuality, rarely is this relationship considered in that context. Yet the relationship between Augustine and the mother of Adeodatus is one of the most poignant of his life. Their union existed for nearly half the period covered by the *Confessiones*.[6] Fifteen years of monogamous relationship must have influenced his thinking about women and about marriage.

This chapter will be concerned with the manner in which Augustine describes this relationship so as to present a particular attitude to sexuality, but it will also use the psychological dynamics of this relationship to elucidate the interaction between Augustine's experience, theology and cultural context. Augustine's philosophical milieu and world-view would privilege certain psychological dynamics over others, in their influence on his early theology. His later Pelagian debates with Julian would force him to wrestle with his attitudes to sexuality at the theological and personal levels.

The legal and ecclesial status of concubinage[7]

Augustine' relationship with Adeodatus' mother is perceived by scholars to be that of concubinage, although the habit of describing her as his mistress creates an inappropriate image in contemporary thought, and is perpetuated by interpretive translations which use 'mistress' for the '*unam*' that Augustine typically uses.[8]

Roman concubinage was a common and acceptable relationship in antiquity.[9] It was usually a stable and sexually exclusive relationship entered into by those excluded from marriage by legal or social constraints.[10] Thus it occupied the middle ground between marriage on the one hand and adultery and carnal knowledge on the other. Concubines, like wives, could bear the title of matron and, if so, could be charged with adultery. All respectable concubines had the status of matron if they did not leave their master-spouse against his will. Hence, a man would protect his rights by making the relationship official. These circumstances make it likely that for his own protection from the charge of carnal knowledge, and to enhance his rights over his partner, Augustine would have established the young woman as his concubine.[11] Concubinage did not affect a man's social standing, his family lineage or, as a general rule, the disposal of his estate. Children were illegitimate but socially acceptable, taking their name and status from their mother and belonging to her *familia*.[12] Their fathers were not expected to be responsible for them, whereas legitimate children remained with their fathers.[13]

The boundaries between marriage and concubinage constituted a grey area, and in situations of conflict the jurists distinguished between them using the criteria of *affectio maritalis*. By late antiquity this connoted both the intention to be married and a degree of marital affection.[14] Where that existed, then a marriage in some sense existed. The intangible intention was assessed by how the couple treated each other – did they regard each other as spouses? If they did, they could consider themselves married without any official ceremony or regularisation.[15] This is an important point to bear in mind in the context of this discussion.

Because of the legal circumstances, the church, like Roman law, tended to assimilate concubinage to marriage, if a couple intended fidelity, procreation and lifelong commitment.[16] In fact, in *Sermo* 224 Augustine says that concubinage was so common a situation that it would be impossible to excommunicate all the men;[17] and the Council of Toledo (397–400 CE) specifically permitted unmarried men with one concubine to receive communion.[18] Those bishops opposed to concubinage required that a man either marry his concubine, manumitting her if necessary, or dismiss her and marry another woman legally.[19] However, if the dismissed partner wished for baptism, she must remain celibate, or be excluded from baptism or communion as an adulteress. It is significant that a man could dismiss his concubine and marry another woman in order to be accepted for baptism, but that the woman, if she wished for baptism, must remain celibate, and possibly indigent, if repudiated. Why it should have been adultery for the women is unexplained.[20] Jerome went even further. He advised concubinage rather than marriage, because it would not be an impediment to later ordination 'if a man came to his senses'. The cynicism of this view, and the lack of concern for the women so exploited, is appalling by any criterion, ancient or modern.[21]

Where a Christian woman was a slave to a pagan master, but held the status of concubine, she would be admitted to baptism if she was faithful to him for her lifetime and reared her own children.[22] As Aline Rousselle points out, this was asking a great deal of a slave. Given the rights of the *paterfamilias*, the rearing of her own children was well beyond her control. Her master/concubine could demand she practise birth control, that she abort, or he could expose or sell her children.[23] Presumably, if he did none of these things, but permitted her to raise her children, he was according her privileges not usually accorded a slave. The church would then recognise their liaison as marriage. However, this would make her status as a Christian dependent on the will of a pagan master, ignoring the woman's intentions and will.

The ecclesial tolerance of concubinage[24] throws doubt on the very common assumption that the only reason Augustine never married this concubine, but became betrothed to another, was because of legal impediments arising from her status, or his desire to receive baptism.[25] If she were a slave he could have manumitted her to marry her legally. Only men of senatorial rank were forbidden to marry freedwomen.[26] Even if she had belonged to a group forbidden to marry legally, the church would have recognised their relationship as marriage given the proper conditions.[27] So we must look for other motives for her dismissal.

Augustine's version of his experience

Augustine offers scant detail about his partner, and never mentions her by name. This is usually seen as significant, and is accounted for by either his respect for her,[28] his wish to spare them both embarrassment,[29] or pain at her memory.[30] However he seems to have a quirk about names in general, only mentioning his mother by name once;[31] and never mentioning the name of his youthful friend whose death so shattered him.[32] In letters he will sometimes resort to extraordinary circumlocutions to avoid mentioning names, yet he frequently names Alypius. There is no discernible pattern to his practice, and it would not seem that any particular interpretation can be placed on his never naming the mother of Adeodatus.[33]

They met when Augustine was still in his late teens, and she was likely to have been even younger. It has been suggested on the basis of *Confessiones* 3.3 that they met in church, and that it is likely that she, too, was at least a Christian catechumen then.[34] This passage is too slight a foundation for such a conclusion, but her vow of continence upon her dismissal, consistent with the church's require-ments for baptism, supports the inference that she became a cat-echumen before her dismissal.[35] If she were a slave, she met all the criteria for baptism – her partner was faithful during the relationship, she raised her own son, who was educated and sponsored as a young man by his father, and she vowed lifelong fidelity. It is likely that as Augustine moved away from Manichaeism towards Catholicism, they began to share a common faith.[36] Although her Christian faith is clear to scholars, neither they nor Augustine raise the possibility that she, like Monica, may have influenced his conversion.

This is not surprising as he consistently represents the relation-ship as sinful because sexual, although the tensions within the *Confessiones* indicate that the reality was far more complex. However, Augustine's intent to depict his conversion as his redemption from the bonds of sexual sin, made manifest in this relationship, renders her a sinner.[37]

Monica's lack of opposition to the relationship also suggests its acceptability, and the likelihood that this young woman, after the birth of Adeodatus, was a respectable matron. If she had been really unacceptable to Monica it is difficult to see Monica sharing a home with her. As already mentioned, Monica refused to share a table or a roof with her son because he had become a Manichee, and that was two years after the beginning of this relationship.[38] And Monica loved Adeodatus.[39]

There is an interesting 'slip of the tongue' in the *Confessiones* 6.14 when Augustine is referring to the men's plans for a philosophic community coming undone when they thought about 'the little women's *(mulierculae)*' reactions. He hastily points out that he was not yet married but had to take his future marriage into account. As his affianced bride was so very young, and as this passage chrono-logically occurs before his concubine's dismissal, it does not stretch the text to include her in the category 'wife'.[40] However, formal marriage to her would have obliterated Augustine's social and vocational aspirations. He could never have cemented his place with Ambrose, or the Milanese Court,[41] and a wifely dowry would have allowed him to pursue his ambitions 'so that the expense would be no burden'.[42]

Augustine describes his attachment in rhetorical language, and so the similes and metaphors tend to extravagance. But in making his confessional prayer public he also has pedagogical intent, and his rhetoric overemphasises negative imagery, because that is most

persuasive.[43] In Augustine's discourse, love is a mixed cup of bitterness and pleasure, fraught with snares and pain.[44] He reduces his
attachment to a 'disease of the flesh'[45] and uses the symbolism of
bondage to present himself as a prisoner of habit, a slave to
insatiable lust.[46] This viewpoint depicts his concubine simply as a
convenience to satisfy his lust.[47] There is something egocentric if
not outright distasteful in his passing reference to his 'ability to
enjoy all the pleasures of the body at the mere nod of the head'.[48]
The text in which he introduces her is illuminating:

> In those years I had a woman. She was not my partner in what
> is called lawful marriage. I had found her in my state of wandering
> desire and lack of prudence. Nevertheless, she was the only one
> for me, and I was faithful to her. With her I learnt by direct
> experience how wide a difference there was between the partner-
> ship of marriage entered into for the sake of having a family and
> the mutual consent of those whose love is a matter of physical sex,
> and for whom the birth of a child is contrary to their intention –
> even though, if offspring arrive, they compel their parents to love
> them.[49]

The text holds within itself a tension born of the contradictions
between lust and fidelity, lack of direction and commitment, avoidance and love of children. It was a strange lust that was faithful for
fourteen years. Rather, scholars agree that, contrary to popular
myth, Augustine's continence in a promiscuous world was remarkable.[50] The uncritical acceptance of his own categorisation of the
relationship has suggested to some scholars that this woman was
an unfit intellectual companion for Augustine, with nothing to offer
but sexual services. In her case, as in Monica's, lack of education
should never be confused with lack of wisdom and stupidity.[51] In the
Soliloquia his ideal wife was educated or teachable.[52] The opposition
between intellect and sexuality is a false one, rooted in the very
paradigms that Augustine himself propounded, and it perpetuates
his own reconstruction of the alliance.[53] Intellectual or not, his
'wandering desire' remained very much directed to her until her
dismissal and he still mourned her loss a decade later.[54]

Similarly, there is a tension in his remarks about children. Allowing for a father's partiality, Adeodatus' charm must owe something
to his mother and the quality of the relationship that nurtured
him, and this Augustine acknowledges indirectly in Confessiones 9:
'I acknowledge that he has all his gifts from you, O Lord my
God ... It was you too, and none other, who had inspired us to
bring him up as you would have him.'[55]

Although Augustine claimed to have had 'nothing in him but the
sin', this contradicts his interpretation of his own rearing, where

he saw his mother and his nurses as the instruments of God.[56] Although Adeodatus undoubtedly loved his grandmother,[57] there is no reason to assume that Monica was responsible for his character and that his personality owed nothing to his mother.[58]

What confused the issue for Augustine was the sexual nature of their relationship which his training and socialisation had taught him to see as inferior to male friendship and potentially dangerous.[59] His concubine could distract him from philosophy more quickly than anything else.[60] This tainted his understanding of his tenderer feelings, as desire would later taint the good of marriage.[61]

A further question is: 'How real is Augustine's opposition between a lustful love and true marriage?' How could he learn to differentiate them from his own experience, if he had only lived one half of the equation? Bk 6 offers one answer. Here he describes his relationship in idyllic terms, distinguishing carefully between Alypius' 'hasty' and 'furtive' youthful experiments with sex, and his own 'settled way of life . . . which required only the respectable name of marriage'![62] It sounds very much as if Augustine and his concubine were indeed living as *de facto* spouses, and that the 'lustful bargain' is a rhetorical device to create a clear boundary between *de facto* marriage and marriage *de jure*.

Augustine operates at two levels when writing about this relationship. *Confessiones* 6.15 relates:

> The woman with whom I habitually slept was torn from my side because she was a hindrance to my marriage. My heart which was deeply attached to her, was cut and wounded, and left a trail of blood. She returned to Africa, vowing never to go with another man. She left with me the natural son I had by her. But I was unhappy, incapable of following a woman's example, and impatient of delay. I was to get the girl I had proposed to only at the end of two years. As I was not a lover of marriage but a slave of lust, I procured another woman, not of course as wife. By this liaison the disease of my soul might be sustained and kept active, either in full vigour or even increasing, so that the habit would be guarded and fostered until I came to the kingdom of marriage. But my wound inflicted by the earlier parting, was not healed. After inflammation and sharp pain, it festered. The pain made me as it were frigid but desperate.[63]

Here Augustine ostensibly accuses himself of sexual licentiousness, but the imagery creates a subversive subtext. Although his portrayal of a festering incision is consistent with that of his sexual sins as running sores, his language is nuanced with meanings of injury and grief.[64] The image of his concubine as hindrance conflicts with the marital image of his cleaving to her in one flesh.[65] As early as

December 386,[66] he had used this symbolism when discussing grief
which 'tries to rend what used to be one. Therefore it is trouble-
some and dangerous to become one with what can be separated.'[67]
It is little wonder that he felt so much shame and guilt at taking
another woman in her place. It would not be surprising, if in his
lacerated heart, sex with another woman felt more like adultery
than anything else. One of the most significant factors is that even
fifteen years later the wound still throbbed.

In *De bono coniugali* there is further evidence that the dissolution
of a *de facto* marriage is at stake.[68] Augustine offers a test case
concerning concubinage which parallels his own situation. His criteria for assimilating concubinage to marriage, are, with one exception, consistent with the *Apostolic Constitutions*.[69] He differs from
the canons in that he denounces as adulterers men who dismiss
their concubines to marry women of suitable rank and fortune. One
must be married to commit adultery. In condemning such men, he
condemns himself.[70] He stipulates that if the woman remains celibate, then although a sinner, she is not an adulteress, and in so far
as she only desired intercourse for children, she is preferable to
many married women! In making such a woman a model of a
faithful spouse, he affirms his concubine.[71]

As Augustine was a Manichee for nine of the years of his concubinage,[72] Manichaean doctrine is also relevant here. From the Manichees' perspective, childless concubinage was considered the least
evil of all sexual relationships, because no souls were trapped in
flesh and partners were legally free to move on to celibate perfection.[73] The Manichaean belief that child-bearing perpetuated evil
raised the question of birth-control for its adherents. Adeodatus
was born just before Augustine became an *auditor*, and they had no
further children. *De bono coniugali* 5.5 implies that Augustine and
his partner practised birth-control, and that she was not happy
about it;[74] if this is an accurate reading, then Augustine's earlier
inference in the *Confessiones* – that she shared his intentions for a
childless, uncommitted partnership – may be simply assumption on
his part, especially considering her vow of fidelity.[75]

It is an ironic twist that the lack of *intentio maritalis*, and the
prevention of children, which satisfied the conscience of Augustine
the Manichee, accused that of Augustine the Catholic. The disconti-
nuity between his two faith perspectives also meant he worried that
fidelity 'employed to commit sin' did not deserve to be called
fidelity.[76] Augustine could have resolved the conflict between baptism and his relationship simply by expressing the *intentio maritalis*
and maintaining lifelong fidelity. His concubinage would have
merged seamlessly into marriage and Augustine could have been
baptised without a worry.

Two factors prevented this: a socially upward marriage was essential to his ambitions, and the Christian ideal he had imbibed from the Milanese presented celibacy as a lifestyle manifesting true 'commitment' to God.[77] True, not all Christians aspired to it, but it was the mark of the best, and Augustine loved to be a winner.[78]

It is not surprising that in 395 he writes to a friend: 'The bonds of this world ... have a real harshness and delusive charm, certain pain and uncertain pleasure, hard toil and troubled rest, an experience full of misery, and a hope devoid of happiness.'[79] Within the space of the next four years Augustine lost not only his lover, but his mother, his son and two intimate friends.[80] These successive bereavements may well have been a driving motive behind his later rejection of affective relationships.[81] He associated affective relationships with grief, and perceived freedom from affectivity, and therefore grief as godlike, for 'no one can part You from the things that You love, and safety is assured nowhere but in You. Grief eats away its heart for the loss of things which it took pleasure in desiring, because it wants to be like You, from whom nothing can be taken away.'[82]

Critical analysis of Augustine's self-evaluation

In the *Soliloquia* Augustine revealed more complex motives for marriage than simply respectable sex. When personified Reason suggested the desirability of a lovely well-educated wife, who caused no inconvenience: a partner on his spiritual journey, who would fund his philosophic quest, Augustine enigmatically asked: 'And where should I dare hope for the like?'[83] Perhaps the knowledge that he had just dismissed her because she could not advance his career through her connections and dowry lies behind his question.[84]

Usually, Augustine's taking of a second concubine is seen as establishing either his addiction to sinful sexuality or his inability to love at all. However both the second relationship and the denigration of the first may be explained in terms of the process of grief resolution. It is typical in the experience of grief that the bereaved experiences denial, anger, bargaining with God and depression, before acceptance is reached.[85] I contend that Augustine never completed this process but short-circuited his grief through the psychological process known as cognitive dissonance.

When people are confronted with a crucial choice between two mutually exclusive but equally desirable options, the conflict creates an internal tension. When a choice is forced, the inevitable grief felt for the lost choice adds to the psychological turmoil. This mental disharmony, or cognitive dissonance, must be resolved, if the person is to continue with an undivided heart. If not, the individual may be unable to function effectively due to nostalgia for the lost desire. There are various mechanisms that can be employed either consciously or unconsciously to resolve the dilemma. One can seek the 'will of God', which creates the illusion that the choice was not really ours to make. One can refuse to choose, and live in a constant paralysis of indecision. Or one can minimise the dissonance by emphasising all the positive and desirable aspects of the chosen option and focusing on all the undesirable and negative aspects of the rejected alternative. In this manner, the chosen alternative is rationalised so as to become far superior to the rejected one, until, ultimately, the rejected alternative is no longer seen as loss, but as undesirable.[86] This can be an appropriate option when followed consciously with due regard for the normal grieving processes. However, there is a very real danger that it will be invoked unconsciously and therefore uncritically so that the grieving process remains stuck in denial. The classic example is Aesop's fable of the Fox and the sour grapes.

There is clear evidence that Augustine tried all three mechanisms. His internal conflict over the choice between ascetic Christianity and public life paralysed him for some time.[87] In whatever he did Augustine had to belong to the brightest and the best.[88] So if he is to become a Christian he will have to become an ascetic philosopher.[89] On the other hand, the possibility of another love, a family perhaps, some material comforts if not luxury, a distinguished career, and social elevation had their own charms. To make this decision he experienced an agony of labour and grief: he could see no haven in the world, yet he could not 'turn back where I might find contentment and satisfaction'.[90] Having made his decision to dismiss his concubine, as a morally and socially upward career move, but still believing his other choices open, he discovered that he had not chosen virtue over lust, but pragmatic ambition over love.[91] Perhaps it was only when he took another woman that he fully realised that whilst another could take her place in his bed, she could not do so in his heart. From now on, only God's love will offer the sanctuary he seeks, the guarantee that what he loves can never be reft from him again.

The grief process can be examined to some degree. His woundedness is manifest, yet he can only for brief moments admit the extent of his loss.[92] It is enlightening to compare Augustine's treatments of other bereavements in the *Confessiones*. About these relationships, sinful and otherwise, he discourses at length. Monica he can talk about comfortably and easily. His grief at the death of a youthful friend receives extended treatment, with Augustine describing and exploring his feelings in detail.[93] In both these cases all 'this is past

and time has healed the wound'.[94] His treatment of Adeodatus'
death is sketchy. He felt no apprehension of his boy's eternal happiness, because Adeodatus was all God would wish him to be, but
the allusive narrative avoids his own feelings of loss. The only
wound that he explicitly said had not healed is that from the loss
of his lover, although his almost cavalier reference to the death of
Patricius in passing suggests that here too he had an unacknowl-
edged grief.[95]

His grief is still unmistakable in the writings of 386, yet his
denial, which appeared to be operative much of the time, prevented
him from resolving it.[96] At the time, he attempted to minimise the
dissonance by convincing himself that what he had wanted and now
missed was a sex object, not a loving relationship. Hence the second
woman who is quite consistent with the dynamic of cognitive dissonance. If she can replace his concubine, he is confirmed in his
rationalisations of his behaviour. That this did not work is clear
from his discovery that lust was now a weak chain that soon snapped
and freed him.[97] In his later reflections, he opted for the 'will of
God' approach. His distress was only a divine goad thrust in his
heart to return him to God.[98] Hence it was the will of God, not a
mistaken choice, the cauterising of the putrid sore of lust, not
a genuine wound of grief for which he was responsible. That both
attempts failed pitifully is apparent from his own anguished cry that
the wound never healed.

But are the other stages of grief in evidence? Anger, the second
stage of grief, is less directly accessible. Sometimes anger turns
inwards, but often the bereaved is angry with the one lost, as if she
or he had in some way been responsible for the separation and
pain. Augustine certainly was angry with himself,[99] and he sees his
concubine very much as responsible for his responses to her. Her
embraces are a snare,[100] her caresses drag him from the manly
heights of philosophy, and sex vitiates his masculine spirit;[101] and
after her dismissal, memories of their sexual life continue to tempt
him, and delay him from embracing asceticism.[102]

Augustine's own experience of his sexuality must not be dismissed
out of hand. What comes through clearly is the feeling of 'drivenness', the experience of compulsion in his sexual need. He conveys
a sense of feeling out of control albeit with only one partner. This
feeling may arise from his conviction that anything which moves a
man beyond conscious control is evil. The less his reason is in
control, the more sinful sexuality is deemed. Psychological theory
would suggest that the more an individual attempts to control by
will power behaviour that is motivated by unconscious needs the
more obsessive the behaviour becomes. If this was true for Augus-

tine it is understandable that he would experience his sexual needs as beyond his control.[103]

He definitely presents his loss as something forced on him, using the passive form of the verbs throughout 6.15. It is a significant omission that, when first discussing his plans to marry, he never mentions the consequences for his concubine. Most scholars, reluctant to hold Augustine responsible for his concubine's dismissal, blame Monica. Those few who do hold him accountable either defend his actions on the grounds of custom or law, or accuse him of never loving his concubine in the first place.[104] Peter Brown blames 'high catholic principles and the great snobbery of the Milanese', but this still tacitly excuses Augustine from blame.[105] Certainly, snobbery may have a great deal to do with it, but it was Augustine's as well. Again, denial of unpleasant reality may have obscured the consequences of his betrothal until they were forced upon him. From the perspective of his young fiancée, it would have been a difficult situation to be betrothed to a man whose household still included a partner of fifteen years standing, and for her family too, a sign of good faith for their daughter's future was not unreasonable. The anger Augustine felt with himself over the whole sordid situation probably reinforced his desire to protect himself from a recurrence of any similar grief.

The bargaining stage of the grief process is found in both the *Soliloquia* and the *Confessiones*.[106] In the former, Augustine offers to tell no more lies about his feelings if Reason will not torment him by probing his heart.[107] In the *Confessiones* he trades exclusive love of God for freedom from grief: 'When at last I cling to you with all my being, for me there will be no more sorrow, no more toil. Then at last I shall be alive with true life, for my life will be wholly filled with you.'[108] Depression and pain resonate in his rhetoric; and he seems to assume that a true life in God will hold no grief. Whether he ever achieved the fourth stage of true acceptance rather than resignation to the *fait accompli* is difficult to assess, but his later writings on prelapsarian sexuality suggest that in his later years he accepted his own sexuality as having some positive value.[109]

The impact on his theology

As bishop, Augustine usually condemns concubinage as sin and considers it marriage only under stringent conditions, although certainly by 418 he is quite aware that the Hebrew Bible uses wife and concubine interchangeably at times.[110] In *De genesi ad litteram* Augustine denies that a man should recognise his need for a wife and receive her as precious.[111] Adams cry that Eve is flesh of his flesh and bone of his bone would have been far more 'tender and loving' if he had said 'soul of my soul'.[112] His misunderstanding of the Hebraic unity of body and soul, his projection of Neoplatonic dualism onto the Genesis text, and his personal rationalisations merge in an exegesis which maintains his fiction that 'rending of what used to be one' was a strictly physical rending of bodies, not persons, and validates his concubine's dismissal as morally acceptable. To do so he has to split marital sexuality from marital affection and intention, and he was one of the few patristic authors to make this distinction.[113] Augustine did this in two ways. First, he followed Ambrose in denying that sexual consummation was integral to the definition of marriage. The essence of marriage was in the intention.[114] Second, he argued that, within marriage, true affection for a spouse did not encompass sexual desire except as an undesirable albeit necessary adjunct to the procreation of children. Men were exhorted to love their wives in so far as they were Christians, but hate them in so far as they aroused desire.[115]

Certainly in his episcopal sermons and treatises he did encourage the possibility of friendship between married couples, but preferred to see it as originating from shared parenting or from the practice of abstinence, which should be increasingly evident as the marriage becomes holier, rather than from sexual union.[116] Perhaps it was not only observation of his congregation but his own experience that taught him the meaning of the companionship which grows between men and women who faithfully share their lives. But in his earlier works, desire so infiltrated even Christian marriage that it could never be really chaste,[117] because spouses could not meet the requirement of true friendship that they love each for their own sakes.[118]

Thus the fellowship of marriage is not enough to constitute marriage a good for its own sake.[119] Goods for their own sake are wisdom, health and friendship. Marriage is only a good for certain ends:[120] procreation,[121] controlling concupiscence,[122] spiritual companionship, and producing numerous offspring to share 'holy friendships'.[123] This means the fellowship of marriage is not of the same quality as that of friendship between men. That is a good in itself, because it constitutes a bonding of souls, whereas marriage is principally as a union of flesh.[124] This is a paradoxical assessment given the primacy of intention over consummation as the true criterion for marriage in his thought. The privileging of intention as the essence of marriage, a minority stance, is essential to maintain the integrity of the *Confessiones*, where he emphasised that he did not intend to be married, although living 'as if' married. Thus the 'cleaving' in one flesh holds no implications as to marital status.[125] His theology empties the biblical imagery of meaning, reconstructing it as the most inferior, although the most dominant aspect of the marriage.[126] Related to this attitude to marital good is his understanding of male friendship as creating community, while marriage is a private good.[127] Augustine consistently opposed private affective relationships and the communal good, for the former may imperil the latter.[128]

His disapproval of concubinage may also have stemmed from his awareness of the exploitation of women inherent in concubinage. Concubines were easily discarded and most were without dowries to reclaim.[129] He was also aware of the wounds women suffered from the infidelity that was often treated as a joke by men.[130] This sensitivity may have reinforced his vehement conviction that men had the same obligations to chastity and fidelity as women.[131] The effect of his own unilateral choices on his son and his partner may have influenced his insistence that sexual rights and obligations are reciprocal,[132] and his preaching that the love of a spouse should be motivated by personal qualities rather than wealth, class or appearance.[133] This aspect of marital love is one of the few which he applies to spirituality. The soul is like a wife who loves her husband for himself, not for his gifts, not for his wealth, not for his honour. She is the model of perfect chastity. She is also an exemplar that might have been inspired by Augustine's partner, who loved him as a youthful student, a struggling teacher, and anguished convert, and who acquiesced in her own dismissal for his benefit.[134]

Augustine tried very hard to maintain the fiction that all committed Christians secretly yearned to be celibate.[135] In De bono coniugali, after discussing the problems of incontinence, adultery and deviant sexual practices within the community, he can still go on to ask rhetorically:

> What Christian men of our time, being free of the marriage bond, having the power to abstain from all sexual intercourse . . . would not choose to keep virginal or widowed continence, than . . . to endure tribulation of the flesh without which marriages cannot be?[136]

However, later in De civitate Dei he conceded that some duly controlled desire may have been present in Paradise, though he would prefer to think otherwise. I would agree here with Clark that it was Julian of Eclanum's perceptive challenges to his position that forced him to confront all the logical implications of his earlier writings and revise them. This is one more example of Augustine's rigorous intellectual honesty and humility. It is important to note that what Augustine repudiated was not desire per se, nor pleasure, but inordinate desire and pleasure not controlled by the will. Perhaps we have his concubine to thank for his willingness to reject the fiercely ascetic belief that sexuality was a result of the Fall. Augustine knew at some level that sexual desire and its expression were not fundamentally evil, but it took the pressure from Julian and the rest of his life to integrate it into his theology.[137]

Given this development in his thinking, the criticism that Manichaeism always influenced Augustine to some extent, is difficult to support unequivocally.[138] Augustine was a man of passionate convictions who set himself the standard of perfection. In his choices regarding both philosophy and religion he was drawn to asceticism, and the rhetoric of dualistic tensions. But he did not teach the dualism of creation, nor that the flesh is inherently evil and eternally opposed to the spirit.[139] The fear of desire when it overwhelms reason permeates philosophy and literature, as well as Manichaeism, and male fear of the debilitating effects of intercourse was rife in the culture.[140] The critical question is: if his interpretation was influenced by an emotional need to be in control of every facet of his life, can the way his personality influenced his interpretation continue to provide a truly theological basis for perceiving sexual desire and pleasure without procreative intent as sinful?[141]

A final point returns us to Augustine's desire to convert others to continence by his own example. This means that he cannot be positive about his concubinage. It is significant that the story he places just before his own conversion is precisely that of two young men who renounced marriage to become celibate Christians. Their fiancées became consecrated women.[142] Their situation parallels that of Augustine and his concubine, although in his case it is she who sets the example.[143]

9

Augustine the cleric

A LL the available sources indicate that, once a cleric, Augustine never had a close woman friend, or allowed women into his personal sphere any more than was strictly necessary.[1] This follows logically from his decision at Cassiciacum, when he abjured feminine companionship. Augustine had felt constrained to choose between his desire for a woman and his desire for God, and he had chosen God.[2] The issues of desire, emotional vulnerability, grief and spiritual death associated with women created a powerful barrier to even Platonic heterosexual relationships in his mature life. Further factors would be his desire to avoid any more scandal about his moral life, especially in the light of the revelations he has made in the *Confessiones* about his struggle for chastity, and the later charges that he had supplied love charms to the wife of a friend with the complicity of her husband. This scandal had led to controversy over his ordination and the accusation that he was still a crypto-Manichee.[3] A further more prosaic pressure was the constraints on his time as a bishop, which may have led him to eliminate scrupulously any relationships he did not see a part of that role.[4]

He never saw a woman alone, would visit widows and orphans only if they were in 'dire tribulation' and monasteries of women only in cases of 'urgent necessity'; Possidius attributes this to his desire to avoid being alone with women.[5] How dire the tribulation or how urgent the necessity one can only speculate, but it is a matter of record that a rebellion of nuns against their prioress was not deemed an urgent enough occasion. Augustine's excuse was that if he visited he would have to be angry with them, and he did not wish to be so.[6] It is possible that he wished to leave the prioress as much autonomy as he could, in the hope that the community could resolve its own problems. On another occasion, he even expelled a young clergyman found speaking to nuns at an inappropriate time.[7]

He did correspond with women, and his letters provide some insights into both the nature of his relationships with them and his perceptions of their role.[8] However, there are few examples of

his correspondence with women. Of the 272 epistles in the Benedic-
tine edition, only seventeen are to women, though the number
increases to twenty-three if epistles to husbands and wives are
included. The surviving epistles to women are written in response
to some query or request for help, in response to a pastoral situation, for example, Demetrias' taking the veil, or to women to
whom he relates as either patron or client. Therefore the genre of
the response helps to structure the content. As the epistles are
quasi-public documents they are likely to be official in tone, corresponding to pastoral epistles rather than to the more personal
expression of private letters. No letters to individual women are
recorded before 408, and no letters from women to Augustine
are extant, despite the fact that we know he had some of them
copied.[9] This does not include his letters to and from Paulinus and
Therasia, a married couple with whom he corresponds. From the
tone of these letters it is clear that the two men are the writers and
friends, although Therasia is included in the honorifics for cour-
tesy's sake. The letters from Paulinus and Therasia are written in
the first person singular, clearly by Paulinus, who refers to 'the
office we both hold'.[10] In his replies, Augustine refers to both
husband and wife as his *brothers* in the body of Christ.[11]

No letters give any clues as to the late dating for the beginning
of his correspondence with women, given that he was ordained
bishop in 395. One might speculate that the therapeutic aspects of
the *Confessiones* may have helped him to deal further with his feelings
and permitted him this avenue of limited interaction with women.
Although this section will focus on letters to women, pertinent
differences between letters to men and those to women will be
discussed, as will letters to men that have a direct bearing on gender
relations, for example, the beating of wives and the betrothal of
young women.

Gender differences in the epistles

The published letters are clear examples of the genre, although his
letters to men contain more intimate and personal passages. Men
and women alike are greeted courteously with honorific titles. However, he often addressed men as his brothers, but never addressed
women as his sisters. Where he goes beyond the honorific 'Lady',
all women are his daughters.[12] This indicates that women are not
his peers in the same way that men are, but are subordinates rather
than colleagues.[13]

Nowhere in his letters to women do we find him speaking to
them with the personal warmth and emotional content he expresses
to his male intimates.[14] A comparison of some letters is revealing.

In a correspondence apparently initiated by Augustine, Augustine responded to Fabiola's regrets that until they share the contemplation of the 'One' they must remain absent to one another. He replied that although they are separated by long distances, in sharing their written thoughts they 'should be more together than if we were in one place, looking at each other but sitting in silence'.[15]

Yet when he wrote to Jerome, he spoke of his burning desire to see him and of the reluctance with which he submitted to the 'remote separation which prevents my mind from having access to yours through our bodily senses, my brother'.[16] Quite unequivocally he wrote to Paulinus, 'God knows how we long to have you corporeally present' and '[I am] curious to know whether you bear with more ease and patience than I do this bodily separation'. Owing to this impatience Augustine feels 'warranted in asking, nay demanding and imploring you to condescend to come over into Africa'.[17] In another he wrote that Paulinus' letter, flowing with milk and honey, both 'permits us to discern and prompts us to desire you'.[18]

Almost the whole of one of his early letters to Nebridius is taken up with the problem of how they can organise to live together.[19] His somewhat lush rhetoric cannot be taken to imply that homosexual relationships existed.[20] Augustine must be trusted in his assertion that his active sexual life ended when he became a Christian. However, it is evidence of what organisational psychology terms homosocial culture, and the kind of masculine camaraderie envisaged by some commentators.[21] The prevailing norms that idealised masculine intellectual friendship meant that Augustine felt free to love and be loved by men in a way that he could not feel free to relate to women. He used the language of *amicitia*, and he was understood as doing so. Women were so clearly identified with sexuality and temptation, and excluded from male *amicitia*, that such language to them would have been misinterpreted. It is more likely that Augustine would have rejected any affectionate feelings towards women as being sexually motivated. About the warmest language that he uses to a woman is in a letter jointly authorised by Alypius; they send a joint reply 'to express our joy in hearing of your welfare, and with sincere reciprocation of your love, to let you know our welfare, in which we are sure you take affectionate interest'.[22] From the evidence, one might say he has male friends and female correspondents.

However, there are some letters which reflect his personal experience and may illuminate our understanding of his prior relationships, and his mature self-understanding.[23] Indirectly, he has a relationship with Therasia, through his letters to Paulinus. He says in praise of Therasia:

In [the letter] the reader beholds a wife who does not bring her husband to effeminacy, but by union with him is brought to share the strength of his nature; and unto her, in you, as completely one'with you, and bound to you by spiritual ties which owe their strength by their purity, we desire to return our salutations with the respect due to your Holiness.[24]

The marked implication of this passage is the danger that a wife, by her very nature, will bring a husband to effeminacy.[25] This is a concrete example of the metaphorical construct he develops some fourteen years later in *De Trinitate*: the soul descends from masculine virtue into sinfulness through the feminine dimension of the mind. In this case Therasia has absorbed something of Paulinus's nature and so is protected by the strength of his masculinity, as the feminine dimension of the mind becomes *imago Dei* once it is united with the masculine dimension.

Epistle 262 provides a foil to the idealisation of Therasia, revealing Augustine's response to a woman who acts on her own authority. Ecdicia had persuaded her unwilling husband into a sexless marriage.[26] She began to dress like a widow, and her husband objected that this was inappropriate to her station in life. Then Ecdicia went even further. Her husband came home one day to discover that she had given all her funds to a pair of itinerant monks. Finally, infuriated by her ascetical practices, he took a mistress. Augustine notes perceptively that her Christian husband had felt unloved, and had used his own self-destruction to wound her. However, far from seeing it as his pastoral duty to call the adulterous husband to repentance, he holds Ecdicia responsible for her husband's behaviour. Having been allowed to have her own way regarding the cessation of sexual intercourse, she should have been moderate in all things, for her husband had lived faithfully with her in continence for a long time. Therefore he ordered her to repent with tears of blood, to apologise and effect a reconciliation. It has been argued that Ecdicia alienated her husband by giving away his property.[27] However, the text is clear that it is Ecdicia's own funds that are given away. Indeed, Augustine specifically says Ecdicia must not dispose of anything that is not hers without her husband's consent. Neither clothes nor gold, neither silver nor money. Rather, she owed it to her small son to consider his future prudently, and see that he should not become a burden on other men.

It is more consistent with the extant evidence to interpret this situation as a clash of models of spirituality and right order, as Brown has done. Brown places Ecdicia in the tradition of Thecla. She is 'dead' to her old life, and alive to Christ, a state of existence which erases her husband's rights over her and her resources. This is totally incompatible with Augustine's ideas of social order, in which the properly governed family is the microcosm of the state and the church. What would have exacerbated the situation for Augustine was that all her resources had been given to itinerant monks, whose role had become a point of tension for the bishops, suspicious of their independent and charismatic character. They were operating outside the institutional structures, draining resources from the diocesan coffers, and like the autonomous women, were potentially dangerous to the proper ordering of society.

As is becoming increasingly clear, Augustine believed the 'natural law' of social relations was divinely inspired, so for a healthy society the natural law must be reflected in the *familia*. The 'true father' was *in loco parentis* for God. Within the Christian ecclesial *familia*, the bishop's role is to be the living embodiment of God, the *paterfamilias* of the church. Certainly throughout this letter Augustine insists on the authority of the husband, orders Ecdicia to return to him with their little son, and even admonishes her that she would be more virtuous to wear fine clothes humbly than poor clothes proudly. Augustine's sensitivity to the complex emotions operative in this marital conflict, and his counsel that Ecdicia should have consulted her husband before giving alms so that they might have shared both the decision and the virtues of the deed, sound reasonable to the modern mind conscious of mutuality in decision-making and equal partnership. But it becomes clear that this type of relationship is not Augustine's intent. To 'consult' meant to 'ask permission' and obey male authority. A woman has no 'head' or authority of her own. Her husband was her head and thus all authority to make decisions lies with him.

In this letter Augustine himself revels in the role of the 'true father' restoring order in his ecclesial household. Verbally, he flagellates Ecdicia with a minatory tone far different from his letters to men who have erred in his eyes.[28] She is not only totally to blame for the whole problem, but the genuineness of her asceticism is even called into question. As Augustine cannot attack her desire for continence and her almsgiving *per se* – they are the epitome of the ascetic piety he espouses – he bases his punitive rhetoric on the assumption that Ecdicia's actions were motivated by pride, not love of God.

This interpretation indirectly confirms the status and honour accruing to ascetic women that was creating tension in the community. Augustine neatly turns this on its head to impute shameful motives to independent ascetic women. Better a sexually active woman who yields the marriage debt to her husband whilst desiring continence, for continence will be imputed to her by God, than a

proud and overly bold continent woman who drives her husband
into eternal destruction. Any good she might have done by her
self-denial is completely outweighed by the scandal of the marital
discord and her disobedience. She has dishonoured her head, and
thus disordered her household. Ecdicia, as she is represented by
Augustine, is clearly about as far from the Monica ideal of slave-
wife as it is possible to get. It is paradoxical that the one area of
mutuality in Christian marriage, the mutual obligation to conjugal
rights and marital chastity, is here used to discourage lay women
from overtly espousing the continent behaviour which was perceived as empowering them with virile status and the capacity for
authority: that is, endowing them with full humanity as it was
understood in late antiquity.

Domestic violence in the epistles

The question of actual corporal punishment for women is raised in
the letters also, but notably, in letters to men. In these letters,
Augustine's attitude is more nuanced than it appears in the *Confessiones*, though he adheres to his conviction that beatings are an
appropriate way for men to maintain authority. The *paterfamilias*
has not only the right but the obligation to punish those who set
him at naught.[29] The sole exception is sons beating their mothers:
that is an offence that invites excommunication.[30] However, he does
point out that in some cases a beating may not be the proper
remedy. There are two specific situations where he stipulates this.
The first example is his direct response to a pastoral situation and
the appropriateness of corporal punishment is the issue in question.
In the second situation, his comments are a device to expose what
he perceived as the exploitation of vulnerable people by astrologers
who did not practise what they preached.

His first example concerned a father beating his daughter to
convert her from Donatism. Augustine does not object on the
grounds of the violence, but on the need for conversion to be freely
willed and chosen, not coerced. This letter was written during the
early phases of the controversy when he was against any kind of
coercion being applied.[31] Later, as the dispute became more violent,
he gradually altered his opinions and justified imperial intervention
to suppress the heresy and compel conversion. Quite probably, a
letter written after the Edict of 405 would not have forbidden the
beating on these grounds.[32]

In his attack on the astrologers, he condemns wife-beating
because it reveals their hypocrisy. His argument was that as astrologers purported to believe that the stars and planets controlled fate
or behavioural circumstances, it was illogical for them to beat

wives or slaves for behaviour that is ostensibly beyond their control. It is difficult to know whether his example of the astrologer who beat his wife for looking out the window really reflected social practice, or whether Augustine has deliberately used a trivial offence to point up the inconsistency between the astrologer's livelihood and his own beliefs, though he does say that he is not jesting.[33]

The personal and the pastoral

Consistently when dealing with personal ties Augustine invokes the 'hatred' of familial bonds found in Luke 14. 26–33.[34] He emphasises that one must 'hate' not the persons themselves, but the personal relationship which is in the nature of a private possession. In the persons, what is to be loved is the 'hope of everlasting blessedness'.[35] It is likely that this is precisely the principle which helped to form Augustine's later relationships with women. It was necessary that he repudiate all temporal relationships with them, yet love in them the hope of eternal blessedness. In fact, as the greetings of the epistles revealed, he saw women as spiritual daughters rather than sisters, and his role was to form them in the faith, until God became their 'interior master', and it seems that this tutoring only took place by correspondence.[36]

In his first letter to Proba, Augustine touches on the nature of friendship. Presumably, given his teachings on the function of women, he is referring to friendship between women here. It may be that in practice, he considered friendship of a sort to exist between ascetic men and women, for his definition of friendship here is so broad that it embraces enemies: 'for the bonds of common humanity require kindly affection'. Indeed, there can be great and reasonable pleasure in a 'pure and holy love' which is requited, albeit at long distance. Such a love is best expressed in persuading the 'neighbour' to love God. However, as he only seems to correspond with women a few times in each case, it seems that even at this level, his personal friendships with women did not extend over long periods and were pastoral rather than personal in nature. This 'friendship' is of a different order from that which he shared with his male intimates, which, he says, surrounded him with the comfort of good men, who contributed to his enjoyment in everything he did.[37]

Patrons and clients

Although Augustine might have sought to avoid personal relationships with women, in his episcopal role he could not avoid their presence altogether. The changes brought about in the transition from private to public structures within the church meant that women and bishops were connected through Christian patron–client networks, the pertinent role depending on their rank in the patronage hierarchy.

One series of Augustine's letters offers an example of how, in late antiquity, bishops' pastoral leadership could cast them in the role of patrons to members of their congregation.[38] Strictly speaking it is not correspondence with a woman but about a 'maiden'. She had been made a ward of the church and Augustine appointed her guardian by a magistrate. The epistles deal with her proposed betrothal. We know little about the girl herself except that she had one living aunt and an uncle by marriage, and her mother's whereabouts were unknown. Both another bishop and her uncle were bringing pressure to bear on Augustine, as was a pagan *paterfamilias* who wished to betroth her to his son. Clearly the other men felt the time was appropriate to betroth her if not marry her. As her guardian, Augustine would have none of it. He would not enter into any arrangements for her marriage, until she was older, nor would he permit her to undertake religious life for the same reason. At this stage, she has told Augustine that if she were 'of full age' she would choose the virginal life. Despite his preference for that choice, Augustine insisted that she wait until she was old enough to make mature choice. Furthermore, he did not consider it his prerogative to choose her husband, but rather to protect her from unsuitable men. Thus he rejected the proposal for marriage to the pagan suitor outright, whilst deferring consideration of suitable Christian suitors until the maid was older. Augustine also stated that should her mother come forward, her wishes would prevail, as would the maiden's if she were of full age.

Clearly, he saw a guardian's role as protective, rather than dictatorial, and considered that women's wishes concerning a husband should be given due consideration. The fact that this girl was much sought after, that two bishops as well as her male in-law concerned themselves with her future, suggests that she was of gentle birth and probably that she was wealthy. That a pagan suitor felt free to approach the bishop suggests that some intermarriage between pagans and Christians was still occurring, despite local conciliar efforts to forbid it.[39] Augustine was adamant that if she chose to marry, any suitable match must benefit the church, and she must be free to choose between eligible suitors. It would appear that in his pastoral practices where Augustine was dealing with his social and spiritual peers, and was not the vehicle for the wrath of God, he was far less high-handed in his approach, and was concerned with the proprieties of rank and the interests of all the major parties involved.

Augustine displayed the same attitudes in Letter 3*. He advises one of his deacons that a woman who vowed her seriously ill baby daughter to the virginal life if she recovered, cannot rescind the vow and substitute it with her own vow to consecrated widowhood. Virginity is more powerful than widowhood and so the inferior cannot be substituted for the superior. However, the child must be free to make her own choice as an adult. If she is not given the charism of virginity then there is no sin in her choosing marriage. Her mother's vow is fulfilled if she rears the daughter to a love of the consecrated life, but it will be broken if she actively seeks a marriage for her daughter who is the last member of her *familia*. Augustine is stern about the mother's selfish desire for grandchildren as opposed to the good of the church. So despite all his genuine belief in marriage as cornerstone of social structures, its needs are nevertheless in tension with the communal good of the church as they were not in tension with the public good of the state in the classical era.[40]

Letter 20* reveals some of the intricacies of ecclesial politics and the involvement of noble landowners in clerical appointments. In so doing it offers a most intriguing insight into Augustine's own dependence upon *patronae* in resolving church disputes.[41] The letter is addressed to his 'most reverent and eminent daughter, the lady Fabiola', whom he petitioned concerning Bishop Antoninus, a young man raised in his monastery. The latter's sudden elevation from lector to the episcopate in his twenties had resulted in arrogant abuse of his power. After being deposed by an African Council he had travelled to Rome to appeal to the Pope. Fabiola, known to Augustine and Jerome, had offered Antoninus hospitality. It is clear that in his attempts at damage control, Augustine was desperately trying to win Fabiola's support for his actions. Augustine was in a particularly difficult situation here, for he had imposed the inexperienced young bishop on Fussala without consulting the congregation there in the first place, and worse, he was in breach of canon law because of Antoninus' youth.[42] He had been appointed when another more suitable cleric fled the post. Augustine entreated Fabiola to counsel Antoninus for the good of his soul. In a stunning reversal of roles, Augustine's abundant tears were now the source of a fountain of mercy poured out for his spiritual son: tears which will make efficacious the ministry of Fabiola, whose kindness will induce obedience and will break down any walls of arrogance the young cleric might erect against her.[43] In this situation, it is Fabiola who will hopefully do the effective pastoral counselling that Augustine had failed to do, whilst Augustine weeps and prays. This diplomatic letter gives evidence of his need to enlist the support of an influential *patrona* for his point of view. It seems almost taken for granted that her counsel would be an important factor in the outcome of the conflict. Under the guise of information, he has proffered his own side of the story, and he has even managed to work in the support that he had received from another feminine ally.

The evidence concerning this second *patrona* emerges from Augustine's narration of the conflict. Augustine describes this woman to Fabiola as a most illustrious woman, the '*fundus*' of her estate, a term which had come to mean the one with authority to approve or ratify decisions. In the argument over the appointment of Antoninus to a smaller church in Thogonoetum after his deposition from his see, both sides claimed her support, and her tenant farmers enlisted her aid to prevent the appointment of Antoninus. So Augustine was wary of making the same mistake again, and indeed went to great pains to try to recoup the situation. In correspondence with Augustine, the *patrona* gave evidence about Antoninus' devious attempts to manipulate the situation. Augustine considered this letter so indispensable that he carried it on his person. Producing it at the crucial moment, he engineered the discomfiture of Antoninus. It is noteworthy that it was to this unnamed woman that her landowners had appealed, not to Augustine himself. She was perceived to have had the right to approve or veto the clerical appointment, and her evidence validates Augustine's case.[44] Here there is a glimpse of a complex reality in which women did not play a subordinate and demure role, and in which they had the power to shame or honour the leaders of their dioceses.

The letters between Augustine and Albina, Melania the Younger and Pinianus offer fascinating insights into the problems caused when Augustine came into dispute with a powerful noble family.[45] Augustine's congregation was accused of entrapping Pinianus into consenting to ordination on account of the immense wealth he would bring to the diocese, and Pinianus was refusing to honour his oath because it was given under duress. It is significant that although the dispute was in fact between Augustine, along with his community, and Pinianus, the letters are addressed in one case only to Albina, Pinianus' mother-in-law, and in the other to Albina, Pinianus and Melania.[46] Horrified at being suspected by such leading lights, he wrote to Albina, very anxious to clear his good name and that of his people, and to hold Pinianus to his oath.[47] It is quite apparent from a letter to his close friend Alypius, who became involved in mediating the conflict, that it was Albina's wrath, not Pinianus', that he feared.[48] His letters to Albina are very direct and natural, with none of the patronising tone found in many of his other letters to women, or of the 'honeyed sword' he was so capable of wielding.[49]

There are several reasons for this. To complicate matters further the family was a patron of Pelagius, about whom Augustine was beginning to have concerns. It was a situation that could have severe implications for his standing in the church on either account; also, Augustine is in a contentious position, and intent on resolving this conflict with these members of the church's élite, whom he called 'vehement flames' kindled into light by the Supreme Light;[50] he cannot afford to alienate them. It is clear from his words to Alypius, that although the accusations have been levelled at the laity in Hippo and they stopped short of accusing Augustine himself, the bishop's honour is at stake, because his authority is pre-eminent, and especially because he is perceived to have the use and enjoyment of the church property as the church's lord.[51] So he prevaricates about calling Pinianus a perjurer, or coward, and tries to create a context wherein Pinianus will keep his word to settle in Hippo, without the constraints imposed by bad faith.

This presents another clear example of women's power perceived as impinging on male honour. Despite the fact that it was Pinianus' ordination at stake, it is clearly Albina and Melania who wield the power and who must be placated, possibly because much of the wealth at stake also derived from Pinianus' (continent) marriage to the heiress, Melania.[52] Like Monica, these women were regarded as 'virile' in mind and soul.[53] This contretemps, which Augustine did not resolve to his satisfaction, is a clear example of the authority and status of such women. It is notable that this was one occasion when Augustine did wish to visit the women, whom he addressed with 'brotherly' rather than 'fatherly' affection.[54] Both are clear indications of their status in his eyes.

Augustine and vowed women

Many of the letters to women were to continent women living within their family home, but there are two extant letters to women living in community. Epistles 210 and 211 were written to resolve a dispute within the women's community, which Augustine's sister had founded. In the first he represents the dispute as a test of love, advising that it be settled quickly before anger corrodes the heart.[55] In the second, he specifically rebukes the community for its 'disorder'. It would seem that the women had been bombarding Augustine with letters demanding that their abbess be replaced. He saw as this as a dangerous precedent, subversive of sound discipline.[56] The women's action in appealing to Augustine, who himself claims that it would have been cause for justifiable protest if he had attempted to remove an abbess from office, gave him the legitimate opportunity to intervene directly in the day to day life of the community. He established a rule for them, modelled on his rule for men.[57] The point of contention was that the recently appointed prior was being so hindered by the sisters' disorderly behaviour that he wished to leave. Apparently, the rumours in the community blamed the discontent with the prioress on the appointment of the prior. It would appear that in Augustine's see, the appointment of a presbyter responsible to the bishop was a means of episcopal control, but one not well received by all the vowed community.[58] The prior was not the only man who felt his honour to be in question. Augustine, too, perceived the nuns' protest as a reflection on his ministry, a product of his work that he has not deserved. Somehow, the fruits of these women's lives accrue to him.[59]

Hence, Augustine carefully defined for them the hierarchy of authority. The nuns owed obedience to their mother, the prioress, and through her, to the prior and the bishop. The prioress is to lead by example, and be cautious in her imposition of rules.[60] In counselling the abbess on the use of power, Augustine's advice derives from his concept of God's dual role as Father and Lord. The wise leader will use both fear and love to guide her community.[61] However, the maintenance of authority is so important that even if the superior made the mistake of being too harsh, she was not to ask forgiveness of the sisters, lest her humility impair her authority.[62] Conversely, the sisters were to admit their shame, and repent of their vexatious behaviour.[63] It is extremely significant that these women are told explicitly that they are not slaves under the law, but free women, established under grace.[64] Similarly, although Augustine uses maternal imagery for the care the abbess gives her sisters, his model is a patriarchal one, utilising the fear and stern affection of the father wielding his absolute authority.

Once again, the issues of honour and shame are raised in connection with clerical relations with women. Both the prior and the bishop are in danger of being shamed quite publicly. In both cases, the ecclesial *paterfamilias* felt he would be popularly perceived as incapable of keeping order in his own 'house', a criterion for ministry first established in 1 Timothy 3. 4–5. This perception would be reinforced by the symbolic link between the virgin woman and the virgin church, which will be developed more fully in the following chapter on Mary. If these women symbolise church, then the bishop is in some respect their spouse, an idea which is implicit in Ambrose's assertion that the priest is the temporal spouse of the church as God is the heavenly one.[65]

There is no indication in Epistle 211 that Augustine instructed the women in any systematic way, but he was willing to instruct women when requested, as attested by his letter to Florentina. He believed that he ought to help to the extent of his ability as a free service to her admirable study. He assumed that there would come a time when she would no longer need his instruction, when God would teach her himself.[66] If his words are not simply to be taken as pious loquaciousness, it may indicate that Augustine truly believed that mature, devout and properly formed women would reach a stage when they no longer needed male tutelage, spiritually as well as economically. His experience of Monica's wisdom is apparent in this context. He had learnt from his shared vision at Ostia that women, equally with men, are open to the revelation and vision of Wisdom.

Influences on his theology

These epistles cover the period between 408 and 423 and form a very small part of Augustine's total correspondence. Taken as a whole, the epistles support the claim concerning the dearth of intimate personal relationships with women during his clerical life. The basis of his rejection of them may be found in a theme that appears in several letters. Augustine persistently returns to the experience of the barriers in this life to total intimacy.[67] The way he expresses it is that no one can know us as we know ourselves in the 'inner man'. Only in the next life will we truly know and be known. Because of this the embrace of Wisdom is the sweetest and strongest of conceivable bonds for it is safe from the pain of loss, whereas the ties of this world are illusory and painful.[68]

But because Augustine isolated himself from everyday contact with women, he denied himself the possibility of 'reality testing', which is the only way the inner demons can be exorcised. Otherwise fears and prejudices grow without any challenges, for any situations which open them to challenge are avoided.[69] The role of pastor by correspondence in which he cast himself meant that he lacked the immediacy of interaction and communication which might have modified his perceptions of women and weakened his tendency to stereotype. Total disclosure and frankness is simply not possible in letters which could well be copied for circulation. The women he could not avoid encountering were the influential *patronae* on whom he depended for financial and political support in the arena of church politics. Their capacity to bring him into ecclesial dishonour would have been as galling as the power of the women who represented sexual temptation. They called into question the 'natural law' he used to prescribe social relations and could well have reinforced his ideal of the subordinate, obedient Christian woman.

In dealing with women, even through letters, it must have seemed to Augustine that he stood on shifting sands. If the natural law was being respected, his relationships with all women should be and would be unequivocally defined as father–daughter, with the bishop holding all the power and honour. But he is constrained by circumstances to be dependent upon the goodwill and support of women, who, in fact, have the ability to compromise not his sexuality but his integrity, jurisdiction and honour. Thus, as copies of his correspondence circulated in Christian communities, the differences in rhetoric and content would have created a complex and ambiguous system of signals to women. Augustine prescribed the subordinate status of even ascetic women, thereby giving due warning to ascetic women who might consider stepping outside of the 'natural law' that they will be held responsible for their husband's sexual sins. Yet his letters to the monastery community, to Fabiola and Albina, also made clear to women that their bishops' dependence on the patronage of powerful women could constrain their honour and their power.

This means that fears about women's sexual or disruptive power would be reinforced during his episcopacy. During the period of his most mature doctrinal formulations, there was no Monica to prick his pretensions and challenge the implications of the philosophic systems he took for granted, no intimate friend or lover to modify the symbols and imagery developed in an almost exclusively male environment. Indeed, his ritual avoidance of women might bind his anxiety about them, but could only serve to reify their role as the symbols of desire.

Theology and social relations

The goal in this section is to draw together the threads of Augustine's thought which appear consistently in his confessional and pastoral writings between the 386 CE and 423 CE. Throughout these writings there is consistency in Augustine's appraisal of women's role and nature. Although the comparison between the *Soliloquia* and the *Confessiones* revealed a change in his thinking about the (uneducated) woman's capacity for spiritual development, the growth in Augustine's thinking seemed to cease with Monica's literary 'death'.

The concept that structures his perception of gender relationships is a cultural, not a theological one, although as Part II demonstrated, he attempted to give this a theological legitimation. His paradigm for the understanding of women's nature and appropriate gender roles was the order of natural law in the Roman honour-shame culture.[70] Where proper order prevails, the superior is rightly dominant over the subordinate and inferior; therefore man is always and everywhere to dominate woman, even a son his mother.[71] But there is one important aspect of Augustine's thinking on marriage and gender relations that is found neither in classical culture, nor in his Christian predecessors Tertullian and Ambrose. Graeco-Roman culture understood marriage as a legal alliance concerned with power, economics and kinship; nevertheless, since the time of Augustus, a sentimental ideal had been developing, emphasising the desirability of affectionate marital concord between spouses. This did not entail an equal partnership, and power still lay within the husband's domain. However, he was expected to exercise it with moderation, to consult with family councils which included his wife, and he had no right to beat his wife in a *sine manu* marriage.

This perception of marital relationships was reinforced by the disparity in age between husbands and wives, for men in their twenties usually married girls in their teens.[72] This would have created an inherent difficulty for true mutuality within marriage, as men tended to see their wives as having to be formed from 'daughter-wives' into mature matrons.[73] It has been noted that this practice was functional for social reasons: a younger woman was physically more suitable for child-rearing; her youth meant that she was no rival to her husband physically or aesthetically; and she was able to care for her spouse in his declining years.[74] Tertullian and Ambrose, whilst maintaining male headship and feminine inferiority, still described spouses as yokefellows, pulling together in partnership. Tertullian was more egalitarian than Ambrose. He described spouses as equal in the house of God, sharing one hope, one desire, one discipline and one service. Where the flesh is one, the spirit is one.[75] Ambrose was more Roman and less Christian. Nevertheless, he exhorted mutual consideration. If a woman must be obedient and affectionate, then men must also curb their curt manners and obstinacy.[76]

Augustine shifts the basis of power relationships far more fundamentally. What earlier writers, both pagan and Christian, had seen as a junior–senior partnership, he transforms into a master–slave relationship.[77] This master–slave rhetoric was possibly inspired by the ambiguity of son versus slave imagery in Christian exegesis. In the sermons the theme of God's Lordship is consistently in tension with Christ's love. Augustine's resolution of this tension is that God's severity is always for our own good. Nevertheless his imagery is revealing. The Lord is a stern master who even 'threatens' his bride when she seeks him, to make sure that she never wanders away from his flock, 'polluted' by unlawful loves.[78] In like manner, God frightens his people in order to save them. This God does by 'crushing' the heart as if it were an olive, so that the virgin oil is captured and the lees discarded.[79] Certainly an imaginative image that would speak to his congregation's daily use of oil, yet nevertheless a violent one.

This is the theological discourse which determines that Monica is not only slave of Patricius, but slave of God. The usual English translation of *ancilla* is 'Your servant', which has different connotations from 'slave' for the modern reader. Previously, women's subordinate status and confinement to the domestic sphere had not been expressed in the discourse of slavery, but of kinship. A young wife had the status of a daughter, not a slave, and the moral power of the older *materfamilias* was certainly not consistent with any social or self-perceptions as slave. There was a huge difference in Roman culture between slave and free status, and between slave and *filiusfamilias* (child of the household). For this reason, even the corporal punishment of sons was more a threat used to control than a power frequently exercised. Furthermore, beatings were not only consistent with the status of slavery, they were virtually the hallmark of it, and thus when a free man was beaten, the symbolic significance was to strip him of honour and mark him as a slave.[80]

Whether intentional or not, the status that Augustine allotted to women included them in the category of virtual non-persons who could be beaten with impunity.[81] It is a status that would have shamed women and further enhanced male dominance. 'You are the lord, she is the slave' (*tu dominus es, illa ancilla*) was the rubric under which he classified gender relations.[82] Woman is to man as man is to God, the slave who may attain to adoptive sonship if he fulfils his duties with obedience and humility. Thus in defining and refining the wifely role, Augustine can think at one remove about the proper demeanour of man (*sic*) to God.

This interpretation is confirmed by an examination of the term *ancilla* in his other writings.[83] A consistent allegorical interpretation, especially in the epistles, distinguishes between the 'free' wife, Sara, and the concubine-slave, Hagar. The former characterises those who had been reformed in Christ, and the latter those who still lived according to the flesh, the carnal and unredeemed state of humanity.[84] In terms of his own later imagery, the distinction is between the City of God and the City of this world, the spiritual over against the unrighteous and deceitful.[85] The symbolic status he ascribed to married women is therefore not only servile, but unspiritual. Thus, consciously or not, his desire to emphasise proper power relations in marriage defined the sexually active woman in terms of the carnal and unredeemed, whilst the husband shares the same title as the Christ, '*Dominus*'. Only the continent woman could symbolise Sara, the free wife, though in other contexts she is the 'slave of God' as is the church.[86] The discourse of Lordship and slavery creates a complex symbolic system where only God is always Lord, man is lord in relation to women and slaves, and married women are always slave, although set above other household slaves.[87] This is one example where the rhetorical language of master–slave to describe marriage cannot be trivialised as simply hyperbole or empty rhetoric. It defines the order of social and spiritual relations, the nature of the allegiance and the punishment for disobedience.

In this way, Augustine has resolved the impasse concerning the virile woman within the community. Intentionally or not, his imagery subverts any solidarity between women within the ecclesia. His slave–free antithesis, embodied in the women of the ecclesia, divides and conquers. The ascetic woman, either virgin or widow, was virile and set apart from her less orderly and disruptive sexual sisters. In this manner, the woman who challenges the stereotyping is defined as an anomaly, co-opted as 'one of the boys' and in fact depends for her own élite status on the humiliating definitions of her secular counterparts as inferior. Her capacities and strengths then become in no way typical of women and cease to challenge the predominant stereotyping. It is extremely significant that in this respect, Augustine stands totally opposed to Ambrose, who had instructed his catechumens, 'You are not her lord, but her husband. You have acquired not a slave, but a wife' (*Non es dominus, sed maritus, non ancillam sortitus, sed uxorem*).[88]

The primary structure of social relations was therefore one defined by power and male honour. The will of the *paterfamilias* was enforced through his authority and dignity, always grounded in his right to inflict corporal punishment to create and maintain household order. Indeed, social historians have argued that slave societies require strong assertion of authority and the exercise of physical punishment.[89] The family model stands as a microcosm of the 'whole web of social control'.[90] Ideally, this paternalistic love is a balance of love and fear,[91] with punishment motivated by love, and God as the ultimate *paterfamilias* is created in the image of the Roman lord and master.[92] Yet kinship relationships were subverted and relegated to the temporal and ephemeral. The Roman mother's status was severely undermined by the Christian restructuring of relationships. Spiritual kinship takes precedence over blood kinship.[93] Hagar the slave woman, representing carnal birth and slavery to sin, came to symbolise woman's maternal role, dishonoured and reduced to the status of stepmother, an unambiguously negative role in Roman perception, and in myth even today.[94]

Desire too fell under interdict because it rebelled against *ordo*. The response of the body to passion, and specifically the male erection, is beyond the control of the will – a disorder felt keenly by Augustine, so keenly, in fact, that in his theological system, the inability to control the genital organs becomes a reciprocal punishment for sin inscribed on the body. As humanity sinned against God, so a man's body rebels against him. The irrefutable sign of humankind's rebellion against God, it becomes the symbol of the primal sin that introduced death into the world.[95] Therefore, desire and death were inextricably linked, and mutual desire between spouses is not a positive aspect of marital relationships, but one which makes marriage ever a hazardous enterprise,[96] overshadowed by sin and death.[97]

However, marriage is essential to control sexual desires and behaviour within the community. Marriage as the necessary means of maintaining the race through a solely procreative function is strictly orthodox Roman thinking which Augustine had inherited. His philosophic training concerning the sinfulness of the non-rational[98] helped him interpret his experience of sexuality as a prison of habit,[99] and contributed to his perception of the married woman as slave to male reason. The result is a concept of marriage as a contract rather than a relationship.[100]

This perception reduces Augustine's presentation of the sexual relationship within marriage to an economic one. Intercourse is a mutual debt owed by spouses, preferably to be called due only for the procreation of children, or to be written off altogether, but tolerated as pardonable sin within marriage if it protects the partners from greater sin such as adultery. Such an attitude stimulates guilt over the inability to overcome desire.[101] Augustine fostered a situation where individuals were supposed to pay their debts willingly, without desiring to do so. Any lack of feminine subordination or non-payment of the sexual debt can be cause for a man to blame his adultery or violence on his wife's behaviour.[102] Shame became the identifying characteristic of intercourse[103] and the women and men who aspired to sexless marriages were invited to view their partners who desired them as akin to brute beasts.[104] Yet when a woman like Ecdicia unilaterally opted for chastity and honour, she was accused of the ultimate sin, disorderliness, and severely chastised.

Whilst some commentators have seen in Augustine 'the great eulogist of Christian marriage',[105] others have perceived him as objectifying both men and women in the sexual act. By presenting non-procreative intercourse simply as a remedy for concupiscence, he inadvertently facilitated relationships in which people used each other for what have been described as 'mutually masturbatory purposes'.[106] This type of mutuality is not altogether edifying; yet it does negate sexual double standards. A more positive aspect is his emphasis on mutual fidelity. It has been suggested that here is a hope of discovering a richer and more positive attitude to marriage, grounded in the imagery of the spousal relationship between God and his people.[107] However, this relationship itself is between spouses of such disparate status and nature that it would be an immense theological task to recover it for a (post) modern world. Augustine's imagery confirms this. As a general rule, he only uses positive imagery, such as Christ and the church, as a symbol of the goodness of lawful marriage to legitimate a husband's authority over his wife. The parallel between spirit–flesh and man–wife, where the man is to love and care for his wife as the spirit does the flesh, must be placed in the earlier context of the war between the Spirit and the lusts of the flesh.[108] There is one text however, which suggests that he never quite forgot the goodness he had experienced in the love of his concubine. A chaste love is like the love spouses feel when they love their partner for themselves alone. In this, a wife is the icon of the chaste soul, who loves God her husband, for his own sake.[109] Although both spouses are mentioned in the human context, only the wife is used in the sacred analogy, because all Christians are feminised in relation to God. So every time 'holy marriage' analogies are used, they reinforce gender dynamics in real life.

Despite such fleeting glimpses of grace, Augustine could not overcome his belief that human relationships hindered his love for God. In loving the other, he is not loving God, but somehow stealing love from him.[110] The sexual dimension of male–female relationships contaminated them so that equal companionship was an impossibility.[111] At best, marriage could be 'a certain friendly and true union of the one ruling, and the other obeying'.[112] If a marriage ended in death or divorce, the bereaved spouse did better to follow Monica's example and remain single, than to marry again. As women who did not die in childbirth tended to outlive their husbands because of the differences in their ages, this meant that in reality a great number of women would ideally remain widows, and they would be the backbone of the church.[113]

Inside and outside marriage, woman is the symbol and object of desire.[114] In this guise, she is in direct competition with God for the hearts of men. It becomes reasonable therefore that chaste men will prefer to avoid them. What is being laid here are foundations stones for later conciliar decisions which will exclude women from the very presence of a bishop.[115] Within marriage, there is the constant danger that unless women become like their husbands, their husbands will become like women.[116] And so the emphasis is on woman's role as slave to man as the passions should be slave to intellect, a paradigm that will emerge again in the symbol system clustering around the *imago Dei*. Roman and Christian culture had utilised woman as the symbol of dangerous desire, but within Christian culture Augustine's use of sexual desire as the lust to sin *par excellence*, heightens the nexus between women and the demonic.

The chaste Roman matron, faithfully bearing children to her spouse and rearing them to the proper appreciation of Roman mores is demoted to the carnal woman, symbolic of worldly as opposed to spiritual values. Her place is taken by mother church, whose children are spiritual and intellectual. The shaming of the sexual is Christian, not Roman. Whatever the concerns about controlling sexuality to protect the purity of citizenship, fecundity and male procreative power were fundamental cultural values. A boy's first ejaculation was a family celebration on the feast of the *Liberalia*.[117] At that time, a boy became a citizen: he put on the *toga virilis* and relinquished the childhood amulet.[118] It was a day for rejoicing and celebration, like modern twenty-first birthday parties, but it was celebrated religiously as well. Augustine himself related his father's joy when Augustine reached puberty. What caused his father joy caused his mother anxiety, and her response was the one Augustine came to share. His disdain for Patricius' joy is but one expression of the slow but inexorable attempt to remove sexuality from the sacred.[119]

Another persistent theme throughout all the texts reviewed is feminine responsibility for masculine emotions and behaviour. With Monica as exemplar, women bear responsibility for their men's honour, their morality, their sexual responses and their relationship with God. They must weep and pray until conversion occurs.[120] Continent women had the power to shame their chaplains and bishop, as the married woman could dishonour her husband. The married woman had to meet all her husband's sexual needs, preferably whilst desiring a sexless marriage. Men can displace responsibility for any sexual sins onto their wives, for presumably if their needs were being met they would not be committing adultery. Likewise, if she is not properly subservient and humble, he is not to be held responsible for his anger or violence. Indeed he is justified in using corporal punishment to restore order. With little regard for consistency, Augustine also instructs women that they must not tolerate their husband's infidelities. This would be a result of the mutual obligation to sexual fidelity and conjugal rights. In the one area where a woman is owed a moral debt, she is free to claim it and can forgo her servile status. It also helps further to shift the responsibility onto her shoulders. If he keeps committing adultery, why is not she doing something about it?[121] Overall, woman's procreative function defined her: Monica's example taught a mother to be obsessively concerned with her children; only in seeking their spiritual salvation will she obtain her own.[122] In this, the Roman tendency to hold young men responsible for their own actions once they don the *toga virilis* is modified. Yet even as the overly responsible mother, she hardly stands in her own right as a individual being, but is presented simply as an agent of God's benevolence, a tool used to carve his channels of grace.[123] Though, putting the best possible implications on this image, it can also reveal something of the feminine face of God, the maternal God of compassion and gentleness.[124]

The Augustine met on this most personal of journeys is a man who has struggled with powerful emotions within himself, ever fearful of the fragility of his chastity and the pain of emotional vulnerability. His sexual experience put him intimately in touch with the archetypal connections between sexuality and mortality. These he wove into a complex theology of sexual desire as the symbol of death. However, the love he had shared with mother and concubine also endowed him with a stubborn belief that marriage was fundamentally good and that, when it came to sexual relationships, men and women were both called to fidelity and chastity.[125] His experience of the mothering and nurturing love of God reveals the power of this divinely maternal presence, and offers the possibilities of a richer and fuller understanding of that love.

PART IV
Woman, man and the imago Dei

10

WOMAN, MINISTRY AND THE *IMAGO DEI*

A TTITUDES and ideals which had their genesis in the unique mix of Augustine's socialisation, education and his personal experiences would gradually be incorporated into his theological anthropology in the two decades after the *Confessiones* (between 400 and 419). Shaped by the theological legacies of Philo and Ambrose, his perception of the stereotypically feminine would find its dogmatic expression in his theology of the *imago Dei*.[1] The goal of Part IV is to determine whether Augustine ever denied the *imago Dei* to women and what implications he considered his theology held for social relations.

That he did deny the *imago* to women was asserted first by Julia O'Faolin, and Lauro Martines, later by Rosemary Ruether,[2] and more recently by Lynda Brownsey.[3] O'Faolin and Martines simply took the passage out of context. Ruether's argument was more sophisticated: she accepted that Augustine taught that women had a redeemable soul but that, given that her specific femaleness was the opposite of divine, she is not theomorphic.[4] She understands Augustine as splitting the *imago Dei* from gender difference, and establishing the male as the normative image of God.[5] Edmund Hill has taken issue with Ruether on this point, asserting that the contentious passage about which they differ is an analogical use of marital imagery.[6] However, Hill, like Jean La Porte and F. Ellen Weaver, has argued that analogies of masculine and feminine, where the latter is always subordinate to the former, hold no implications for women's subordination or inferiority in the real world.[7] These are complex issues and more nuanced understandings will emerge in the course of this analysis. However, first it is necessary to make a brief excursus into the church politics which influenced the emergence of this as a theological question in the fourth century.

The exegetical conflicts

One approach taken by certain bishops of late antiquity to the 'problem of women' was to invalidate their ministry by invalidating their very humanity. Women did not bear the image of God, only the pale reflection of it as the moon reflects the light of the sun. Such clerics took literally the Pauline text in 1 Corinthians 11.7: 'For a man should not have his head veiled since he is the image and reflection of God: but woman is the reflection of man.'[8] They placed this text ahead of Genesis 1.27–8: 'So God created human-kind in his image, in the image of God he created them, male and female he created them.' They perceived no tension between the texts, interpreting 1 Corinthians as an explication and clarification of Genesis. As one step away from full humanity, women had no authority. Without authority, they could not act as ministers of the sacred.

As is common in modern debates concerning the ordination of women, what may be in evidence here is a response to feminine reliance on egalitarian texts such as Galatians 3.28 and the *Acts of Thecla*, which laid claim to the witness of the Pauline tradition, and on the cult of Mary which had received strong support from the Empress Helena.[9]

The discourse of headship

The discourse of Christian power in antiquity was couched in terms of headship. Christ is the head of the church, the bishop is the temporal head of the church, man is the head of woman. 'Head' stood for source, authority, rationality, wisdom and intellect in philosophic and theological discourse. Ambrose had declared that a body without a head is totally dishonoured and debased, for the head contains the whole human essence, being the dwelling place of the soul. Ambrose was not denying the *imago Dei* to women; ostensibly the body in *Hexameron* 6 is ungendered. Nevertheless, in the context of the discourse of authority, his imagery holds symbolic implications for the status of women. Women only become fully human when in relationship to a male head, be he *paterfamilias* or bishop, or in the case of the virgin, the divine Bridegroom.[10]

What is often lost on modern readers is the nuance that would be heard by people of that era. 'Head' was a euphemism for penis, and it was customary for Greek and Roman homes to have a symbolic phallus placed in their inner gardens.[11] This symbolic representation of (pro)creative power, authority and rationality by male genitalia offers an instructive insight into the full criteria for entry into public office, and later into ordained ministry. One guarantees the other in a circular reciprocity.

Symbolic masculine and feminine

Philo
A model which used masculine and feminine as symbols for superior and inferior capacity for rationality, morality, power and strength, was so common in the ancient world that it permeated the majority of classical and Judaeo-Christian texts. Late in the first century it had been theologised into Jewish spirituality by Philo, variations of it are found in Methodius and Origen; and, most significantly, the Philonic system was incorporated into Christian thought by Ambrose.

Philo himself did not include woman in the concept of full human being.[12] His assumptions about women are not derived from the biblical texts but imposed on them. In his attitudes to women, he followed Aristotle rather than his usual mentor, Plato, even citing the former's remark about women being 'imperfect males'.[13] This is seen most clearly in his sexualised interpretation of the sin of Adam and Eve. For Philo, that sin was almost inevitable once Eve was created.[14] Before she was made, Adam was innocent, virtuous and single-minded in his devotion to God. With Eve came sexual desire, which divided Adam's heart and made him susceptible to temptation.[15] Although myths attributing the world's evil to women were common in antiquity, Philo's account of all evil traits as having their origin in Eve's softness, irrationality and moral frailty, brought myth into the realm of 'history'. For Philo, Masculine and Feminine symbolise two aspects of the soul: the masculine always represents *Noûs* or Mind, the feminine *Αἴσθησις* or Sense-perception. *Noûs* is virtually infallible in the wise man, when untainted by *Αἴσθησις*.[16] The salvation of Mind is the goal of the spiritual life, with the Sense-perception being relevant only to the temporal and the ephemeral. Though both are aspects of the soul, only *Noûs* is immortal.[17] Philo thus genders the whole paradigm of salvation.[18] He adds a further nuance. As woman is to man, and Sense-perception is to Mind, so man is to God. He is the frail one in comparison with God's virtue and transcendence. He must be obedient to God as woman is to man. In the total hierarchy of religious relationships, man is feminised in relation to God. This symbolic universe is mirrored in social relations where there is a moral imperative that man dominate woman so that the spiritual life of the community will not be under threat.

Ambrose

Following Philo, the Christian Fathers utilised a system of gendered stereotypes. Both Origen and Ambrose took the mind as masculine *Noûs* and the faculty of perception as feminine *Aἄσθησις*.[19] Both took for granted the intellectual inferiority of women as a class, although Ambrose was at great pains to assure his readers that women's creation was a good, and not a source of evil in itself.[20] When it comes to patristic understanding of the gendered Mind-Perception symbolism, Ambrose is the most significant source for he stands in the direct line of transmission to Augustine. For Ambrose, the masculine–feminine dyad within specific individuals is reflected in the ambiguous soul imagery: the soul, whose goal is masculinity, is usually symbolised as feminine because of its tendency to slide into sin through sense perception.[21] The androgynous gender allows for the soul's ultimate status to be masculine, whilst retaining Philo's feminisation of the soul in relation to God. This is extremely important for any understanding of the significance of gendered symbolism in patristic thought. In being rendered feminine in relation to God, men were forced to confront their own frailties and vulnerabilities, interiorised as feminine, while human reason is characterised as masculine. Inward self-control is then played out socially in heterosexual relations at the individual and communal level. Indeed they must be so if the symbolic order is to be maintained and there is to be congruence between cultural symbols and personal identity, for human beings share the structures of the cosmos.[22]

Augustine

When it came to his theologising concerning the *imago Dei*, Augustine, typically, refused to privilege one scriptural text over another. There had to be a way to reconcile them. The following analysis of his doctrine will progress by way of his own exposition of the masculine and feminine as aspects of each human being; the relationship between woman and the feminine and man and the masculine; and the relationship between masculine and feminine aspects of the person and the *imago Dei*. In so doing the characteristics of the feminine and masculine will be closely examined. In the final chapter, the manner in which his understandings of the feminine inform his theological anthropology and his attitudes to women will be demonstrated.

Augustine's concept of masculine and feminine within the human psyche

As early as the *Confessiones*, Augustine employed the concepts of Masculine and Feminine to describe dimensions of the human mind.[23] In *De Trinitate* he repeats almost word for word Ambrose's statement that as human beings have no helper like themselves in their animal soul that is able to undertake the conscious and rational management of daily life, part of the 'rational substance of our minds by which we adhere to the intelligible, unchangeable truth' is diverted to handle and direct these inferior things.[24]

He names these two functions of the rational soul not mind and sense-perception but *Sapientia* (Wisdom) and *Scientia* (Knowledge/ skill/science).[25] *Sapientia* is concerned with the contemplation and knowledge of God, *Scientia* with the administration of the corporeal and the temporal.[26] Although both are linguistically feminine, ana-logically, *Sapientia* is masculine and *Scientia* is feminine. Like Philo and Ambrose, Augustine uses Adam and Eve as the paradigmatic couple, and as in their texts, *Sapientia* relies on *Scientia*, for even the most spiritual of beings must live in, and interact with, the world. Consequently, just as Eve was created as a helpmeet for Adam, so *Scientia* was created a helpmeet for *Sapientia*:

> And as the twain is one flesh in the case of male and female, so in the mind one nature embraces our intellect and action, or our counsel and performance, or our reason and rational appetite, or whatever other more significant terms there may be by which to express them; so that, as it was said of the former, 'and there shall be two in one flesh,' it may be said of these, they are two in one mind.[27]

This nomenclature for the masculine is quite a revolutionary departure from early usage. In the Judaic and pagan traditions, Wisdom is not only feminine linguistically, but symbolised by the Feminine. In biblical symbols little distinction is made between the Feminine and the womanly (Prov. 7.4; 8.1–9; 9.1–6; Wis. 6.12–22; 8.2–3; Eccles. 1.1–25). The attributes of the Feminine in the book of Wisdom are powerful and evocative (7.12–27), but it will become apparent from the following discussions that, for Augustine, such images could have no relationship with the Femi-nine as he perceived it. Therefore he insisted that there is no association between the linguistic feminine and the Feminine dimension of the mind, virtually ignoring the symbolic content of the Hebrew Wisdom imagery. Wisdom Christology and its assimi-lation to the Λόγος Christology previously discussed, meant that all scriptural references to Wisdom denote Christ.[28] One with the

Father in essence and wisdom, the Christ then further reinforces male monopoly of wisdom. It is notable that Augustine departs from Philo's paradigm here. Philo represents Wisdom as the mother of creation, as God is the Father of the universe.[29]

The late antique identification of the ascetic Christian with the *vir sapiens* of the philosophic tradition would have over-determined the perception of Wisdom as a masculine attribute, and displaced the encratic tradition of Wisdom as a female virgin. Augustine may have feared any Feminine symbols as either heretical or dangerously close to idolatry for two reasons. First, many of these texts come from a Gnostic setting; second, the very popular goddess, Isis, was also a Wisdom figure, whose cult had many parallels in the Wisdom literature and John's Gospel.[30]

Masculine, Feminine and the *imago Dei*

Augustine may have been responding to objections to his break with the tradition of *Sapientia* as feminine, when he argued his case explicitly in *De Trinitate*. He was most concerned to distinguish between the corporeal reality of male and female sex, which pertains only to the bodies of man and woman, and the masculine and feminine gender stereotypes which are functions of the mind. For him, sex is a bodily distinction only,[31] because 'a common nature is to be acknowledged' in the mind.[32] It would appear that Augustine perceived this distinction as essential on two counts: on the first count, he did not wish the feminine aspect of the mind to be tainted by female sexuality. He went to great pains to explain that even though corporeal imagery may be used in the case of 'things spiritual',

> when he [*homo*] begins to ascend upwards from thence [corporeal reality], under the guidance of reason, in order to attain to the unchangeable truth itself through which these things were made, he may not draw with himself to things above what he despises in things below. For no one ever blushed to choose for himself wisdom as a wife, because the name of wife puts into a man's thoughts the corruptible connection which exists in begetting children; or because in truth wisdom itself is a woman in sex, since it is expressed in both Greek and Latin by a word of the feminine gender.[33]

Femaleness is here described as that which has no place on the pilgrimage to Truth, as that which is to be despised, as that concerned with the corruptible processes of procreation, and as that which must be distinguished from Wisdom herself, although both share linguistic gender.

On the second and most important count, he cannot afford that woman and feminine be entirely interchangeable because he depends on the distinction between them to resolve the conflict he perceived between Genesis 1.28 and 1 Corinthians 11.7. Augustine understood Genesis 1.28 as clearly establishing that woman is made in the image of God. But he understood 1 Corinthians 11.7 as establishing just as clearly that she is not.[34] So the fundamental question he faced was 'how is woman *imago Dei*?' Augustine's response was that the *imago Dei* of both man and woman is found in the mind, the highest faculty of the rational soul.[35] Within this part of the 'interior being' 'where we are renewed in the newness of our minds, there is no sex',[36] so Augustine will not allow that women are separated from the human image of God 'in that place [where] the human being was made to the image of God, where gender is not . . . in the spirit of his mind'.[37]

This non-sexual and incorporeal image is essential to declare his independence of Manichaean or anthropomorphic ideas which Augustine believed debased God by asserting that He (*sic*) was circumscribed and limited by the shape of bodily members.[38] Also, if bodily being participated in the image, then the female form itself would reflect some aspect of divine being and destroy the integrity of One God. Augustine concurs with the prevailing belief that the upright stance of human beings is a sign of their dignity as *imago Dei*, and symbolic of the fact that they are not to seek earthly pleasures like cattle who are bent towards the earth.[39] As such the body is appropriate for the rational soul, for it represents the good will of humanity before the Fall.[40] Nevertheless, the true *imago* is found neither in the body, nor in the mind as a whole, but only in that part of the mind where the 'knowledge of God can exist'.[41] Augustine is quite explicit that

> although the physical and external differences of man and woman symbolize the double role that the mind is known to have in one man, nevertheless a woman, for all her physical qualities as a woman, is actually renewed in the spirit of her mind in the knowledge of God according to the image of her creator, and therein there is no male or female.[42]

It is absolutely clear that Augustine understands woman's mind to bear that imprint of *imago Dei*, just as man's does, although given the gratuitous comment, 'for all her physical qualities as a woman', he clearly sees those qualities as implying otherwise, rendering the female body as even less capable of imaging God than the male. But having taken this fundamental option, he must then deal with the exegesis of 1 Corinthians 11.7. He does so by interpreting Paul in a symbolic manner.

How then did the Apostle tell us that the man is the image of God, and therefore he is forbidden to cover his head: but that the woman is not so, and therefore is commanded to cover hers? Unless forsooth, according to that which I have said already, when I was treating of the human mind, that the woman together with her own husband is the image of God, so that whole substance may be one image; but when she is referred to separately in her quality of help-meet, which regards the woman herself alone, then she is not the image of God; but as regards the man alone, he is the image of God as fully and completely as when the woman is joined with him in one.[43]

This is the crucial Augustinian text which has been understood by feminist theologians as asserting definitively that woman is not *imago Dei*. However, there are ample texts to prove that Augustine was unequivocal on the question of woman's equality with man in her interior being.

The key to understanding this passage is its context. As his own words indicate, both in introducing and concluding the analogy, Augustine is referring the Pauline passage back to the masculine–feminine analogy of the mind, which he had developed earlier in *De Trinitate* and which later he will call 'that hidden and secret marriage, which also takes place and can be discerned within a single human being'.[44] The point most germane to the question under discussion is that it is only the masculine *Sapientia* that represents the image of God. Feminine *Scientia*, not totally separated but 'diverted so as to be a help to fellowship', does not and cannot bear the image of God.[45] This is because only that part of a human being is *imago* to which God alone is superior. As the *Sapientia* is superior to the *Scientia*, the feminine *Scientia* cannot image God.[46]

This interpretation confirms that in this passage Augustine is alluding to the analogy of the dual aspects of the mind; otherwise he is flatly contradicting all that he has to say about women as *imago Dei*, and about the masculine and feminine dimension within each person. This is explicitly ratified in *De opere monachorum*: 'Therefore the injunction given to men about not covering the head is expressed in a corporeal figure, but the words indicate that the injunction is carried out in the mind where the injunction exists.'[47] Augustine reinterprets Paul so that 1 Corinthians 11.7 refers not to the actual status of women as *imago Dei*, but the status of *Scientia*. Thus he is able to maintain the absolute veracity of both scriptural statements, whilst resolving the tension between them. This textual conflict therefore forced Augustine to reject an explanation of the *imago Dei* similar to his own, but which understood that the *imago* resided in the very unity of masculine and feminine within the individual.[48] He rejected this aspect of the theory, precisely because he wanted to argue that it is the distinction between *Sapientia* and *Scientia* that Paul had in mind when he wrote that 'only man is the image and glory of God, but woman is the glory of man'.[49]

This resolution of the exegetical problem made it imperative that from the very beginning Augustine had to maintain a distinction between the explanatory symbolism of man–woman, and the intellectual realities of the masculine–feminine which had to be explained. The identification between them must be close enough so that he can apply Paul's words about woman to the feminine, yet the difference must be maintained so that the Pauline statement cannot apply to woman as human beings (*homo*).

Such an identification is facilitated by Latin usage itself. It provides the word *homo* to indicate humankind or human being, *mas* or *vir* to denote man/husband and *femina* or *mulier* to denote woman/wife. This allows Augustine a sophistical distinction between woman as *homo*, created in the image of God, and woman as *femina*, created from Adam, second and therefore subordinate.[50] As *homo*, there is no distinction between man and woman,[51] but as *femina*, 'the woman, then, with the appearance and distinctive characteristics of her sex, was made for the man from the man'.[52] The maintenance of the necessary difference underlines why there can be no implication of female sexuality in the feminine, because Augustine is adamant that sexual difference pertains only to the body and not to the mind.[53] It is this fact of sexual difference, with its concomitant physical characteristics, which renders woman inferior. It also explains both why Paul can say that man is the image and glory of God, but woman is the glory of man, and why Augustine can use woman to symbolise the inferior dimension of the mind.[54]

This rather complex system which manipulates sexual difference and language to create a gendered symbolic partnership, which distances itself from embodied sex, can be represented schematically thus:

human being (*homo*)	= *imago Dei*
man (*homo* and *vir*)	= *imago Dei*
woman (*homo*)	= *imago Dei*
woman (*femina/mulier*)	≠ *imago Dei*

The issues raised at the beginning of this chapter can now be addressed. Augustine employs the concept of masculine and feminine dimensions within the human psyche to explain the *imago Dei* in both sexes but distinguishes corporeal man and woman from *Sapientia* and *Scientia* by the purported absence of sexuality in the latter pair. In a sense one could argue that Augustine has here anticipated the feminist distinction between biological sex and social gender roles. *Sapientia* and *Scientia* are gender roles which Augustine argued were totally severed from any connotation of biological sex. Yet his use of Adam and Eve as the paradigmatic example ties them to social gender which was definitively tied to biological sex. *Sapientia* performs the contemplative function of the mind, as male performs the rational and reflective functions in society. *Scientia* performs the active function of dealing with corporeal and temporal existence, as a wife keeps the home fires burning to permit her husband the freedom to concentrate on higher matters. Therefore, *Scientia*, which is not concerned with God in any way, only images God when it is united to *Sapientia*; that is, when its rational capacity ceases to be diverted to temporal matters and joins *Sapientia* in the contemplation of God. Then it ceases to have an independent function or identity. A more detailed description of the characteristics of these functions will offer pertinent insights into Augustine's perceptions of gender roles.

Characteristics of the masculine *Sapientia* and feminine *Scientia*

The characteristics of the masculine-*Sapientia* and feminine-*Scientia* are determined by the way Augustine has deployed them to resolve his exegetical conflict. The criterion for allotting characteristics to either function is whether Augustine perceives the characteristic as capable of imaging God, because only *Sapientia* is capable of doing so. This manner of defining each aspect then structures the relationship of masculine and feminine. Because *Scientia* cannot image God, it is necessarily the inferior function. Yet *Scientia* is essential because she contains the healthy knowledge of human affairs, and so assists *Sapientia* to achieve eternal life. As the higher power, *Sapientia* is the lord to which *Scientia* is subject, because it is fitting that the lower serves the higher.[55]

The basic criteria which distinguish between *Sapientia* and *Scientia* are those of masculine and feminine gender roles. As noted earlier, the analogy of Adam and Eve is frequently used to explain the relationship between the functions of the mind. *Scientia* is a 'consort'[56] or helpmeet[57] to *Sapientia*, just as Eve was to Adam.[58] The term Augustine employed is *adiutor*: a subordinate who sustains or assists the dramatic hero or army general.[59] *Scientia*'s role as *adiutor* is purely auxiliary. It is not concerned with the most significant aspect of human life, the true end of human being, which is 'to depend upon and cleave to the supernal and inward truth'.[60] This is reserved to *Sapientia*, rational wisdom.[61] The more the masculine aspect reaches towards eternal values, the more closely it conforms to the image of God.[62]

The qualities of *Sapientia*'s assistant, *Scientia*, are described in various terms. It is action as opposed to intellect, performance as opposed to counsel, and appetite as opposed to reason.[63] The distinctions are always between the practical and the intellectual, the temporal and the eternal, the superior and the inferior. The former are always attributed to *Sapientia*, the latter to *Scientia*. Augustine found his categories in Job 28.28: 'Behold, fear of the Lord, that is wisdom: but to depart from evil, that is knowledge'.

Ignoring the parallelism of the text he applies fear of the Lord to *Sapientia* and knowledge to *Scientia*. *Sapientia*'s role is defined and refined through a chain of associative reasoning: fear of the Lord is a contemplative fear, manifested as worship of God; worship of God manifests love for God 'by which we now desire to see Him, and we believe and hope that we shall see Him'. So *Sapientia* is essentially the love of God, an aspect of human being that no feminine function of the mind can manifest.

Inherent in Augustine's understanding of *Sapientia* is not only a yearning for God, but also a positive reaching out towards the One who is the most truly excellent of eternal things: to discourse on eternal matters is the discourse of Wisdom itself.[64] Hence *Sapientia* belongs to the sphere of the changeless, to things that have 'absolute being', which do not abide in any fixed place, 'but as intelligible things in incorporeal nature' are as visible to the mind as created things to the eye.[65] If *Sapientia* is committed to absolute good, then it remembers, understands and loves the God who made it.[66] It loves by worshipping, and ultimately by partaking of God.[67] It is precisely in and through this, the greatest capacity of human nature, that the mind is the image of God.[68] When it finally cleaves totally to God and becomes one spirit with him, 'It will live unchangeably, and will see as unchangeable all that it does see. Then as divine Scripture promises, "His desire will be satisfied with good things," good things unchangeable, – the very Trinity itself, its own God, whose image it is.'[69]

Augustine's imagery and language are reminiscent of his narrative about the vision he shared with Monica at Ostia. Discoursing on wisdom they were carried upwards to glimpse Wisdom itself. Truly, Monica, filled with good things, relinquishing all attachment to any one place, then reached out for eternal happiness, literally dying to temporal happiness, and so personifying *Sapientia* at its most noble and yet its most virile.

Through faithful commitment to its purpose, the rational soul is made wise,[70] capable of loving God and neighbour. Once capable of rightly ordered love in its relationships *Sapientia* not only exists, but is renewed and restored and beatified with youth, righteousness, holiness and happiness.[71]

The nature of *Scientia* is similarly determined by Augustine's exegesis of Job: *Scientia* is defined as the knowledge that chooses between good and evil. This language evokes the biblical image of Eve and the tree of knowledge of good and evil in Genesis. The association becomes quite explicit in *De civitate Dei* when Augustine discusses the Fall.

> The eyes of them both were opened, not to see, for already they saw, but to discern between the good they had lost and the evil into which they had fallen. And therefore also the tree itself which they were forbidden to touch was called the tree of knowledge of good and evil from this circumstance, that if they ate of it would impart to them this knowledge.[72]

Having eaten of the tree first, it becomes the lot of the feminine to tend the fruits of the tree. As good and evil relate only to mortal life, *Scientia* is confined to the 'rational cognisance of temporal things', which 'we touch by corporeal sense, placed as they are without us'.[73] Through this intertextual interpretation, Augustine intimates that *Scientia* itself is, in a manner of speaking, a product of the Fall. If Eve had not eaten of the tree, there would have been no evil will within the soul to reject, and no temporality in the same sense, for Adam and Eve would have been immortal. On this point there is a clear distinction between *femina* and the feminine. Woman was created gendered and subordinate before the Fall. *Scientia* then fulfils a role in the temporal sphere which was modelled on Eve as helpmeet, but which now must continually discern between good and evil, the task Eve failed in paradise. So that it is not simply temporal affairs that *Scientia* manages, but precisely the faculty of discernment of good and evil within the temporal sphere.

> And therefore, whatsoever we do prudently, boldly, and justly belongs to that knowledge or discipline wherewith our action is conversant with avoiding evil and desiring good: and so also, whatsoever we gather by the way of knowledge that comes from inquiry, in the way of examples to be guarded against or to be imitated, and in the way of necessary proofs respecting any subject, accommodated to our use.[74]

Scientia must cover the wide range of behaviours required for the individual to interact with the world. The subject matter of its knowledge is whatever matter is accidental to the mind, acquired either through learning, sense experience, or reflection.[75] The content of such knowledge is factual and historical, and as such inferior to the content of *Sapientia*, which is love of God. Given the diversity of temporal affairs, *Scientia* is more clearly explicated than *Sapientia*. *Sapientia* has the integrity of unity – one *telos*, one goal, to which all its functioning is directed, and it often appears that that function is defined in opposition to *Scientia*'s. *Sapientia* is what *Scientia* is not.

Feminine as repository of faith

Augustine makes it clear that faith belongs to the realm of *Scientia*. However, he does not explicitly identify faith with feminine symbols or imagery as he does other characteristics, so it is not self-evident that faith is a feminine attribute. However, as he reiterates that the *imago Dei* does not reside in the faith aspect of *Scientia*, it is consistent to consider it a feminine attribute. As aspects of knowledge, faith and the virtues flowing from it are accidental to the mind because they are learnt, even though they do not exist objectively of themselves outside individuals.[76] Faith is that *by which* truth is believed, not *what* is believed. It is true faith and virtue which empower one to live so well in this life that one will gain the reward of immortal blessedness in the next.[77]

It may seem strange that faith belongs to the temporal sphere and not the eternal, but as it will pass away in eternity, it belongs to the temporal.[78] Once one has been granted the beatific vision, faith 'will be reckoned among things past, when sight shall have succeeded, and itself shall have ceased to be'.[79] Faith as instrumental to the blessed life will no longer be necessary.

> Undoubtedly, so long as the just man (*iustus*) lives by faith, howsoever he lives according to the inner man, although he aims at truth and reaches on to things eternal by this same temporal faith, nevertheless in the holding, contemplating and loving this temporal faith, we have not yet reached a trinity as is to be called an image of God: lest that should seem to be constituted in things temporal which ought to be so in things eternal.[80]

Within time, therefore, the just live by faith which 'works' by love and generates the virtues. If a virtue cannot be referred back to faith, then it is not a true virtue.[81] Believing and loving the truth permits one to live well, because people usually live according to whatever they love. And the truth that faith acknowledges is the risen Christ, who frees us from death in the 'abiding place of the devil'. Thus faith cleanses the heart and promises immortal blessedness.[82] For Augustine it is the most necessary and important human attribute for it is the only one which permits people to begin to order the will rightly and to obtain what is rightly willed.[83] The absolute purity of that will that constitutes true blessedness is ultimately only attainable with immortality.[84] Until then, the intimations of blessedness in this mortal life are those of hope.[85]

An important facet of Augustine's thought here is that faith is a gift, shed in our heart by the Holy Spirit.[86] Thus love cannot be received directly by *Scientia*, but must be mediated by *Sapientia*. Although the good works of *Scientia* are directed towards God, only *Sapientia* reaches towards God immediately. But Augustine does not explain how this mediation takes place. Loving appropriately is a characteristic of *Sapientia*, and love is also the empowering force of the most necessary characteristic of *Scientia*. It would appear that within its own sphere, *Scientia* is not autonomous, but dependent upon *Sapientia* for the fundamental capacity to choose correctly between good and evil.

The feminine as desire

This dependence has an interesting parallel, which also supports the argument that *Sapientia* is ultimately responsible for the individual's choices. A constant theme in Book 12 of *De Trinitate* is that *Sapientia* must constantly restrain *Scientia* or it will inevitably rage out of control.[87] With respect to this restraint *Sapientia* is variously called 'the head', 'the watch tower of counsel',[88] the one who 'rules', and 'dominates',[89] 'the sovereign power in the mind'.[90] *Scientia* is thereby the one 'ruled' and 'subdued'.[91]

Where *Sapientia* is an unequivocally positive aspect of the mind, although it can fall into sin, *Scientia* is far more ambiguous. As corporeal and temporal knowledge, *Scientia* is very close to the appetites and senses, which provide the information for it. So the feminine acts as an intermediary between the world of the senses and the reason of wisdom.[92] When the feminine is appropriately ruled, then the gaze of the inner being remains focused on eternal things.[93] However, if the inner being does not restrain the feminine, the demonic will seize control:

> Then he waxeth old because of all his enemies, *viz* the demons with their prince the devil, who are envious of virtue; and that vision of eternal things is withdrawn also from the head himself, eating with his spouse that which was forbidden, so that the light of his eye is gone from him.[94]

When this happens the inner being seeks no longer the love of wisdom, but rather lusts for inferior sense knowledge. Such knowledge cannot edify but corrupts, giving free rein to bestial appetites.[95] Prostrated and degraded,[96] the mind rests in false happiness,[97] because it lives not by will but by sensual desire.[98] In contrast to the discussion of faith, where the feminine is not directly invoked, in the discussion of sin in *De opere monachorum*, we find the explicit identification of the feminine, and woman, with concupiscence: 'What therefore, in one person are mind and concupiscence (for the one rules, the other is ruled, the one dominates and the other is subdued), that in two human beings, man and woman is represented according to the sex of the body.'[99]

That the one dominating and the one subdued are the same aspects of the Mind as *Sapientia* and *Scientia* is apparent from the previous citation. It is in the metaphorical repetition of the 'eating of the apple', a fruit closely connected to sexual desire in antiquity, that *Sapientia* withdraws from the eternal vision, its inner life not renewed but decrepit with sensual gratification. In the latter citation, the feminine becomes a locus of meanings that tie the sexless aspect of the mind to both sexed bodies and sensual desire. Like *Scientia*, concupiscence is an ambiguous concept. It may refer to any desire: if a good object is desired, the desire is good; otherwise it is bad. But although Augustine uses lust to describe any illicit desire, sexual desire is lust *par excellence*. The terms he uses regularly for desire are *libido* and *cupiditas*, but he uses *libido* and *concupiscentia* as parallels in *De civitate Dei*,[100] and *libido* and *concupiscentia carnalis* consistently as synonyms in *De nuptiis et concupiscentia*.[101] *Concupiscentia* is not sin itself in the redeemed: 'However, as by a certain manner of speech it is called sin, since it arose from sin, and, when it has the upper hand, produces sin, the guilt of it prevails in the natural man.'[102]

So the feminine, and the female sex, are linguistically identified with the dubious nature of sexual desire and its proximity to sin, especially if it/she gains the 'upper hand'. Clearly, this is the great danger which requires restraint, as he wrote in *De nuptiis et concupiscentia*: 'A man turns to use the evil of concupiscence, and is not overcome by it, when he bridles and restrains its rage, as it works in inordinate and indecorous motions: and never relaxes his hold upon it except when intent on offspring.'[103] Here are the same images and the same dynamic as *Sapientia* bridling *Scientia*, to prevent the body acting against the will. Here, too, is a further reference to the disorderly nature of male sexual responses where the unwilled erection is the *poena reciproca* for original sin. For Augustine the punishment did indeed fit the crime, and he seemed to assume that women's experience of sexual desire paralleled that of men.

The feminine as locus of temptation

The feminine, identified as concupiscence, is the locus of temptation, especially sexual temptation. Whenever *Scientia* is tempted to enjoy 'private and personal good, the serpent addresses the woman',[104] for *Sapientia* can only be brought to bestiality through its own 'intermediate grade'.[105]

This descent into sin is grounded in 'apostatising pride' which leads the soul to stop following God as its ruler and, in doing so, to substitute one 'part', its own, for the whole that was God's. Through love of its own power, the soul slips away from God. By lusting for more, it becomes less, 'whence also covetousness is called "the root of all evil" '.[106] This has one of two consequences: sinners either become arrogant from spiritual achievements, and think themselves superior to other souls given up to the corporeal senses, or else are 'plunged into a foul whirlpool of carnal pleasure'.[107] There are parallels here to Augustine's portrayal of Eve's role in the Fall. In Augustine's eyes, Eve would not have been susceptible to temptation 'if there was not already within her heart a love of her own independence and a proud presumption of self which through that temptation was destined to be found out and cast down'.[108]

Adam, on the other hand, was motivated not so much by pride, but by that attachment and affection 'by which it often happens that we offend God while we try to keep the friendship of men'. Therefore, he complied with her actions because he did not wish to make her unhappy, 'fearing that she would waste away without his support, alienated from his affections, and that this dissension would be her death'.[109] So Adam virtually joins Eve in sin through misplaced love. Augustine teaches that Eve was seduced by the serpent 'to accept as true what in reality is false'. Adam, whatever his motivations, did not believe that God had given his command about the tree out of envy for mankind.[110]

However, even the power of the feminine to sin is limited. If *Scientia* is tempted, but the sin is limited to the pleasure of thought, then 'the woman' alone sins, but if the body becomes actively involved in the sin, then, like Eve, she has given the fruit of temptation to her husband. Only *Sapientia* has the authority to engage the members of the body in physical action, or to restrain them from one.[111] Augustine does not deny that sin occurs in thought, but it is far less serious than if the thought was followed by action:

> And yet, certainly, when the mind is pleased in thought alone with unlawful things, while not indeed determining that they are to be done, but yet holding and pondering gladly things which ought to have been rejected the moment they touched the mind, it cannot be denied to be a sin, but far less than if it were also determined to accomplish it in outward act. And therefore pardon must be sought for those thoughts too, and the breast must be

smitten, and it must be said, 'Forgive us our debts': and what follows must be done, and must be joined in our prayer, 'As we also forgive our debtors'.[112]

This discrimination between desire which provokes the body to active sin, and desire which remains an internal pleasure, subverts the dominical teaching that adulterous lust is as sinful in the thought as in the deed (Matt. 5.27). This distinction allows him to define all passive sins of the mind as feminine. If the desire is pleasing but not acted upon, the masculine aspect of the mind is never implicated. In this way, responsibility for sin can be shifted to the feminine dimension of the mind, as responsibility for original sin was consistently blamed on Eve, from the moment God asked Adam to account for himself.

To nuance this idea further Augustine distinguishes very carefully between the dual aspects of the mind and sexed bodies. If Eve only had eaten of the forbidden fruit, she alone would have died, for Adam and Eve were separate human beings, each responsible for their own persons.[113] But within one human being 'the woman cannot be condemned without the man' even if action does not follow thought, if evil thoughts are deliberately retained with pleasure in the memory. Only if 'those things which, as lacking the will to do, and yet having the will to please the mind with them, are perceived to be sins of thought alone, are pardoned through the grace of the Mediator'.[114]

This is a fine distinction here. What it pleases the mind to contemplate is not serious sin, but deliberate retention of such thought is. Once the will consents to thought, i.e. *Sapientia* accedes to *Scientia*, then serious sin has been committed. Augustine defines this as anything done to achieve sensual satisfactions, or to gratify lusts, which replace God as the final good of the soul.[115]

Sin is a process of descent from highest to lowest which happens by degree.[116] The soul fails little by little, losing sight of Truth and Wisdom until all divinity seems to reside 'within the deceitful images of corporeal things . . . combining them in vain thought'. What begins as 'the perverse desire for the likeness of God, arrives in the end at the likeness of beasts'. Once the descent is complete, there is no return. The soul is condemned to 'the trial of its own intermediateness', from which it is powerless to extricate itself. Its only hope is in 'the grace of its Maker, calling it to repentance and forgiving its sins'.[117] It is completely lost in the feminine world of bodiliness, change and time.

The feminine as both faith and concupiscence points to the choices confronting the soul in the temporal world, and is a 'generic' feminine which contains within itself the ancient symbols of

woman as Pleasure and Virtue. Both Philo and Ambrose had
described conflicts of the will as the conflict between these two
'women'. This gendered paradigm of desire and temptation reflects
to some degree the complexities of his theology of grace. The
feminine can lead the rational mind to sin for, like Eve, it is more
susceptible to error, being so closely associated with the body. Once
the masculine faculty assents to the sin of thought and wills action,
then serious sin is committed which is totally the responsibility of
the sinner.[118] But if the masculine will cleaves to faith as gifted
by God, in Christ, through the Holy Spirit, then the feminine,
appropriately bridled, assists the soul's ascent to righteousness. Here
the feminine is not so much intermediary as instrument, like the
horse to which it is compared. The soul does not ascend to eternal
things through the feminine but by means of the feminine. The
feminine can assist only through obedience and humility. The individual must be totally governed by grace, for all the goods which
lead to blessedness have their source in God.[119]

The grace of God empowers human beings by teaching them
what has to be done, and helping them to do with love what they
have learned. There can be no good will in anyone except that
helped by the grace of God.[120] In this context, Augustine directly
opposes grace to physical desire; 'Further, since on account of that
one [Adam] the devil held all who were begotten through his
corrupted carnal concupiscence, it is just on account of this one
[Jesus] he should loose all who are regenerated through his immaculate spiritual grace.'[121] So grace also is operative in the sphere
of the feminine, which is the temporal battleground of faith and
concupiscence.[122] Like faith, grace is unmerited gift of God and so
descends to the feminine via the masculine.

The paradox implicit in Augustine's concepts of *Sapientia* and
Scientia is that the feminine is defined as activity, performance
and rational appetite, but it has no power to initiate action on its
own behalf. It is a recommending body, without executive authority.
It cannot be autonomously responsible for either good or evil,
although it is the only aspect of the mind which can be tempted,
because 'she alone spoke with the serpent, and she alone was led
away by him'.[123] Activity belongs to *Scientia*, yet the feminine can
only offer the fruits of its knowledge, whether good or evil, for the
judgement of the masculine, wherein the will to action resides.[124]
If the knowledge of good is offered, then the soul is nourished to
greater life with the flowering of faith; if temptation, then the soul
is lured towards its own death.

The resolution of the paradox is now more clearly apparent. It
pertains to the feminine faculty to act only under the direction of
the masculine. Feminine activity does not include the power and

authority of decision-making. The full force of the concept of *adiutor*, which orders the relationship between *Sapientia* and *Scientia*, emerges here. *Scientia* has a prominent role, but it is at all times subordinate. It is literally 'under orders'. If the responsibility for serious sin does not lie upon it, neither does the praise for virtue. That is the prerogative of the masculine.[125]

In summary, *Sapientia* and *Scientia* are two dimensions of the human mind, concretely symbolised by man and woman. The analogically masculine has as its function the contemplation of the eternal and changeless, defined as the love of God. The analogically feminine has as its function the knowledge of good and evil in the administration of the corporeal needs of mortal life, but it cannot actually initiate action on its own behalf. The crucial relationship between them is that of master and assistant. Because *Scientia* is the intermediary whereby the highest faculties of the person interact with the world, it may be said to possess an instrumental but not decisive function for either good or evil. Augustine thus consistently expresses his understanding of the feminine via its dichotomy with the masculine: the feminine can only be defined in relationship to the masculine as 'other'. The masculine is taken as the standard from which the feminine is 'diverted to help fellowship',[126] and thus the feminine can only be understood in relation to that standard, to which it is consistently inferior, subordinate and potentially dangerous. In the realm of eternity, only the masculine functions will perdure. The feminine role will have ceased to exist with time and mortality.

Interconnections between Woman and the Feminine

It is clear then, that women bear the imprint of the *imago Dei*, because they too possess both aspects of the mind. They too are capable of living according to *Sapientia* and controlling the passions of *Scientia*. However, it remains to be judged whether Augustine has succeeded in severing the connection between *Sapientia* and *Scientia* as the abstractions of the feminine and masculine, and real women and men whose lives express the concrete realities of gendered existence and experience. This is the most significant issue for, if the answer is in the negative, then pastoral authority would require that gender relations should be structured according to the archetypal pattern of the human soul.

The first point to be made is that the effectiveness of any analogy depends on the existence of parallels or correspondence between what has to be explained and the example used to explain it. These similarities may be either physical behaviours or the fact that both follow similar rules, or have similar structures. Thus the effectiveness of Augustine's analogy of the two functions of the mind being related like a husband and wife hinges on the existence of similarities, or congruences, or corresponding structures between the symbolic relationship and the proper relations of the sexes as perceived by Augustine.[127]

The fundamental relationship between woman and man is the same as that between the feminine and the masculine, and it is this very factor which made the analogy apposite for Augustine. From his earliest writings Augustine had asserted that proper order required male headship and control, and female subordination, service and obedience. Women were typically the same and their role was sexualised and domesticated. Further both 'marriages' are dominated by the concept of woman/feminine as *adiutor*.[128]

An examination of some of Augustine's mature writings from this same period, which illustrate his reasoning and give content to this concept, are enlightening. Women would not have been created to help till the soil, for labour was not toil in paradise, so she is not co-worker; if a helper was required a male would be better because 'how much more agreeably could two male friends, rather than a man and woman, enjoy companionship and conversation in a life shared together?' Thus generic woman is not companion either. It is a given for Augustine that she was not created to exercise authority or power.[129] Having exhausted the reasons why women have no other function in society and relationship than the procreative, he concluded: 'Consequently, I do not see in what sense the woman was made as a helper for the man if not for the sake of bearing children.'[130] This is a consistent stance that appears in his earlier writings and remains unchanged in the later works. This perception of women is actually a dual vision. Although equal as *homo*, woman is subordinate as *femina* (i.e. non-*vir*) because she was created second, and her subordinate status is reinforced because she was made from man.[131] Like the feminine, as *adiutor* she is essentially passive, that is, not in control of her life, her emotions and her actions. Passive does not necessarily connote lack of activity, but being subject to feelings and to authority beyond the control of the self. Within the context of procreation, passivity denotes the ancient belief that woman held no procreative power. That was the biological male power which legitimated all male social and political power. Man creates life as God creates life. Woman simply received the vivifying seed of man.[132] Indeed, Augustine compares her to the earth which nurtures the seed of the plants.[133] In *De genesi ad litteram* the analogical association of woman and earth is placed in the context of the command to increase and multiply and fill the earth and subdue it.[134] The implication is that men must subdue women as they subdue the earth. Therefore the language reinforces the inferiority and subordination of women to men. The only aspect of woman–man that is not shared by the masculine–feminine is biological sex. Otherwise the shared properties of the spiritual marriage and the human partnership are total. It is implicit in Augustine's reasoning that woman fills the same function physically that the feminine does mentally. In the same way that some rational capacity has been diverted to manage temporal affairs, so woman has been 'diverted from man', literally being taken from man's side, to fulfil a temporal function. He has already made it clear that her function is procreative, and that woman also stands as a symbol for *concupiscentia* as well as *Scientia*. This fusion of woman, *Scientia*, sex and sin becomes even clearer in the 'feminine' texts which prescribe the veiling of women.

First, the texts in *De Trinitate* regarding the veiling of women. 'Because she differs from man by her bodily sex, that part of reason which is turned aside to regulate temporal things, could be properly symbolised by her corporeal veil.'[135] Although its larger context is still the discussion of the mind, it is concerned with the question of veiling of real women. In Book 15 Augustine states that he has explained the meaning of 1 Corinthians 11.7 in Book 12.[136] Man is the image and glory of God; thus he may not cover his head for he symbolises the masculine *Sapientia*, which 'is so much the more formed after the image of God, the more it has extended itself to that which is eternal, and is on that account not to be restrained, so as to withhold and refrain itself from thence; therefore the man ought not to cover his head.'[137]

However, woman symbolises the feminine *Scientia* which must be veiled 'because too great a progression towards inferior things is dangerous to that rational dealing, that is conversant with things corporeal and temporal; this ought to have power on its head, which the covering indicates, by which it is signified that it ought to be restrained.'[138]

We see here the restraint of the feminine, explicitly identified with the veiling of real women. Corporeal veils symbolise the restrained and controlled mortal soul. Augustine says that Paul's instructions about veiling being for the sake of the angels remain empty words unless they have a figurative and mystical meaning.[139] This hidden 'sacrament' is the hidden marriage of the mind within one person. The visible sacrament is the 'visible wedlock'[140] of the two sexes whose bodies reveal two functions in their common human nature.[141] Once there is an explicit identification, as there is now, between man and the masculine, and woman and the feminine, historical consequences must follow.

Texts from *De opere monachorum* and the *Confessiones* express this thought in different ways, and their earlier dating indicates that the doctrine in *De Trinitate* expresses long held opinions. In *De opere monachorum* (400 CE) he wrote:

> Do women not have this renewal of the mind where the image of God is? Who said that? But they do not signify it in the sex of their body, for which reason they are bidden to veil themselves. Truly in so far as they are women they show that part which can be called concupiscible, which when a woman lives according to God's law and order, is dominated by the mind subject to its God.[142]

That to live according to God's law and order is not only to have the masculine element of the mind dominant, but the male sex also, is clear from this passage in the *Confessiones*, which also blurs the boundaries between the hidden and visible marriages.

> Just as in man's soul there are two forces, one which is dominant because it deliberates and one which obeys because it is subject to such guidance, in the same way, in the physical sense, woman has been made for man. In her mind and in her rational intelligence she has a nature the equal of man's, but in sex she is physically subject to him in the same way our natural impulses need to be subjected to the reasoning power of the mind, in order that the actions to which they lead may be inspired by the principles of good conduct.[143]

In these texts there is as close a connection between woman and concupiscence as there was between the feminine and concupiscence. This identification is facilitated by woman's procreative function because the very name of wife brings sexual desire and intercourse to a man's mind.[144] By association, woman comes to symbolise the 'law of sin' which encompasses all irrational appetite,[145] and especially sexual sin and desire,[146] which 'subjugated man to herself when he was unwilling to remain subject to his God'.[147] Concupiscence is not the servant of the will but a punishment of the will which disobeys. Here too Augustine uses woman as symbol: 'Concupiscence is the daughter of sin as it were; and whenever it yields assent to the commission of shameful deeds, it becomes the mother of many sins.'[148]

Sexuality is understood as demonic, for it is only when a man came to desire the opposite sex and lost his virginity that his heart turned from God and evil gained control of him.[149] The psychological connection here is that between concupiscence, sin and death. The lack of control of his genitals was, for Augustine, a constant reminder that humankind had lost its innocence and thereby had been condemned to death.[150] Women, then, were the 'seductive stimuli' that reminded men, and especially ascetic men, that they were still a part of nature.[151] Those who aspired to live like angels were constantly reminded that they were still mortal men.[152]

Woman, genitality, concupiscence and shame are linked by the discourse of the veil. Just as woman is to be veiled to symbolise her temporality and proper subordination, so Adam and Eve covered themselves with fig-leaves, that 'at the very least, by the will of the ashamed offenders, a veil might be thrown over that which was put into motion without the will of those who wished it: and since shame arose from what indecency pleased, decency might be attained by concealment'.[153]

The discourse of the veil which recurs in other contexts consistently links shame, unseemliness, sex and impurity as the things which must be covered. In anti-Pelagian texts Augustine consistently argues the necessity for shameful things (*pudenda*) to be veiled in order that the shameful might become seemly and separated from God. Sexual desire, like the genital response it arouses, is intrinsically shameful and also requires veiling.[154] Proximity to God is also expressed by the presence or absence of a veil. Early in *De Trinitate* Augustine has cited 1 Corinthians 12.2 to establish that in this temporal life Christ cannot be seen face to face, but only through symbols which constitute the dark mirror.[155] He returns to this verse in Book 15 and interprets it through 2 Corinthians 3.18 – the human soul is transformed when unveiled it sees God's face. Thus the image grows from glory to glory. It is important to note that here he specified that the image, which moves from the glory of son to the glory of being like God, from that of faith to sight, from that of creation to justification, is symbolised by man (*vir*) who is forbidden to cover his head. The blurred image of God that a man saw when he looked in the mirror would be replaced by a clear image when the glory of God shone full on him.[156]

In a similar manner, the veil of the Temple symbolised the veil that separated carnal humanity from God before the death of Christ. For those who live in Christ, this veil is now removed.[157] This usage of the veil is related to a theme which runs through several sermons against the Donatists. Consistently citing the Song of Songs 1.7 he interprets the verse 'Lest I come as one veiled', to mean that if the bride wanders away from her Groom's flock she will then be veiled, which signifies that he will not recognise her, because she pollutes herself with unlawful loves.[158] The only way that this danger can be averted is for the bride to 'recognise herself': her choice is 'be manly or be thrown out'.[159] The veil is the barrier which separates true church from heretic. It is the shadows in which the heretics lurk, but which disappear when the noon sun of Christ shines on his flock.[160] This shadow veil means that heretics are unrecognised by Christ and they are no longer able to recognise him. Heretics are bad daughters – not bad wives – yet heresy is 'bad desire' and symbolised by the same putrescent sores used for sexual desire in the *Confessiones*.[161] These variations on a theme appear in sermons from 396 until 412, often in almost the same words.

The veil constitutes a boundary which divides the temporal from the eternal, the carnal from the spiritual, Christ from the unredeemed, the heretic from the faithful, the chaste bride from the lustful shamed daughter, and the sun of wisdom from the shadows of error. It might be summed up as the core symbol which separates the sacred from the profane, clean from unclean. As a symbol it is most effective. But as real women must wear a physical veil because they symbolise concupiscence, it may be taken that the veil serves to render women seemly, and yet remind them and their menfolk that they represent the shameful, sinful carnality which put the barrier between God and humanity in the first place. As they are equally *imago Dei* in their inmost (masculine) being, it is their female bodies which are thus designated. If they wish to see the image of God they must look not in a mirror but at their husbands. There is irony in the fact that the institution which has continually proclaimed that women are not to be exploited as sex objects has done so much to sexualise women's bodies as entities divorced from their essential human being. These texts create a discourse in which woman symbolises sexual desire, the 'unclean' power which shames and dishonours men by subverting male rationality, authority and structures. The 'disorderly' male response to sexual stimuli was a constant reminder of this 'unclean' or shameful power of women. The roles of *Scientia*, woman, and even desire were essential for the continuance of the state, the *familia*, and for the comfort of individual men, yet these roles were perceived as a diversion from the only truly significant human endeavour.[162] Their very necessity, connoted in the ancient use of 'the necessity' for the sexual act, meant that the subversive power they possessed must be tightly constrained, lest woman, like concupiscence, literally rage out of control.[163] So although the shameful response is a function of the male body, it is the female face which must also be veiled as shameful stimulus.[164]

It is as if Augustine has taken the Pauline dictum that the more shameful parts of the body are clothed with more respect and applied it to women (1 Corinthians 12.22). The matrix of meanings converging on femininity link together desire, the uncontrollable genitalia, and the veiling of real woman. Women represent fallen human sexuality, and in a more focused way, sexual desire, and this necessary but inherently tainted aspect of human being must be concealed for the sake of honour, so that masculine rationality will not be deterred from its higher calling. This contention immediately calls to mind his remark that the caresses of his lady could bring his mind down from the manly heights of philosophy quicker than anything else.[165]

Indeed, in Augustine's thinking, woman from her very creation was a vitiating influence on man. When writing about the miraculous nature of woman's creation, he queries why God would use a rib rather than flesh, which would have been more appropriate 'for the formation of the woman who belongs to the weaker sex';[166] this use of the rib made woman strong, because she was strengthened by man's bone, 'but he was made weak for her sake because in place of his rib it was flesh, not another rib that was substituted'.[167] In a new guise, what appears here is Philo's perception that it was the very creation of woman which led to man's destruction.

Indeed, as was said above (p. 133), the whole paradigm of *Sapientia* and *Scientia* owes a great debt to Philo. Augustine's paradigm differs from that of Philo in two major aspects. First, the feminine is not irrational, but a rational power diverted from the mainstream of rationality to interact with the corporeal world, like a temporary business manager appointed for the duration of a project, so that senior management can focus on corporate planning and vision statements. As the 'go between' between *Sapientia* and physical reality, *Scientia* still hovers dangerously close to the sensual passions, and thus possesses a spiritual vulnerability and the power to entice the masculine into sin.

Second, by naming the masculine *Sapientia*, he claims Wisdom as an exclusively masculine, though not male, attribute. It was noted above that Wisdom had become coterminous with Jesus, and the human Jesus did have a feminine function operative during his earthly life. But this aspect of his mind did not perdure into the Resurrection.[168] It is difficult not to conclude that Augustine did not take the Incarnation too seriously. Or rather, that he took it seriously as the gift of grace which redeemed humanity, but Christ's humanness is for him simply an instrument of God's saving act, not a blessing of the very humanity God chose to join. Indeed, it is highly significant that when Augustine attacks those who believe God holds some bodily form of shape, he never mentions the Incarnation, which influenced such thinking for the monks of the East, if not for the Manichees. If God has become human, if Jesus was a real human being as Nicaea held, then it is harder to argue that human images debase God as Augustine persistently holds. Jesus, for him, is not the risen man but the risen Word.

Augustine, like other Christian Fathers, had to face the question, 'What happens to women's bodies at the resurrection?' Those who took the status of the masculine to its logical conclusion posited that all the faithful would be resurrected as men. Augustine denied this because he believed that the biological sex of women was part of the natural order. However, women will be altered in some way that is 'superior to carnal intercourse and childbearing' as they are 'translated to the mind of the Son of God'. Women's bodies 'shall remain adapted not to old uses but to new beauty, which so far from provoking lust, now extinct, shall excite praise to the wisdom and clemency of God who both made what was not and delivered from corruption what he has made'. Thus the 'corruption' inherent in the female function will be eliminated by God. Women will be resurrected to true beauty in the image of the masculine mind of Christ which holds no danger for spiritual men; this erasure of the definitively female will be a cause for rejoicing. Needless to say the bodies of men will not need to alter as they already image the eternal.[169]

By incorporating Philo's system into his doctrine of the *imago Dei* Augustine made it one of the foundations of what became orthodox Christian theological anthropology. Ambrose's references to the symbolic function of Adam and Eve are simply that – references, and he does not amplify the symbolism into any systematic doctrine. A theology that did not espouse the ontological inferiority of women might be able to displace the sexist imagery, though not without difficulty. But from Augustine onwards, it becomes acceptable doctrine that women as women, cannot represent the eternal Holy One in their human person.

Before the consequences of this doctrine are explored more fully, there is one further important conclusion to be drawn. If immortal, masculine *Sapientia* is the image of God, then God's nature is characterised by masculine rationality, if not maleness. This is consistent with the perceptions of philosophy as a male domain, and the privileging of intellect and rationality over feeling and experience. If the feminine cannot reflect God, then nothing that can be attributed to the feminine exists within the divine nature, and indeed, as I have argued, that was an a priori assumption for Augustine's definitions of *Sapientia* and *Scientia*.

The only thing about women that reflects the image of God is one aspect of their minds. This dogmatic position marks a significant shift in Augustine's thinking. Between the publication of the *Confessiones* and of *De Trinitate* Augustine has purged the eternal of any vestige of the feminine, even analogically. To do so he had to ignore his own spiritual experience. In the *Confessiones*, his first experience of God was as mother. His spiritual experiences close to his conversion included visions of Continence and Wisdom as female figures.[170] Feminist theological method which posits experience as one datum of theology calls into question the validity of his relegation of the feminine to the purely temporal and earthly, when his own experience had been of God as both Mother and Father.[171] It is likely however that Augustine's response would be that God is neither, human beings simply interpret their experience of God according to human knowledge and categories. One cannot really engage with Augustine's argument, because his a priori assumption is that if anything can be predicated of God then it is analogically masculine. Thus his arguments, however logical, spring from presuppositions that constrain his premises.

11

THEOLOGY AND SOCIAL RELATIONSHIPS

THERE is no doubt Augustine has elevated the spiritual status of women above that ascribed by certain other Fathers, because he insists, vehemently at times, that they, too, are the image of God. It has been suggested that he allots them higher standing than Ambrose, because he posits the feminine as an aspect of mind not of sense-perception, but as the latter was taken as a function of the mortal soul by Ambrose the difference is not great.[1] The operative dynamic in both symbolic systems is the same. The rational masculine must control and constrain the irrational feminine in order to attain salvation, and the source of its death, both spiritual and physical, lies in the realm of the feminine.[2] Only the masculine dimension of any soul bears the *imago Dei*. The feminine aspect of being is purely temporal and will lose its independent existence once the soul enters immortal life. More ironically, whatever difference may remain, it held no real impetus for change in social relations because of the distinction between woman as *homo* and woman as *femina*.[3] Indeed, Augustine flatly contradicts the Ambrosian dictum that a wife is not slave and a husband is not a master.

Masculine–feminine: symbolic partners

This symbolic partnership is tied to real gendered people at three levels: first, philosophically, by the belief in the hierarchical cosmos within which each grade of being shares the same laws and structures. This is particularly true of the Neoplatonists, for whom the material world was a reflection of the spiritual ideal Forms, though these had been thoroughly Christianised. When Wisdom became incarnate in the Christ, his human form was male, and *Sapientia* ruled *Scientia* in and to perfection. So if the spiritual paradigm is masculine ruling feminine, then the social cosmos must participate in that paradigm.[4] Second, at the level of discourse, it is tied to gendered people by the marital imagery, by the constant appeal to Adam and Eve as paradigms of the relationship, and third, at the concrete level, by the veiling of historical women to signify the control of desire. It could not help but have repercussions on the perception of women and the structures of gender relations. Despite woman's eschatalogical status as *homo*, Augustine's perceptions of women and the feminine are consistently and overwhelmingly pessimistic. In this mortal world, woman to all intents and purposes is *femina* when it comes to any relationship. She is a 'vessel' to be possessed rather than a person to be related to.[5] Her physical being is inferior, her position is subordinate, her moral fibre is suspect and, however unwittingly, she provides the preferred access of the demonic through her sexuality.

This doctrine is the ultimate theological abstraction of patriarchal, honour–shame culture. The feminine has the power to bring the ultimate dishonour, eternal damnation, upon the masculine soul both individually and in the body of Christ. Woman, through her sexual function, can subvert the purity of the *familia* and the state by bearing children with no right to inheritance or citizenship; she can manipulate male power structures by tempting men to compete for her sexual favours or seducing them into adulterous relationships, and can threaten male headship if permitted to assume clerical office. Likewise the feminine can subvert the purity of Wisdom's gaze by luring it to the contemplation of carnal and worldly beauties. It can seduce the masculine into carnal sexuality, or manipulate masculine order if it seizes the leadership in the mind, asserting itself as identity rather than function. And yet in both domains, the assistance of women for masculine goals is essential. The masculine-man is dependent upon the feminine-woman to provide an earthly 'home', to bear and raise his children, spiritual and carnal, and to meet his most personal and intimate needs. Masculine-male success depends upon feminine-female co-operation. Thus in both the internal and external world, redemption from disorder and sensuality demands male headship and the subordination of women.[6]

Practical consequences
Therefore, concrete consequences for real men and women must follow, and some of these are prescribed explicitly by Augustine. Firstly, men must dominate and restrain women or further corruption will occur and sin will multiply. It is the inverse of the command to increase and multiply and subdue the earth. For earth and woman to be fruitful, and directed to eternal values, they must first be subdued.[7] Women, like the feminine through whom temptation comes, are clearly the weaker vessels in the human alliance. Augustine ordained that women had no moral rights over children, property, lifestyle or even the manner in which they dressed, although

they may have had legal rights.[8] A woman might not expend money without her husband's consent, although women must bear with feckless husbands wasting their possessions.[9] He also gave men the right to beat their wives in the pursuit of order. This stance put the Christian values as articulated by the bishop at odds with civil law, which had granted women economic rights, protected women in *sine manu* marriages from violence, and permitted them to conduct their own business and personal matters.

Paradoxically, one right that woman had was her sexual right in marriage. A woman had a right to the marriage debt, just as a man did, and she had a right to forbid his adultery.[10] Augustine did not support the view that men could leave marriage for the ascetic life but that women could not.[11] This mutual obligation was a novel idea in the Roman empire, but one faithful to the Christian tradition which from its earliest days had abolished the double sexual standard regarding adultery (Mark 10.1–12 and par.).[12] Men who fail to be as chaste as women were no longer regarded as virile, but are shamed by the virtue of the inferior sex.[13]

Secondly, the identification of woman and concupiscence had enormous consequences for intimate personal relationships by shaping the perception of gender stereotypes. Augustine's precepts created a truly conflictual situation. As women had no integrity of body and spirit, but were divided between spiritual *homo* and physically carnal *femina*,[14] men must learn to love the one and hate the other. Husbands were told,

> in one and the same woman to love the creature of God, whom he desires to be renewed; but to hate the corruptible and mortal conjugal connection and sexual intercourse: i.e. to love in her what is characteristic of a human being, to hate what belongs to her as a wife.[15]

Nothing could be clearer in this text than the identification of the wifely role with concupiscence and temptation. This love/hate injunction to husbands has been perceived as a parallel to the Platonic discrimination between the rational essence of man and the temporal conditions of existence. Indeed, it is clear that Augustine's whole distinction between woman as *homo* and woman as *femina* falls into this category. Eternally, in relationship with God, woman is man's equal, in essence. Temporally, in relationship with man, she is his inferior. Thus Augustine transmutes the philosophic journey from sexuality to the *via sapientiae* into the ascetic path from sexual desire to sanctity.[16]

The Augustinian dilemma

It is a journey which leaves little room for the sanctity of relationships between men and women, especially those which include genital expressions of love. Having reduced the feminine role to the purely temporal and largely sexual, this role is to be hated by the Christian.[17] Thus Augustine implicitly legitimated a split between love and sex which facilitates the depersonalisation of sexual intercourse. This depersonalisation may be reflected in both hedonism and asceticism. An impossible situation was created for the devout Christian. Carnal concupiscence, that is, sexual desire not motivated by the desire for children, is never acceptable even in marriage, although it may be tolerated and forgiven. But 'it is not a good which comes out of the essence of marriage, but an evil which is the accident of original sin'.[18] Thence intention becomes all important.[19] Intercourse for the sake of children means that the will is rightly ordered and desire controlled by the will. If intercourse is motivated by sexual desire, the will is evil,[20] although the sin is only 'venial'.[21] In *De mendacio* Augustine is quite clear that sex is corrupting if enjoyed.[22] In fact, a man who loves his wife with passion is an adulterer with his wife.[23] The split between love and sexual desire means that men, at a very deep level, are taught to hold woman in contempt for their very desirability.[24] And women learn to hold men in contempt for desiring them, and to hold themselves in contempt for desiring to be desired.[25]

Augustine, and the ascetical masters of his era, set standards of sexual behaviour which no one could live up to without crippling emotional cost, and which engendered failure, shame and guilt.[26] Women who expressed passion were considered shameful yet, without it, marriages became tortured and adultery a constant problem. Ascetic men could become prurient voyeurs, ever vigilant to detect sexual temptations from even the most innocent of women.

> Your very dress, cheap and sombre as it is, is an index to your secret feelings. For it has no creases and trails along the ground, to make you appear taller than you are . . . as you walk the very creaking of your black and shiny shoes attracts the notice of the young men . . . And when in public you for modesty's sake, cover your face, like a practised harlot you only show what is likely to please.[27]

Though Augustine rejected Jerome's extremes, his understanding of the evil of sexual desire uncontrolled by the will means that there is no possibility of sexual or married love imaging God or divine love.[28] As Børresen expresses it perceptively:

> Augustine shows that, for him, the sexual relationship has no real

value. Governed as it is by the penalty of sin, it will finally be removed by the work of redemption. The goodness proper to marriage exists in its purity only in the state of innocence, an ideal which has never been fulfilled. The condition of the human race after the fall and during the time while it waits for its complete renewal, involves a sexuality which is deeply disfigured. The Christian can only employ this evil for a good end by directing it towards the three goods of marriage.[29]

There is no room in Augustine's attitude to sexuality for Judaism's view that intercourse on the Sabbath reflects the divine ideal. The notion that man is most like God when he makes love with his spouse would not only be alien but totally abhorrent to ascetic Christianity.[30] Rather, Augustine offers the ideal of sexless marriage,[31] and interprets coitus and childbirth as corruption and loss of integrity.[32]

The 'Augustinian emotion'

It is poignant commentary on Augustine's experience, or his interpretation of it, that he could posit shame as the only motivation for the privacy that lovers sought, even when consummation was licit. He speaks of lust requiring darkness and secrecy[33] for 'all are still ashamed, and seek out secret retreats for cohabitation'. So strong is his emphasis on shame that one commentator has called it the 'Augustinian emotion'.[34] Shame is focused on the genitals, because the penis is not controllable at will. This shame is particularly attached to sexual feelings even when unsought, because they symbolise the rebellion of humankind against God.[35] At first reading, Augustine's argument could seem inconsistent. If the modest woman is one who keeps to the private sphere, and screens herself from public, i.e. male gaze, then how can the maintenance of that privacy for sexual intimacy be proof of shame? The resolution of the paradox is that sexuality itself was considered unseemly in the milieu of the scholar and the ascetic. Woman's honour is the equivalent to concealing her (potential for) shame. Thus her acceptance of seclusion to the privacy of her home indicates her acceptance of her own capacity for shamefulness.

Recently, this Augustinian view of marriage has been invoked to argue that the sexual act has an inherently evil aspect which renders it most vulnerable to the abuse of chastity, including conjugal chastity.[36] Appealing to Augustine's argument from shame, it was held that the desire for marital privacy results from the awareness of sexual desire's propensity to become selfish and exploitative and the consequent wish to conceal this disordered element from others.

This argument is faulty on several grounds. First, it begs the question in assuming that Augustine is correct in his assumptions about shame and privacy. Other motives, such as the intimate nature of the experience, its very importance to the couple, are not even considered. What is considered most personal and valued is rarely exposed to indiscriminate public view. Second, it consistently opposes instinct and will in the realm of sexual behaviour without any acknowledgement of the learned values and attitudes, and apparently without any awareness of the cultural construction of sexual meanings.[37] The argument from an inherently flawed sexual instinct has important consequences and will be fully addressed in the final chapter. Third, it accepts the Augustinian evaluation of disordered sexual desire as the ultimate expression of disordered desire. It is a similar mindset to the one that understands rape as a sexual crime and ignores the will to power that dominates the act. All human desires have the potential to be disordered and exploitative.

It has been further suggested that Augustine's limited notion of the 'private' is understandable in the context of Graeco-Roman society, where it meant those personal aspects of life on the margins of public life, which was the arena of communal welfare and personal honour and accomplishment.[38] This does not account though for Augustine's emphasis that privacy for the sexual act is motivated solely by shame, in a culture which had venerated fertility, honoured the fruitful, and made a god of Priapus. Augustine's own father had seen nothing shameful in proclaiming Augustine's sexual maturity to his wife and family. Sexual maturity was an occasion for celebration, not shame.[39] But, for Augustine, the desire for private as opposed to communal good is the sin of pride. Indeed, this was the sin of Eve and of Ecdicia; even Adam's sin though not motivated by pride, but affection, still comes under the rubric of his private good, his relationship with Eve. This privileging of the personal disrupts the social order and therefore the communal good.[40]

Use and enjoyment

Augustine's ordering of all relations distinguishes between those things that can be 'enjoyed for themselves' and those that are to be 'used' (*uti*).

> Since the creature therefore is either equal or inferior to us, we must use the inferior for God, and enjoy the equal, but in God. For just as you ought to enjoy yourself, but not in yourself but in Him who made you, so you ought to enjoy him whom you love as yourself.[41]

He distinguishes between use and enjoyment thus: 'We enjoy things known, in which things themselves the will finds delight for their own sake and so reposes, but we use things, which we refer to some other thing which we are to enjoy.'[42]

Woman, as *femina*, was inferior, and therefore could only be used and not enjoyed. It is impossible to enjoy women, as one can enjoy a friend, because the will can never rest in women for their own sake. Rather women are to be used for procreation. It will be helpful to examine more closely the meaning of the Latin *utor*. Although it could refer to instrumental use as in English, its most usual meaning was 'to serve oneself with'. Its meaning 'to possess', 'to control', or 'to possess the usufructs of', foreshadows and is retained in the language of the traditional marriage service, 'to have and to hold'. It could also mean 'to associate with', and was sometimes employed as a synonym for 'enjoy', although the latter had a more restricted meaning.[43]

In actual popular usage the boundaries may have overlapped. But Augustine clearly intends the two concepts to convey different categories of relationship. He amplifies the meaning of *utor* in *De Trinitate*: what is used, is used at the discretion of the user's will, for a specific purpose, but no pleasure is found in it for its own sake. What is enjoyed is also willed, but it is found joyful in itself.[44] This is the basis of his belief that a man is always preferable for companionship: one can find a pure delight in friends for their own sake.[45] His 'use' of women can be read off *Sapientia*'s 'use' of *Scientia* to achieve temporal goals within the divine will. Woman as *femina* or *mulier* is the sex that in a manner of speaking is turned aside from man for procreative purposes, as Eve was literally taken from Adam's side.[46] As *femina*, woman's function is '*adiutor*': she was made 'for man',[47] as man was made for God. A man cannot desire her for her own sake, for that would be to desire her sexually, with no procreative goal. Augustine's split between the redeemed soul that must be loved and the wifely carnality that must be 'hated' makes this very clear. The will could never be sure it rested in a female companion for her own sake, for even in marriage there can never be absolute surety that procreative desire is never contaminated by sexual desire. As inferiors, women are debarred from non-sexual relationships also; in this Augustine practised what he preached, never having a female as close personal friend. Thus for Augustine the 'use' of women is not so much manipulative exploitation as the proper control of a person over whom one had rights, a person who had been created for the role of assistant and sustainer, and for whom one was responsible. Thus the masculine in its intrapersonal, individual and social manifestations is served by the feminine and the female.[48] The irony of his position is that the order of male–

female relationships as he perceived them could so easily slip into a procreative use of woman totally severed from affection and personal respect.

The objectification of women

Whilst Augustine would have intended otherwise, his encouragement of virginity and celibate marriage in the hope that it would enable a truer spiritual affection to develop held the seeds of a less positive attitude to women. The language of use, the devaluing of non-procreative sexual intercourse, and the instrumental function assigned to both *Scientia* and *Femina* facilitate an objectification of women, especially in cultures where women are already considered to be male possessions. The insistence on feminine inferiority denies the possibility of truly mutual heterosexual relationships, genital or otherwise. A concomitant problem of such an approach to sexuality is that heterosexual relationships lack depth. Moreover, when sexual needs are denied validity they may express themselves in more bizarre attitudes and behaviours, such as prurience, or an obsession with sexual sin to the detriment of conversion in other areas of life.

When man is made the symbol of the spiritual masculine, then man/masculinity is named not only as the normative standard of the human, but as the characteristic of the divine being. Even physically men's bodies were closer to being the image of God,[49] because it is the sexual characteristics of women which are thought to mark their difference from God's image.[50] For men, there was no split between the 'inner man' and the 'outer man' as there was for women. Therefore: 'Man experiences no conflict between soul and body from the point of image, but woman is in a permanent squeeze between soul which is image and body which is not; therefore in Paradise, woman is closer to Satan than man.'[51]

Symbolising the masculine faculty of the mind, men were perceived as more closely conformed to the image of God they represented. Thus they were symbolic of the true purpose of humanity; they were physically stronger,[52] more intelligent,[53] and theoretically less susceptible to moral temptations.[54] What temptations they experienced were displaced from their truest self onto the external or internal feminine. The obverse of this is that when women experienced temptation, they were being socialised to interpret it as the normal expression of the female and feminine nature. For *femina* – read sexual being – is the door to the devil. What virtue woman achieved, was displaced onto the external or internal masculine. The association of women with disorder and evil reinforced the cultural impetus for placing women in circumscribed spheres such as the home and the cloister for the purpose of introducing order into the sexual lives of men.[55] The superiority of the masculine is the basis of male headship which intervenes between God and woman. According to Augustine, whatever is separated from God cannot be totally in God's image, 'for the image is only then an expression of God in the full sense, when no other nature lies between it and God'.[56]

For Augustine, the relationship between man and woman is very much of the order of that between masculine and feminine: 'It is not difficult to decide which is to be preferred, or placed after which.'[57] The result is that the masculine is always at one remove from sin, as woman is always at one remove from God. It must be noted at this point that although Augustine's symbolic gender has strong roots in the tradition, he himself was aware that others believed the *imago* to rest in the union of masculine and feminine within the soul. This alternative view shared his belief that the masculine was the planner and the feminine the part that obeyed, yet he rejected it out of hand.[58]

The woman ascetic – an exception?

The ascetic woman, of course, was almost exempt from these strictures because she left the feminine role behind her and was engaged in the masculine pursuit of the contemplation of God.[59] Her virginity was not an affirmation of her being as a woman, but an assumption of the nature of the male which is identified with the truly human: rationality, strength and courage, steadfastness and loyalty.[60] Thus she fulfils the same role for Christianity as she did for Philo – she was the symbol of the soul which transcended its feminine component and symbolised the virile soul before God.

Contemporary studies are unanimous that asceticism was a liberating experience for women, although it could become ambiguous.[61] It must always be kept in mind that the manner in which symbols functioned for each gender was not necessarily the same.[62] The tensions attached to Thecla as a model, the case of Ecdicia, the heroines of the Apocryphal *Acts*, and the erotic hagiography which revelled in the violence done to women's bodies all indicate that different agenda were at stake for men and women.[63] A recurring theme in the Apocryphal *Acts* and later patristic literature, as in Augustine, is the obedience and subordination of women and the emphasis on male headship. As the earlier exploration of the religious and cultural trajectories of Augustine's context have shown, attempts were being made to erode the freedom of ascetic women in the late fourth century.

Marital teachings

One cannot conclude a discussion on Augustine and marriage without considering the significance of Jovinian for his marital teachings. Recent scholarship has indicated that ascetic spirituality did not sweep through Christendom opposed only by a few heretical sects, as the Catholic tradition once held.[64] As early as the second century Clement of Alexandria had condemned encratism,[65] and in late antiquity there were grave concerns that ascetic bishops were introducing Manichaean beliefs into Christian orthodoxy. Helvidius, Ambrosiaster and Jovinian all defended marriage in Rome, responding to what they perceived as a threat to orthodoxy. Jovinian had a particularly high profile and was regarded as the instigator of the dangerous doctrine that marriage had equal status with virginity. Although Jovinian was an ascetic himself, he was held responsible for many ascetics who renounced celibacy for marriage.

The clerical church's response was swift.[66] He was denounced by the Roman synod, the Milanese synod, Jerome and Augustine, and condemned as a heretic.[67] The bishops would not countenance his anti-ascetical views, his teaching that Mary was virgin before birth (*ante partum*) but not during birth (*in partu*), or his belief that the baptised were incapable of serious sin.[68] By presenting marriage as equivalent to virginity, Jovinian was denying the hierarchical order of the sacred, and enhancing the status of married women. However, Jerome's response to Jovinian was so caustic, and so demeaning to women, that his own friends took it out of circulation in Rome, and Augustine was moved to write *On the good of marriage*. The response to Jerome's defence of asceticism clearly indicated to Ambrose and Augustine that his rhetorical strategies were inappropriate, and so they moved to the argument that whilst marriage was good, virginity was better. This preserved both the acceptability of marriage and the status of the continent, for if marriage had not been a natural good, then to reject it would not increase the honour due to the ascetic.

Hill's statement that Augustine's theology does not imply that women are either subordinate or inferior is not supported by the evidence, which confirms Ruether's conclusion that Augustine teaches that femaleness as such cannot be the image of God. Woman and feminine are perceived as inferior, subordinate and instrumental.[69] In order that humankind be kept centred on God and sin be controlled, woman and feminine must be ruled by those who know themselves to be superior, man and the masculine.[70] Børresen concluded:

> Certainly, woman possesses the image of God in her rational soul, and so she is *homo*. But in so far as she is *femina*, differen-

tiated from man on the bodily level, she does not reflect this image. On the contrary, man, in so far as he is *vir*, represents the superior element of the soul where the image resides. By such exegesis does Augustine succeed in explaining Paul's statement that man alone is the image of God, whilst equally allowing this quality for the woman.[71]

This is a more nuanced understanding of Augustine's teaching on woman and the feminine as *imago Dei*. The concept of *ordo* within the context of ancient interpretations of sexual difference limited his ability to develop an anthropology in which women were perceived as the peers of men. Nor is the body–mind dualism that informs Augustine helpful any longer. It has been damaging for both sexes to understand their sexual desire as the *poena reciproca* of original sin, and for women especially to have lived within a construct which understood their bodies as the contradiction of the image of God.

PART V
Mary

MARY IN THE THOUGHT OF AUGUSTINE

IN the previous chapters the impact of Augustine's culture, life experience and his doctrinal exposition have delineated three specific stereotypes of women. First, there is the post-sexual, formidable *matrona*, virile in her status and honour. These women are characterised by fidelity, faith and humble obedience, and exemplified by Monica and Augustine's concubine after her dismissal. Second, there is the proud autonomous woman, a demonic instrument in her potential wilfully to disrupt familial and social order through her pride. She was exemplified in Eve and Ecdicia, who both caused their husbands to sin. Third, there is the sexual woman, the locus of desire and danger, yet essential for procreation; she too is potentially demonic and in need of restraint. The evil of uncontrolled libido, which she symbolises, can be restrained within marriage for the good of the individual and the state in the procreation of children. Her positive ideal is exemplified by the modest wife and mother, and her sinful *alter ego* by the shameless woman. The tensions between the two extremes are well exemplified in his representation of his concubine – two in one flesh yet sexual and sinful, and in *Scientia*, partner and helpmeet of *Sapientia*, yet the avenue of access to carnality, worldliness and sin.

However, no real woman could be used as an exemplar of any one 'type', thereby creating a problem for Augustine. Monica had loitered around Babylon in her youth, his concubine had embraced both passion and continence, and the socially unruly Ecdicia was a personal model of continence and self-denial. What was needed was a feminine 'meta-symbol', a model woman who could exemplify the ideal *Scientia*.

So within the tensions of a church where women's spirituality was perceived to be developing forms outside cultic ritual and institutional control, where bishops and clergy found themselves not only patrons of women but their clients also, and where networks of male authority acted to eliminate alternative models of Christian spirituality and to restrain the subversive power of women, there emerged one amongst women deserving of the highest praise: Mary, mother of the Christ.[1] Marian doctrine created a vision of a woman with complete integrity of being, who could serve as a basis for clear categories of good and bad women, and who would erase any competing symbolism.

This was not such a radical step as it may appear. Judaism had opposed Wisdom and Pleasure in feminine guise and Roman culture had symbolised Virtue and Vice as feminine. Christianity personalised them in Eve, the spiritual whore, and Mary, the spiritual virgin, thus bridging symbolic and historical categories.[2] A study of Augustine's Marian writings will offer some insights into the nature of the ideal woman, and the symbolic meaning that she held for Augustine. The behaviour of the properly Christian woman of the late fourth and early fifth century as Augustine saw it can be read off her icon.

The era of Augustine saw the foundation of Mary as icon in episcopal thought. Prior to the fourth century, the status and nature of Mary had been an open question, a sure sign that the theological and cultural circumstances which led to her enthronement had not yet arisen. She was portrayed by the Antiochene school as an ordinary woman, typically weak and needing reproval;[3] for others she was the 'Holy virgin', whose purity was paralleled by her moral integrity.[4] Most Fathers taught the perpetual virginity of Mary, but some, such as Tertullian, denied her virginity during childbirth (*in partu*) and (*post partum*) after childbirth in order to provide the true humanity of Christ.[5]

The received wisdom has always held that Marian theology was totally dependent upon christological issues; that although Augustine deliberately used Mary as a model for others, he never set out to develop a Marian theology independent of other doctrinal issues.[6] However, the dating of the majority of the Marian texts reveals that, while references to Mary appear regularly from 393 onwards, and are found consistently in the homiletic material, references to Mary in his treatises cluster in two sets of writings on the question of sex and gender within the order of creation – against Jovinianism (*c*. 401) and against the Pelagians, specifically, against Julian of Eclanum (*c*. 420–1).[7] The context of these Marian writings and other evidence arising from feminist scholarship's search for texts illuminating the lives of women, hint that other issues might have been at stake, issues that involved Mary in her own right as a significant and important Christian exemplar.

Certainly, from the second century on, a consistent patristic witness is to Mary as the new Eve: her role is an aspect of the doctrine of recapitulation first articulated most clearly in the teachings of Irenaeus, though he was influenced by Justin Martyr. The concept of recapitulation holds that the failure, fall and sin of Adam and Eve are paralleled in the saving incarnation, death and resurrection of Jesus. Recapitulation develops the Pauline opposition between the old and new Adam to include an Eve–Mary dualism, envisioning Mary as the true 'mother of the living' (Genesis 3.20). This is therefore one of the earliest affirmations of Mary's universal motherhood.[8] Although the doctrine of recapitulation is a christological one, the Pauline model saw no reason to include Mary as the new Eve, which indicates that the later theologians felt the need for a female role model to parallel that of the Christ. Previously the church as bride had filled the role now granted to Mary.

The appearance in late antiquity of apocryphal Gospels about the infancy of Mary, which present Mary's birth as divinely ordained and accomplished after the model of Hannah and Samuel, further attest to a growing interest in Mary and her life for their own sake. This literature has an ascetic cast, and there is a great deal of emphasis on Mary's seclusion from social contamination from her birth, her dedication to a religious life from the age of three, and her asexual marriage to Joseph. The description in these texts of ritual ordeals by which the innocence of Mary and Joseph are proven suggests the need to counter scepticism about the emerging belief in the perpetual virginity of Mary.[9]

Moreover, the all-women liturgies which so scandalised Epiphanius in the fourth century were either within the context of a Marian cult, or justified women's liturgical role from Mary's example. Empress Helena, a leading light in the establishment of the martyr cult, built a shrine to Mary in 325, which also suggests a cultic role for Mary years before the birth of her great clerical advocates, Ambrose, Jerome and Augustine. Possibly, like Thecla, Mary was already an exemplary figure within certain strands of women's ascetic spirituality, but outside episcopal networks and control.

A further factor was the exegetical shift from Christ's birth from a virgin in the Synoptic Gospels, to a virginal birth in patristic exegesis. That is, Jesus was conceived without sexual intercourse and born without rupturing his mother's hymen. The virgin birth was apt for melding with the Philonic image of the virgin as the symbol of the virtuous soul before God.[10] As ascetic thought came to dominate Christian spiritual categories, a virginal God-bearer would provide the ideal symbol for its value system. And as suggested, the polemical debates with Jovinian and Julian of Eclanum (and Helvidius before them), have Christian anthropology, and specifically the nature of human sexuality, at their heart. One of the prime issues contested in the Jovinian debate was whether celibate lifestyles were spiritually superior to married life. The *post-*

partum sexual status of the mother of God was one of the crucial questions at stake. Mary as the archetypal celibate was an influential figure to deploy against the opposition, as battles over Mary's *in-partu* virginity, and *post-partum* continence acknowledge. Similarly, in the debates with Julian, the goodness of human sexuality, and again its status *vis-à-vis* continence, was still at issue.

As other scholars have noted, what is at stake is models of church: a one-tier inclusive model, or a hierarchical model within which different lifestyles earn different eternal rewards.[11] The institutional church, both virgin and mother in the theological tradition, needed a vibrant feminine symbol that tied the winning model to history. Mary, in both cult and doctrine, was to hand. If Mary were perpetual virgin as the ascetics held, then the church, the corporate virgin bride of Christ, exemplifies celibacy and continence as the highest Christian ideal. If Mary had other children, as Helvidius and Jovinian argued, then both virginal and maternal expressions of sexuality are equally appropriate for Christians.[12]

Thus the conflict over ascetic spirituality and its perceived rejection of social roles and of the sexual body, which would have engaged women particularly, was one arena where a specifically female model of the believer was of cardinal importance.[13] This is not to dispute that the christological debates, which highlighted the significance of Mary in determining the status of Jesus, would have interacted with the move towards asceticism and the needs to define the internal structures of the post-Constantinian church and to clarify the role of women. Other modern commentators have postulated both the need for a feminine ideal sanctioned by ecclesiastical authority, and the decline of pneumatology as factors in the development of Mariology.[14]

Augustine would have been exposed to all these pressures, and was clearly familiar with those groups that denied Mary's perpetual virginity. Given his love for the ascetic life, and his theological debt to Ambrose and, to a lesser extent, Tertullian and Cyprian, it is not surprising that he found in Mary the ideal woman to symbolise *Scientia* and to be exemplar to his flock.[15] However, the imagery and rhetoric surrounding Mary changes dramatically. From Ambrose's lush eroticism from the Song of Songs, Augustine moves to a more sedate symbolism of the heart, although, as will become clear, the heart itself is a mask for the original sexual images.[16]

Against this background, and within ecclesial debates over asceticism, sexuality and the Incarnation of Christ, Augustine will develop his Mariology, which elevates Mary well beyond the 'ordinary', and creates the potential for doctrines such as the Immaculate Conception and the Assumption.

Mary as virgin and mother

For Augustine, it is of paramount importance that Mary is a perpetual virgin and a mother. He will persistently reiterate the formula: 'a virgin conceived, a virgin bore, and after the birth was
virgin still'.[17] So significant is this doctrine to him, and so confident
is he of its acceptance, that he made virgin birth part of the rule of
faith, and therefore essential orthodox doctrine.[18] The true human
motherhood of Mary was essential to the Nicaean doctrine of the
Incarnation. If Christ was not truly born of woman, then he has
not, in truth, freed those who believe in him, because his passion
was not real either.[19] Also, this temporal plan ennobled both sexes
because God was born of a woman and he took a male nature,
which it was certainly incumbent upon him to do. Thus God
showed concern for the sex he 'represented' and the sex from which
he took human nature upon himself.[20]

This stance has two serious and related logical consequences.
The temporal aspect of Mary's role means that she is the mother
of his human person, but not of his divine nature. The latter comes
from the eternal Father and is united to his human nature in the
womb; thus God is the Father of the divine nature, and Mary is
the mother of his humanity: 'He was in extraordinary manner
begotten of the Father without a mother, born of a mother without
a Father; without a mother he was God, without a Father he was
man; without a mother before all time, without a father in the end
of times.'[21]

Although Augustine's primary concern here is to keep distinct
the two natures of Christ, his use of 'motherlessness' is heir to
Philo's understanding of motherlessness as a sign of purity.[22] The
Word has no need of a mother at all. Only the human Jesus needs
a mother. Hence Jesus was both Lord and son of Mary – her son
after the flesh, and her Lord after his majesty.[23] This distinction is
used to explain the manner of Jesus' words to Mary at the marriage
feast of Cana. There, where he functions in his divine role, he
denies her the title, mother, to emphasise that she did not give
birth to his divine nature; but at Calvary he recognised her as his
mother because there the weak flesh of his human nature, derived
from her, was dying.[24] Hence Augustine is wary of the title Mother
of God, as implying the divinisation of Mary, and as a parallel to
the pagan titles for the goddess.

Even as the ideal woman, she does not symbolise the *imago Dei*,
Sapientia, in any way in her motherhood. Like *Scientia*, Mary's role
is only significant within time as she assists God in bringing
Wisdom to birth, but there is nothing of her in Wisdom personified.
Rather, she is the source of Jesus' mortality. Mary provided only

the vessel within which the Spirit formed his flesh and the matter from which it was formed, matter which conveyed the seeds of Jesus' death.

The second consequence is that Jesus, as the Word made flesh, 'represents' specifically the male sex, rather than human nature. His argument shows that from Augustine's point of view, Mary's role is linked to Christology because Christ does not represent women. However, she is not simply a peripheral aspect of the discussion to prove Christ's divinity. Rather she is essential to rationalise a place for women within the economy of salvation.[25] To argue that women were not represented by the Saviour should raise serious questions about women's redemption for Augustine, since from the time of Irenaeus, the tradition held that what is not caught up in Christ is not redeemed. Augustine never addresses the question directly, though his mariology indicates that he intuited a problem. His solution would probably lie in his distinction between woman as *femina* and woman as *homo*. Woman as *homo*, through her masculinised image of God, is caught up in Christ. As *femina*, she is not. Like all women, Mary is both. But it is as the ideal *femina-scientia* that she represents women: Christ is the representative of *Sapientia* as man, and its source as seminal Word.

Once again, sharp boundaries are drawn between woman and the sacred to make it quite clear that the feminine contributed nothing to the divine nature, and manifests nothing of it. Men are eternally ennobled in that they are represented by divine Wisdom incarnate, whom they symbolise on earth. Women are temporally ennobled through Mary's motherhood, but they are not represented by the human Jesus, so clearly they could not represent him within the ecclesia.

But Mary's human motherhood of itself was not enough. Her virginity was of overwhelming importance. Even before Augustine accepted the divinity of the Word he had accepted the virgin birth. He had understood it as the basis of Jesus' special authority as the teacher of Christians because it revealed the divine care that despised worldly goods in order to win immortal life for human-kind.[26] After accepting the Incarnation, Augustine would move away from its scandalous humility to proofs of divine honour. Around the turn of the fifth century, his arguments were not derived from Scripture but proceeded from premises about what is due to divine rank. Therefore it both befitted a God to be born of a virgin,[27] and the birth from a virgin attested to the nobility of the child.[28] He also developed a metaphorical interpretation of the virgin birth at this time: it signified that the spiritual members of Christ should be born spiritually of the virginal church.[29] So, up until the beginning of the fifth century, the virgin birth signified the elevation of

the spiritual over the material world, and developed to become the
foreshadowing of the rebirth of Christians from the virgin church.
Mary is to Augustine a symbol of the church as bride from his
earliest Christian years, the legacy of his education by Ambrose.

From 414 Augustine adduced a further justification which was of
immense significance. The Word became true flesh, but was never
sinful because the virgin birth was untainted by concupiscence.[30]
Augustine based this on the Pauline text that Jesus came in the
'likeness' of sinful flesh. All readings that took this text to indicate
that Jesus was not truly human were ruled out as heretical. So it
had to have another meaning, which was that the likeness Jesus
shared was human mortality, the result of sinfulness, but was not,
himself, sinful. Thus the use of 'likeness'.[31] Logically, this argument
does not demand a virgin birth, simply the human sinlessness of
Jesus. But Augustine's assumptions about the role of concupiscence
in conception made a normal birth corrupted with its taint totally
unacceptable. In a sense, the distancing of Jesus' birth from human
copulation, which attested to Jesus' obedience to divine values in
Augustine's earlier writings, is transmuted into an essential aspect
of the Incarnation, for sexual intercourse has become the means
for the transmission of original sin, and sexual desire has become
the *poena reciproca* for that sin. So all aspects of the sexual except
being born of woman must be distanced from the humanity of
Christ in every particular. Jesus must have had a virginal birth to
be free of original sin.[32] He could never feel sexual desire for this
could never be fully pure. Augustine's argument further reinforces
the connections between virginity and the eternal, and marriage
and the temporal, which are made explicit in other passages on
virginity.[33]

His arguments are connected to scriptural precedents by the
most tenuous of ties. He muted the Pauline emphasis on the self-
emptying of God in favour of the dignity of God.[34] A virgin birth
was essential for the sake of divine honour. Christ is therefore
miraculously born. His miraculous conception distances him from
the taints of sexual desire; Mary's virginity even during the birth
distances God from the bloody pollution of human birth; and her
perpetual continence is the only fitting behaviour for a woman
whose womb has held God. Sexual desire has become that antithesis
of the holy which is portrayed as virginal innocence and integrity.
Augustine's insistence on the virgin birth as part of the rule of faith
owes more to classical values than to scriptural ones. His symbolic
web which embraces Mary, the Incarnation and the church under
the rubric of Virgin is undergirt by his increasingly articulate explication of the theology of original sin.

This raised the question of the extent to which Mary was totally

free of its pollution. As there were absolutely no grounds for arguing Mary's virginal birth, Augustine taught that Mary herself was
not free from original sin but she was so graced from birth that
she was sinless and merited singular honour.[35] Although some commentators have seen the seeds of the doctrine of the Immaculate
Conception in this stance, it is clear that Augustine's belief in the
universality of original sin transmitted by concupiscence will not
permit an understanding of an Immaculate Conception in his own
mariology.[36] The corruption of the seed that begot Mary is what
introduced death into the flesh formed from her.

To understand why Augustine could not perceive the transition
from virgin to matron as a rite of passage from potential to fruitfulness, but saw the physical alteration as a loss of integrity, it is
necessary to understand something of what integrity meant in the
ancient world. It signified unity, not plurality, purity of essence
rather than admixture,[37] beauty, goodness and autonomy – self-
containment and self-sufficiency of the highest order.[38] Just as God
is one who can never need, so the fully mature man is one who
never needed anyone or anything outside himself. He might be
part of a tight social structure but, in Christian terms, his only need
was God.[39] In the *De virginitate* Augustine wrote that, once perished, the integrity of virginity is irrecoverable, although five years
earlier he had written that through continence 'we are made as one
and regain that unity of self which we lost by falling apart in the
search for a variety of pleasures'.[40] In the *De Trinitate*, it is the Word
himself, the One incarnate, who gathers together both the individual soul, and the individual members of the body, into the unity
of one body under one head, inflamed by one Spirit, charity.[41]

Though this spiritual paradigm need not in theory have moral
concomitants, it does in practice. Augustine always spoke about
the conception of Jesus within the context of Mary's and Joseph's
marriage. Yet the fruitfulness of marriage is only a limited and
temporal good. Irrevocably tainted by concupiscence, every child
born of the union of the flesh is touched by evil and under the
dominion of Satan.[42] Even chaste Christian wives were perceived
as marred by the nuptial embrace, and this is one of the tenets
underlying the theological necessity of the virgin birth. 'Christ
would never have granted to his mother the blessing in which wives
delight in such a way as to deprive her of the better gift for which
virgins forgo motherhood.'[43]

Particularly potent is the language of *De bono viduitatis*: 'He
knoweth how to make fruitful without marring of chastity, a wife,
a virgin, whom even in the flesh itself his mother could without
violation of chastity conceive (*sine corruptione*).'[44] In this latter text,
the loss of integrity is nuanced by overtones of violence, which

appear elsewhere in Augustine's writings.[45] The rhetoric of corruption was not a new development in Christian discourse. *Corrumpo* was used by Roman orators as a euphemism for sexual intercourse, usually with virgin or wife as object of the verb. Its violent implication was weakened by the male belief that women really enjoyed sexual violence, and so 'violation' came to be perceived as just somewhat of an exaggeration for normal sexual relations. Nevertheless, it was this nuance that gave it its appeal for Christian moralisers in late antiquity.[46] Therefore, whilst the language of violation may not have been heard by a Roman audience with the same effect as it would have on a modern reader, it does contain a pejorative meaning in the Christian context.

Unlike Ambrose, Augustine does not attempt to answer the physiological problems raised by the virgin birth, and indeed, becomes somewhat irascible when asked to do so.[47] Ambrose stated clearly that the Word himself opened his mother's womb, fertilising it with the immaculate seminal Word/seed (σπέρματικος Λόγος), which Ambrose translates into Latin as the *immaculatum semen*.[48] Augustine shied away from such language and such imagery. To him the virgin birth was a miracle explicable only by faith.[49] Mary conceived through the power of the Holy Spirit,[50] and her own faith.[51] Faithfulness of heart was Mary's most significant and valued attribute, for it enabled her to conceive through hearing the Word.[52] However, he did attempt to explain Mary's virginity during childbirth (*in partu*) by using the analogy of Jesus' post-Resurrection appearances through closed doors. He apparently had no difficulty attributing to the infant Jesus the qualities of the glorified body of Christ.[53]

Mary is faith personified: her faith is even more powerful than her blood kinship to her son, and it is the foundation of her status as the ideal Christian.[54]

> Therefore, Mary is more blessed in receiving the faith of Christ than in conceiving the flesh of Christ, [for] . . . her nearness as a mother would have been no profit to Mary had she not borne Christ in her heart after a more blessed manner than in her flesh.[55]

As faith and continence are the primary temporal virtues of properly regulated *Scientia*, Mary is therefore the exemplar of *Scientia* as she should be in every individual soul. Her virginal body symbolises her integrity of heart.[56] As Mary believed ardently, what she believed was accomplished with her.[57] Through faith, the virginal womb became the bridal chamber of God and humanity. The eternal Word was united to human nature, as husband to wife, and emerges as the bridegroom, the spouse of the church.[58] The birth leaves the mother's body as inviolate as the conception.[59]

Nuptial imagery

This nuptial symbolism is reserved for the Incarnation; the marriage of Christ and his church is a spiritual one, and best expressed for Augustine through images of continence and spiritual fruitfulness. Yet the virginal integrity of heart which is implicitly opposed to the multiplicity of worldly desires, functions as a masked symbol for the virginal hymen. In *De continentia*, Augustine developed a chain of reasoning whereby continence of the loins is discursively tied to continence of the mouth and lips; this in turn becomes the continence of the 'mouth' of the heart, which is to be understood in the psalmist's plea to God to 'set a watch to my mouth, and a door of continence around my lips' (Ps. 141.3). In antiquity, oral symbols were often used for genitalia, and Augustine sees the meaning of continence as most chiefly and properly the bridling of the 'parts that beget'.[60] Ambrose had had no such hesitation in instructing the virgin explicitly to keep the door to the genitals barred,[61] but Augustine shifts from a sexual discourse to the language of the heart. The heart is the source of the will to continence. It is the mouth of the inner being from which issues good or evil. The latter part of the treatise is specifically concerned with the battle of desires within the heart between those of the spirit and those of the flesh. In turn, this leads him to the proper union or order of flesh and spirit which is manifested spiritually in Christ and the church, and materially in husband and wife. The ideal union is virginal and spiritual; in the human realm where flesh must be considered and appropriately cared for, husband and wife stand as a paradigm of the spirit and flesh. Within that paradigm, it is the role of continence to restrain and heal all delights of lust which are opposed to the delights of Wisdom.[62]

Death imagery

A darker symbol attached to Mary is the assimilation of her womb to a tomb.[63] Her womb represents the 'new tomb' in which Jesus will be laid. This underlines the destiny of the bridegroom, and the mortality that is his legacy from his mother. Even Mary's virginity cannot save her son from the destiny of the sinful flesh of which he bears the likeness.

Earth imagery

The most consistent image of Mary is of 'earth giving birth to truth' (Ps. 84.12). In the Incarnation, human and divine truth are united in the One who is the living Truth, thus bridging the chasm between heaven and earth.[64] As the earth of paradise was watered by a spring, so Mary is watered by the holy Spirit and truth is spoken from the earth, by the enfleshed Word of God.[65] Elsewhere Augustine interprets the rain on the earth as the mercy of God engendering spiritual fruit; it is probable that this mercy can be construed as the spring of grace empowering Mary's virtue, which then merits the virginal birth.[66] Unlike her son, she is not sinless by virtue of her birth, but by virtue of the grace and mercy of the Father.[67] This grace has prepared her for her privileged position, not simply as Jesus' mother in the flesh, but as his sister and mother in the spirit.[68] Hence she is humble, obedient, and loving as well as faithful and chaste.[69] But notwithstanding this graced virtue, the images of earth, marriage and death, and her virtues of faith and continence define Mary as a temporal symbol. The rain–earth imagery also had a sexual import in a culture which still retained the memory and practice of the older gods. Although transposed into a Christian key, the imagery is that of the sky father fertilising the earth mother, not to mention the fertilisation of Danaë by a shower of gold. This imagery is also found consistently in Ambrose as well, and indicates that old mythologies die hard, if they really die at all.[70]

The innovative vow

It has been considered that one aspect of Augustine's mariology that was truly innovative was his interpretation of Mary's words, 'I know not man', to indicate that she took a vow of virginity long before the Annunciation.[71] He was well aware that this was not Jewish practice, which explains why Mary was betrothed to Joseph, despite her vow. Mary needed a husband and Joseph was prepared to marry Mary to protect her.[72] The vow was consequential to Augustine for several reasons. It revealed Mary's great humility and faith,[73] and that she chose virginity freely, rather than accepting it by command, or as a necessary aspect of being the mother of the Messiah. Therefore Mary's virginity was all the more acceptable and pleasing to God 'in that it was not that Christ being conceived in her, rescued it beforehand from a husband who would violate it, himself to preserve it; but before he was conceived, chose it, already dedicated to God, as that from which to be born'.[74]

As the gospel of pseudo-Matthew (attributed to the first four centuries) states that Mary rejected marriage freely to choose virginity, it cannot be certain that Augustine was totally original in this, but, as Hilda Graef has pointed out, it is significant that Mary's vow did not enter Christian writing until a formal vow of virginity had become an established custom in the church.[75] That he found it necessary to assert Mary's virginity as perpetually vowed indicates how far Augustine would prefer to distance sexuality from the sacred.

References to Jesus' brothers in the Scriptures, which Helvidius and Jovinian took to indicate that Mary had other children, are dealt with by taking brother and sister to mean cousin.[76] In this he is probably taking his cue from Jerome.[77] It would seem that one argument against Mary's perpetual virginity was the use of the word woman (*mulier*), rather than virgin, to describe her. The use of *mulier* indicated a wife in every sense to the opponents of asceticism. To counter this objection, Jerome had argued that *mulier* was used of a betrothed woman. Ambrose and Augustine defended Mary's continence on similar grounds, but do not directly follow Jerome.[78] *Mulier*, they argue, is a synonym for *femina* and is used thus of Eve when she was first formed, and so was still a virgin. Therefore it cannot be used to argue for a normal married life between Joseph and Mary.[79]

Mary as the new Eve[80]

In Augustine's later writings, original sin, like the virgin birth, became one of the foundations of the Christian faith.[81] Steeped in a culture where even pagans saw human life as a punishment for sin committed in a higher life, Augustine struggled to develop a sound way to account for human suffering. The Gnostics blamed the demiurge, the creator God of the Hebrew scriptures, for the sufferings of infants, a heretical explanation that damned the goodness of created matter altogether. Augustine found Cicero's explanation that nature was to blame no more helpful, though he would appropriate the image of nature as a stepmother, because her children suffer. Augustine could not explain evil without recourse to the doctrine of original sin unless he called into question the justice or the omnipotence of God.[82] He understood the Scripture to indicate that those who died unbaptised, even infants, would go to hell.[83] Furthermore, even new-born infants suffer terribly sometimes. That would be dreadfully unjust if they had done nothing to deserve it. A just God would never let anyone suffer who did not deserve it, unless God was powerless to stop suffering. Both tenets were anathema to Augustine. Therefore, if anyone suffers, they must deserve it, and if tiny babies suffer, then they must be born carrying a sin requiring punishment. Original sin had created an unbridgeable abyss between humankind and God. Only baptism into new life could bridge the chasm, although the body would bear the intimate sign of its punishment for life.[84]

Prior to this rebellion all creation had been good. Sexuality and gender existed in paradise, and Augustine, pushed by Julian, could even permit the possibility of the presence of desire under the control of the will, although he preferred to think that desire would have been totally absent.[85] Human beings embraced in peace of soul and integrity of body, and Eve remained *virgo intacta*, receiving Adam's seed in the same way that a virgin menstruates.[86] In a bizarre manner, Augustine virtually separated desire from pleasure. If there is no lustful desire, only the desire for children, then a certain 'grave pleasure' accompanying intercourse is permissible. Augustine argued this strongly against Julian, who asserted that sexual desire was from God, because without desire there would be no intercourse.[87] For Augustine any pleasure should lie in the desire for children, not sexual yearning.[88]

This scenario indicates the extreme importance of bodily integrity for Augustine. Even when sexual intercourse is idyllic and totally as intended by God, intercourse will not rupture the hymen. The body would remain in its virginal state.[89] Augustine's concessions to Julian's arguments place him light years from Ambrose and Jerome, who firmly believed that there had been no sexual desire or intercourse in paradise. As far as they were concerned, sexual desire and relations were the result of the Fall, and as Brown has noted, for radical ascetics, even marriage re-enacted the Fall in miniature.[90]

Thus the first Eve was created good, but she fell victim to pride and listened to the serpent.[91] In Augustine's earlier treatises the tempter deceived her, and she led her husband into sin. Augustine was very careful to say that Adam was neither deceived nor seduced, but influenced by his attachment to Eve to join her in rebellion, offending God to keep her friendship, and to protect her in exile.[92] Symbolically, Eve represents the carnal appetite of the body, deceived by the senses (the serpent), which lures reason (Adam) into consenting to evil.[93] Augustine believed that, in sinning, Adam and Eve made indecent what God by creation made seemly.[94] They had to cover their nakedness in case they were shamed by the pleasure aroused by it,[95] a pleasure made all too visible by the spontaneous erection of the penis.[96] (Augustine did acknowledge that the female response differed from the male's, but argued it was the same internally.[97]) Henceforth, every child would be born to death, the penalty of the primal sin.[98] The Fall had altered human nature to a 'wild' state, as seeds from a cultivated olive tree can revert to 'wild olives'.[99]

Interestingly, although in Augustine's paradigm, Adam as senior partner had to consent to sin, in Augustine's writing on the Fall, Eve carries the brunt of the responsibility. It is this responsibility which requires a new Eve to recapitulate her role.[100] 'Since through the female sex man fell, through the female sex man was reinstated, for Christ was born of a virgin.'[101]

This does not imply that Eve was not virginal at the time of the Fall. Nor does Augustine say that the serpent had intercourse with Eve; rather, he seduced her mind, but Augustine uses the metaphors of sexual intercourse and conception. She had faith in the evil one, and conceived (*concepit*) in her heart the venom of the serpent,[102] because her virginity of heart had been destroyed.[103] From incontinence of heart proceeded incontinence of the body.[104] Hereafter,

> evilly did Eve give birth, thereby leaving to women the inheritance of childbirth, and the result that everyone formed in the pleasure of concupiscence and conceived in it in the womb and fashioned in it in blood, in it wrapped as in swaddling clothes, first undergoes the contagion of sin before he drinks the gift of the life-giving air . . . to weep at birth for the guilt he contracted before his birth.[105]

The remedy for a corrupt soul can only come through a virginal body.[106] Physical virginity here is of unmistakably symbolic importance. It stands as the antithesis of corruption and death. Note that it was not Mary's virginity of heart that was opposed to Eve's corrupted soul, but her virginal body. It as if the damage must be undone in reverse. As an incontinent heart led to an incontinent body, a continent body leads to a continent heart, despite his affirmation cited earlier that her faith took precedence over her physical motherhood. Birth from a virgin repairs the damage done by birth from Eve.

> The first birth holds man in that bondage from which nothing but the second birth delivers him. The devil holds him, Christ liberates him; Eve's deceiver holds him, Mary's son frees him: he holds him who approached man through woman; he frees him who was born of woman that never approached man. He holds him who injected into the woman the cause of lust; he liberates him, who without any lust was conceived in the woman.[107]

Again he uses sexual metaphors for Eve's sin. The serpent injects venom, venom that leads by way of Adam's seduction into sin, to a demonic seed which will be transmitted to their children in perpetuity. Eve's sin of pride is repaired by Mary's freedom from sexual desire, an almost seamless shift from pride to concupiscence which unites them in the autonomous woman and sexualises the Fall, through the movement from pride to venom to lust. Following 1 Timothy 2.14–15, patristic exegesis consistently used the language of seduction or deception virtually interchangeably, to describe Satan's successful temptation of Eve,[108] with the result that even in writers like Augustine who consciously reject a sexual interpretation of the Fall, it appears in their metaphors and their discourse of desire.[109] All women, even Christian women, are daughters of Eve, and can only give birth to children in bondage to Satan.[110] Augustine had argued as early as 400 CE that only through being 'dyed in his sacraments' will children be born of Christ, and that 'mothers run to have their children baptised, 'for they know what they have given birth to'.[111] A practice, incidentally, which is precisely what Monica failed to do in his own case.

In opposition to Augustine, Julian argued that as God commanded Adam and Eve to multiply before the Fall, then their children were born innocent because born by God's command, though their parents might be guilty of lust.[112] Julian also believed sexual intercourse was not sinful because it was an aspect of our created nature.[113] It is striking that Augustine replied to many of Julian's challenges with an appeal to the authority of Ambrose, whose orthodoxy was impeccable, and who, Augustine argued, supported completely the doctrine of original sin. But his actual responses to Julian bear investigation. He seemed to agree with Julian that desire aroused by the desire for children is a godly will, and not reprehensible. But if aroused by the turbulence or agitations of lust, where the control of the will is ineffectual, this is a wound of nature inflicted by the devil through the original sin. He therefore concludes with the ambiguous statement that 'therefore I had a good reason for saying that "the semination of children in the body of that life would not have been without the disease without which semination cannot exist in the body of this death" '.[114]

This is a convoluted and opaque sentence in any language. A short digression into ancient biology may shed some light on his meaning. Although the analogy of the procreative seed was widely used, it was a biological shorthand for spiritual essence. In ancient medical paradigms, the seed was simply the vehicle for the spiritual principle, the vital heat, which like a spark of the seminal word instilled life, ordering and forming the blood in the mother's uterus as a potter forms clay or a carpenter a building. In some schools of thought, this vital heat was even thought to convey the soul (Traducianism).

The semen which carries this vital heat has different origins in different models, but in all of them, at some stage, the blood was involved. Sexual desire was necessary to form semen from the blood or body tissue. Augustine was not a Traducianist, but his belief in a vitiated seed is easier to understand when it is recognised that if the primal couple's sin created a quantum shift which rendered them mortal, then some part of their vital essence must have been altered and corrupted. And this is exactly what he argued against

Julian.[115] If semen is created from the blood or brain matter of corrupted male flesh, then the spirit carried within the semen cannot escape its taint.[116] Both he and Julian agreed that pleasure was a necessary aspect of conception, but what Julian called 'reproductive heat', Augustine called lust.[117]

Julian was not a libertine. He and Augustine agreed that sexual desire could become excessive and therefore sinful. Julian believed that the excesses of sexual desire were like those of the other appetites, and were controllable by the will. Augustine believed sexual desire was not like the other passions because one never totally loses control of rationality, as one does when engaging in sexual intercourse. Then one cannot think at all. But it is ironical that the very thing that convinced Augustine that concupiscence was not totally under the control of the will was not its excess, but its impotence. Therefore, the sin was inherent in the desire itself.[118] In reading his rebuttal of Julian it is difficult to escape the conclusion that these two fine minds argued often at cross purposes, and that their personal misunderstanding held tragic consequences for Christian anthropology.

This is what makes it so interesting that Augustine attributes death to Eve. To Augustine, Eve's name, 'Life', conferred because she was 'mother of the living', could only be construed as an ironical title. The name reveals the labour for which she 'had been provided', but Eve's travail leads only to death.[119] By contrast, Mary is the true spiritual mother of the living.[120] However, there is one very important distinction between the power of Mary and that of Eve. Mary does not have the power to confer life, as Eve had the power to confer death. Mary had an instrumental function, she was the vessel of the Life-bringer. There is a radical inconsistency in this attribution of death-dealing power to Eve through original sin for, in ancient thought, only Adam could create the children whom Eve will bear to mortality. Logically, if Eve brought death to the world, then Eve's role should be equated to that of Jesus the Life-bringer in the doctrine of recapitulation. However, this would not only give Eve too much power, but would contradict the Pauline equation and the dominant biological paradigms of the culture. So in the formal articulation of the doctrine, Eve's role, like Mary's, was only instrumental.

Although Eve conceived lust from the venom of the serpent, she had no seed to be corrupted. It was Adam's seed which was corrupted when he joined Eve in sin. Adam remained the final arbiter of sin. Yet as temptress and ally of Satan, Eve is made to bear full responsibility for death, but Mary is never conceded similar power over, or responsibility for, life. This is where the Adam–Eve, *Sapientia–Scientia* parallels break down. Within one agent, Adam/

Sapientia controls action, Eve/*Scientia* cannot act alone. Where the two functions are projected onto separate persons, then ultimately, the woman can act alone. Hence the enormous energy expended to keep women under control.

The language that Augustine used with regard to Mary and Eve is significant. It is redolent of sexual imagery, and reinforces the psychological association between women, sex and sin. Eve's sin is implicitly adultery against God, when she allows her heart to be corrupted. To renounce evil is to renounce Eve.[121] The significance of Mary's physical virginity reinforces the links between the discourse of the heart and the discourse of desire as different levels of meaning which inhere in the Augustinian texts.

Mary and the church

Mary's relationship with the church is complex and mystical.[122] As mother of the human Christ, she is also mother of his 'members',[123] but the church fulfils this role on earth. As Mary, the fruitful and untarnished earth of the new creation, through the rain of divine grace gave birth to the sinless Word made flesh, so does the church give true birth to Christians through the water of baptism and sinful flesh becomes Word.[124] In a paradoxical manner, Mary is both mother of the church and mother of the church's spouse, for Jesus is espoused to his own body.[125] The Body of Christ as a whole is masculine, for Christ is male, but the body's internal dynamics are gendered. Christ is then male head, and within the feminised body, everyone takes on the feminine gender role:

> Each sex is called woman because each sex, that is, the church, is called a virgin. 'I have espoused you to one husband, that I may present you as a chaste virgin to Christ' (2 Cor. 11.2). And few have virginity in the flesh: all ought to have it in the heart. Virginity of the flesh is a body unsullied: virginity of heart is a faith uncorrupted. The whole church is therefore called a 'Virgin', and in the masculine gender, 'the people of God', and 'one people' and 'a single people' . . . [126]

This text elucidates Augustine's attitude to consecrated virginity. The physical virginity of Mary and the church's virgins provides a bodily symbol of the church's virginity of heart present in all the faithful. The notion that even Christian women who adhere strictly to the church's teachings on legitimate marital intercourse are corrupted in body, and by implication, in spirit, is also present in the parallels between virginity and integrity, lack of virginity and the poisoned corruption of desire that does not arise from the will to procreate.

That the laity were sensitive to such implications in his own time is clear not only from his responses to the Pelagians, but from his spirited defence of the holiness of the bodies of wives in other texts. His early answer was that holy in spirit the faithful may be, yet modesty cannot be attributed to the flesh.[127] Over a decade later he would come to affirm that when the spirit is sanctified, it sanctifies even the body. All members of Christ are holy because they are united to Christ. Nevertheless, some members of the body are preferred to others.[128] However, his consistent teaching that the less sex the holier the marriage, and that the virgin has greater holiness in body and spirit, reinforces the idea that holiness of spirit is incompatible with sexual activity.[129] Augustine's pervasive pessimism means that although he could follow Clement of Alexandria in arguing that all the faithful are holy, he rejects Clement's affirmation that if the spirit is sanctified, then the semen of the faithful is holy.[130]

Both Mary and the church represent chastity, purity and sanctity, and compassion in uncorrupted fruitfulness.[131] Thus the church, virgin forever, 'scorns earthly nuptials',[132] preferring the spiritual fruitfulness of virginity,[133] which reintegrates the self,[134] and is expressed in doing the will of the Father,[135] with true poverty of heart.[136] The love of the church for the bridegroom makes her obedient and fearful of offending.[137] United with Jesus in his glory she is like a queen at the right hand of God, clothed in the glory of a King's daughter, and companioned by a train of virgins who are not captives, but brought into the temple in joy and gladness.[138] All these texts are applied to the church in Augustine's writings. Yet given the texts on Mary's vow, and the apocryphal stories that she lived in the temple until puberty, in this image the eternal Virgin (Mary/church) returns to the temple at the right hand of God.[139]

This holy marriage between Christ and the church, untainted by any carnal imagery, is the ideal marriage, and explains why divine spousal imagery is not used by Augustine to illuminate human marriages. The contamination of concupiscence in earthly marriage means that the analogy of Christ and the church is more suitable for the church and virgins in spiritual marriage with Christ than for sexual marriages.[140] Nuptial imagery is used most frequently of the union of Word and flesh, which is repeated again on the spiritual plane in the union of the resurrected Christ and his body.[141] The belief that intellectual procreation was superior to physical procreation was as old as Plato, and from a feminist perspective the benefits accruing to male power from this belief system are difficult neither to see nor to understand.[142] Like so many other originally Platonic ideals, it was theologised into the Judaeo-Christian tradition through Philo, Origen and Methodius, and reinforced by the resurgence of Neoplatonism in late antiquity through Ambrose, Jerome and Augustine.[143]

In speaking of the church as mother, Augustine appropriates the nurturing attributes of Mary's physical motherhood. The church is the one who truly gives birth to Christians. However, her labour, unlike Mary's, is painful, perhaps due to the sinful nature of her embryonic children (cf. Gal. 4.19). In her womb/font of grace, sin is washed away and the faithful are reborn, freed from the power of the devil and regenerated through Christ's 'immaculate, spiritual grace'.[144] Like Monica, her breasts flow abundantly with milk that loosens the tongue to speak Jesus' name.[145] As Monica cared for Augustine physically, the church nurses, feeds and nourishes the faithful in age and wisdom.[146] With God as Father, and the church as mother, human beings move from human to spiritual birth, from death to life, and from woe to joy.[147] As far as Augustine is concerned, this is not a 'rebirth', but the authentic birth of Christians as members of Christ's body. All the positive aspects of mothering are ascribed to the spiritual mother who becomes the only the true mother, while human mothers are debased. They can only bear children to misery and death.

Eve too appears as a model for the church, but it is significant that it is always in a context where she saps life from a man whose strength is vitiated. The creation of Eve symbolises the creation of the church. Both are built up from the substance of another.[148] Both are the daughter/wives of their spouses, being formed from their husbands' sides. Adam's sleep prefigures the death of Jesus; Adam loses a rib-bone, which weakens him, and Jesus is pierced in his side, 'the place of sin', from which Eve was born. The lance that kills Jesus symbolises the sin of Eve. From the first side came death, from the second, life everlasting.[149] Hence the Eve/church symbolism assumes more fully the womb/tomb imagery found elsewhere of Mary. Eve symbolically kills Christ, in a narrative permeated with sexual symbols and euphemisms.[150] The phallic lance and the womb fluids of blood and water invert the normal gender roles. The suffering body of Jesus, penetrated by the lance, opens itself and pours out virginal life. Yet the blood can stand symbolically for sacred seed also. As God, the Christ contains within himself the fullness of creative power. The church remains the faithful bride, whilst Eve is cast in the role of the church's adversaries, allied with Satan for the overthrowing of humanity.[151]

Mary as a model for virgins
As Mary's canonisation and ascetic exhortation were so interdependent, it was inevitable that Mary became the model for virginal women. Conceivably, episcopal sponsorship of her cult may have

arisen to develop a less autonomous, less powerful model than Thecla. Mary was also harnessed to the legitimation of asceticism by establishing that this form of Christian life had its inception even before Christ was actually born. Augustine says specifically, and often, that 'with Mary begins the dignity of virgins',[152] although Christ himself is the chief instigator and pattern of virginal purity.[153] Continence comes from Christ as a gift,[154] which empowers the virgin to live in abstinence from unlawful sense by reason of her 'integrity'. This abstinence applies not only to sexual chastity, but to unlawful sight, hearing, smelling, tasting and touching.[155] Keeping their sense life to a minimum permits the continent to 'think more richly on the Lord, hope more happily, serve more instantly, love more ardently and please more attentively'[156] – in other words, to live more fully the life of *Sapientia*.

These strictures concerning chastity apply to virgins and to widows consecrated to serving the Lord.[157] Augustine structures the *ordo* of the body of Christ from the martyrs (virgin then married), through virgins and widows to the married (continent then incontinent).[158] Virginity is a life that must be freely chosen even by women, although they may be given in marriage.[159] Mary's vow, freely made without any awareness of the honour to fall upon her, is the model for the virgin. In real life, such 'freedom' may have depended in large part on the virgin winning the approval of her family in order to avoid marriage or to achieve the financial security to remain celibate.[160] Perhaps this is why it has been concluded that celibacy attracted the 'noblest women of the time'.[161]

Therefore, virginity is honoured because, like Mary, it is dedicated to God.[162] As first Mary and then the virgin live the sapiential life, it is noteworthy that virginity is not explicitly given as an exemplar of *Sapientia*. Nor was Augustine able to see the earthly and everyday service of women to their families as dedication to God.[163] That the loss of a family and especially children was a difficult one for Christian women is clear from Augustine's need to argue his case over decades. He offers different reasons in different texts.

First, in *De bono coniugali* he argued that if her husband was present, then much of a wife's time was taken up with pleasing him.[164] In this text particularly he could not afford to criticise marriage too heartily and, as he always intended the companion piece, *De sancta virginitate*, to follow on its heels, then people would soon have access to all the reasons why the better had become the enemy of the good. In the second treatise he argued from women's sorry lot in society. If they were not betrothed when young, they would be despised and rejected till too old to marry; yet even if they were chosen, their destiny was still not a happy one. They either feared childlessness or were burdened by bearing and nurturing children.[165] Their peace of mind would be disturbed by fearing false reports about themselves, or offended by false suspicions of their husbands.[166]

In 414 he invoked the further reason that wives were often abandoned by husbands who set off for foreign countries and, if they returned at all, returned aged.[167] It would seem that this latter argument had some merit. Ambrose devoted some space in the *Hexameron* to resolving tensions between spouses in just this situation, and it is supported by evidence from other sources.[168] From this perspective, it is not difficult to see that a life of moderate asceticism, with time for prayer, study and works of charity, in the company of like-minded women, who all controlled their own finances and sexual choices, was a liberating new role for Christian women.[169]

Virgins, then, should not be sad that they cannot be virginal mothers like Mary. Since they identify with Mary, Jesus' virgin birth is an ornament to them all, and they too become 'mothers of Christ' doing the will of the Father.[170] As the virgin cannot conceive Jesus in the flesh, she reserves her flesh for him conceived in her heart.[171] She is spiritual mother and bride. Her spiritual conception results in a greater fruitfulness than mere physical child-bearing,[172] for the integrity of the flesh is not lost.[173] Indeed, theirs

> is a richer and more fruitful condition of blessedness, not to have a pregnant womb, but to develop the soul's lofty capacities; not to have breasts flowing with milk but to have a heart as pure as snow; not to travail with the earthly in the pangs of labour but with the heavenly in persevering prayer.[174]

In fact, they give birth to the spirit of salvation, and lavish on Christ the love they would bestow upon a husband,[175] who is fairer than all the sons of men.[176] In a somewhat mixed metaphor, the older notion of the soul conceiving Jesus is conflated with the spousal imagery of Mary's womb as the bridal chamber where God unites with flesh, and the marriage of Christ and the church, so that Mary as church and the consecrated virgin conceive their own Bridegroom. This is underlined by his statement that the Christ who is healing in them the pride and concupiscence of Eve, would be the last to violate in them the purity they have loved in Mary. Therefore, the virgins need not fear as ravisher the Christ who comes as the redeemer/bridegroom.[177] Scholars have recently begun to highlight the erotic motifs in the martyr hagiography and women's conversion stories, and erotic imagery is present in Ambrose's virginity texts. It is much more subtle in Augustine.[178]

It is important to Augustine to emphasise that marriage is a good.

Experience had clearly demonstrated that the strategies of Jerome had alienated his own constituency. It was far more effective to argue from the good to the better. If marriage were not a good, virgins would only be doing what was right and appropriate, and all should be virgins. As it is, they earn their greater glory by transcending the good of married life, rather than by shunning marriage as an evil.[179] Not only do they have a better earthly life, but their rewards in the next life will also be greater.[180] Furthermore, they can compensate by their virginity for their mothers' loss of integrity; nevertheless, mothers of virgins remain inferior to their daughters because they have lost *integritas*.[181]

Just as Mary symbolised paradise regained, the virgin symbolises the angelic life on earth, because integrity, sanctity and truth bear the image of the heavenly.[182] The fact that it is still 'on earth' explains why this eternal dimension of virginity does not exemplify *Sapientia*. The virgin, like Mary her exemplar, shows how woman is to live the angelic life, to recreate paradisal human life within time; they still are bound by their mortality and their feminine form and so they still may only image *Scientia*, although perfected. The angelic dimension of virginity also reinforces Augustine's connections between virginity and holiness of body. It is not that married women's bodies are not holy at all. He hastened to assure his directees that, like marriage, the bodies of chaste Christian wives are holy. But as a class, they are not, and can rarely be, as holy in either body or spirit as a virgin.[183]

By arguing for the holiness of married women in both body and spirit, Augustine preserves the élite status of virginity which then merits special standing in the church, and greater rewards in heaven. There are two exceptions to this *ordo* of holiness for women. The first is the virgin who belongs to a heretical sect,[184] and the other is a disobedient or carnal virgin who substitutes other worldly pleasures for sex.[185] They were totally outside the Kingdom of God.[186] Spiritually dead, their choice of virginity was attributed to their desire for licentious freedom.[187] For, in spite of their sacred character, Eve is still present, 'even as we have known many sacred virgins, talkative, curious, drunken, litigious, covetous, proud: all which are contrary to precepts, and slay one, even as Eve herself, by the crime of disobedience'.[188]

From the number of times that Augustine adverts to it, pride appears to have been a major problem for the ascetic woman. Was it that the élite status of virgins led to some of them developing a self-image of impregnable moral superiority?[189] Or did asceticism empower women with spiritual authority which could impinge on the power and authority of the bishop, as is clear from Augustine's own correspondence with Fabiola? Was it simply that pride had become the core and source of sin so that this became his focus? If pride could be conquered, then so could the lesser sins. For Augustine the ultimate touchstone of sanctity was readiness for martyrdom, and no virgin could be sure that she was readier to accept martyrdom than a married woman until she was confronted by a life or death situation.[190] The example he uses of virgin *vis-à-vis* married woman martyr does suggest that at least some women were using their spiritual rank to claim social superiority over other women.[191] His strictures on the different aspects of pride suggest that the abolition of class distinctions within ascetic communities where noble and peasant women shared a communal life were not without their problems. The noble clung to pride in their kinship systems and the peasants aggrandised themselves, as peers of the nobility.[192] All proud virgins 'puffed themselves up', a signal failing of *Scientia* when she gets above herself and divorces herself from love.

However, Augustine may have contributed to this very pride with his reversal of the status of mothers and daughters, and his subversion of *patria potestas* to permit a girl to choose freely between virginity and marriage. Nor would it have been conducive to humility that he refused to send virgins to learn anything from repentant sinners, because even though penitents have been cleansed, they are not worthy to be 'patterns' for undefiled virginity. Hence the touchstones for the virgin were Christ, meek and humble of heart,[193] and Mary, humble and faithful.[194] Paradoxically, another fear he expressed was that because of the holy and circumspect lives led by gently reared virgins, they would take their status for granted and would not 'love much', as do those who are forgiven much.[195]

But even in consecrated women, there is the danger that Eve still invites desire. There is discreet mention of the struggles with the libido.[196] Virgins are cautioned about the way they walk and talk, and the custody of the eyes, but this seems more to prevent them becoming objects of desire who tempt others, than a recognition that sexuality and sexual needs might occasion real spiritual struggles for these girls.[197] Even to regard a man with more than a passing glance is forbidden.

> For it is not only by touch that a woman awakens in any man, or cherishes towards him such desire, this may be done by inward feelings and by looks. And say not that you have chaste minds though you may have wanton eyes, for a wanton eye is the index of a wanton heart.[198]

In certain texts the implicit assumption seems to be that in gently reared girls who have never experienced a sexual relationship their innocence is a protective shield. Yet this is unusual in the culture.

It would be more customary to expect that the 'flower of youth' in full bloom would seek sexual outlets if not channelled into marriage. This had been Augustine's own experience, and may be the source of the judgement that those who do not keep their eyes submissively lowered are sexually motivated. At the physical level, fasting is important so that no superfluous food fuels the sexual appetites.[199] Augustine certainly believed that the will must co-operate with grace, and prescribed constant prayer as proof of this good will.[200] Then the grace of their divine spouse will enable them to live as befits him.

However, there are certain veiled warnings to widows about what 'remaineth to overcome',[201] to convents about the dangers of carnal affection among themselves,[202] and explicit warnings about the dangers, for virgins, in the company of lustful widows who repent their vows and hold to them only through pride.[203] Presumably because such women have been sexually active in the past they are more at risk of temptation.[204]

Hence continent women are not to be idle,[205] nor are they to be involved in the public work of the church.[206] They are to discipline themselves by prayer, alms, vigils and fasting, and a modest dress. They are to occupy themselves with reading, prayer, psalms, good thoughts, good works, hope of the world to come, and raising their hearts to God,[207] but the chief business of continent women is prayer.[208] One notable aspect of Augustine's instructions to women with regard to ascetic practices is his constant insistence on moderation. They are only to fast, to watch, to pray even, in so far as it is not injurious to their health.[209] Augustine is not a fanatic, and he does not require women to destroy themselves physically to overcome their sexual nature.[210] In this he follows Ambrose, who believed that whilst very young women required more rigorous discipline, older women like his sister, spiritually mature and past the bloom of youth, should minimise their austerities beyond the prescribed fasts so that they could protect their health to teach the young.[211]

Mary as a model for married women
The influence of Jovinian was still a factor when Augustine wrote his treatises on *The good of marriage* and *The holiness of virginity*.[212] The titles themselves encapsulate his position. Marriage is a human good, virginity is holy. As a married woman and mother, Mary was the model for the married woman also, but it must never be assumed, as Jovinian did, that married and continent women were equals, simply because each reflected one aspect of Mary's role. To do so, he said, would in fact destroy Mary's sacred virginity.[213] The equality would only be 'endurable' if they gave birth to Christians

in the flesh, instead of to the children of Eve.[214] To maintain the hierarchy of virtue and reward within the Christian community Augustine, like Ambrose and Jerome, had to overlook several strands of biblical tradition.

First, Augustine had to account for and dismiss the fertility of the Hebrew patriarchs: in times past fruitfulness compensated for the loss of virginity. Now the holy women of the Old Testament were no longer suitable models for Christian women.[215] The Jewish matriarchs married under obedience from God so that the prophets might be born. There was no lust in them. But the times were ending now. And if the world was perishing, 'the married woman, for whom beareth she?'[216] Second, he totally ignored the Pauline injunction that the faith of the parents sanctifies the children (1 Cor. 7.13). Third, so adamant was Augustine about the privileging of virginity in the Christian era that he argued that when the Pauline letters spoke of apostles' wives that this could not possibly be the right translation. The correct word would be sister, or a woman as a sister. The idea of the apostles having wives could not be countenanced.[217] Finally, gospel passages which reveal that the generosity of God does not discriminate between workers in the vineyard (cf. Matt. 20.1–16) are neglected in favour of interpretations of the parable of the sower and the seed which assume that differences in the yield of the seeds are indicative of difference in rewards and honours (Matt. 13.3–23).

Therefore, as the end-time approaches, procreation becomes a self-indulgence for Christians, little more than an excuse for concupiscence.[218] Hence, Christian mothers must always honour the moral superiority of sacred virgins. Augustine said that a woman who bought slaves in order to make them Christians gave birth to Christ more fruitfully than any mother by the fruit of her womb, yet even she would not dare to compare her money to the gift of virginity.[219] So a mother's honour is not only less than the virgin's, but less than that of a Christian slave-owner. Nevertheless, in its chastity, procreation and fidelity, marriage too is a gift from God.[220] Even in its goods, marriage belongs to human duty and therefore the temporal, whilst virginity belongs to freedom and therefore the angelic realm.[221]

What the married woman can and must emulate is Mary's virginity of heart, even though she has already lost its bodily symbol.[222] Such 'virginity of faith' will lead to wedded chastity and, ideally, to a continent marriage.[223] To objections that total continence in the church would eliminate the good of marriage from the body of Christ, Augustine had two responses. The earlier was that the married goods of the past would suffice Christ's body. Marriage did assist in fulfilling the number of true believers, and not all receive the grace of chastity, but his inference to Juliana was that if pagans could be converted, the predestined number of saints would be accomplished and the end would come.[224] His later argument used the classical understanding of marriage to subvert its traditional function far more fundamentally. This argument was that marriage did not need physical consummation to be a true marriage; rather marriage inheres in the contract, not the consummation.[225] His exemplar is the virginal marriage between Joseph and Mary.[226] Thus he separated the *intentio maritalis* and the *affectio maritalis* from the purpose of marriage – to raise heirs for the *familia* and citizens for the state. In chapter 8 it was argued that this distinction between intention and consummation was essential to permit him to navigate the resolution of his own concubinage which he described as two in one flesh, a description which henceforth could be used to define marriage.[227] Therefore, despite the virginity of Mary and the continence of Joseph, this is a true marriage of the spirit, a far more binding bond than that of the flesh.[228] Joseph is no less Jesus' father for not inseminating Mary.[229]

Another aspect of Augustine's use of the Marian exemplar is the most subtle connection he established between Mary's subordination and her chastity. The former testifies to the latter. This stems from the fact that although Mary was the earthly mother of the Lord she was subject to Joseph.[230] She acknowledged the authority of the *paterfamilias*,[231] and his place of honour in the marriage.[232] Therefore Mary fully subordinated herself to Joseph in obedience to the order of marriage, disregarding the extraordinary honour deriving from her motherhood. The humble Christ would not have taught his mother to be proud.[233] The most chaste woman created was the most obedient. For women, the lesson is that the more subject they are to their husbands, the purer they are. Obedience becomes the prerequisite for, and criterion of, chastity.[234] Following Mary's example, holiness for the married woman is to be subject to her husband and therefore to be chaste. Only then she will be holy in body and spirit.[235] Again the point of connection between pride and chastity is order. Personal honour, no matter how elevated the woman, disrupted the social order.

Mary as a model for the faithful

Mary is also the model for all believers as the epitome of the integrity of faith, hope and charity.[236] She is the ideal 'faithful one'. All can follow her example in believing the Word, and conceiving it in their hearts.[237] Their imitation of her would manifest itself in two ways. First, Mary's faith is tied firmly to the accomplishment of the Incarnation. Because she believed the Word, what she believed was achieved. The faithful, too, must believe that what has been achieved in Mary will be efficacious for them.[238] Second, everyone doing the will of the Father in 'most fruitful charity' would become the mother of Jesus, and his sister and brother.[239] Augustine exhorted:

> His mother carried him in her womb, let us carry him in our hearts. The virgin was heavy with the incarnate Christ, may our hearts be freighted (*gravida*) with belief in Christ. The virgin brought forth the saviour, may our souls bring forth salvation. May we bring forth praise also. Let us not be sterile, let our hearts be full of fruitfulness in the Lord.[240]

13

MARIOLOGY AND SOCIAL RELATIONS

MUCH of Augustine's mariology develops neither from Scripture[1] nor early tradition, but from a 'must have' argument based on his cultural assumptions.[2] The chasm between heaven and earth, eternity and time, sacred and profane, masculine and feminine, demanded that a God be born in a manner fitting to a God. A culture based on honour could not accept a God with total disregard for his personal honour. God had to act in such a way that God's honour was manifest. Thus to be born miraculously was a proof of divine honour. To Augustine, God is humbled enough by becoming human at all, let alone being born like the rest of humanity.

His mariology is a classic example of the manner in which female shame is harnessed in the service of masculine honour. In a world in which the godly is symbolically masculine, then the feminine must be bound by ritual or social constraints from shaming God's honour. Thus Mary is constructed as the asexual woman, who conceived directly through a pure spiritual principle, rather than one contaminated by original sin. Her *post-partum* virginity then prevents the womb that has been sacralised by God being debased by normal sexual intercourse and birth processes.[3] The miraculous birth not only protected the godly from pollution, construed as feminised sexuality, but attested to the honour of Jesus Christ himself. Assumptions about sexuality, influential in both philosophic and ascetic discourse, melded seamlessly in Augustine's marian writings to discriminate radically between the sacred and the profane, the 'true' Christian and the politically expedient, and the spiritually masculine and feminine.

In a circular argument, the virgin–mother dualism theologically justifies philosophic body–soul dualism.[4] As the model of faithful discipleship, and mother of Jesus, Mary belongs to the realm of the temporal and the transient. As eternal virgin, she belongs to the angelic realm, foreshadowing the nature of feminine resurrection. Hence men, feminised before God, can be exhorted to imitate her faithful heart, her integrity. if *Scientia* is disciplined like Mary, there will be no fear of her seducing *Sapientia* into sin. Instead the soul will bear spiritual fruit. As the virile woman, the ideal which transcends all human women, she is an acceptable model for male Christians, and yet her humility, obedience and modesty all serve to reinforce the subordination of Christian women.

Through marian ideology, the chastity of both virgins and married woman is defined by their obedience. Disobedience to a male head, be he bishop or husband, indicated an unchaste soul.[5] Some such criterion had been made necessary during the ecclesial debates through which the church came to realise a new 'orthodox' self-identity. Once, to be simply a virgin was the mark of divine grace. But when two parties are anathematising each other as heretics, and both groups include virgins and widows, then consecrated virginity or widowhood *per se* is no longer proof of divine favour. In addition, traditions later defined as heretical were often groups which deviated from the cultural norm and permitted women to hold charismatic or clerical offices. This flouting of social roles was unacceptable in the post-Constantinian church, which came to control its virgins by defining them as 'brides of Christ'. This very title had been one of the issues that Jovinian debated with Ambrose and Jerome. He believed that the prestigious symbol of the Virgin Bride was far too powerful for individual women to bear. It belonged to the church as community. Within that community, all Christians were equal, and all acts equally virtuous if done for the glory and love of God. Thus Jovinian had no need of a strong mariology to idealise virginity or reinforce feminine stereotypes. His theology belonged to an earlier age of the Roman church, more egalitarian, and formed more by the tradition of the Pastoral Epistles than that of desert asceticism.[6]

Nevertheless, Mary was an impossible model for women to follow completely. No ordinary human woman can be both virgin and mother at the same time. Whilst male theologians debated their roles and rewards, women made choices. Either choice presented sacrifices. To choose marriage and motherhood meant the acceptance of the lowest level of discipleship within the church. Although superior to sinful virgins, sexually active married women were still the lowest class within the church because sinners were outside the church altogether.[7] Furthermore, within Augustine's theology, it meant the loss of the dignity of being birthgivers. This had been the one role that gave women a *raison d'être* and respect within the patriarchal society, and it had defined their nature and role within Augustine's own anthropology. Not even giving birth to virgins elevated the natural mother, because all females are born virgins and subject to the devil; they are not born 'sacred virgins'.[8] A mother becomes 'stepmother' to her own children, because she cannot give them true life. Augustine spiritualises all the life-giving aspects of the mothering role and attributes them to the church who is *virgo*. From another perspective, the 'fact' that married women are corrupted by intercourse and childbirth[9] implies that they have less integrity than men who do not lose a hymen, do not menstruate, and do not give birth.[10] There is never any intimation that men as a class are 'corrupted' by marriage.

The attraction of virginity was subtly reinforced by the language Augustine employed to discuss conjugal relations. The very language of defloration and intercourse suggested that women liked a bit of rough handling in the bedroom, not surprising perhaps in a culture which located the origins of Roman marriage and gender roles in the story of the rape of the Sabine women.[11] Perhaps this was one reason why the Fathers had to argue that women should only choose virginity for pure motives like the love of God, and not because it would enhance their status or because they disliked marriage itself. This reading of the language is supported by the recent explosion of scholarship on social history and women's lives in antiquity, which offers considerable evidence that tenderness and concern for women was not a given within Roman marriages.[12] Certainly it cannot be assumed regarding the sexual practices of husbands often many years older than young brides, husbands who were encouraged to see women as 'slaves' in Augustine's own writings.[13]

For the virgin, the choice was more positive. She gained status and a degree of personal freedom, depending on her own specific situation.[14] She might be as independent as Thecla or Egeria, or as sheltered as the virgins who never left their family. But all had to relinquish their identity as *femina*. Given that procreation had defined her nature and role, and that virginity elevated her to the virile heights of virtue, the virgin lost her feminine identity.[15] What remained was to be chastised through penance and veiled from the rest of humanity. There is, though, a contradiction at the heart of this transcendence of the feminine. In the orthodox context, virgins were forbidden to cut their hair, because short hair symbolised the masculine estate, although they should aim for their soul to be 'short-haired'.[16] They are removed from the quasi-sacerdotal status given them in some contexts and defined as brides of Christ, a specifically private, feminine role. Though eulogised as the incarnation of angelic life, their bodies were often eroticised and textually exposed to the public gaze they were commanded to shun. Augustine avoids the latter by shifting from sexual imagery to the discourse of the heart. Their virgin status must never be taken for granted, lest the shadow of Eve fall over them and stain the purity of their souls.

Virginity functioned symbolically to create a bridge from the temporal to the eternal, from the human self to the immortal self. In terms of the analogy of *Sapientia* and *Scientia*, *Sapientia* is dominant in the souls of virginal women. As a cosmic communal *Scientia* they mediate between the earthly and the heavenly as individual *Scientia* mediates between the material and the incorporeal.[17] Their unruptured hymens symbolise this heavenly reality. Yet they cannot defy the feminine stereotype enough to symbolise wisdom. That is still symbolised by the male sex. From the clerical perspective, the virgin's equality in Christ did not invite her to change the world, but to leave it.[18] That this was not taken for granted by the virgins and widows themselves may be assumed as the motivation for much of the insistence that they do so.

It has been argued that, for Augustine, the physical virginity of Mary and the virgin who takes her as exemplar did not represent a sacred boundary unbreached by a polluting world, but rather the ideal of physical and spiritual harmony and untroubled obedience on every level: an ideal human soul, where the body (and community) remains undivided by the 'dark twist of the human will'.[19] Certainly, Augustine moves right away from the Ambrosian symbol of the womb as the heavenly court of modesty, the garden enclosed. The undivided heart rather than the immaculate womb is the significant symbol for Augustine. Undeniably Mary's virginity is the pristine symbol of the intact heart, the integrity of faith; and the apogee of Mary's discipleship was her faithful obedience, which recaptured the paradisal union of will and body. Yet – although not in the foreground – the *virgo intacta* remains a potent symbol of human integrity untainted by concupiscence. Hence, in paradise, intercourse would have taken place without rupturing the hymen,[20] and Augustine prohibited the consecration of women who had been raped, because they could not symbolise the *sacramentum* of virginity in the body.[21]

The symbolic shift from womb to heart holds implications for Augustine's ecclesiology. For Augustine, the purity of the church was a problematic issue. In his debates with the Donatists he defined the church as a hospital for sinners not a church of the pure. Thus the virginal womb, which is an all-or-nothing symbol, was not appropriate because it did not reflect his ecclesial reality. The discourse of the heart, with its veiled allusions to sexual continence, permits him more flexibility. The heart is a mixture of virtue and dross. It will be pressed like virgin oil, and its lees discarded. The heart, like the mouth, can be open to God's nourishment and grace, and closed to all that would poison it. The mouth/heart analogy also connects readily with the eating of the fruit which was motivated by Eve's contaminated heart. As Augustine's church was a mixture of wheat and tares, the heart conveyed this more appropriately than the womb. One can have a heart that is mostly good, but not have a womb that is just a little virginal. The shift from physical body to spiritual heart allows him to distance real sexual bodies and the pollution they incur from virtue and grace. The heart may be virginal even if the body is not.

This radical disjuncture between desire and integrity did not require a Copernican revolution on the part of Roman aristocracy. Roman moralists had long distinguished between the chaste wife a man acquired to bear legitimate children, and the mistress he took for fun and pleasure. They were the first to articulate the conundrum that a man who loved his wife with passion played the adulterer with his own wife, an idea that found fertile ground in asceticism.[22]

Negative attitudes to sexual passion for one's wife, the personal experience of many young brides, and ascetic ideals both philosophic and Christian contributed to marital relationships where frigid women became morally preferable to passionate women, and women believed that frigidity in sexual relationships kept them uncorrupted.[23] The chance to embrace a way of life that made women the equals of men led some married women to choose continence unilaterally, and this posed great problems for Christian husbands.[24] The solace of concubinage was denied them, and they risked being seen as morally inferior to women.[25]

The unilateral practice of continence by a husband may similarly have caused problems for wives, and there is extant evidence that men put aside their wives to follow the eremetical life. For Augustine, however, such a decision would not be a husband's prerogative. His insistence on the mutuality of the marriage debt meant that if such a decision led to moral problems for a woman, even a continent husband would be obliged to put his wife's needs first.[26] On the other hand, if wives were passionate, there was the insidious suspicion that they were morally suspect.[27]

If the mutuality of conjugal relations was taken as a starting point, without the negativity Augustine attaches to desire, a more reciprocal model of marriage might be developed, with regard not only to intercourse, but other aspects of the relationship such as nurturing and mutual companionship.[28]

Fiorenza has argued that rather than transform structures such as patriarchal marriage in terms of Christian equality and freedom for women as well as men, the patristic writers restrict such equality to those who remained free from the bondage of marriage that was cursed by the Fall. I would qualify this conclusion as far as it concerns choice. The constraints of cultural mores based on the ubiquitous assumptions about the ontological inferiority of women made the choice of a more egalitarian model virtually impossible for the fourth-century writers. Those ascetics who tried to live as brother and sister, still modelled their lives on a continent spousal relationship though no marriage took place. The scandal these couples caused in the ancient communities, which placed no credence in sexual innocence, led to a universal prohibition.[29] The suspicion that no cohabiting couple could really live continent lives resulted in conciliar decrees that bishops and their wives sleep in different rooms, accompanied by their same-sexed servants or associates as chaperones.

In this regard, one aspect of Augustine's teaching on the marriage of Mary and Joseph merits special attention: the union of souls. Although Augustine always saw sexual union and the union of souls as almost antithetical, in a different context the concept holds richness for a theology of marriage. The perception of marriage as a relationship that has the potential to engage all aspects of being at deep personal levels is a strand of his thought that holds great potential. Emotional and spiritual intimacy is still problematic for many couples, and it is often confused with genital intimacy. Ideally, the goal of such a marriage would be authentic intimacy where sexual delight was a reflection and an outcome of a loving interpersonal relationship, and a joy in one another that can encompass all facets of interpersonal relationship, including the physical, the emotional and the spiritual.

The shift to ritual cultic purity and the concurrent idealisation of the virgin had specific effects on marital life. It was in the fourth century that the church actually began to legislate on sexual abstinence within marriage. Abstinence was required on all feast days, all Sundays, during Lent, during Advent, twenty days before Pentecost, during menstruation, and during pregnancy. These restrictions were particularly to be enforced for sex during menstruation.[30] Clerics began to blame still births, birth defects, leprosy and epilepsy on unlawful sex.[31] Thus parents of disabled or ill children were publicly shamed because everyone 'knew' that they had had illicit sex of which the child was living proof. It is quite probable that these very prohibitions designed to free Christians to pray undistracted and to achieve ritual purity to commune with the divine would have had the opposite effect, charging marital sexuality with both a heightened awareness of desire and a freight of sexual guilt.

Augustine's theology may well be related to his own loss of intimate feminine companionship after his ordination about age thirty-seven. His rejection of his own concubinage as a lustful relationship unredeemed by marital intention, and the loss of his mother, may have led to his projection of his ideal women onto

Mary and the institutional church. The portrayal of Monica as figure of the church in his earlier writings, and the shared characteristics of Monica and Mary throughout the *Confessiones*, offer strong support for this hypothesis.[32] In Mary, Augustine recovers the feminine, but disembodied, asexual, and virtually non-human in her perfection and capacity for virginal motherhood.[33]

His theology is related also to Augustine's image of God as *paterfamilias*. His doctrine of original sin, his theology of baptism and his order of sanctity presume a God who is identified with the masculine, who will condemn infant children to everlasting hell if they die without baptism, whose grace is irresistible and who yet withholds it from some individuals according to his predestined will. The paradox is that a doctrinal formulation developed to protect the justice of God led to a God whom Julian of Eclanum would challenge as supremely unjust.[34] To the Pelagians it seemed that not only was Augustine showing decidedly Manichaean tendencies toward the sexed body, but that he was encouraging moral laxity and irresponsibility by denying any true freedom of the will. So much so that Augustine devoted a whole treatise to free will to establish that the will must co-operate with divine grace.

His mariology further shapes his perception of God. His *Sapientia–Scientia* model erases the feminine from God to the degree that Jesus cannot represent women at all. Thus the teaching of Augustine helped to shape attitudes that conceived of the feminine as not only inferior, but essentially unattributable to God. This was compounded by the doctrine of the virgin birth, which had implications for trinitarian theology. In some traditions, particularly in the East, the holy Spirit had had a feminine face. The dynamic of the virgin birth wherein the spirit of God overshadowed Mary made it essential that the Spirit be masculinised. A feminine Spirit, no matter how holy, could simply not make anyone fecund; a feminine Spirit would come perilously close to the Gnostic Sophia, who gave birth to the creator of evil matter because she tried to conceive alone. Furthermore, there was a perceived indecency in the idea of a feminine principle fertilising a woman's womb, and this reinforced the gendering of the holy Spirit.[35] Hence the way in which Augustine and the Fathers understood reality affected the way they understood God; and the way they thought of God affected the way they felt about reality. As Tony Kelly concluded, 'The result was a vicious circle of masculinity'.[36]

The emergence of Mary as the symbolic woman did not radically alter the gendered structure of the cosmos. The most important aspects of Mary's *fiat* were her obedience and faith. Faithful discipleship belongs to the temporal order, and has no place in eternity. As a model, Mary's primary significance was as virgin, and therefore a virile woman, who met the standard of virtuous masculinity. This androcentric thinking, allied to the concept of *ordo* which permeated all Augustine's thought, made it impossible for him not to stratify and rank the Christian community after the pattern of the Roman empire. So it is crucial that, when he assigns the *ordo* of the church, virgins take precedence over obedient Christians in the order of sanctity. Lest this conjure up images of women leading the community, all clergy ranked over all virgins. Male virgins ranked over female virgins. Female virgins ranked over incontinent men. This emerging hierarchy of the church totally destroyed the ethos of equality expressed in some communities of the apostolic church and created barriers between ascetic and married, clerical and lay, and clerics and women.[37] The danger of spiritual arrogance was serious enough for Augustine to have to address it on several occasions, as was clear above; his certainty about the true *ordo* of virtue made alternative visions an impossibility for him. Specific consequences followed. Institutional male celibacy effectively distanced women from the priestly caste and stated explicitly that the church, in its hierarchical expression, had no need of women.[38] The deliberate avoidance of women's presence led to a situation which promoted stereotypical fantasising about women, with no opportunity for testing reality. The dynamics of sexual symbols created a hierarchy of gendered power, where the superior is always masculinised and the inferior feminised. Thus God is symbolically masculine as Father and concretely masculine as Son and the church and the individual Christian soul are symbolically feminine as bride. The bishop is masculine in body and soul as the vicar of Christ; all other men are feminised in relation to him. Ascetic women are masculinised *vis-à-vis* other women, which makes them the spiritual peers of ordinary men, but does not permit them leadership roles. Men rule over their women, children and slaves, who are legally and spiritually their inferiors. As the social cosmos and the 'natural' world was created according to a divine paradigm, then natural law reveals that the feminine is ontologically inferior to the masculine.

Mary and the virgin-mother goddesses

Any discussion of Mary as the ideal of Christian virginity would be incomplete however, without an exploration of the debt mariology owed to ancient religious beliefs in virgin-mother goddesses. Christianity has always insisted that Mary is not worshipped, and certainly in late antiquity there is little to suggest that Mary received divine honours, although later pious Catholic practice came dangerously close. In addition to the significant personal and ecclesial factors which influenced Augustine's formulation of the virginal ideal, the fact that Mary emerged as a critical figure precisely when the old goddesses were being overthrown suggests that an exploration of the pagan meaning of virginity and virginal motherhood as an aspect of the holy would be fruitful with regard to Mary. This was also a time when the cults of Isis and Cybele were among the strongest rivals of Christianity, and both attracted condemnation from Augustine.

Belief in the power of the virginal did not begin with Christianity, but was a polyvalent religious belief in the practice of continence as a source of spiritual strength and power. Under the Republic and Empire, however, the ideal of celibacy was seen as anti-Roman.[39] Nevertheless it was current in both philosophy and pagan cultic practice. What Augustine did do, like the other church Fathers, was to elevate abstinence from a position of rare charismatic choice, exemplified by the Vestal Virgins or the Delphic priestess, to the general virtue required of many.[40]

Though the place of Mary in Christian discourse may have been construed as a specifically Christian phenomenon, the social sciences and theology have explored the transcultural and transhistorical mythos of the virgin-mother.[41] The use of archetypal language in this analysis acknowledges the transcultural and transhistorical presence of the archetype, but it will be argued that specific contexts shape and modify the content of the archetype according to cultural or organisational needs, both conscious and unconscious. By comparing Mary to the Graeco-Roman virgin-mother goddesses, the patristic modification of the archetype will emerge.

The feminine archetype was originally a trinity: woman perceived as virgin, mother and wise woman (crone).[42] The Great Goddess summed up the unity and multiplicity of feminine nature.[43] She was not a symbol of anti-physical purity, but rather of a reality that was spiritual and pneumatic.[44] She encompassed youth and age, birth and death, joy and sorrow. Sometimes she had eunuch priests. The waxing and waning moon was her symbol. She differed from the masculine Christian Trinity in that through the stages of the female life cycle she mediated a cyclical view of time. Isis is an exemplar here, as are the *Bona Dea* whose symbol was a serpent, and Cybele the *Magna Mater*. The Christian Trinity represents three distinct persons, albeit with one essence, in a patriarchal relationship, Father, Son and the Spirit that proceeds from them, thus mediating a linear view of time. Doctrines of immutability exclude change from the divine masculine, whereas the Goddess's nature encompassed change within itself. Thus in a culture where there can be only one God, the rhythmic natural cycle of time manifested in the Goddess had to give way to a Trinity which expressed linear progress from change to eternal stability.[45] As cult and culture developed, aspects of the goddess were often individualised as separate cults – Artemis the virgin, Aphrodite the goddess of fertility and procreation, Demeter the grandmother, Persephone virgin and daughter, the wise Norns, and Ariadne the spinner of fate.

In classical antiquity, the virgin as the one who does not change from girl to woman often stands as the symbol of timelessness, which in the Christian articulation is expressed as living 'the heavenly life' on earth.[46] Virginity denoted not chastity but integrity, being true to one's own nature.[47] Virgin because unexploited.[48] Thus virgin goddesses were not necessarily continent. The virgin goddess might freely give of herself to a beloved though she walked alone. She was not the adjunct of a male deity, but a deity in her own right. Her relationships were egalitarian and represented in terms of sibling rather than spousal relationships. Her virginity symbolised unity with the rhythm of the universe, the passage from death to life. Her symbols were the tree, and light. The patristic exegesis of the texts from Revelation which identified Mary as the woman standing on the moon would have provided a link in popular imagination with the virgin deities also worshipped as moon goddesses (Rev. 12. 1–6). It was in Ephesus, the centre of the cult of Artemis-Diana that Mary was first proclaimed Θεοτόκος (the Godbearer), a phenomenon traditionally dismissed as having no significance apart from the christological. It would appear that the Christians who paraded her image through the streets of Ephesus just as Artemis had once been carried might have felt otherwise.[49] Certainly the links between Diana's feast day early in August and the feast of Mary's Assumption can be historically traced,[50] and the Purification of the Virgin[51] (clearly not a tradition with Augustinian origins) celebrated on February 15, has clear links to the Lupercalia, a purification and fertility rite.[52]

The word virgin originally meant the one who belongs to no man, or the woman who is one-in-herself.[53] This meaning and title is still found in hunter-gatherer societies. Whilst virgin she retains her freedom of choice, and may not be compelled either to continence or to sexual encounter.[54] The Christian appropriation of this archetype altered it to symbolise the person who was spiritually and physically totally at God's disposal, living solely by the gift of God's grace, whilst rejecting any vestige of sexual desire or activity.[55] However, the connotation of self-containment and self-possession is very strong in Ambrosian texts, even the notion of autonomy of movement being retained for the mature virgin.[56] Later prescriptions, possibly influenced by the extreme youth of women choosing virginity in preference to marriage, dissociated the virgin from her independence – its remnant lies in the freedom of the young Roman woman to choose celibacy rather than sexual relations. Its attrition is reflected in the tendency to denigrate the independent female ascetic in favour of women under rules in formal houses.[57] The harsh condemnations by patristic authors of the pagan virgins, especially the priestesses of Apollo, suggest that to the ordinary Christian the consecrated virginity of select women may have been perceived as a Christian expression of the same virginal ideal. Patristic authors defined pagan virgins like the Pythian priestess as demonic, or, if virginity was not a lifelong commitment, as with the Vestals, as lacking in integrity.[58]

The Romans worshipped the virgin-mother under the name of *Bona Dea*.[59] She was not only associated with aged wisdom but the divine child, a daughter or son. The mother–son dyad is especially interesting in relation to Mary. The God King as the son/spouse of the Great Mother is a development of this ancient image. The great mother was life-bestowing, bearing a saviour who rescued humanity from death, a function the male gods could fulfil alone.[60] The King reigned over the world from the lap of his mother/spouse.[61] Her mystery was such that man often turned away, an experience which was often interpreted as 'shame'.[62] The original son of the divine mother was frequently symbolised by an ear of wheat,[63] or perceived as the mother's breath/spirit, the symbol of wisdom.[64] This breath was later articulated as the *Logos*.[65] Isis was often portrayed bearing Horus on her lap, and her wisdom and compassion towards all the suffering are traits which came to be identified with Mary in later tradition. Some early statuettes of Mary and Jesus were so indistinguishable from similar images of Isis, that some Isis images were venerated in Christian churches as Mary.[66]

The congruity between the classical imagery and that of Augustine is striking. The bridal-chamber symbolism, the Mary/church/spouse overlap, all speak of the presence of the archetype of the Great Mother. Augustine could not remain untouched by the religio-cultural symbols of his age, even though he was so hostile to goddess worship.[67] His very hostility suggests that the symbol strongly engaged his fears of the autonomous, fertile, maternal woman. He replaced her with Mary, a woman devoid of sexuality and personal power who would yet, in and through the church, love him like a mother. Neumann has argued that the patriarchal evaluation of spirit as eternal, a priori denies the genetic principle of the Great-Mother myth and murders the mother, undertaking a patriarchal appropriation of the *Logos*. (One is reminded of Augustine constantly exhorting Laetus to 'kill' all affection for his mother.[68]) The Logos is then identified with the father, and the masculine becomes the source of the feminine. We see this not only in the Father-Son/*Logos* relationship but in the origin of Eve from Adam. The virgin birth of the Word celebrates and defines the ideal father–son and mother–son relationship, but mother–daughter and father–daughter relationships are obliterated.[69] Traditionally, the holy marriage of the mother and son was celebrated in the union of fire and water. One has to look no further than the rite of blessing the holy water at Easter in the older Catholic liturgy to find this symbolism still active and quite explicit.[70]

The final face of the archetype was the wise old woman who saw beyond appearances. She spoke wisdom and truth without fear. She was midwife and healer. She was the face of death before life was renewed in the virgin. She could be intimidating, was no respecter of persons and, when necessary, would demand the abandonment of immature emotional dependency and attachment in her son. Her refusal of self-gratification through maternal possessiveness and her demand for his concomitant relinquishment of narcissistic dependence is symbolised as her demand for the death of the son. In mythic terms, the son who accepts the death demanded is resurrected as the fully mature man.[71] Hence she was perceived as an ambiguous figure associated with death as well as wisdom. On the human level, the older woman who concretely filled this role could be construed as witch as easily as wise woman and was often feared and fled from as well as honoured.[72] It is not surprising that Augustine, in unconsciously beginning to recreate the archetype in Christian terms, would prefer to ignore the crone, or represent her earthy symbolism as the likeness of Eve. Eve then stands for the independent, decision-making, sexual woman, who threatens the submissive model of Mary, and reminds humankind that it is mortal; and pagan wise women were condemned as diabolical.[73] Yet, even for Augustine, Mary was Earth, and universal mother. Instead of the feminine symbolism maintaining its integrity, aspects of woman's nature were set in opposition to one another. Death was rejected as part of the human experience and natural pattern and connected to sinful femininity which cursed masculine humanity.[74]

Conclusion

The split in women's identity between their eternal nature as *homo* and their temporal role as *femina* was now complicated by the split within the role of *femina* itself. Submissive, chaste women are idealised and good, like the 'good mother' who never fails to love the child and never thwarts the child's wishes. Autonomous, and/or sexually desirable women are Eve and dangerous, like the 'bad mother' who disciplines the child, is emotionally attached to the father and who fails to meet the child's every need.[75] The problem was, as Augustine observed to Laetus, that it was almost impossible to tell them apart. Both groups of women become depersonalised, isolated and alienated from the public life of the community, and from each other. Patristic authors commonly instructed virgins and widows that they were not to visit even Christian homes, and good wives were also supposed to stay home as much as possible. What differentiated these groups became far more significant than their shared femininity. Or rather, they no longer share femininity but simply the name, woman. Women learn to be suspicious of each other in such a culture.[76] The idealised virgin, particularly Mary, became an object for the projection of sublimated sexuality and the glorification of 'safe' aspects of womanhood.[77] She is the woman who is totally obedient to her son, and who remains devoted to him in a spiritualised spousal relationship. But she is not a fully human figure, and is used, by implication, to demean married women.[78] The sexual woman becomes either an object to be avoided, or used for procreative purposes where unavoidable. It has been picturesquely noted that placing women in either heaven or hell is a good way of excluding them from earth.[79] Virginal women hold 'clean' if limited power, sexual women wield only the power which pollutes. Virgins are sacred, wives are profane. Virgins are the most Christian of Christians, the faith of wives is compromised by sexual desire. Both groups of women are locked into ascribed roles that are defined by an androcentric view of womanhood,[80] which, over time, will allow them less and less freedom to break stereotypical preconceptions of what it means to be a nun, a mother, or a sexually active woman.

The split between *homo* and *femina* due to the inability of women's bodies to image the divine, resulted in Augustine's belief that Jesus did not, and could not, represent women.[81] The sexual difference had so much more weight than the common humanity of Jesus and women, that the full humanity of women is implicitly queried.[82] His position raises important theological questions. If Jesus did not represent half the human race, are women really redeemed? Augustine, of course, assumes that they are, but his position on the *imago Dei* does not necessarily follow from his incarnational theology. It is logical then, that if Jesus cannot represent women, women cannot image Jesus as God incarnate, and this attitude was, and still is, the basis for objections to the ordination of women.[83]

Augustine's writings on Mary are singularly devoid of affect, in contrast to Ambrose. Yet I have argued that his own unresolved feelings about women were a very important influence on his theology. The mothering God he erased from his later theology would reappear in Mary's universal motherhood, and his vision of

Continence, holding out her arms to him in 'serene, unsullied joy' conveys something of his emotional response to Mary. The beauty of Continence is a radiant image of what Mary must have stood for in Augustine's imagination: the grace that set him free from corruption and mutability, which he could serve as mother church for the rest of his life.[84]

PART VI
Conclusions

14

Augustine's symbolic universe

Ｆｒｏｍ the late 390s until his death, Augustine refined the symbolic
system inherited from his theological and philosophical predecessors. He melded it with doctrine and spirituality forged from
personal experience and familial traditions into a consistent, integrated cosmology and theological anthropology. The foundational
principles are consistent over time, and the result is extremely
coherent.

Prelapsarian creation

His was a hierarchical universe, built by the divine Architect to an
incorporeal plan. This harmonious universe was the paradisal setting for the primal couple, whose sexual difference and union were
part of the divine plan, and whose gentle pleasures and joys never
disrupted the order maintained by a will ever focused on their God.
In Eden, human integrity of heart was paralleled by the integrity
of the virgin body of Eve that could engage in intercourse without
rupture of the hymen.

His was an ordered cosmos, its structural principles reflecting the
'natural law' embedded in creation by the Creator, and appearing at
each level of being, the ancient version of 'fractal theory'. To maintain this law, those more naturally endowed with wisdom, rationality
and creative fertility held the responsibility for their inferiors, both
to care for their needs and to control their passions. Thus God
ruled the cosmos, humanity ruled the animals, man ruled woman,
and soul ruled body. This order was justified by the biological and
philosophical tenets which argued that the superior formation of
males in the womb endowed men with a form more ordered, a
mind more rational and a power more (pro)creative – the human
counterpart of the creative power of God.[1] Both God and man
were father and pre-eminent by reason of their creative power.[2]

The Fall

The Fall threw the order and harmony of this exquisitely balanced system into chaos. The natural world no longer graciously provided either food for the body or refreshment for the spirit, but had to be subdued and dominated. The soul's desires were in constant tension between God and material satisfactions, and the original sin was inscribed on male bodies as the eternal stigma of human rebellion. Women were no longer subordinated by bonds of affection but rebelled against the natural order, and social relationships deteriorated to permit wars and even slavery. The young Augustine had fondly believed that a properly ordered will might permit the restoration of order. But his meditations on grace in Scripture and personal experience in the late 390s led him to believe that only a freely graced intervention by God, to whom the soul must cling with desperation, could offer salvation.

His repudiation of his earlier position led him to become a hostile opponent to any anthropology which placed emphasis on the capacity of the will. Two scriptural texts – Psalm 51. 5, 'Indeed, I was born guilty, a sinner when my mother conceived me', and Romans 7. 23, 'I see in my members another law at war with the law of my mind, making me captive to the law of sin that dwells in my members' – became the scriptural lenses through which he interpreted other scriptural texts and read his patristic forebears. These texts particularly provided the justification for his conviction that it was through inordinate sexual desire and sexual pleasure that original sin was passed from generation to generation. The very seed of humanity had become twisted from its true essence and become the carrier of death, not life.

It is undeniable that the experience of the divided will that was the driving force of Augustine's theology is a real human experience. But he could not allow that such a will could have existed before the Fall, because he could not countenance a divided will or an incontinent heart in Eden. He believed that the will before the Fall had to parallel the redeemed integrity of the will in heaven. Yet a divided will and a heart incontinent there undoubtedly was, according to his own exegesis. Adam and Eve had the free will to make choices, and choices they made. Augustine's image of Eden where the will always chose the best without constraint or conflict is idyllic, but inconsistent with the biblical text.[3]

Post-lapsarian humanity

Even after redemption, the state of fallen humanity, its integrity violated by conflicting desires, required strong control over desire in all its forms to prevent sinful desires manifesting themselves in the body. The price of continence was eternal vigilance and faithful obedience to God's will.[4] Thus, although the graced and redeemed will cannot restore order of its own volition, nevertheless it must *choose* to observe the order of love in order to love chastely. Augustine's *ordo amoris* rests on his philosophic assumptions about the nature of God. For the philosopher, God was perfect and autonomous in every aspect. Therefore change could not exist in God, because 'true being' is changeless perfection.[5] Any change would impute a loss of perfect Being to God. Thus temporal change also imputed corruption. Therefore, spiritual conversion was interpreted not as change but as true birth into human being, but all material change was seen as corruption away from an original state.[6] God has no need of any other Being, and so the perfect man had no need of any other being.

With God at the apex, the Augustinian hierarchy of human love proceeds from all that is above us, to ourselves, then our equals, and then all that is below us.[7] The goal of love is very important. Augustine saw it as healing, as leading to the fulfilment of the beloved.[8] For Augustine, love itself was expressed as enjoyment or use. Enjoyment connotes some need of the other, use does not, at least not in the personal sense. Because true friendship embraces both enjoyment and use, it can only exist between peers. A superior can never enjoy an inferior, because such enjoyment would indicate a personal need. How then was Christian love to be expressed between inferiors and superiors? In that situation, Augustine decided, love was expressed as use. Thus 'use' of a wife does connote a lack of need and a certain detachment of heart on the part of the man, but it was not incompatible with love.[9] To the contrary, Augustine argued that as God loves us, but cannot need us, then God can only use us for our own good. There was no other way that Augustine could understand how God loves us.[10] Hence God uses, but does not need human beings. Men enjoy and depend on God and their peers, and use women and slaves. Free women enjoy and are dependent on God, men and their peers, and use slaves. The corollary of this is that the man who is emotionally and spiritually independent of all others is the closest to God. Women dependent on men can never achieve such autonomy in this life, unless they choose consecrated virginity that confers autonomy in the spiritual realm.

The manner in which love is expressed as use may be extrapolated from Augustine's instruction on how the spirit loves the body: it gives it wise care within reasonable limits, and keeps it safe and sound, and above all, controls its desires.[11] Thus even the flesh, which connotes not simply the physical body but carnal desires, can be loved in this manner while it is being appropriately cared for and being healed although total healing is only possible in the next life. So there is a sense in which love of the subordinate means maintaining proper order in the object of love.[12] God, as Christ the Bridegroom, loves the church and the soul by caring for their needs, disciplining them and bringing forth spiritual children from them. Similarly, men care for and control women. As long as the analogically masculine commands on every level, then grace reigns at every level of the cosmos. Where desire rules, then sin and death prevail.[13] As these three exemplary unions are consistently portrayed in spousal imagery, wifely authority is constructed as intrinsically evil. In the context of male–female relations, the Augustinian emphasis is on God's control as *paterfamilias* rather than the Bridegroom's love-driven death. Even in his exegesis of the Song of Songs it is the Bride who desires, the Bridegroom who threatens and rebukes her to ensure that she will remain faithful.

What has become overwhelmingly clear is that the very structure of the universe was metaphorically gendered, with masculinity always being the attribute of the superior in any relationship and femininity that of the inferior, independent of biological sex. On the temporal plane, the masculine is defined as contemplative wisdom and the feminine as knowledge of the material world. When evil shredded the fabric of the world, its polluting power, perceived as alien to wisdom, rationality and order, was therefore perceived as feminine, and the result of a real woman acting immodestly and pridefully beyond her station in life. Disaster struck when the female took precedence over the male. Thus women were identified with sin, concupiscence and death in a way men were not. Sexuality, sin and the power to enervate unite in women in a powerful way. Only rigid control of the heart, body and women will provide the climate wherein souls may cleave to God and co-operate with divine grace to maintain the established and appropriate order within the individual and society.[14]

Furthermore, as women's bodies change more often and more dramatically in their menses, in pregnancy and lactation, their bodies were identified with change more closely than men's, with each change implying the loss of an original good. Virginity giving way to sexual activity is not a transformation into a fuller experience of, and potential for, female human being, but a corruption of spiritual and physical integrity. This capacity for bodily transformation, and particularly the power to bleed without dying, could not express for ancient men the transformative mysteries of Christianity, but is interpreted as evidence of women's distance from the ideal of immutability.

Thus the doctrine of original sin wove into the seamless garment of a spirituality of control. Whatever was out of one's conscious control was dangerous, especially if it was perceived as having the power to subvert sanctioned and holy power and to cause moral chaos. The irrational emotions and passions which held this power – pride, lust, anger, fear – were perceived as feminine and feminising. The pervasive fear of Roman men of sliding into effeminacy, of their rationality being enervated by desire, or their bodies by loss of vital heat, was mirrored in the paradigm of masculine *Sapientia* descending into pride, sin and chaos the more it became enmeshed in the realm of feminine *Scientia*.[15] This fear of being overwhelmed by emotion – gendered as a feminine mode of being – is directly related to the functionality of *apatheia* in Augustine's own era.

To conquer the fear of death and to cultivate self-restraint were essential disciplines for social order and personal tranquillity in an age when normal life expectancy was less than twenty-five years and 'death fell savagely on the young';[16] when men held enormous power over their dependants and when war was not only a way of life for many men, but was increasingly disrupting the established order of the Empire. Even under normal circumstances, given the suppressed violence inherent in a slave economy, when slave-owners of both genders (including Christians) were known to beat slaves to death, impulsive behaviour required strong moral restraints where there were no legal ones. What was destructive for social relations was to have all gentler emotional responses distanced from masculinity to the extent that a patrician patriarch like Ambrose could even chide men for their emotional rigidity in marital relationships.[17]

The yearning for a divine order so clear in Augustine was not only a means to understand his own spiritual dynamics but a response to the anxieties posed by the crumbling imperial structures and the need to erect new Christian replacements. As different models of church and their attendant cultural assumptions were pitted against each other in the debates over orthodoxy in belief and practice, and as the older more charismatic leadership models were displaced by hierarchical leadership conferred by the episcopate, Augustine baptised the structures of Roman bureaucracy. Ironically, the City of God came to be a mirror of the secular city which he so feared and criticised.

Androcentric theology

What is most significant about this doctrinal system is its androcentrism. Could such a construction of sin-drenched sexual desire, which considered a lack of control over the movements of the penis to be God's punishment for sin, have been derived from women's experience of their own sexual responsiveness?[18] As it was a punishment women stimulated but did not have to bear, it would not be surprising if those who accepted Augustine's arguments felt that this was extremely unfair when a female was responsible for sin – or desire.

Moreover, although the *ordo amoris* placed women lower on the hierarchical ladder than men, thus indicating that men had no need of women, sexual desire and its bodily manifestation continually reminded men that in reality, they did need women as lovers, wives and mothers, to perpetuate the *familia* and the state and to run their homes. From a feminist perspective 'use' appears to be a euphemism which conceals men's emotional and physical dependence on women and those subordinate to them in the hierarchy. If dependence is taboo for those in power, who 'use' but do not need their inferiors, then God too, as the ultimate power, must use those inferior to the Godhead. So it would be even less surprising that a certain anger, conscious or unconscious, was directed towards the women who reminded them both of their dependence and of their inherent propensity to rebel against God.[19] Shame and death were the twins born from Eve's conception of sin in heart. Shame about the indiscriminate sexual response is really shame about death.[20]

Much of this aspect of Augustinian thought has been masked by the traditional male scholarly approach, to which Augustine's experience of his body may have spoken more intimately. The physicality of the experience on which the doctrine is built remained discreetly veiled by the discourse of the 'failed will' or the 'flawed instinct', which usually does not even hint at the bodily concomitants. Although the incontinent heart was the source of lust, its effects were physical.[21] The Augustinian discourse of the flawed instinct virtually precludes any change in sexual behaviours, by tying sexual politics to the distortion of instinct via original sin inscribed in the body.[22] This discourse also maintains the perception of sexual abuses as motivated by 'instinctual' sexual desire, ignoring issues of power and violence. If it is a 'flawed instinct' then there can be no hope for change. But the 'flawed' instinct which exploits others sexually, which inscribes sexual violence on the body as punishment or retribution, which needs to control, to assert its individual and social power over others, may well be a learned behaviour, manifested to maintain control or to respond to frustration, anger or rejection. If not it would appear to be a gendered flaw, as women and children are disproportionately the victims of rape, sexual harassment and serious domestic violence.

The most far-reaching consequence of androcentrism was the

dictum that Jesus, as the Christ, did not represent women. This argument privileged sexual difference over common humanity in the Incarnation. Whilst it is understandable in the Roman context, a patriarchal context does not necessarily demand such a view. Clement of Alexandria, who so often dissented from the ascetic condemnation of women and marital relations, gave primacy to Christ's humanity, not his male sex. So it is not surprising that Clement spoke of God choosing to become a mother out of love for humankind, or that he used feminine images for Jesus.[23] Even Ambrose could comfortably write that the womb of the Father is the innermost dwelling of the Father's love.[24] Augustine, on the other hand, eliminated all trace of any feminine trait within the Trinity, rationalising away his own experience to do so. God stood in no need of any nuptial union to beget the Son, not even a union between the analogically masculine and feminine within God's self which is found in both Clement and Ambrose. Rather God's heart uttered the Word, as a man's heart begets its own counsel, *without need of a wife*.[25]

Then, to recoup his position on women and the *imago Dei*, Augustine had to render the *imago* intrinsically masculine. As the female bodily form was at odds with the masculine *imago*, women lacked the constitutional integrity of mind and body which characterised men. Furthermore, like *Scientia* they held in tension the personas of Mary and Eve. They represented the locus of the divided will, the incontinent heart. Women lacked authority within human temporal communities, and clearly, if Christ did not represent them, they could not represent the Christ. In eternal life, woman's purpose and nature will have to be radically altered in a way that man's will not. Augustine was not able to reconcile his perception of woman's mind–body dichotomy without doing fundamental damage to the full dignity of her humanity. From another perspective, it was a feat of reconciliation within his own era which permitted him to eat his scriptural cake and have it too. He managed to placate both those who wished to retain power asymmetry and those who argued for women's status as the image of God. Anything more would have been impossible to achieve within that cultural context, as the rejection of Jovinian's vision of a non-hierarchical church indicates. This question of the *imago Dei* is of vital importance to theology and spirituality because our subjective and objective images of God are interdependent and reciprocal. What is rejected as less than human will not be present in our image of God. What is feared as vitiating will not be present in our image of God. Rather God's image may be created from the distortions deep within the human person. Augustine's rejection of the spiritually feminine in God, and therefore his rejection of all creatureliness, all temporality, all contingency, all emotion from the divine image in the human person prescinds from the subjective *imago Dei* all that is distinctively human. Taken to its logical conclusion, the person is most like God who is least like a human being – finite, fallible and contingent. And if God treats people instrumentally, they are justified in treating each other so.[26] Certainly, the categories of *Sapientia* and *Scientia* are no longer appropriate to express the nature of the *imago Dei*. And if woman *qua* woman bears the image of God, then the Augustinian notion of God must also undergo amplification and enrichment.

Mary: the new feminine ideal

However, as Christ could not represent woman, a mythic woman, Mary the ever virgin, was constructed from sparse scriptural evidence, from popular legends, classical stereotypes and, above all, Monica, to portray Augustine's ideal mother, and to insert the feminine into the new creation. The appeal to Mary to justify ascetic spirituality and reinforce the doctrine and spirituality of original sin provides the classic example of what Mercia Eliade has called the *regressus ad uterum* (the return to the womb) to mark the moment of a new creation.[27] The new creation did not begin with the cross of Christ, but with his conception in Mary's virginal womb. The Spirit of God did not rest over the waters of chaos but over the immaculate fluids of Mary, so that from its very inception there was no gateway for the devil into the new Eden. Mary was also utilised to serve the ideology of male headship. In her, the ideal woman was revealed as one who could conceive without intercourse, was subordinate to all men, including her son, and whose chastity was only exceeded by her humility.[28]

Through Mary's virginal motherhood, Augustine provided a spiritual basis for the rejection of carnal blood kinship, in favour of spiritual Christian kinship systems. This was now composed of Father God, Mother church, and the Christian children born to them.[29] This was the ecclesial manifestation of the fantasy family in the *Confessiones*: God the Father, Monica, his chaste and obedient servant, and Augustine, the prodigal son. Post-Freudian and Jungian psychoanalytic theory have both developed the thesis that the symbol of the virginal mother allows the male psyche to reclaim the mother free of the incest taboo. In fact it has been asserted that 'true celibacy, if rightly understood, is the most complete expression of transferred sexual instinct'.[30] The language of instinct and transcendence intimates the classical heritage of psychoanalysis, but if the propositions concerning mother–son relationships hold a valid insight, and the union of virgin and mother in Monica-Mary-church suggests that it does, then use of the virginal symbol has served the needs of the male psyche at the expense of the female. It is also consistent with the virtual eradication of sexual desire in Augustine's exegesis of the Song of Songs. The shift of all mothering images from God to church in Augustine's later work erases feminine imagery for the divine and demotes it to the temporal and human sphere, no matter how elevated. With the feminine rooted firmly in creatureliness, there can be no danger of women claiming to have the authority to act for God as they are incapable of authoring anything.

The contrast between Mary's humility and Eve's pride has significant implications for gender relations. If the Augustinian understanding of pride is, in the words of David Hunter, of 'a perverse self-love that chooses isolating, deadening independence in place of life-giving creaturely dependence',[31] then the ideology of headship would require that women accept that same creaturely dependence on man, which men accept in relation to God. The point where the gospel message of creatureliness becomes distorted for women is the symbolic matrix which places women in the same relation to men as men are to God. In Augustine's social and spiritual order the male and the masculine must of necessity mediate between women and God. Any self-assertion of women in relation to men is then perceived as the choice for a 'perverse self-love', leading to an 'isolating, deadening independence'.

Dorothy Dinnerstein, building on the work of Klein, has suggested that such polarities in feminine symbolism indicate an unintegrated image of the mother, where the 'good Mother', experienced as selflessly responding to all the child's needs like an ever-giving breast, is opposed to 'bad Mother' who disciplines, denies and withholds. As long as the feminine remains unintegrated in the psyche, then female authority will continue to engage the hostility directed to 'bad Mother'. While the feminine is interiorised as inferior and irrational it is far more likely that men, as a class, will continue to project it onto women and will perpetuate the dichotomy of Eve and Mary. Women who accept the androcentric definition of the good woman, will likewise project bad mother onto other women and be unable to integrate the rejected aspects of the feminine self.[32]

Augustine, Wisdom and patriarchy

I have said that in defining *Sapientia* as masculine, Augustine defied a long history of religious tradition that had perceived Wisdom as feminine.[33] The sapiential traditions of Hebrew Scripture and popular pagan Wisdom figures reveal a feminine/maternal wisdom that

is never abstract or disinterested. She is a Wisdom of loving participation, who delights to dwell with the children of God (Prov. 9.
30–1; Wis. 7. 22—8. 1; cf. John 1. 14), or whose being is devoted
to compassion.[34] By contrast, Augustine's *Sapientia* is an abstract,
unworldly and detached attitude of mind that contemplates God
disengaged from the created world.[35] But feminist scholarship has
noted that Athena as goddess of Wisdom is a father-identified figure
who legitimates the rights of the father over the mother, precisely
because the father is the source of life.[36] Philosophy was committed
to an abstract Wisdom also. So there were other traditions for
Augustine to call on.

The *Sapientia*/masculine identification is significant in terms of
Augustine's own spiritual experience of a mothering God who con-
soled, healed and nourished, and of a feminine Wisdom who was
totally alluring.[37] But when what he knew came into conflict with
what he experienced, he could not trust experience.[38] The experience of his mothering God yielded first to the Father-God who
taught through punishment and discipline, who in turn was displaced by the God who was eternal Wisdom, devoid of any feminine
component.[39] Augustine's paradigm of spiritual development is
fairly typical of Roman child-rearing patterns. Children would be
reared gently, although always with an eye to their role in life, until
weaned, when a harsher discipline was considered more appropriate. Schooling for young boys was often a painful experience, as
Augustine attested, but with age and freedom from tutelage the
educated young man was expected to seek the joys of Wisdom.
The fear of effeminacy would have been a further factor in his
interpretation of his experience. To sustain a mother–son relationship with God would be to stigmatise oneself as a man who could
not relinquish infantile and unmanly relationships.[40]

Yet patriarchal systems do not demand such relinquishment of
the father–son relationship whilst the father lives.[41] Instead the
authority of the *paterfamilias* meant that any man whose father was
still alive and who had not been emancipated could still be under
his father's authority and dependent on him financially well into
middle age.[42] The trinitarian doctrine according to the Nicene
formula offered a model that reshaped the power imbalance of
traditional patriarchy, which was preserved in Arian theology. It
posits a Father and Son who share a common essence and common
power. The Father hands all authority to his Son, who responds by
being in perfect amity with the Father's will. This doctrine is
extremely pertinent to the wielding of power within the culture, as
the Fatherhood of God permits all the disparate nations of the
empire to be perceived as one family united in essence, where
power and resources are a male prerogative. The common goal of

Father and Son in creating and maintaining the cosmos provides the exemplary model for relationships between powerful men, whilst the abyss between God and humanity, rapidly being bridged by patronal saints, preserved the basis of hierarchy in the community.

Augustine reinterpreted cultural systems which persistently and deliberately, though not necessarily maliciously, taught the ontological inferiority of women and their susceptibility to sinfulness. Augustine's stature has been such that he is often perceived as single-handedly changing the face of Christianity and culture. Far from it. Augustine's self-appointed role in his own era was not only that of the vigilant defender of asceticism, but that of the protector of the City of God, in which, despite his disclaimers, the social mores show a striking resemblance to classical ideas of sexual and gender roles, hierarchical structures and male honour.[43] His great vision of a Christian *societas*, formed in the ascetic mould yet respecting the role of the *familia* in establishing a strong social order, meant that he had to find a median path which could foster the ascetic ideals which captured his heart without breaching the bounds of ascetic orthodoxy or alienating his congregations.

As heir to Plato, Augustine could argue that asceticism and continence were the true grounds for honour and he could spiritualise sexual being so that fruitfulness was of the heart, not of the loins. But, like every thinker, he could not think outside the categories of his time and, even more powerfully, could simply not comprehend the possibility of a society in this world or the next in which women, *qua* women, held equal status with men. The élite classical attitudes to sexual practice, the Christian acceptance of virginity as the basis of feminine autonomy and transcendence of the natural order,[44] and the adoption of a hierarchical structure of sanctity combined to create a climate in late antique Christianity that rejected both the egalitarian views of Jovinian, and the polemical advocacy of ascetical virtue by Jerome.[45] Augustine's exaltation of virginity tactfully preceded by his defence of marriage gained him the middle ground. This would have been fostered by his own theological reputation, the congruity between his position and strong social customs, and the moderation of his stance *vis-à-vis* both Jerome and Jovinian.[46]

It has been suggested that despite his permanent allegiance to the Neoplatonic view of sexual desire, and the enormous negativity invested in it because of its association with concupiscence, Augustine was an innovator in that he understood sexuality as an issue appropriate to theology. Rather, I would suggest, the push to articulate anew the essence of Christian identity, embracing both the need to preserve its historic links with Judaism and to reject the pitfalls of heterodoxy, meant, as always, the return to the Genesis texts to interpret their meaning for the particular historical context. Asceticism itself raised the issue of sex and desire in its attempt to discern what a redeemed human life would look like. Its models were naturally Adam and Eve before the Fall. Augustine's position was forged and tempered in debates over theological anthropology with Jovinian, Jerome, Pelagius and Julian.

Nevertheless, he was with the minority opinion in ascetic circles in accepting a sexual relationship for Adam and Eve in paradise. By positing sexual relationships as the basis for the first natural society, Augustine broached the notion that the origin of sexual relations is divine; if it is, then sexuality holds significant meaning for human beings about their created nature, and the nature of God.[47] Augustine's perception that the sexual nature of human beings is intrinsic to their humanity and not the result of sin is of perduring value. In his presentation of woman as sharing the *imago Dei* and his understanding of sexuality as intrinsic to human nature, Augustine revealed his ability to stretch the thinking of his era.[48] Detached from a spirituality obsessed with control, and from a concept of original sin tied to the procreative process, sexuality and sexual experience is open to being understood as an arena for the experience of God.[49]

Yet, in the final analysis, what emerges from his writings is not a new heaven and a new earth, but the consecration of cultural assumptions and value systems. The Jewish and pagan feminine personifications of virtue and vice have been adapted to Christian agenda in the archetypes of Mary and Eve. In Augustine's thought woman remains as the antithesis of virtue, but her capacity to represent Wisdom in Hebrew thought is erased in favour of secular knowledge and maintenance of the temporal and ephemeral.

This intellectual paradigm was, *au fond*, a male claim to culture, and to the superiority of culture over nature where nature equalled woman. It legitimated masculine power as that which transcended and controlled feminised nature, desire and self-indulgence. There can be no argument with the will, masculine or feminine, to discipline both destructive self-indulgence and the indiscriminate use of power. However, too often the gendering of the cosmic structures legitimated the self-serving use of male power over women and slaves, whose personal worth was often deemed of little value and whose moral and social inferiority did not merit the *amicitia* which could only flourish among male cadres. The symbolic matrix which juxtaposed God-Christ-Man to Soul-Church-Woman in spousal relationship created not simply a gendered cosmos, but a sexualised one. But it is distinguished from other 'holy marriages' in the fertility religions by its Neoplatonic bias. The fertility of the

Christian dispensation is spiritual. All erotic imagery disappears from the language of Augustine, and the ideal marriage imitates the heavenly one in its continence. On earth, mother church is in fact ruled by her earthly sons, the final sublimation of the reclamation of the mother.

Women, church and Graeco-Roman culture:
reprise

It is now appropriate to relate Augustine's beliefs and concerns to the wider social and ecclesial issues raised in Part II. By relating his prescriptions for social relations and female behaviour to the developments in the fourth-century church it is possible to demonstrate that his symbolic systems reinforced the structures they were drawn from, for practical consequences were not only recommended but implemented.

Marital relationships

The consequence of the doctrine of original sin meant that although Augustine himself taught that marriage was the fundamental building block of society, marital sex was irrevocably tainted by desire. To guard against the rule of sin, symbolised as female authority, Augustine returned rights to married men which they had lost in law. Marriage was redefined as a master–slave relationship and freeborn and freedwomen were metaphorically stripped of their status.

Because of their differential status, men and women cannot share the mutual friendship and enjoyment that exists between peers. The exception was the mutual conjugal debt that spouses owed to each other. Augustine's fidelity to this position meant that even sexually active marriages where there was no intention to have children were licit because concupiscence was confined within the fidelity of marriage.[1] It would be sinful, but not mortally so. But the dictum that unilateral withdrawal of conjugal rights by women meant that they were responsible for male adultery held serious physical consequences for women. In medieval church law not even danger of maternal death from repeated pregnancies was grounds for a woman refusing to sleep with her husband.[2] The focus here solely on male well-being is invidious, but also subtly insulting to the male character. The unexamined implication is that no man is capable of existing without sex, so that vulnerability to adultery, which Augustine called 'the male disease', is a spiritual danger more real and more serious than maternal death.[3] Because this position implies that their sexual drives must be fulfilled whatever the cost to others, it encourages in men the persistence of the infantile emotional demand for instant gratification.

Nevertheless the principles that conjugal rights were the one aspect of married life wherein there was mutual obligation, and that men should manifest the same standards of chastity which they expected of their wives was a decidedly Christian innovation, though not an Augustinian one. It was, however, a principle hon-oured more in the breach than in the observance, because the fathering of bastards with no legal rights did not disrupt either the *familia* or the state financially or politically.

One of the less tangible effects of Augustine's use of the feminine to symbolise concupiscence was the emotional confusion he created by the split between woman's status and lovability as human being and as wife. This is compounded by the split between pleasure and desire. Thus a man had to love his spouse, but preferably not her body, and both parties were permitted an ordinate sexual pleasure in conjugal relations as long as they were not motivated by desire. This is like saying it is acceptable to enjoy eating, but not to feel hungry. At least the ascetics were consistent in this, but for lesser mortals the consequence was a constant anxiety about the legitimacy of their physical needs and temporal concerns.

Outside the bedroom wives became possessions, more clearly defined as an extension of the male self; if the situation warranted it, a man had not only the authority but the obligation to beat his wife in the interests of domestic order.[4] In so structuring the marital distribution of power Augustine legitimated a situation where vio-lence of men to women became progressively more acceptable, and the definitions of order progressively more subjective.[5] The corollary of this was the control of female assertiveness through the discourse of Eve's pride. Any woman who exercised authority, who asserted any claim to autonomy, was vulnerable to condem-nation as proud, therefore insubordinate, therefore unchaste. There had surely been a strong cultural foundation for this edifice, but now desire and insubordination have entered the moral realm, and ancient perceptions of women as inferior are grounded in the creative decision of God to make them so. It is this nexus of pride and sexuality which blurs the boundaries Hunter wishes to draw between lust as sexual libido and lust for power, defined as 'arrogant pride', in his project to reclaim Augustine for contemporary thought. As Hunter himself acknowledges, this 'arrogant pride' was introduced by the first sin, which Augustine described as the *concep-*

tion of evil in the conceited heart of Eve. It was Eve's sin of pride
which flawed the foundations of the earthly city by introducing
concupiscence into the human heart and inscribing it on the sexed
body as uncontrollable sexual desire.[6] Pride and feminine desire are
united in a symbolic network that feminised the material, the physical, the irrational and the sinful to establish the physically or spiritually feminine as disorderly, proud, irrational and in the Christian
context sinful and heretical.[7]

Therefore, as the individual body must veil its genitals, so the
body politic veils its social equivalent. Ultimately, in the discourse
of the veil, woman became the *pudenda* of the ecclesial body. She
represented the shame-inducing sexual desire that resulted from
her sin, and which ever more tempted the human – read man –
away from God. Hence she must be veiled and silenced to protect
the honour of the church's head.[8] Her veil, far from being a trivial
cultural requirement, was the physical reality that signified the
separation of the sacred from the profane, the godly from the
ungodly, polluting desire from licit desire. Metaphorically speaking,
it veiled from the gaze of Christ and man the carnal concupiscence
which had so defaced the image of God in humanity. Man as
intermediary between God and woman connects her to Christ.

The sin of rape

Where Augustine did differ from cultural mores, and his perception
of women as incitement to desire, was his defence of Christian
women who had been raped. While Ambrose had seen it as ideal
that Christian women would commit suicide rather than risk rape
when arrested for trial during the persecutions, Augustine argued
that the sin was solely that of the perpetrator. Women were innocent before God and were not required to commit suicide to establish their chastity and their shame at being defiled. Indeed, why
should they bear a heavier penalty than their violators, who were
only exiled? 'If she is chaste, why slay her?' was his question. Indeed,
such suicide adds homicide to the crime of rape.[9] Roman mores
expected such a response to 'prove' that there was no blot on
the family's honour.[10] For Augustine rape was an ordeal, not base
corruption, because there was no passion on the woman's part to
cause it.[11] Though he assumed that even persons who experienced
forced sex, could not help feeling some pleasure, if a woman felt
pleasure unwillingly, she still remained chaste.[12] Where his focus
on the reproductive good of sexual activity did shape his thinking
was on the relative evil ascribed to female and male rape. Rape of
the female was less reprehensible for two reasons. First, the intercourse was 'natural' and open to procreative ends, and second, the

male body was closer to the image of God than the female body.[13] Augustine perceived the evil to be spiritual rather than physical, and women were taught that they may not lie to escape rape, though such a lie is less culpable than others.[14] To lie would violate the chastity of truth in the mind, which must be preserved at the expense of the body, for if the chastity of the soul is lost then the chastity of the body will soon follow. Where the soul is incorrupt, the body remains incorrupt, for the mind is more superior to the body than man's body is to woman's body.[15] This dualism could not appreciate the consequences of bodily violation, for the body itself is esteemed as of inferior value to the mind.

Augustine's exemplar was the story of Lot and the angelic visitors, and this hierarchy of values, reinforced by the value of hospitality, explained why Lot had offered his daughters rather than his guests to the mob.[16] In his later years, he judged that Lot's action was sinful, his judgement affected by fear, so he permitted a lesser evil to prevent a greater.[17] But Augustine's view was that he should have permitted neither. Despite this, Thomas Aquinas used Augustine's treatment of Lot to argue that it is permissible to do the lesser evil to prevent the greater. Nevertheless, Augustine's uncompromising stand on the innocence of the raped woman is a positive aspect of his thought which requires acknowledgment. It demonstrates that when his critical faculties were really engaged, as they were by pagan criticism of Christian women raped during the fall of Rome, he was capable of rejecting Roman custom and freeing women from the odium attached to their victimisation.[18] Sadly, the later culture informed by Christian tradition only partially realised his insights in social practice. Women were not required to commit suicide, but still bore the burden of proof to establish their chastity rather than the perpetrator's guilt.

Marriage as a master–slave relationship

Augustine was the first of the Fathers to include the sacramental bonding of the partners in the goods of marriage, and he established the groundwork for marriage to be given religious status.[19] The personal and spiritual bonding he understood as an aspect of marriage may not have seemed contradictory to his rhetoric of male headship, or perhaps even his master–slave rhetoric, in his own time. Ancient writers customarily used the imagery of father-daughter to express both the imbalance of power, the differences in ages and the affective dimension of marriage, but there is a great shift from daughter to slave status. However, men were also known to be capable of affectionate relationships with slaves, sometimes even freeing them to marry them. It is highly unlikely that Augustine would have expected real marriages to be alliances where women were literally treated as slaves, but the rhetoric can appear to justify such an interpretation, and he did justify the beating of an insubordinate wife.[20] Rather he would have envisaged that wise headship and humble subordination would have resulted in a harmonious relationship with strong affective ties which deepened as the marriage became less dependent on sexual desire and found its full fruit in marital continence.

The order of love dictates the nature of marital love. It predicates emotional, physical, social and spiritual need of married women and emotional, physical, social and spiritual independence of men. If such love is not based on mutuality, it cannot be fully life-enhancing for the subordinate partner.[21] It must be accepted that this theology of marriage has maintained women in dependent and often infantilising relationships.[22] From the perspective of an era in which feminism has only comparatively recently established gains for women's autonomy, and which is barely beginning to cope with the sexual abuse of women and children, neither a master–slave nor father–daughter model is acceptable for marriage.

Augustine himself divorced the definition of marriage from the biblical image of one flesh, because he needed to be able to exclude his concubinage through that image, and Ambrose had set him the precedent. It should be noted that this was one aspect of ascetic theology that orthodox tradition did not eventually accept. An unconsummated marriage has traditionally been grounds for annulment, and a marriage where sexual relations were impossible was not permitted within the Catholic church. Augustine's use of the spiritual marriage of Christ and church as the paradigm for real marriages turned the scriptural understanding on its head. The Ephesians text makes human marriage the paradigm for understanding the spiritual one, not the other way around. In a Jewish context, this would include sexual love and desire, as the Song of Songs attests. Indeed, it is notable that one aspect of his Ambrosian heritage that Augustine almost totally disregards is the former's reliance on the Song to explore the meaning of the virginal life. Augustine does not appeal to it to illuminate either Christian marriage, or Christian virginity. In his moral treatises there are only three citations. Two are used to describe the church as bride and one is to exhort the monks to seek Christ. None of the texts he used explicitly express desire.[23]

However, he does use the Song in sermons to elucidate the relationship of church and Jesus. In one sermon he argued that all believing Christians are caught up in the bride's desire for Christ. Those who are fervent in spirit and brilliant in doctrine are those in whom the church cleaves to Christ, who are led into the bed-chamber of the bride.[24] However, his consistent habit is to employ the Song to teach humble obedience, rather than the mutual desire of the spiritual spouses. There is no certainty about this bride's fidelity and so, from the time she comes seeking her beloved, her self-directed choice of love meets not with welcome but warnings of the harsh penalties of infidelity.

Nevertheless, despite his avoidance of erotic imagery, inherent in Augustine's view of sexuality as divinely created, in his teaching that even a childless but sexually active marriage is a true marriage, and in his perceptions of marital love as a sacramental bonding directed towards wholeness, is the possibility of a new perception of sexual relationships, where mutual love both creates and heals the 'one flesh', bringing it to perfection in God.[25] This aspect of his theology of marriage preserves his insights based on experience that loving partnerships bond in a deeper manner than those liaisons founded on sexual attraction only. The limits to his ability to transcend his culture meant that the only way he could see to preserve such a relationship from being corrupted by desire was to keep women subordinate and sexual relations to a minimum. But his insistence on the *caritas coniugalis* that bonds husband and wife offers fruitful possibilities for a contemporary theology of marriage. When a marriage is understood as a partnership of equals, it then expresses the full friendship of peers who can enjoy each other. Therefore marriage becomes a good in itself. It is not then dependent on procreation for its intrinsic value. Thus in a more qualified manner I would agree with van Bavel and Hunter that there is potential in the Augustinian concept of marital friendship for modern theologies of marriage, but these positive implications in his thought await development.

Asceticism and the demotion of cultural kinship systems

Augustine's ascetic agenda established élite standards of spirituality which harnessed honour–shame culture, androcentric in itself, in the interests of the church. In this way asceticism functioned to detach primary allegiances from Roman kinship systems and ascribed familial honour in favour of spiritual kinship and the achieved honour of the ascetic. Ambrose himself had pointed out that the martyrs, and their heirs the ascetics, were the new patricians, the new nobility.[26]

By demanding the freedom for young women and men to choose virginity, Augustine undermined the male headship and familial structures he supported so diligently elsewhere. The rights of God as the ultimate *paterfamilias* took precedence over the power of the earthly *paterfamilias* to dispose of his children in marriages which would enhance the *familia* economically, socially and politically.[27] This freedom had enormous social consequences and it was one that Augustine practised as well as preached.[28] The freedom to reject marriage was a giant step towards female autonomy, though often obscured by the androcentrism of the rhetoric and the episcopal attempts to curtail ascetic women's power. Ascetic renunciation not only opened the door for women to achieve personal status by heroic action but also for men to rise to ecclesial power who might otherwise have remained on the fringes of political power – Augustine being a case in point.

To achieve this, and to harness support for some of the genuinely revolutionary changes asceticism entailed, Augustine reassured those anxious about the changing order that fundamentally, apart from inserting the Christian *familia* as a higher good than the civic one, nothing would change. Even more, he cast his vision in rhetoric that appealed to sentimental and nostalgic Roman ideals when all women were chaste matrons and Roman public life was controlled by philosophically sophisticated patrician men devoted to the fatherland. The new Christian culture would be marked by a return to modest, submissive behaviour on the part of women, and dedicated commitment to the communal good on the part of men. It would be ruled by philosophically oriented Christian ascetic men, devoted to their heavenly fatherland.

In this world, a woman's obedience would become the criterion for her chastity and her husband's honour. If she achieved the virtuous life she was, by definition, achieving the virile life. Women who were prepared to forgo physical motherhood were elevated to masculine status, though attempts were made to exclude them from the public life of the church by constraining them in socially acceptable feminine roles. Hence their virile status merited them the role of 'brides of Christ' while male ascetics were 'friends of Christ' or 'soldiers of Christ'.[29] Human child-bearing was dishonoured in favour of the spiritual birth conferred by mother church, and mothers were demoted to 'stepmothers'. Augustine never likened a father's role to a 'stepfather's', though he did say that an unbaptised child with both parents living is more destitute and wretched than an orphan.[30]

Women and public life

Although the desire for greater social and ecclesial control of women had been evident as early as the apocryphal *Acts*, and was clearly on the agenda of the Synod of Elvira, Augustine's definitive identification of women with the purely temporal and their symbolic status as concupiscence gave added impetus to the exclusion of women from public life and clerical office. He himself provided an early example of the exclusion of women from clerical friendship and residence which entered canon law in later Synods. His intent that women hand over all their financial and business affairs to their husband's sole control would have closed another door to the public domain for those who adhered to his maxims.

However, when women are excluded from public life and public spaces, women's space becomes defined as private space, women's concerns become defined as private concerns – and concern for the private as opposed to the public was the criterion of sinful pride in Augustine's lexicon. The more fully love flourishes, the more concern will be for the communal good, the domain of Jesus.[31] Indeed, Markus has argued that 'privacy', self-enclosure, was the 'most insidious form of pride' in Augustine's mature thought.[32] If Markus is correct, then the confinement of women to the private life constructed their sphere of influence and their legitimate domestic concerns as inherently in tension with the public good and at least potentially sinful. Several cases have already been mentioned and it was a point Augustine hammered home in his sermons as well.[33] However, if the feminine is appropriately controlled by a male head, with its proper awareness of public values, then right order can be maintained by the grace of God within the Christian *domus* and ecclesia.[34]

The shift from ritual to moral impurity

Augustine's anthropology would also have given impetus to the demands for a celibate clergy because he shifted the emphasis from the classical concern with ritual purity to a concern with ontological and moral purity. This meant that the purity of the priest was doubly important. These concerns were especially significant when it came to women, for they were not only polluted by sexual fluids, but by child-bearing and menstruation. Following Philo and Ambrose, Augustine perpetuated the use of menstruation as a symbol of the worldly passion stemming from carnality. This unformed fluid represented the flood of chaos overflowing from an excess of matter, knowing neither boundary nor order. Free-floating shame attached to menstruation reinforced the extant cultural taboos, again moving from ritual to moral pollution. Women's bodies thus become a living locus of disorder and passion, unfit and unable to represent the Christ in liturgical ministry.

Augustine's construction of Christian identity

At the end of chapter 6 the categories of sacred and profane, pure
and impure, orthodox and heterodox, clean power and polluting
power were given content according to broad social developments
and questions of ecclesial identity and structure. How does Augustine's perception of gender fit against that broader background?
This study of Augustine's understanding of women and the feminine
reveals that it not only has implications for the status of women in
the church and in society but for the self-understanding of the
church, for it is constituted as feminine.[35] Although masculine as
the total people of God, the ontological purity which that implies
can never be realised on earth, and so for Augustine the focus tends
to be on the internal dynamics of the church as body of Christ in
subjection to its head. What the imagination supplies is a feminine
image, head and all. But Christ is the church's head as man is
woman's. Metaphorically speaking, the church and woman are
'headless', unless under male control. And as Ambrose told his
catechumens, there is nothing more dishonourable or ignoble than
a headless corpse. It is in fact lifeless, for all human and spiritual
essence resides in the head.[36]

The femininity of the church conveys its ambiguous standing as
the temporal connection between eternal Wisdom ascended to
heaven and the created world. As for the other Latin Fathers, the
church is the virgin bride, but for Augustine its role as virgin
mother takes the foreground. As virginal mother the church is the
only authentic mother on earth, for it offers the only true birth
which he could acknowledge.[37] The waters of the font supersede
the waters of the womb, its catechumenate supersedes a mother's
milk, and it confers life where human mothers confer death.[38] The
focus on its maternal role diminishes the aspect of the holy marriage
which is only brought to the fore when Augustine needs to explain
the dynamics of human power in inter- and intra-personal relationships. Thus the spiritual birth is sacred and pure, the physical is
profane and polluted. Spiritual marriage is more sacred and totally
pure, but carnal marriage has lost its pristine purity since the Fall.
Like the human heart and the curate's egg, it is good in parts.

Both spiritually and carnally, clean power is masculine and feminine power in any aspect is polluting. Mirroring social relations,
masculine power is symbolised as that of the patriarchal husband.
In a dynamic analogous to biofeedback, husbands provided the
metaphor for Christ as spouse to the church, an intrinsically
unequal relationship, which then becomes the model for husband
as spouse of woman, soul as spouse of body and mind as spouse of
knowledge. The imagery also works conversely. If the good woman

is a loving slave to her husband, so the church is the humble and obedient slave of its spouse. This may seem quite appropriate when humanity is espoused to divinity, yet it trivialises the Incarnation in which God freely chose to relate to humanity as a human being, and it alters free human co-operation with the divine will to the coerced obedience of the slave. In his later years, Augustine would had seen this as perfectly acceptable. The Donatist controversy had seen him change his attitude about imperial intervention in church controversy. He came to accept physical coercion to orthodoxy as preferable to the soul's eternal damnation for heresy.

The virginal bride-mother is the core symbol of ecclesiology for Augustine and it is the one which mediates all other ecclesial relations. The bishop is temporal 'head' or 'spouse' of his church, *in loco Christi*. All the faithful are feminised in relation to their bishop, to whom they metaphorically owe the obedience of the slave.[39] The power of the bishop is clean spiritual power, all other civil power is suspect, and female sexual power is both ritually and spiritually polluted.

The church as virgin bride represents the incandescent holiness of the chaste and virile soul, but the temporal reality of sexual activity means that there are degrees of holiness within its body. The church's consecrated virgins are the living symbol of the purity to which the church is called, their spiritual activity and progress the fruit of the church's spiritual fecundity. By rejection of their sexual relationships these women wielded the clean power of virility, but under the stern and watchful eye of their spouse and his proxy, the bishop. Augustine's doctrine of original sin, and his ascetic hierarchy of virtue means that wives and mothers cannot be living symbols of the church as mother. Rather they stand in antithesis to it as the daughters of Eve and the mothers of death.

For Augustine, the church is a field wherein the weeds grow with the wheat. The Donatist controversy and his experience of graced redemption led him to perceive the church as a hospital for sinners, not a community of impregnable purity. Therefore the virginal heart rather than the virginal body provided a more appropriate core symbol for Augustine, as it is less absolute than the hymen.[40] The virgins may be closer to the sacred and the sexually active more profane, but still, all the orthodox are within the church and to a greater or lesser degree holy in mind and body. Those who are not reborn of mother church are the truly profane. Those whom Augustine defined as heterodox were not profane but damned.

Conclusion

Brown has concluded that in matters sexual, Augustine became the 'sorcerer's apprentice', who canonised the unconscious fears and prejudices of the average man in order to convert him to the ascetic viewpoint.[41] This conclusion leaves unexamined just why the unconscious fears and prejudices of the average man would lead him to fear women, who were defined as his social and spiritual inferiors. The anthropologist George Devereux argued that the source of such fears and prejudices was not in the individual psyche but in the need for male social hierarchies to protect their own interests.

> The innumerable 'invidious' restrictions imposed upon women and slaves clearly indicate where genuine as distinct from fantasised and spurious, power really rests: in women, who *propagate* the species, and in the masses, who *are* the species. Were they less powerful, the owners of spurious and infantile power would not find it necessary to hem them in with innumerable and 'degrading' restrictions.[42]

With this swingeing attack Devereux reverses the patriarchal definitions of clean and polluting power to argue that real achievement and power is manifested in the feminine capacity to give birth. His comments about women and slaves are pertinent to cultures where power is held by a few, and predicated on the domination of others. Furthermore in a slave culture, the rebellion of the enslaved is a constant fear. Hence the constant rhetoric to inculcate subordination and fear of punishment for threatening communal order. Augustine could see the human injustice of slavery. One man should not have the right to own another, and in the paradisal world, he did not. It is puzzling that he should then construct marital relationships around that image. It would seem that the feminine pride Eve unleashed into the world meant that no woman would voluntarily keep her subordinate place, unless forced to do so. It is less surprising that Augustine used master–slave imagery for God and human beings, as God the creator and source of all life would have the right of ownership over all created beings.

Yet it still remains that a culture that was not established on slave labour could not think in these categories and would have had to find some other way to talk about being in relationship with God. Is it appropriate for a religious institution which claims the high moral ground in condemning social injustice, to continue to argue from traditions which assume slave culture as the proper context for male–female relations? In the case of Augustine, my research indicates that it was not simply individual fears and prejudices, but the archetypal symbolism of woman as interpreted by patriarchal culture that Augustine shaped, articulated and sanctioned.

It has become clear that women, sex, sin, shame and death are intimately connected within the matrix of meanings that constitute Augustine's writing on woman and the feminine. It has been imposs-ible to discuss his writings about women's nature and role without raising doctrinal issues such as original sin, free will and grace, the symbolic identity of the church and humanity's relationship to God. Thus questions of gender are not peripheral to 'mainstream theology'. This is consistent with the anthropological research which locates sexual meanings at the heart of cultural systems. Hence any theological or historical analyses of the early church which ignore gender analysis offer an impoverished theological understanding. There is a poignant irony in the fact that it was Augustine, the man who argued so powerfully, and eventually per-suasively, that sexuality belonged in Eden, who also made the desire to be loved by the beloved so suspect and so shameful, rendering it so tainted and dangerous that the erotic could never be permitted to symbolise the divine.

Notes

Chapter 1

1 *Con.*, 10. 27. *PL* 32. 795, Chadwick, p. 201.
2 *Gaudium et spes*, 60, *Vatican council II; the conciliar and post-conciliar documents*, ed. Austin Flannery (Dublin: Dominican Publications, 1975), p. 965; Pope John Paul II's Apostolic Letter *Mulieris dignatatem*, 10, *L'Osservatore Romano* (Eng.) 40, 3 (October 1988), p. 5.
3 The Broverman study revealed that health professionals assessed 'Healthy men' and 'healthy adults' by identical criteria. However, 'healthy women' were defined as more submissive, dependent, excitable, vain, vulnerable and subjective than men, while 'feminine' traits such as non-aggressive, less dominant, emotionally expressive, were not deemed well-being in the healthy adult, sex unspecified. Scarf draws the logical conclusion that to behave both as a 'healthy adult' and a 'healthy female adult' is a contradictory task for women. See Maggie Scarf, *Unfinished business: pressure points in the lives of women* (New York: Doubleday and Company Inc., 1980), pp. 359–65.
4 Peter Brown argues that Augustine's mind was so powerful that he himself, in large part, created the 'reality' which we now like to think his doctrines merely attempted to 'explain'. See 'Augustine and sexuality', *Colloquy* 46 (1983), p. 13.
5 Gedaliahu Stroumsa, ' "*Caro salutis cardo*": shaping the person in early Christian thought', *HR*, 30, 1 (1990), p. 31.
6 See my review of Peter Brown, 'Women, sex and sin: Peter Brown on early Christian attitudes to asceticism and sexuality', *Eureka Street* 1, 5 (June 1991), pp. 40–2, 44.
7 Sherry Ortner and Harriet Whitehead, *Sexual meanings: the cultural construction of gender and sexuality*, Cambridge: Cambridge University Press, 1981. See 'Introduction', esp. p. 21–4, 27. Jeffrey Weeks also adds the development of 'cultures of resistance': see *Sexuality and its discontents* (London: Routledge, 1985), p. 27. Cf. Victoria Goddard, 'Honour and shame: the control of women's sexuality and group identity in Naples' in P. Caplan, ed., *The cultural construction of sexuality* (London and New York: Tavistock Publishers, 1987), p. 196.
8 Hence 'heresies' are the opinions of competing groups: cf. R. A. Markus, *The end of ancient Christianity* (Cambridge: Cambridge University Press, [1990] 1993), p. 33.
9 Mary Douglas, *Purity and danger: an analysis of the concepts of pollution and*

taboo, London and New York: Ark Paperbacks, [1966] 1988; *Natural symbols: explorations in cosmology*, Middlesex: Penguin Education, [1970] 1973; *Risk and blame: essays in cultural theory*, London and New York: Routledge, 1992. Douglas's work has also been used to explore Christian texts by Ross S. Kraemer, who uses her 'group' and 'grid' paradigm to plot the connections between community structures and belief. See *Her share of the blessings: women's religions among pagans, Jews, and Christians in the Greco-Roman world*, New York: Oxford University Press, 1992.

10 Douglas, *Purity*, p. 115.

11 Douglas, *Natural symbols*, pp. xiii, xix; *Risk*, pp. 55–6.

12 Caplan, *Cultural construction*, p. 9. On gender as a prestige structure see Ortner and Whitehead, *Sexual Meanings*, pp. 6–24.

13 Douglas, *Purity*, p. 114.

14 Douglas, *Purity*, p. 94 in particular and ch. 6 *passim*.

15 Caplan, *Cultural construction*, p. 9; Douglas, *Purity*, pp. 56–7. See Athanasius, *Contra gentes*, 22.30; 28.1–4; 29.1. Text and trans. R. W. Thompson, pp. 61; 79.

16 Ortner and Whitehead, *Sexual meanings*, p. 26.

17 Early surveys were done by George H. Tavard, *Women in the Christian tradition*, London: University of Notre Dame Press, 1973; and Roger Gryson, *The ministry of women in the early church*, trans. Jean Laporte and Mary Louise Hall, Collegeville MN: The Liturgical Press, 1976. Kari Børresen provides an excellent survey of the literature, 'Women's studies of the Christian tradition', *Contemporary philosophy*, ed. Guttorm Fløistad (Dordrecht: Kluwer Academic Publishers, 1991), pp. 901–1001.

18 See Bibliography (p. 314) for major writing in this field, most notably by Peter Brown, who has done much to bring out the social implications of antique asceticism and of Augustine's work on sexual meanings; Robert Markus, for his work on the late antique church's articulation of its self-understanding; David Hunter, on the rise of asceticism in western Christianity; Elizabeth A. Clark, especially for her insights in her more recent work into the structuring of power through gendered symbolism in late antiquity; the posthumously published work of Kerstin Aspegren on the ideal of the male woman; Kari Elisabeth Børresen, for her systematic examination of Augustine's and Thomas Aquinas' writings on women under thematic headings, with a comparison of their anthropologies; C. E. McLeese, for her rhetorical analysis of *The good of marriage* and *Holy virginity* to determine whether Augustine's theology as found there can be called sexist; Gerald Bonner, Tarcisius van Bavel and Donald Burt, who along with McLeese offer various alternative views on the significance of Augustine's anthropology in evaluating marital affection and *amicitia*; Jean La Porte and F. Ellen Weaver, and more recently Edmund Hill, who maintain that Augustine's theoretical anthropology had no practical consequences for women; in the sphere of Roman social history, the work of Beryl Rawson on the Roman family and of Suzanne Dixon on the Roman mother; Aline Rousselle's researches on 'desire and the body in antiquity'; and Thomas Laqueur's history of the medical construction of sex and gender in late antiquity.

19 Roger L. Gould, *Transformations: growth and change in adult life*, New York: Simon and Schuster, 1978.

20 Melanie Klein, *The psychoanalysis of children*, ed. Ernest Jones, trans. Alix Strachey, London: Hogarth Press, 1950.
21 I wish to emphasise that a Freudian psychoanalytic model of sexual development is not presumed. I agree with Elizabeth A. Clark that the differing child-rearing practices in late antiquity make such a model most problematical. 'Theory and practice in late antique asceticism: Jerome, Chrysostom and Augustine', *JFSR*, 5, 2 (1989), p. 29.
22 Dorothy Dinnerstein, *The rocking of the cradle and the ruling of the world*, London: Souvenir Press, 1978.
23 E. Neumann, *The great mother: an analysis of the archetype*, trans. Ralph Manheim, Princeton NJ: Princeton University Press, 1963.
24 Joanne Stroud and Gail Thomas, eds., *Images of the Untouched*, Dallas, Tex.: Spring Publications Inc., 1982.
25 Neumann, *Great mother*, p. 13. For critique see Naomi Goldenberg, 'Archetypal theory and the separation of mind and body: reason enough to turn to Freud', *JFSR*, 1, 1 (Spring 1985), pp. 55–72.
26 Carl Jung, *Man and his symbols* (London: Aldus Books [1964], 1979), pp. 47, 69–82.

Chapter 2

1 See Thomas Laqueur's excellent study, 'Organism, generation and the politics of reproductive biology', *Representations*, 14 (1986), pp. 1–41.
2 Although there were specific Gnostic sects, echoes of Gnosticism are found in Platonic texts, Jewish texts and 'orthodox' Christian texts. It had certain affinities with the Manichaean religion which strongly influenced the young Augustine and which, some scholars assert, maintained some influence on his thought even after he consciously rejected its doctrinal tenets. Those affinities centred on the antithesis between spirit and matter, the rejection of sexual intimacy, and hierarchical levels of holiness.
3 I confine my perspective to that of First World feminist theology.
4 Heije Faber, *Psychology of religion* (London: SCM Press, 1976), p. 281; Tissa Balasuriya, 'Women in the church', *Commonweal* (16 January 1976), p. 41. Traditional scholars such as W. Oddie agree: *What will happen to God? feminism and the reconstruction of Christian belief*, London; SPCK, 1984.
5 Sheila Briggs, 'Women and religion' in *Analyzing gender: a handbook of social science research*, eds. Beth B. Hess and Myra Marx Ferree (California: Sage Publications, 1987), p. 414; Faber, *Psychology*, p. 281. This is inconsistent with the fact that church membership and attendance in all mainstream churches is predominantly female, and that, in 1988, women received over one third of all degrees and diplomas conferred by the Melbourne College of Divinity.
6 Also noted by C. E. McLeese, *Augustine and sexism: interpretation and evaluation of* The good of marriage *and* Holy virginity, unpublished thesis, Université de Montréal, 1994.
7 *Con.*, 1.6; 6.14; cf. 2. 3. *PL* 32. 655; 751; cf. 678; P-C, pp. 26, 131; cf. 46.) Lewis and Short, *A Latin dictionary*, define *muliercula* as mere woman, little woman or common working girl. G. Bonner, 'Augustine's attitude to women and *amicitia*' in *Homo spiritalis: Festgabe für Luc Verheijin*, ed. Cornelius Mayer and Karl H. Chelius (Würzburg: Augustinus Verlag, 1987), p. 269, and Edward B. Pusey, *Con.* 1. 6 ([GB 18, p. 3a;) translate

muliercula as 'weak woman', although in 6.14, Pine-Coffin, Pusey and Watts all translate it simply as 'wives'. The translators either perceive the terms 'weak woman', 'mere woman' and 'wife' as synonymous, or they change the text to avoid giving offence to modern sensibilities, which masks attitudes which the text conveys.

8   *Ep.* 48. 2. *PL* 33. 188, WAA 6, p. 183.

9   *De trin.*, 8. 6. 9; 9. 6. 11. *PL* 42. 955–6; 966–7, WAA 7 pp. 211–15; 232.

10 As we shall see, Augustine does include women in the category *homo*. But Philo does not include them in the equivalent Greek category of ἄνθρωπος. See Dorothy Sly, *Philo's perceptions of woman* (Atlanta: Scholars Press, 1990). pp. 59–70.

11 Concerning Christian women, see Bernadette J. Brooten, 'Early Christian women and their cultural context: issues of method in historical reconstruction' in *Feminist perspectives on biblical scholarship*, ed. Adela Yarbro Collins (Chico, Calfornia: Scholar's Press, 1985), pp. 67, 70.

12 See Jo Ann McNamara, 'Muffled voices: the lives of consecrated women in the fourth century' in *Medieval religious women*, Vol. 1, eds. John A. Nichols and Lillian Thomas Shank (Kalamazoo: Cistercian Publications, 1984), p. 12; and Rosemary Rader, *Breaking boundaries: male/female friendship in early Christian communities* (New York: Paulist Press, 1983), pp. 111–12.

13 Cf. Elizabeth A. Clark, ed., *Ascetic piety and women's faith: essays on late ancient Christianity*, Studies in women and religion 20. (Lewiston, Queenstown: Edwin Mellen Press, 1986), p. 47, on Marcella, a scripture scholar of repute.

14 *Ep.* 130. 16. 31; cf. 130. 1. 1; 130. 10. 19. *PL* 33. 507, 494; 501; WAA 13, pp. 165; 156; 142.)

15 'Peregrinatio', *CSEL* 39, trans. and ed. Patricia Wilson-Kastner, 'Egeria's pilgrimage' in *A lost tradition: women writers of the early Christian Church*, Lanham: University Press of America, 1981. This question is taken up in detail in Part II.

16 Ernst Fortin, 'Reflections on the proper way to read Augustine the theologian', *AS*, 2 (1971), p. 260.

17 So Roland J. Teske, '*Spirituales* and spiritual interpretation in Augustine', *AS*, 15 (1984), pp. 74–7.

18 *Con.*, 1. 16. *PL* 32. 672, P-C, p. 37.

19 One exemplar is Graham Gould, 'Women in the writings of the Fathers: language belief and reality' in W. J. Shiels and Diana Wood, eds., *Women in the Church* (Oxford: Basil Blackwell, 1990), pp. 1–13.

20 R. J. O'Connell warns of trivialising problems in interpreting Augustine as 'momentary extravagances of language'. See *The Confessions of St Augustine: the odyssey of a soul* (Cambridge Mass.: Belknap Press, 1969), pp. 179–80.

21 Augustine, *De ord.*, 2. 13. 38. *PL* 32.1013, FC 5, p. 315. On the significance of rhetorical imagery see Paul de Man's 'Introduction' to Hans Robert Jauss, *Towards an aesthetic of reception* (Brighton, Sussex: The Harvester Press Ltd, 1982), p. xx. On Augustine and rhetoric see M. O'Rourke Boyle, 'Augustine in the garden of Zeus: love, lust and language', *HTR*, 83, 2 (1990), pp. 118–19.

22 *Tract. in Ioh. ev.*, 124. 8. *PL* 35.1976, PNF 1/7, p. 452b.

23 See Alberto Pincherle, 'The Confessions of St Augustine: a reappraisal',

AS, 7 (1976), p. 131; Richard Fenn, 'Magic in language and ritual: notes on Augustine's Confessions', *JSSR*, 25, 1 (March 1986), p. 80.

24 I am dependent here on Pamela Bright, 'The Scriptures as firmament: the multivalency of truth in Books 12 and 13 of the *Confessions*', *NAPS*, Chicago, May 1994.

25 *Con*. 1. 1, 4–5. *PL* 32.659–663, P-C, p. 21–25. The questions I ask of the text in the following section were drawn from the categories used by Paul Ricoeur, 'Philosophical hermeneutics and theological hermeneutics: ideology, utopia and faith', *Colloquy* 17 (1975), pp. 1–28.

26 *Con*., 1. 1. *PL* 32. 661, P-C, p. 21.

27 *Con*., 2. 3. *PL* 32. 678, P-C, p. 45. See Pincherle, 'The Confessions', p. 124.

28 *Contra litt. Pet*., 3. 16. 19. *PL* 43. 357, PNF 1/4, p. 604a; *Contra Cresc.*, 3. 80. 92. *PL* 43.545. See Peter Brown, *Augustine of Hippo: a biography* (Berkeley: University of California Press, 1969).

29 Paula Fredriksen sees Augustine as claiming the Pauline tradition for Catholicism against the Manichees in a radical way through hs autobiographical exegesis. See 'Paul and Augustine: conversion narratives, orthodox traditions and the retrospective self', *JTS*, n.s. 37/1 (April 1986), p. 24.

30 Cf. Ricoeur on the Hebrew Scriptures, 'Philosophical hermeneutics', p. 10. E. Clark's observations on narrative form as a means to construct an ideological position are also relevant here: 'Ideology, history and the construction of "woman" in late ancient Christianity', *JECS*, 2, 2 (1994), pp. 162–5, 172–8.

31 It also allows Augustine to develop implicit parallels with Scripture. Like the biblical narrator, he hinges his story upon a specific event which encapsulates the meaning of the experience of deliverance and offers the interpretive key to the whole. Ricoeur, 'Philosophical hermeneutics', p. 10, terms this experience the 'kernel event'.

32 *Con*., 8. 6–7. *PL* 32. 754–7, P-C, pp. 167–9.

33 Cf. Lonnie D. Kliever on autobiography as parable: 'Confessions of unbelief: in quest of the vital life', *JSSR*, 25, 1 (March 1986), p. 107.

34 *Con*., 8. 1; 9. 1; 10. 1. *PL* 32. 749; 763; 779, P-C, pp. 157; 181; 207. Fredriksen pursues this question, 'Paul and Augustine', pp. 3–24. Andrew Hamilton concluded that Augustine's honesty in the *Confessiones* strengthens the reader's conviction that his interpretation of the meaning of his life is subjectively correct. See 'The Confessions: autobiographical theology', *Colloquium*, 17, 1 (1984), p. 38.

35 See Pincherle, 'The Confessions', p. 119; and Fredriksen, 'Paul and Augustine', p. 21, on the differing accounts.

36 Therefore, Eric Osborn misses the mark in his contention that childhood events with a strong emotive content in the *Confessiones* may be discounted. See *Ethical patterns in early Christian thought* (Cambridge: Cambridge University Press, 1976), p. 145.

37 Including Augustine's relationship with God the Father. This is explored in both Fenn, 'Magic in language', pp. 77–91, and James E. Dittes, 'Augustine: search for a fail-safe God to trust' in *JSSR*, 25, 1 (March 1986), pp. 57–63.

38 John C. Cooper 'The basic philosophical and theological notions of Augustine', *AS*, 15 (1984), p. 93.

39   Fredriksen, 'Paul and Augustine', p. 24.
40   Ricoeur, 'Philosophical hermeneutics', p. 12. Ricoeur points out that fiction and poetry as well as objective history have the power to create a world that embraces and explores the projection of our own 'utmost possibilities'.
41   *Con.*, 4. 6; 4. 7; 4. 10; 4. 12; 9. 12. *PL* 32. 697; 698; 699; 700; 776, P-C, pp. 77; 78; 80; 82; 200–1. Several secondary themes appear in this world-view. Cf. Pincherle, 'Confessions', pp. 124–9.

Chapter 3

1   The Hexameral literature is an excellent source of the integration of Scripture and philosophy.
2   Plato, *Republic*, IV.441. GB 7, p. 353.
3   Douglas, *Risk*, pp. 104–6.
4   Valuable sources of primary material on Roman social relations are found in Jo-Ann Shelton, ed., *As the Romans did: a source book in Roman social history*, New York: Oxford University Press, 1988, and Mary R. Lefkowitz and Maureen B. Fant, *Women's life in Greece and Rome: a source book in translation*, Baltimore: Johns Hopkins University Press, 1982.
5   Jane Gardner, *Women in Roman law and society* (London: Routledge, [1986] 1990), p. 11.
6   In this sense, Christ is the 'head' of man, as man is the head of woman. Eve born from Adam is the scriptural expression of the belief.
7   Cf. Ortner and Whitehead, *Sexual meanings*, esp. pp. 21–4.
8   Trans. James Donaldson in *Woman: her position and influence in ancient Greece and Rome, and among the early Christians* (Frankfurt/Main: Minerva Verlag GMBH, [1907] 1984), p. 126.
9   Judith Evans Grubbs, 'Constantine and the imperial legislation on the family' in Jill Harries and Ian Wood, eds., *The Theodosian Code: studies in the imperial law of late antiquity* (London: Duckworth, 1993), pp. 137–9.
10 *The constitutions of the Apostles*, I. II. 7–I. III. 10. *ANF* 7, pp. 393b–5b. Aspegren traces the classical ideals and demonstrates how they were incorporated into Christian thought in Kerstin Aspegren (ed. René Kieffer), *The male woman: a feminine ideal in the early church*, Stockholm: Almquist and Wiksell, 1990.
11 *Codex Theodosianus* 9.7.1 of 326 CE, discussed by Grubbs, 'Constantine', p. 137.
12 Plutarch suggested that a wife should see respect for herself in her husband's taking a mistress for debauchery. See Lefkowitz and Fant, n. 16, p. 156. Cf. Ambrose, *Cain* 1. 4. 14–1. 5. 19. *CSEL* 32/1, pp. 348–57, FC 42, p. 370–7.
13 Suzanne Dixon, *The Roman mother* (London and Sydney: Croom Helm Ltd, 1988), p. 8.
14 Dixon, *Roman mother*, pp. 41–70.
15 Suzanne Dixon, 'The sentimental ideal of the Roman family', in B. Rawson, ed., *Marriage, divorce and children in ancient Rome* (Oxford: Clarendon Press, 1991), pp. 99–113.
16 There is still debate about exactly how to define the 'family' in Roman antiquity. It was a legal construct, not defined by blood kinship. Cf. Beryl Rawson, 'The Roman family' in *The family in ancient Rome: new perspectives* (London and Sydney: Croom Helm Ltd, 1986), *passim*.

17 Keith R. Bradley, 'Wet nursing at Rome: a study in social relationships' in *The family in ancient Rome*, pp. 214–16.

18 K. Power surveys the medical assumptions about the nature and causes of gender in 'Godly men and medicine', *Woman-Church*, 15 (Spring 1994), pp. 27–30.

19 For Roman law and Jerome see Antti Arjava, 'Jerome and women', *Arctos, separatum expressum*, XXIII (1989), p. 9. For Ambrose, see *Hexameron*, 5. 7. 18. *Opera omnia di Sant' Ambrogio*, Vol. 1. [*OO* I], ed. G. Banterle (Milan. Biblioteca Ambrosiana, 1979), p. 260, FC 42, p. 173. For Augustine, see below, Part III.

20 *Con.*, 1. 6. PL 32. 664, P-C, p. 25.

21 *Con.*, 1. 14. PL 32. 671, P-C, p. 35.

22 P. Garnsey, and R. Saller, *The Roman empire: economy, society and culture* (Berkeley and Los Angeles: Duckworth and Son Inc., 1987), pp. 130–1.

23 Gardner, *Roman law*, pp. 11–14, 45.

24 Ulpian, *Rules*, 11. 1, 21, 27–8. See Shelton, *Romans*, p. 34.

25 Dixon, *Roman mother*, pp. 72, 89.

26 Gardner, *Roman law*, pp. 6; 156–8.

27 Garnsey and Saller, *Empire*, p. 132.

28 P. Brown states that young women could face widowhood for up to forty years: see *The body and society: men, women and sexual renunciation in early Christianity* (New York: Columbia University Press, 1988), p. 148.

29 Karen Jo Torjesen, *When women were priests: women's leadership in the early church and the scandal of their subordination in the rise of Christianity* (HarperSanFrancisco 1993), pp. 120–8.

30 Although to bequeath her estate away from her children would have incurred social disapproval. See Dixon, *Roman mother*, p. 211 and *passim*.

31 Ambrose, *De excessu fratris Satyri*, 2.15. PL 16. 1376, PNF 2/10, p. 176 A; *Hexameron*, 5. 18. *OO* I, p. 260, FC 42, p. 174.

32 *Con.*, 3. 4. PL 32. P-C, p. 59.

33 Dixon, *Roman mother*, pp. 6–7.

34 Dixon, *Roman mother*, p. 194. Certainly Monica will be seen to do all three.

35 Dixon, *Roman mother*, p. 143.

36 Dixon, *Roman mother*, pp. 216–17.

37 *Con.*, 2. 3; 1. 9; 8. 12. PL 32. 677; 667; 762, P-C, pp. 45; 30; 178–9.

38 Rawson, 'Roman family', pp. 25, 51 note 69. Cf. Mary Beard, 'The sexual status of the Vestal virgins', *JRS* (1980–81), pp. 12–27.

39 Gryson, *The ministry of women*, p. 113. Gryson's arguments in the Christian context apply equally well to classical society. Cf. Torjesen, *Women priests*, pp. 167–8 on Livy.

40 Garnsey and Saller, *Empire*, p. 131.

41 Dixon, *Roman mother*, p. 9.

42 James A. Brundage, *Law, sex and Christian society in medieval Europe* (Chicago: University of Chicago Press, 1987), pp. 33–5.

43 Dixon, *Roman mother*, pp. 213, 180.

44 To mourn with abandon was the lot of the bereft mother. See Dixon, *Roman mother*, pp. 4, 200–1. Cf. Ambrose, *De excessu fratris Satyri*, 2. 12. PL 16. 1376 A, PNF 2/10, pp. 175b–6a.

45 *Con.*, 5. 8. PL 32. 713, P-C, p. 101.

46   Dixon, *Roman mother*, pp. 192–202. Cf. the interchanges between Monica and Augustine at Cassiciacum. See pp. 87–9.
47   *Con.*, 1. 11. *PL* 32. 669. P-C, p. 32.
48   Dixon, *Roman mother*, pp. 172–3.
49   *Con.*, 2. 3. *PL* 32. 677, P-C, p. 45.
50   Aline Rousselle, *Porneia: on desire and the body in antiquity*, trans. F. Pheasant (Oxford: Basil Blackwell, 1988), p. 63.
51   Gardner, *Roman law*, p. 46.
52   Rousselle, *Porneia*, pp. 34, 101. However, the Synod of Elvira in Canon 65 prescribed that if the wife of a cleric commits adultery and he, knowing this, does not dismiss her, then he shall not receive communion, even on his death bed, for it would seem as if the community's models should seem to collude in sin. Canon 70 prescribes that a layman in the same situation may receive communion after ten years. See Samuel Laeuchli, *Power and Sexuality: the emergence of canon law at the Synod of Elvira* (Philadelphia: Temple University Press, 1972), pp. 133, 124.
53   Dixon, *Roman mother*, pp. 72, 85, 94, 101 note 23.
54   Aristotle, *History of animals*, 7.1. This was one belief that Greek and Roman doctors shared about nubile females.
55   Rousselle, *Porneia*, pp. 59–69.
56   Rousselle, *Porneia*, pp. 72–3. Some doctors held that virginity inflamed desire.
57   Dixon, *Roman mother*, p. 62.
58   Rousselle, *Porneia*, p. 55.
59   Rawson, *Roman family*, p. 27.
60   Thomas Laqueur, *Making sex: body and gender from the Greeks to Freud* (Cambridge: Harvard University Press, 1990), pp. 25–62.
61   Brown, *Body and society*, p. 24.
62   CIL 6. 1527, 31670 (ILS 8393) in Shelton, *Romans*, pp. 293–6, indicates the scope of this woman's activities as a valued partner to her husband.

Chapter 4

1   Justin's *Apologies* and other writings are translated in ANF 1, pp. 159–302. The assimilation of the classical doctrines of the Λόγος is treated by Ragnar Holte in his excellent article, 'Logos spermatikos: Christian and ancient philosophies according to St Justin's Apologies', trans. Tina Pierce, *Studia theologica*, XII (1958), pp. 109–68.
2   Jerome, *Ep.* 70. 3. *PL* 22. 667, PNF 2/6, p. 150a. On the influence of Philo on the Christian tradition see David T. Runia, *Philo in early Christian literature: a survey*, Minneapolis: Fortress Press, 1993; On Philo's understanding of gender see Sly, *Philo's perceptions*.
3   Ambrose, *Hexameron*, 1. 1. 1–3; 1. 3. 11; 1. 6. 22; 1. 7. 25–7 *OO* I, pp. 24–6; 34; 54–8. Cf. Basil of Caesarea, *Hexameron*, I. 7. *PG* 29. 18. PNF 2/8, pp. 55b–6a.
4   Jerome lists seventeen Christian authors who interweave the Scriptures with the doctrines and maxims of the philosophers in their books, *Epistola* 70. 4. *PL* 23. 667, PNF 2/6: 150a–51a.
5   See *Civ. Dei*, 10. 2. *PL* 41. 279–80, GB 18, pp. 299b–300a; *De trin.*, 13. 4. 7; 13. 5. 8; 14. 9. 12; 14. 19. 26. *PL* 42. 1019; 1046; 1056–58, WAA 7, pp. 316; 317; 359; 375. The secondary literature is voluminous. Examples are R. J. O'Connell, *Augustine's early theory of man: A.D. 386–391*

(Cambridge, Mass: Belknap Press, 1969), for Augustine's dependence on Plotinus; Marcia Colish, *The Stoic tradition from antiquity to the early middle ages: II, Stoicism in Christian Latin thought through the sixth century* (Leiden: E. J. Brill, 1985), p. 156 and pp. 144–62, for Stoic influence; William Alexander, 'Sex and philosophy in St Augustine', *AS*, 5 (1974), pp. 197–208.

6   *Civ. Dei.*, 14. 9. *PL* 41. 413, GB 18, p. 391b.

7   *Con.*, 7. 9. *PL* 32. 740, P-C, p. 144.

8   See discussion on the Neoplatonic origins of Augustine's concept of the hypostatic union in Kari E. Børresen, *Subordination and equivalence: the nature and role of women in Augustine and Thomas Aquinas* (Washington: University Press of America, 1981), p. 24.

9   *Con.*, 7. 9–10. *PL* 32. 740–42, P-C, p. 144; 146–7.

10 Henry Chadwick, 'The role of the bishop in ancient society', *Colloquy* 35 (1980), p. 7.

11 Peter Brown, 'The philosopher and society in late antique culture', *Colloquy* 34 (1980), pp. 6–7. Also Rader, *Breaking boundaries*, p. 14, on the equivalence of the '*vir sapiens*' and the Christian religious man.

12 Brown, 'The philosopher and society', p. 1. Cf. A. Henricks, 'Response to Peter Brown', *Colloquy* 34 (1980), p. 29.

13 M. Shepherd, 'Response', *Colloquy* 34 (1980), p. 27.

14 Brown, 'The philosopher and society', pp. 13–16, esp. p. 14.

15 *Con.*, 6. 14. *PL* 32. 731, P-C, pp. 130–1.

16 Brown, 'The philosopher and society', p. 16.

17 Chadwick, 'Role of the bishop', pp. 2–5, 8, 10. See below on changing ecclesial structures.

18 *Civ. Dei*, 19. 14–16. *PL* 41. 642–5, GB 18, pp. 520–2.

19 *Civ. Dei*, 12. 5; 12. 2. *PL* 41. 352–3; 350, GB 18, pp. 345a; 343b.

20 Origen, *In canticum canticorum*, 3. 13. 27. *SC* 376, p. 640. In cant. cant., 9. ACW 26, p. 223; Athanasius, *De Incarnatione*, 54. 11, Thomson, p. 269; Ambrose, *Hexameron*, 6. 8. 49. *OO* I, p. 394; Basil, *Hexameron*, 5. 6. *PG* 29, 106–12, PNF 2/8, p. 78.

21 Osborn, *Ethical patterns*, p. 182. Cf. Colish, *Stoic tradition*, pp. 219–20 on the *ordo amoris* as a transformation of the Stoic doctrine of virtue.

22 Cf. Chadwick, 'Role of the bishop', p. 14, and Peter Brown in his response, p. 18, discuss the tension between institutional authority and charismatic power in the bishop's role.

23 *Contra litteras Pet.*, 2. 73. 163–4; *PL* 43. 309-10; *Ep.* 185. 2–9. *PL* 33. 793-6, both in *Writings in connection with the Donatist controversy*, ed. M. Dods (Edinburgh: T. & T. Clark, 1872), pp. 342–3 and p. 486; *Ep.* 51. *PL* 33. 191–4, FC 12, p. 214; *De nupt. et con.*, 2. 3. 9. *PL* 44. 441–2, PNF 1/5, p. 286b; cf. *Ep.* 185, 2. 6–6. 21. *PL* 33. 794-802, WAA 13, p. 468.

24 Osborn, *Ethical patterns*, p. 182.

25 *De trin.*, 10. 5. 7. *PL* 42. 977, WAA 7, p. 250. Cf. Aristotle, *Politics*, 1. 13. [40] 1260a. GB 9, p. 454b.

26 *Civ. Dei*, 19. 14–15; *PL* 41. 642–4, GB 18, pp. 520b-1b. Aristotle, *Politics*, 1. 1. [5] 1252b. GB 9, p. 445b.

27 Aristotle was well aware of dissenting opinions: *Politics*, 1. 5., cf. 1. 3; GB 9, p. 447ab. Augustine, *De gen. ad litt.*, 11. 37. 50. *PL* 34. 450, ACW 42, p. 171.

28 *Civ. Dei*, 19. 15. *PL* 41. 644. GB 18, p. 521b.

29 *De gen. ad litt.*, 11. 37. 50. *PL* 34. 450, ACW 42, p. 171.

30 *De gen. ad litt.*, 11. 37. 50. *PL* 34. 450, ACW 42, p. 171. Cf. *Civ. Dei*, 19. 15. *PL* 41. 643–4, GB 18, p. 521ab.

31 Cf. Ambrose, *Hexameron*, 5. 7. 18. *OO* I, p. 260, FC 42, p. 174.

32 Cook and Herzman, *The medieval world view: an introduction* (New York: Oxford University Press, 1983), p. 31.

33 *De trin.*, 13. 19. 24. *PL* 42. 1034, WAA 7, p. 340.

34 Plato, *Republic*, 7. [514]-[518]. GB 7, pp. 388a-9b.

35 Plato, *Timaeus*, 69. GB 7, p. 466a.

36 *De trin.*, 14. 17. 23; *PL* 42. 1054, WAA 7, p. 372. *Civ. Dei*, 9. 17. *PL* 41. 271–2, GB 18, p. 295a. It is because the eternal and the temporal cannot 'hold intercourse' together that Jesus the mediator was needed.

37 *Con.*, 7. 10. *PL* 32. 742, P-C, p. 147.

38 *De cont.*, 9. 23; *PL* 40. 363, PNF 1/3 p. 388b; *Civ. Dei*, 19. 14. *PL* 41. 642–3, GB 18, p. 520b.

39 *De nupt. et con.*, 1. 9. 10. *PL* 44. 419, PNF 1/5, p. 267.

40 In Christian thought also; cf. Athanasius, *Contra gentes*, 39. 1–4. Thompson, p. 107.

41 *De bono con.*, 20. *PL* 40. 387, PNF 1/5, p. 407b-8a.

42 *Contra Iul.*, 4. 12. 59; 4. 15. 75; 5. 8. 33; 5. 9. 38. *PL* 44, 767; 776; 804; 807, FC35, pp. 217; 231–2; 277; 281–2. His inconsistent treatment of natural law is discussed by Colish, *Stoic tradition*, pp. 159, 167–8.

43 *De bono con.*, 20. *PL* 40. 387, PNF 1/5, p. 408a. The context may well have been a Christian man's right to keep a concubine, rather than outright polygamy.

44 *De nupt. et con.*, 1. 10. 9. *PL* 44. 419–20, PNF 1/5, p. 267.

45 *De bono con.*, 15. *PL* 40. 384, PNF 1/5, p. 406a.

46 *De nupt. et con.*, 1. 10. 9. *PL* 44. 419, PNF 1/5, p. 268.

47 *Civ. Dei*, 16. 38. *PL* 41. 517, GB 18, p. 466a.

48 *De bono con.*, 19. *PL* 40. 424–5, PNF 1/5, p. 407b. Colish, *Stoic tradition*, pp. 161–2, discusses Stoic influence on Augustine's treatment of patriarchal marriages in *Con.*, 3. 7. *PL* 32. 688, P-C, p. 63.

49 *De con. adult.*, 2. 8. 7. *PL* 40. 475, FC 27, p. 108–9. Men should be punished more severely, in fact, because of their superiority.

50 *De con. adult.*, 1. 6. 6. *PL* 40. 454–5, FC 27, p. 67. Augustine argues here against second marriages for women (after divorcing the first husband for adultery) on the grounds that all men are so inclined to adultery that the second husband will be just like the first.

51 *De con. adult.*, 1. 4. 4. *PL* 40. 453–4, FC 27, p. 65.

52 *Ep.* 262. *PL* 33. 1077–82, FC 32, pp. 261–9.

53 *De con. adult.*, 2. 10. 9. *PL* 40. 477, FC 27, p. 113.

54 *Serm.*, 9. 9. 12; 9. 3. 3; 132. 2. *PL* 38. 84; 77; 735.

55 Plato, *Symposium*, [208–209], GB 7, p. 166b.

56 Augustine, *De nupt. et con.*, 1. 13. 14; 1. 16. 18. *PL* 44. 422; 424, PNF1/5, pp. 269, 271; *De bono con.*, 18; *PL* 40. 386, PNF 1/5, p. 407b. *De con. adult.*, 12. 12. *PL* 40. 478, FC 27, p. 116. Cf. *Acts of Thomas*, ANF 8, p. 538ab.

57 *De nupt. et con.*, 1. 11. 12. *PL* 44. 420, PNF 1/5, p. 268.

58 *De bono con.*, 27–8. *PL* 40. 392–3, PNF 1/5, pp. 410b-11b.

59 *De bono con.*, 5. *PL* 40. 377, PNF 1/5, p. 401b.

60 Alexander, 'Sex and philosophy', pp. 198–9.

61 See Brundage, *Law*, pp. 12–21, for a survey of the sexual ethics of the various philosophic schools. Apart from the Cynics, they held that the wiser the man, the less importance he placed on sexual behaviour and feelings.

62 Plato, *Laws*, VIII. 838. GB 7, p. 737a.

63 Alexander, 'Sex and philosophy', pp. 198–9.

64 See Elizabeth Spelman, 'Woman as body: ancient and contemporary views', *FS*, 8, 1 (1982), pp. 109–31.

65 Plato, *Symposium*, [206] GB 7: 165A; Plotinus, *Third Ennead*, 5. 1; *Fourth Ennead*, 8. 2. GB 17: 101a; 202a.

66 H. Marrou, *St Augustine and his influence throughout the ages*, trans. P. Hepburn Scott (New York: Harper and Bros, 1957), p. 24.

67 See Brown, *Body and society*, pp. 7–8; 179–80.

68 Alexander, 'Sex and philosophy', p. 197–208.

69 *De nupt. et con.*, 1. 4. 5. *PL* 44. 415–16, PNF, 1/5, p. 265.

70 *Civ. Dei*, 14. 10. *PL* 41. 417, GB 18, p. 285b.

71 *De nupt. et con.*, 1. 13. 14–1. 14. 16; *PL* 44. 422–3, PNF, 1/5, pp. 269–71. *De sermo. dom. in monte*, 1. 15. 41. *PL* 34. 1250, WAA 8, p. 32.

72 Alexander, 'Sex and philosophy', p. 208.

73 *Civ. Dei*, 14. 16. *PL* 41. 425, GB 18, p. 390a. Cf. 1 Thess. 4.4.

74 *De bono con.*, 10; 31. *PL* 40. 381; 394, PNF 1/5, pp. 404, 412a.

75 Freedom from passion or feeling, insensibility, the Stoic principle of morals (Lewis & Short, p. 135).

76 Colish, *Stoic tradition*, pp. 221–5, compares Stoic and Augustinian treatments of ἀπάθεια.

77 Augustine defines *pathos* in *Civ. Dei*, 8. 17; 9. 4. *PL* 41. 242; 258–60, GB 18, pp. 276a; 287–8.

78 *Solil.*, 1. 10. 17; *PL* 32. 878, FC 5, p. 365. *De nupt. et concup.*, 1. 6. 7. *PL* 44. 412, PNF, 1/5, p. 266. and *passim* in Book 1; *Civ. Dei*, 14. 10. *PL* 41. 417, GB 18, p. 285.

79 Examples are: Irenaeus, *Adv. Hær.*, 4. 38. 4; *PG* 7. 1109, ANF 1, p. 522a. Clement of Alexandria, *Strom*, 4. 4; 6. 5. *PG* 8. 1231; PG 9. 258–64, ANF 2, pp. 410a–11b; 489a. See J. M. Hallman, 'The emotions of God in the theology of St Augustine', *RTAM*, LI (1984), p. 5. Hallman lists twelve early Fathers who held this concept 'Impassibility', *Encyclopaedia of early Christianity*, ed. Everett Ferguson, New York: Garland Publishing Co. 1990, pp. 458–9.

80 His mature writings on *apatheia* follow the Origenist controversy, which had anthropomorphism as one of its central issues. Cf. Elizabeth A. Clark, 'New perspectives on the Origenist controversy: human embodiment and ascetic strategies'. *CH*, 59 (June 1990), pp. 145–62.

81 *Civ. Dei*, 9. 5. *PL* 41. 260–1, GB 18, p. 289a.

82 *Tract. in Ioh. ev.*, 124. 5. *PL* 3. 1973, PNF 1/7, p. 449b.

83 *Civ. Dei*, 5. 9, *PL* 41. 149, GB 18, pp. 213–15 rejecting Cicero's arguments against this.

84 *Civ. Dei*, 15. 25; 22. 2; 21. 24; 14, 11. *PL* 41. 472; 753; 736–8; 418–19; GB 18, pp. 419a; 587; 577–9; 385b-6a.

85 *Civ. Dei*, 14. 7. *PL* 41. 410, GB 18, p. 381ab.

86 Origen, *In canticum canticorum*, Prologue, 2. *SC* 375, p. 105, ACW 26, p. 35.

87 Note on Jerome's Preface to Bk 4 of his *In Hieremiam. CCL* 74. 174

PNF 2/6, p. 499. Jerome condemned it as a Pelagian revival of Origenist doctrine.

88 *Civ. Dei*, 14. 9; 9. 5; *PL* 4 1. 413–17, 260. GB 18, p. 383a-4a; 288a-9a. *Tract. in Ioan. ev.*, 60. 3. *PL* 35. 1798, PNF 117, p. 309.

89 Creating an interesting paradox for Augustine which he does not address in *Civ. Dei*. God's *impassibilitas* is of a different order apparently to human *impassibilitas* during life on earth.

90 Irenaeus, *Adversus haereses*, 4. 38. 4. *PG* 7, 1109, ANF 1, p. 522a.

91 *Civ. Dei*, 14. 9; 9. 5. *PL* 41. 418–19; 260, GB 18, pp. 383b; 288a-9a.

92 In the blessed life love and joy remain, utterly directed to God. Cf. *Civ. Dei*, 14. 9. *PL* 41. 418–19, GB 18, pp. 384ab.

93 Lewis & Short, p. 1997.

94 Plato, *Timaeus*, 42 b-c. GB 7, p. 453.

95 Garnsey and Saller, *Empire*, chapter 6, 'The social hierarchy', pp. 107–25.

96 Viz. Ambrosiaster, Chrysostom and Diodore below.

Chapter 5

1 Brown argues that the demonic was to antiquity what viruses are to modernity; see *The world of late antiquity* (London: Thames and Hudson, 1971), p. 55.

2 Gordon J. Laing offers a valuable treatment of 'Roman religious survivals in Christianity', in John McNeill et al., eds., *Environmental factors in Christian history* (Port Washington NY: Kenuckat Press, 1970), pp. 72–90.

3 Useful and succinct introductions with ample primary sources are Everett Ferguson, 'Demons', and Frances Young, 'Atonement', *Encyclopedia of early Christianity*, Garland reference library of the humanities, Vol. 846 (New York: Garland Publishing, 1990), pp. 259–61 and 117.

4 Origen, *In canticum canticorum*, Prologue, *SC* 375, p. 105, ACW 26, pp. 34–5.

5 Paul's use of 'powers' is more neutral in Romans 8.38 (cf. Eph. 6.12). There they are simply part of a list of things, including life and death, angels and human rulers, which cannot keep us from Christ.

6 Stoics also had guardian angels.

7 Augustine reprimands those who claim that to venerate a tutelary deity of a city is not idolatry because it is not a god. Cf. *Serm.*, 62.10. *PL* 38. 421–2. PNF 1/6, p. 301b. Laing also shares my conclusions, 'Religious survivals', pp. 78–80.

8 Jacques Aubert presents the archaeological evidence in 'Threatened wombs: aspects of ancient uterine magic', *GRBS*, 30. 3 (Autumn 1989), pp. 439–40.

9 *Civ. Dei*, 10. 9–11. *PL* 41. 286–291, GB 18, p. 303–6. Some philosophers believed that demons could be used to purify souls.

10 *Civ. Dei*, 22. 8. *PL* 41. 759–71, GB 18, pp. 596b-7a.

11 *Civ. Dei*, 10. 11–12. *PL* 41. 291, GB 18, pp. 305b-6b.

12 Brown, *Late Antiquity*, pp. 53–4.

13 As *daemones* and women were also associated with tempestuous emotions, women's similar association would have strengthened the linkage between women and the demonic. See *Civ. Dei*, 9. 3. *PL*. 41. 258, GB 18, p. 286b.

14 Justin Martyr, *Apology I*, 5. 2–3 (29). ANF 1, p. 164. Cf. Eric Fuchs on the associations between sexuality and the sacred in *Sexual desire and love:*

origins and history of the Christian ethic of sexuality and marriage, trans. M. Daigle (Cambridge: James Clark & Co., 1983), p. 22.

15 Epiphanius *Panarion*, 79. 8. *PG* 42. 751–4, *Mænads*, p. 57. Cf. Genesis 3.12; cf. 1 Tim. 2.14; Tertullian, *De cultu feminarum*, 1. 1. 2 *PL* 1. 1417. FC 40, p. 118; Justin Martyr allied demonology and witchcraft; Nancy Van Vuuren, *The subversion of women as practised by churches, witch-hunters and other sexists* (Philadelphia: Westminster Press, 1973), p. 74.

16 Gregory the Great, *Ep.* 9. 106. *PL.* 77. 863–4. PNF 2/13, p. 26.

17 Aubert, 'Threatened wombs', p. 424.

18 On the taboos and superstitions surrounding childbirth, B. Rawson, 'Adult-child relationships', in *Marriage*, pp. 10–15.

19 According to Samuel Terrien, the Fathers adopted the post-exilic code of Judaism which was restrictive towards women: 'The numinous, the sacred and the holy in Scripture', *BTB*, XII, no. 4 (October 1982), p. 100. Certainly, Augustine cites Leviticus, *Quaest. in Hept.*, 3. 6. 4. *PL.* 34. 706. Judaic regulations of the third century are found in the *Niddah*, in Eugene J. Lipman, ed., *The Mishnah* (New York: Schocken Books, 1976), pp. 269, 284–96.

20 One such community is reflected in Eudokia's *The Life of St Cyprian of Antioch*, trans. G. Ronald Kastner in Wilson-Kastner *A lost tradition*.

21 R. Mortley, *Womanhood: the feminine in ancient Hellenism, Gnosticism, Christianity and Islam* (Sydney: Delacroix Press, 1981), p. 84.

22 For another historical perspective see J. Morris, *The lady was a bishop* (New York: The Macmillan Publishing Co., 1973), Appendix 1; also Aubert, 'Threatened wombs'. For a social science perspective see George Devereux, 'The psychology of feminine genital bleeding: an analysis of Mohave Indian puberty and menstrual rites', *IJP*, 21 (1950), p. 252; on Judaism see Leviticus 15.19–24; 18.19; 20.18 and also Terrien, 'Numinous', p. 99.

23 See Penelope Washbourne, 'Becoming woman: menstruation as a spiritual experience', in Carol P. Christ and Judith Plaskow, eds., *Womanspirit rising: a feminist reader in religion* (San Francisco: Harper and Row, 1979), p. 251. On ancient Judaism see Lipman, *The Mishnah*, pp. 269–70.

24 Aubert, 'Threatened wombs', pp. 431–5.

25 Rawson, 'Adult–child religion', p. 14.

26 *Civ. Dei*, 6. 9. *PL* 41. 487–8, GB 18, p. 239b-40a.

27 Except for some Byzantine depictions, such as the birth of Mary, in the crypt of the Church dedicated to Anna in Jerusalem.

28 *Quæst. in hept.*, 3. 40. *PL* 34. 694–5.

29 *Ep.* 167. 1.1; 166. 3.6; 166. 7. 18. *PL* 33. 733; 723; 728, WAA 14, pp. 318; 300–2. See chapters 12 and 13 for detailed discussion on original sin.

30 The *Ethiopic Didascalia* and the *Apostolic constitutions* both had to defend the right of menstruating women to participate in Eucharist. See David Brakke, 'The problematization of nocturnal emissions in early Christian Syria, Egypt and Gaul'. I am grateful to David for permitting me to see his prepublication MSS.

31 Dionysius of Alexandria, *Epistle to Bishop Basilides*, II. PNF 2/14, p. 600.

32 Dionysius of Alexandria, *Epistle to Bishop Basilides*, II. ANF 6, p. 96. Similarly Jerome, *Ep.* 48. *PL* 22. 505 and *Commentarium in Zachariam*, 3. 13. 1. *PL*. 25. 1517.

33 *Quaedam in semine quasi materialis informitas, quae formata corpus hominis*

redditura est, in significatione posita est vitae informis et inerudatae. Menstrua feminarum . . . significari per illam lex voluit animum sine disciplinae forma indecenter fluidum ac dissolutum (De bono con., 23. PL 40. 389, PNF 1/3, p. 409ab). PNF translates 'soul', but the text has *animum*, signifying mind rather than soul: see Augustine's distinction in De trin., 15. Prologue. PL 42. 1057, WStA 1/5, p. 395.

34　Cf. *Con.*, 7. 1. PL 32. 733, P-C p. 133–4.

35　*Con.*, 4. 16. Cf. 7. 1–15 *passim*. PL 32. 704–6; 733–44, P-C p. 88; cf. 133–50.

36　Philo, *Quod deterius potiori insidiari solet*, 9. 28; Yonge, p. 115A. Ambrose, *De virginitate*, 16. 100. OO 14/2 p. 80, trans. Callam, p. 49. Augustine, *Serm.*, 62. 7–8. PL 38. 420, PNF 1/6, p. 300a-1b.

37　Brown, *Body and society*, pp. 145–6.

38　John E. Lynch, 'Marriage and celibacy of the clergy, the discipline of the western church: an historico-canonical synopsis', *The Jurist*, 32 (1972), p. 26–9.

39　*Pace* Daniel Callam, 'Clerical continence in the fourth century: three papal decretals', *TS*, 41 (March 1980), pp. 48–50, who argues that the absolute celibacy demanded of clergy and upheld as the Christian ideal owed more to ascetic ideals than to notions of ritual impurity, although Pope Siricius appealed to that concept in his decretals on clerical celibacy.

40　Brown, *Body and society*, p. 146. More recently, Elizabeth A. Clark has discussed the function of the rhetoric of shame and the 'Gaze of God' in feminising men in the Christian community: 'Sex, shame and rhetoric: en-gendering early Christian ethics', *JAAR*, LIX, 2 (1990), pp. 221–45.

41　Tertullian, *De anima*, 27.5–6. CCL 2. 823, FC 10, p. 244. Cf. Rousselle, *Porneia*, pp. 15–20, 4; Brown, *Body and society*, p. 19.

42　So Brundage, *Law*, p. 53.

43　See my article, 'Body and gender in the Fathers of the church', *Proceedings: Hildegard of Bingen and the gendering of theology*, ed. Constant Mews, Clayton: Institute for the study of religion and theology, Monash University, 1995.

44　Brakke, 'Nocturnal emissions'.

45　*Serm.*, 205. 2; cf. 208.1; 210. 6, 9. PL 38–9. 1039; 1044–5; 1052. Brundage, *Law*, p. 67, Brown, *Body and society*, p. 149 on the prolonged periods of abstinence recommended for Christians. My thanks to Denis Minns for his insights on ritual purity.

46　See figure 4.1 in Brundage, *Law*, p. 162.

47　Canons 27 and 33 of the Synod of Elvira (Laeuchli, *Power and sexuality*, pp. 129–30). In like vein, the Synods of Carthage, 390 and 391, Council of Toledo, 397–400. See Lynch, 'Marriage', pp. 26–9.

48　*Apostolic canons*, 5 (6). PNF 2/14, p. 594.

49　Brundage, *Law*, p. 69.

50　It is necessary to understand that mandatory celibacy was not achieved for many centuries. Chalcedon in 451, Canon 14, permitted minor orders to marry. See Brundage, *Law*, pp. 11, 110.

51　Lynch, 'Marriage', pp. 20–9.

52　Brundage, *Law*, p. 70.

53　Brown, *Body and society*, pp. 146–7; Tertullian, *Exhortatio castitatis*, 13. 4. CCL 2, p. 1035, ANF 4, p. 58.

54 S. Perowne, *The Caesars' wives: above suspicion?* (London: Hodder and Stoughton, 1974), pp. 19–20. See Beard, 'Sexual status', on the Vestals.

55 W. K. Lacey, '*Patria potestas*' in Rawson, *The family*, pp. 126–9.

56 *The Martyrdom of Perpetua*, trans. Rosemary Rader in *A lost tradition*, pp. 11–12.

57 Rosemary Radford Ruether, *Womanguides: readings toward a feminist theology* (Boston: Beacon Press, 1985), pp. 85, 109, 138, 160. Cf. Eusebius on the word of God and the Christian emperor, #318 in J. Stevenson, ed., *A new Eusebius: documents illustrative of the history of the church to AD 337*, p. 391.

58 M. Miles, 'The evidence of our eyes: patristic studies and popular Christianity in the fourth century', *Studia Patristica*, XVIII, Vol. 1 (1985), p. 60.

59 See F. Cardman, 'The emperor's new clothes: Christ and Constantine' in G. Fagin, ed., *Above every name: the Lordship of Christ and social systems* (Wilmington: Michael Glazier, 1984), pp. 202–3.

60 Henrichs, 'Response to Peter Brown', p. 29.

61 *Ep.* 93. *PL* 33. 321, FC 18, p. 57.

62 Paul Keresztes, 'Constantine: called by divine providence' in *Studia Patristica*, XVIII, Vol. 1 (1985), pp. 48–51.

63 Markus, *End*, p. 89.

64 Eusebius, 'Oration of the tricennalia of Constantine', 2. 1–5 in *A New Eusebius*, p. 391. Cf. Augustine, Letter 10*. Divjak, J. *Lettres 1* 29** (Œuvres de St. Augustin, 46 B, 6 Série, Bibliotheque Augustinienne, Paris: Etudes Augustiniennes, 1987), pp. 167–82, esp. pp. 176–7.

65 Brown, *Late Antiquity*, p. 55.

66 For specific parallels see Laing, 'Religious survivals', pp. 78–80.

67 *Civ. Dei*, 8. 26–7. *PL* 41. 253–4, GB 18, pp. 284b–5b. On mediation see Peter Iver Kaufman, 'Augustine, martyrs and misery', *CH*, 63, 1 (March 1994), p. 7.

68 Brown, *Body and society*, p. 183; cf. *Augustine of Hippo: a biography* (Berkeley: University of Califoria Press, 1969) , p. 249, where he makes the point that this distinction is made architecturally, e.g. in liturgy, the virgins being separated from the laity by white marble balustrades.

69 Eudokia, *Cyprian*, trans. G. Ronald Kastner, *A lost tradition*, pp. 149–72.

70 Eudokia, *Cyprian*, Bk 1, p. 149.

71 Eudokia, *Cyprian*, Bk 2, p. 167.

72 In this attitude Eudokia is very close to Augustine who saw his conversion as a choice between continence and lust: *Con.*, 8. 11–12. *PL*. 32. 761–2, PC, pp. 176–7. Cf. Aspegren's study on the Apocryphal *Acts*, *Male woman*, pp. 115–42.

73 Eudokia, *Cyprian*, Bk 2, p. 164.

74 Eudokia, *Cyprian*, Bk 1, pp. 150–2.

75 Eudokia, *Cyprian*, Bk 2, pp. 164–6.

76 On the necessity to take or enlist the numinous, see Terrien, 'Numinous', p. 99.

77 Oddie, *What will happen to God?* is an excellent example of the fear of women raised to consciousness by the women's movement.

78 This happened slowly but inexorably. The witch hunts of the fifteenth to the seventeenth centuries were its pernicious nadir. Brown, 'The philosopher and society', *Colloquy* 34 (1978), p. 8; Charles Robert Phillips,

'Magic and politics in the fourth century: parameters of groupings' in *Studia patristica*, XVIII, 1 (1985), p. 67.

79 Athanasius, *Contra gentes*, 10. 10. Thompson, p. 29.
80 Dody H. Donnelly, *Radical love: an approach to sexual spirituality* (Minnesota: Winston Press, 1984), p. 4; Van Vuuren, *Subversion*, p. 160.
81 M. I. Finley, 'The silent women of Rome', *Horizon*, 5 (1965), p. 57.
82 On Isis, *Civ. Dei*, 8. 26; on Cybele, *Magna mater*, 2. 4–5; 7. 24–6. *PL.* 41. 254; 49–51; 215–16, GB 18, pp. 285b; 152ab; 258a-9b.

Chapter 6

1   Torjesen, *Women priests*, p. 3.
2   Ambrose, *Secundum Lucam*, 2.7 CCL 14: 33.
3   See Tatian's eulogy of Christian women in his *Oratio ad Graecos*, 33. PG 6. 874, ANF 2, p. 79a.
4   *Constitutions of the holy apostles*, II. 26; 57, Kraemer, *Maenads*, pp. 231; 241 ff. Kraemer translates several epitaphs of women elders and deacons, pp. 221–3. Tertullian, *Exhortatio castitatis*, 13. 4, CCL 2, p. 1035, ANF 4, p. 58 speaks of women in ecclesiastical orders who have gained the honour through continence.
5   It is accepted by reputable scholars that Gal. 3.28 is a pre-Pauline baptismal formula that proclaimed real change in social relations within the church. See Wayne Meeks, 'The image of the androgyne: some uses of a symbol in earliest Christianity' in *HR*, 13 (1973), pp. 165–208, esp. pp. 181–2; also Elisabeth Schüssler Fiorenza, *In memory of her: a feminist reconstruction of Christian origins* (London: SCM Press, 1983), pp. 208–9. Reuther, *Womanguides*, p. 180, asserts that prohecy was the only acceptable role in Judaism and early Christianity. This overstates the case, as in early Christianity there were also female presbyters, deaconesses, canonesses, widows and priests.
6   Epiphanius, *Panarion Ad. Collyridianos*, 79. PG 42. 739–56, *Maenads* pp. 51–8.
7   Power, *Medieval women*, p. 10.
8   Tavard, *Woman*, p. 74.
9   See Fiorenza, *In memory*, pp. 245–334.
10 For the full ramifications of Jovinian's condemnation see David G. Hunter, 'Resistance to the virginal ideal in late fourth century Rome: the case of Jovinian', *TS* 48, 1 (March 1987), pp. 45–64; 'Helvidius, Jovinian, and the virginity of Mary in late fourth century Rome', *JECS*, 1, 1 (1993), pp. 47–71.
11 Alexander Souter, *The earliest Latin commentaries on the epistles of Saint Paul* (Oxford: Clarendon Press, 1927), p. 41.
12 Synod of Laodicea, (c. 343–81) Canon XI, PNF 2/14, p. 129–30. This canon was replicated at the Synods of Orange (441), Epaon (517) and the second Synod of Orleans (553). See note PNF 2/14, pp. 129–30.
13 *Acts of Paul and Thecla* in *New Testament Apocrypha*, Vol. 2, eds. E. Hennecke and W. Schneemelcher, trans. R. McL. Wilson (Philadelphia: Westminster Press, 1965), pp. 322–90. S. Davies argues that the *Acts* were used to legitimate women's authority to teach and baptise: *The revolt of the widows: the social world of the apocryphal Acts* (Carbondale, Illinois: Southern Illinois University Press, 1980), pp. 50–69, 95–109.
14 Aspegren, *Male woman*, pp.112, 129–31.

15 Torjesen offers an excellent exposition on the interdependence of church structure, leadership and Roman political models in the case of Tertullian, *Women priests*, p. 161. Cf. E. A. Clark, *Women in the early church* (Delaware: Glazier Press, 1983), p. 20, on the different roles permitted women in charismatic communities and in the institutional church.

16 Synod of Gangra, Canons 13 and 17, PNF 2/14, pp. 97, 99.

17 Synodal letter of the Bishops of Gangra, PNF 2/14, p. 91.

18 Synod of Gangra, Canon 17, PNF 2/14, p. 99.

19 Note on the Synod of Gangra, Canon 17, PNF 2/14, p. 99.

20 Ps. Clement, *Two epistles*, 2. 9–13, ANCL 14, pp. 389–92.

21 *Epistle of Dionysius* (*c.* 247), Canon 2; this letter was approved as canonical in the Synod of Trullo; Synod of Laodicea (*c.* 343–381), Canon 44, PNF 2/14, p. 153.

22 Second Synod of Nicaea (*c.* 787), Canon 18, PNF 2/14, p. 567.

23 Synod of Trullo (692) 18, PNF 2/14, p. 388. The council of Trullo was not ecumenical but many of its canons were ratified at the second Council of Nicaea. However, there was a perceived gap between law and practice, notes pp. 356, 409.

24 Both citations from Ambrosiaster, *Questions on the Old and New Testament*, Question 45, Sections 21 and 26, CSEL 50, p. 82, trans. Gryson, *Ministry of women*, p. 95. Hunter has explored the milieu and teaching of Ambrosiaster extensively in 'The paradise of patriarchy: Ambrosiaster on women as (not) God's image', *JTS*, n.s. 43, 2 (1992), pp. 447–69; 'On the sin of Adam and Eve: a little known defence of marriage and childrearing by Ambrosiaster', *HTR*, 82 (1989), pp. 283–99.

25 Diodore, *In Genesum*, PG 33. 1564D.

26 Chrysostom, *Hom. VIII on Genesis*, 1. 4. PG 53. 73, ANCL 14 p. 38.

27 Aristotle, *Politics*, 1. 13. 1260a [10]. GB 9. p. 454 B.

28 *Acts of Thecla, New Testament Apocrypha*, pp. 322–90, *The martyrdom of Perpetua and Felicitas, A lost tradition*, pp. 19–32. The story of Blandina is in Eusebius, *Historia Ecclesiastica*, 5. 1. 33–5. 1. 47. PG 20. 407–434, trans. G. A. Williamson, pp. 144–5.

29 Jerome, *Commentarius in epistolam ad Ephesios*, 3. 5. PL 26. 567.

30 See ch. 3, n. 10 above on classical Stoicism. However, the Stoics did regard women as inferior physically.

31 Clement of Alexandria, *Paedagogus*, 1. 4. PG 8. 259, ANCL 2, p. 121.

32 Epiphanius, *Panarion Ad. Collyridianos*, 79. 1. PG 42. 739–42, *Mænads*, p. 51.

33 This is supported by the research of Mary Ann Rossi, 'Priesthood, precedent, and prejudice: on recovering the women priests of early Christianity. Containing a translation from the Italian of "Notes on the female priesthood in antiquity", by Georgio Otranto', *JFSR*, 7, 1 (Spring 1991), pp. 73–94.

34 Epiphanius, *Panarion Ad. Antidicom.*, 78. 23. PG 42. 735, *Maenads*, p. 50.

35 *Panarion Ad. Collyridianos*, 79. 2. PG 42. 742–3, *Maenads*, p. 51–2.

36 Synod of Laodicea (343–81), Canon XI; 1st Synod of Orange (441), Canon XXVI; 2nd Synod of Orange, Canons xvij and xviij. PNF 2/14, Percival's 'Excursus on Deaconesses', p. 42.

37 So Karen Armstrong, *The gospel according to woman: Christianity's creation of the sex war in the west* (London: Pan, 1987), p. 64, refuted by Uta Ranke-

Heinemann, *Eunuchs for heaven: the Catholic church and sexuality* (London: Andre Deutsch, 1990), p. 168.

38   Ambrose, *Hexameron*, 6. 8. 46. *OO* I, p. 388. FC 26, p. 258.
39   *De haeresibus*, 1. 17. *PL* 42. 30–1. He cites Quintilian as giving women the priesthood. His source was Epiphanius.
40   My work in the following section is indebted particularly to Markus, *End*, pp. 1–136.
41   P. Brown, *The cult of the saints: its rise and function in Latin Christianity* (London: SCM Press, 1981), pp. 67–8, and *Society and the holy in late antiquity* (London: Faber & Faber, 1982), p. 7. Markus, *End*, pp. 87–94, and 'How on earth could places become holy? Origins of the Christian idea of holy places', *JECS*, 2, 3 (1994), pp. 257–71.
42   Brown, *Society*, pp. 15–19.
43   Markus, *End*, pp. 22, 32ff.
44   Brown, *Cult*, p. 44.
45   Maureen A. Tilley, 'The ascetic body and the (un)making of the martyr', *JAAR*, LIX, 3 (1991), pp. 467–79; cf. Augustine, *Civ. Dei*, 14. 9. *PL* 413, GB 18, p. 383.
46   Methodius, *Symposium*, 7. 3; *PG* 18. 127–30, ANF 6, p. 332b; Augustine, *Con.*, 8. 6. *PL* 32. 754–6, P-C, p. 168. Cf. Torjesen, *Women priests*, p. 217.
47   Ambrose, *De institutione virginis*, 4. 31. *OO*, 14/2, ed. Dom Gori (Milan: Biblioteca Ambrosiana, 1989), p. 132.
48   Ambrose, *De virginibus*, is replete with examples. *OO* 14/1, pp. 101–241, trans. H. de Romestin, PNF 2/10, pp. 361–87.
49   *Edict of Constantine I on rescission of penalties for celibacy and for childlessness*, trans. P. R. Coleman-Norton, *Roman state and Christian church: a collection of legal documents to AD 535*, Vol. 1 (London: SPCK, 1966), pp. 77–9.
50   Ps.-Athanasius, *Canons of Athanasius, Patriarch of Alexandria*, 98, trans. and ed. W. Reidel and W. E. Crum (London: William and Norgate 1904; Amsterdam: Philo Press, 1973), pp. 62–3. See discussion in Brown, *Body and society*, p. 264.
51   Hagith Sara Sivan, 'On hymens and holiness in late antiquity: opposition to aristocratic female asceticism at Rome', paper presented at the joint SBL/AAR International Conference, Melbourne, Australia (July 1992).
52   *Constitutions of the holy apostles*, III. I. 6; ed. and trans. James Donaldson, ANF 7, p. 428a. Ambrose, *De virginibus*, 1. 3. 13; cf. 1. 8. 40. *OO* 14/1, pp. 116; 140, PNF 2/10, pp. 365; 369.
53   Augustine's *Ep.* 262 deals precisely with this issue. *PL* 33. 1077–82, FC 32, pp. 261–9.
54   Synod of Gangra, Canon 14; 2nd Canonical epistle of Basil of Caesarea, Canon 35, PNF 2/14, pp. 98; 607.
55   Ambrose, *De institutione virginis.*, 4. 31; cf. 3. 16. *OO* 14/2, pp. 132; 122. Cf. K. E. Power, 'The rehabilitation of Eve in Ambrose of Milan's *De institutione virginis*', *Religion in the ancient world*, ed. M. Dillon, Amsterdam: A. Hakkert, 1995, pp. 367–82.
56   So argued by Brown, *Body and society*, p. 404. Cf. Davies, who argues that this ideal of feminine continence was partly a reaction to discovering that Christian men still 'apprehended them in sexual terms': *The revolt of the widows*, pp. 50–69.
57   What Augustine has to say on this question will emerge over the succeeding chapters.

58 Synod of Trullo, Canon 5–6. The latter Canon was incorporated into the *Corpus Iuris Canonici* and Gratian's *Decretum*, Pars I. Dist. 33, c. 6, PNF 2/14, p. 364. Philip Rousseau offers an excellent study of eastern asceticism and the focus of power in the celibate cleric, *Ascetics, authority and the church in the age of Jerome and Cassian* (Oxford: Oxford University Press, 1978), pp. 5, 29, 62–7.

59 K. E. Power, 'What do we mean when we say *"ministry of the laity"*?', *Compass*, 20 (Spring 1986), pp. 10–14.

60 Fiorenza, *In memory*, p. 303.

61 Brown, *Cult*, p. 28.

62 Markus, *End*, p. 41.

63 On class and episcopal leadership refer to Ramsay MacMullen, and on the mediation of imperial patronage, see Peter Brown, *Colloquy* 35 (1980), pp. 27 and 16, 20, for their response to Henry Chadwick.

64 Brown, *Colloquy* 35 (1980), p. 21. As ever there was often a gap between the prescriptions and the lived reality, and women were known to hold magisteries, and to be honoured as patrons of cities. Cf. Gardner, *Roman law*, pp. 67–8; Torjesen, *Women priests*, pp. 90–106.

65 *CT* 16. 2. 20, Coleman-Norton, *Roman state*, Vol. 1, p. 326. *CT* 16. 2. 7, Vol. 2, p. 429, repealed 390 and 455. *CT* 16. 2. 28, *LNMarc.* 5. Vol. 3, p. 849. *LNMaior*, 6, repealed 463 *LNS* 1, Vol. 3, p. 866. The clergy were often accused of soliciting funds.

66 CI 1. 2. 22; CI 1. 3. 45. Coleman-Norton, *Roman state*, Vol. 3, pp. 1040 and ß1072.

67 Augustine, *Ep.* 262 also provides useful insights into the way traditional society and its order could be undermined by ascetical women. PL 33. 1077–82, FC 32, pp. 261–9.

68 *Egeria's pilgrimage* indicates the high regard in which ascetic, powerful women were held by the monks of the holy land; trans. P. Wilson-Kastner in *Lost tradition*, pp. 85–134.

69 Torjesen, *Women priests*, p. 91.

70 Torjesen, *Women priests*, p. 107, n. 3.

71 Von Harnack, *Expansion of Christianity*, Vol. II, pp. 235–9. According to Harnack, this was true especially in the upper classes.

72 Brown, *Cult*, p. 46.

73 All three wrote to Demetrias or her family upon her taking the veil: Augustine, *Ep.* 150; PL 33. 645, WAA 13, pp. 249–50; Jerome, *Ep.* 130, *Ad Demetriadem* PL 22. 1107–24.

74 Dorothy Irvine, 'The ministry of women in the early church: the archaeological evidence', *Duke Divinity School Review*, 45, 2 (1980), pp. 76–86.

75 Brown, *Cult*, p. 32; cf. *Society*, pp. 15–19.

76 On power, see Brown, *Cult*, pp. 32–9; *Society*, p. 8.

77 Brown, *Society*, p. 8. Brown's insights are further nuanced by Markus, 'How on earth?'

78 Brown, *AH*, p. 205, cf. *Ep.* 33. 3. PL 33. 130, WAA 6, p. 102.

79 Synod of Laodicea (343–81), Canon 9, PNF 2/14, p. 129, provides one example. The Canons of this Council were received at ecumenical Synods. PNF, p. 57.

80 Re candles, Canon 34; re cemeteries, Canon 35; re confessors, Canon 25. The title of confessor was to be removed from all such letters to save the confusion of simple folk: Laeuchli, *Power and sexuality*, pp. 130, 129.

260   VEILED DESIRE

81 *Con.*, 6. 2. *PL* 32. 719–20, P-C, pp. 112–13.
82 Clement of Alexandria, *Paedagogus*, 2. 2; 3. 11; *SC* 108, pp. 55–9, ANF 2, pp. 243a; 287a; Gregory of Nyssa, *De opificio hominis*, 30. 18–23; *PG* 44. 247ff. PNF 2/5, pp. 424b-5a; Jerome, *Ep.* 54. 9–10; 22. 8–11; *PL* 22. 554-5; 399–401. *Contra Iovinianum*, 2. 11. *PL* 23. 313–315, PNF 2/6, pp. 105b-6a; 25b-6b; 396a. This biological connection is missed by Joyce Salisbury, *Church Fathers, independent virgins* (London: Verso, 1991), *passim*, and so she cannot account for the ascetic insistence on fasting except as hatred of the body.
83 *Con.*, 6. 2. *PL* 32. 719–20, P-C, pp. 112–13.
84 Davies, *Early Christian church*, p. 274.
85 R. Markus, *Christianity in the Roman world* (New York: Scribner's Sons, 1974), p. 111.
86 *Civ. Dei*, 22. 8. *PL* 41. 760, GB 18, p. 592a (my italics).
87 *Civ. Dei*, 22. 8. *PL* 41. 759–71, GB 18, pp. 591b-8a.
88 P. Brown, 'A social context to the religious crisis of the third century AD', *Colloquy* 14 (1975), p. 2. For similar non-Christian contexts see Jay Bregman, 'Response to Peter Brown', *Colloquy* 14 (1975), p. 17.
89 *Civ. Dei*, 22. 8. *PL* 41. 761, GB 18, p. 592ab.
90 Ambrose, *De institutione virginis*, 1. 3. *OO* 14/2, pp. 110–12.
91 Brundage, *Law*, p. 2.
92 Laeuchli, *Power*, p. 48.
93 R. A. Padgug, 'Sexual matters: on conceptualizing sexuality in history', *RHR*, 20 (Spring/Summer 1979), p. 11. I have applied Padgug's categories to Roman culture. Cf. Plato, *Laws*, VIII. 838, GB 7, p. 737a.
94 Laeuchli, *Power*, p. 107.
95 This offence does not include breaching ritual celibacy. For fathering children within marriage, a bishop lost his office: Canon 13, Laeuchli, *Power and Sexuality*, pp. 126–35.
96 Cf. Ambrose, *De institutione virginis*, 16. 100–17. 114. *OO* 14/2, pp. 180–94, for an example of one such ceremony.
97 Council of Chalcedon, Canon 4, legislates episcopal control over monasteries, PNF 2/14, p. 270. This was a greater problem for women, for monks could also be priests and bishops and be regulated by one of their own. The tensions of powerful men dealing with powerful abbesses are addressed by Joan Morris, *The lady was a bishop*, *passim*.
98 *Ep.* 211. *PL* 33. 958–65, WAA 13, pp. 392–404.
99 Douglas, *Purity*, pp. 5, 35.
100 Douglas, *Purity*, p. 104.
101 A helpful discussion of this process is Virginia Burrus, 'The heretical woman as symbol in Alexander, Athanasius, Epiphanius, and Jerome', *HTR*, 84, 3 (1991), pp. 229–48.
102 Epiphanius, *Panarion Ad. Collyridianos*, 79. 1–9. *PG* 42. 739–56, *Maenads*, p. 51; Ambrose, *Hexameron*, 3. 12. 51; 6. 8. 49. *OO* 1, pp. 164; 394, FC 42, pp. 106; 263; Augustine, *Ep.* 126. *PL* 33. 480, FC 20, p. 266–8.
103 Aristotle, *On the generation of animals*, 4. 1. 766b [15–25], GB 9, p. 308a. My recent research indicates that this model was so dominant in the culture that Christianity incorporated most of it uncritically. The preliminary findings are in Kim E. Power, 'Philosophy medicine and gender in the ascetic texts of Ambrose of Milan', *Proceedings: Ancient history in a*

modern university: in honour of Edwin A. Judge, eds. Tom Hilliard et al., Sydney: Primavera Press, 1995.

Chapter 7

1   G. R. Evans, *Augustine on evil* (Cambridge: Cambridge University Press, 1982), p. 9.
2   Brown, *AH*, p. 19.
3   Sr Mary Inez Bogan, 'Notes on the *Retractiones*', FC 60, p. 13.
4   Sources noted in full below in relevant discussion, p. 271, n. 104.
5   Eugene Te Selle, 'Augustine as client', p. 92. George Lawless, *Augustine of Hippo and his monastic rule* (Oxford: Clarendon Press, 1987), p. 20.
6   Evans, *Evil*, p. 21.
7   Henry Chadwick, *St Augustine: Confessions. A new translation* (Oxford: Oxford University Press, 1991), p. xviii.
8   O'Connell, *Early theory*, p. 280.
9   Sources on Monica's childhood: *Con.*, 9. 8–9. *PL* 32. 771–3, P-C, pp. 193–9.
10 *De doct. Christ.* 3. 11. 17. *PL* 34. 72, GB 18, p. 662a.
11 I thank Mark Vesey for these insights: 'St Augustine: Confessions', *AS*, 24 (1993), pp. 163–81.
12 *Con.*, 2. 4–6. *PL* 32. 678–81, P-C, pp. 47–50.
13 *Con.*, 2. 3. *PL* 32. 676, P-C, p. 45.
14 *Con.*, 6. 10. God as the desirable food of the soul: 3. 1; 7. 17–18; 9. 3. *PL* 32. 683; 744–6; 765–6, P-C, pp. 55; 126; 152; 184. *Serm.*, 21. 2. *PL* 38. 142, WStA II/2, p. 31. On the equivalence of food and learning, *De doct. Christ.* 4. 11. 26. *PL* 43. 100, GB 18, p. 683b.
15 *Pudor: Letter 2*.* 4. Divjak, p. 64, FC 81, pp. 20–1.
16 O'Connell, *Odyssey*, p. 114. Cf. *Con.*, 9. 9. *PL* 32. 772, P-C, p. 194.
17 *Con.*, 9. 9. *PL* 32. 772, P-C, p. 194.
18 *Civ. Dei*, 19. 25. *PL* 41. 656, GB 18, p. 528a.
19 *Serm.*, 392. 4–5; cf. *Serm.*, 82. 8–11; 332. 4. *PL* 38–9. 711–12; 511–13; 1463.
20 *Con.*, 9. 9. *PL* 32. 772, P-C, p. 195.
21 Brown, *AH*, p. 208. Cf. *Con.*, 9. 9. *PL* 32. 773, P-C, p. 195.
22 L. Ferrari, 'The boyhood beatings of St. Augustine', *AS*, 5 (1974), p. 4.
23 *Con.*, 9. 9 and 2. 3. *PL* 32. 773 and 677, P-C, pp. 195 and 45.
24 Cf. *Con.*, 9. 11. *PL* 32. 775, P-C, p. 199.
25 *Con.*, 1. 9. *PL* 32. 667, P-C, p. 30.
26 *Ep.* 211. *PL* 33. 958–65, WAA 13, p. 392–403. He applied this to both men and women.
27 *Con.*, 9. 9. *PL* 32. 772, P-C, pp. 194–5 . . . *quibus ancillae factae essent.*
28 Saller, 'Corporal punishment', pp. 152–3. Monks in Augustine's monastery were beaten for misbehaviour; cf. *Letter* 20*. 5. Divjak, p. 298, FC 81, p. 137.
29 J. J. O'Meara, *The young Augustine* (London: Longmans Group Ltd, 1954), p. 36. Cf. B. Shaw, 'The family in late antiquity: the experience of Augustine', *Past and present*, 115 (May 1987) p. 28.
30 *Con.*, 1. 9. *PL* 32. 667–8, P-C, p. 30.
31 *Con.*, 9. 9. *PL* 32. 772–3, P-C, pp. 194–5.
32 *Con.*, 9. 11. *PL* 32. 775, P-C, p. 199. Whether he is the brother mentioned in *Letter 6*.* 2 is hard to say. Divjak p. 128, FC 81, p. 54.

33 *Ep.* 211. 4. *PL* 33. 959, WAA 13, p. 394. Possidius, *S. Augustini vita*, 26. *PL* 32. 55, FC 15, p. 105.

34 *De beata vita*, 2. 7; 14. *PL* 32. 963; 966, FC 5, p. 51; 61. If it is Navigius in *Letter* 6* then his description is very different. He writes that they are as one person.

35 *Con.*, 9. 11. *PL* 32. 775–6, P-C, pp. 199–200.

36 *Con.*, 10. 4. *PL* 32. 781, P-C, p. 209. He calls Alypius his brother in *Letter* 20*.15. Divjak, p. 316, FC 81, p. 141.

37 For wet nurses see *Con.*, 1. 6; cf. 1. 7. *PL* 32. 661; 666, P-C, pp. 25; 28.

38 *Con.*, 1. 6. *PL* 32. 664, P-C, p. 25.

39 *Con.*, 1. 6. *PL* 32. 664, P-C, p. 25.

40 *Con.*, 2. 3. *PL* 32. 677, P-C, p. 45.

41 *Con.*, 3. 4–5. *PL* 32. 686, P-C, pp. 59–60. It is significant that in this context he does not mention his nurses, but only his mother (*lacte matris*). Marsha L. Dutton takes this as a representation of God as mother: ' "When I was a child": spiritual infancy and God's maternity in Augustine's *Confessiones*', *Collectanea Augustiniana: Augustine: 'Second founder of the faith'*, eds. J. C. Schnaubelt and F. Van Fleteren (New York: Peter Lang, 1990), pp. 113–40.

42 *Con.*, 1. 7, 14. *PL* 32. 665; 671, P-C, pp. 27–8, 35.

43 I first encountered this lovely image in O'Connell, *Early theory*, p. 84. *Con.*, 7. 14; cf. 4. 1; 5. 2; 5. 5; 6. 10; 7. 18. *PL* 32. 744; 693; 707; 709; 728; 745, P-C, pp. 149–50; 71; 92; 96; 126; 152. The maternal image of God is greatly developed by O'Connell in his later articles, 'The God of St Augustine's imagination', *Thought*, 57 (March 1982), pp. 30–40, and 'Isaiah's mothering God in St Augustine's *Confessions*', *Thought*, 58 (1983), pp. 188–206. A more recent study traces the changes in God imagery which Augustine sees as pertinent to spiritual maturity: Dutton, ' "When I was a child" ', pp. 113–40.

44 *Con.*, 1. 9. *PL* 32. 667. P-C, p. 30.

45 *Con.*, 2. 3; cf. 1. 9–10, 19; 2. 2; 6. 11. *PL* 32. 678; cf. 667; 674; 677; 729, P-C, pp. 46–7; 30–1; 39; 126. The text in 6.11 is the only passage where Augustine even intimates that his father helped set him on the right path.

46 *Con.*, 2. 3; 3. 4. *PL* 32. 678; 686, P-C, p. 46–7; 59.

47 *Con.*, 1. 9–10. *PL* 32. 667–8, P-C, pp. 30–1. Ferrari notes that Augustine represents God as a flagellating God at least twenty times: 'Boyhood beatings of St Augustine', pp. 1–14.

48 The former is directed at Monica, for his pagan father could not be expected to seek his baptism.

49 *Con.*, 2. 2–3. *PL* 32. 676, 678, P-C, pp. 44, 46.

50 *Con.*, 2. 2; 6. 12. *PL* 32. 670; 730, P-C, p. 44; 129. Cf. *De bono con.*, 5; *PL* 40. 377, PNF 1/3.3, p. 412b, *Solil.*, 1. 10. 17. *PL* 32. 878, FC 5, p. 365. In this context, it is interesting to note Klein, *Psychoanalysis*, p. 340. Klein argues that the love of children derives from the feminine phase of early childhood, and that the male tendency is to regard a wife as a child/lover. If her psychoanalytic model is applicable to antiquity, such tendencies would have been reinforced by the Roman practice of marrying young girls to older men, which encouraged men to see their wives as daughter-like: Quintilian, *Institutio Oratoria*, 6. Praef. 5, in H. E. Butler, ed., *Quintilian*, Loeb Classical Library, Vol. II (Cambridge: Harvard University Press, 1922), p. 375. See Brown, *Body and society*, on daughter/wives, pp. 10–13.

51   *Con.*, 3. 1. *PL* 32. 683, P-C, p. 55.
52   *Con.*, 2. 3. *PL* 32. 678, P-C, p. 46.
53   *Con.*, 1. 11–12. *PL* 32. 669–70, P-C, p. 32.
54   *Con.*, 1. 11. *PL* 32. 669, P-C, p. 32. *Et in hoc adiuvabas eam, ut superaret virum, cui melior serviebat, quia et in hoc tibi utique id iubenti serviebat.*
55   *Con.*, 9. 9. *PL* 32. 667, P-C, p. 195. Roman fathers did not usually take over supervision of their sons until the latter were adolescents. Patricius died when Augustine was sixteen. Emiel Eyben, 'Fathers and sons', *Marriage, divorce and children in ancient Rome* (Oxford: Clarendon Press, 1991), p. 114.
56   *Con.*, 2. 3. *PL* 32. 677, P-C, p. 45, cf. 1. 19; 2. 5; 3. 3; 3. 4. *PL* 32. 674; 679; 685. *P-C*, pp. 40; 48; 58.
57   *Con.*, 9. 9; cf. 3. 1–3. *PL* 32. 772; 683–5, P-C, pp. 194; 55–7. Augustine tended to react passive-aggressively as *Con.*, 5. 8 illustrates. *PL* 32. 712–13, P-C, p. 101.
58   *Con.*, 3. 3–4. *PL* 32. 683, 685, P-C, pp. 55, 59.
59   See P. Brown, *Augustine and sexuality*, p. 3. on 'fleshly' versus 'spiritual' bonding.
60   *Civ. Dei*, 19. 16. *PL* 41. 644, GB 18, p. 521b (my italics). I have amended the translation to become gender inclusive. The unamended translation creates the impression that only men were beaten, where Augustine's own texts indicate otherwise. Note particularly, *Speculum*, 1. *De libro legis* [xxi] *PL* 34. 890c.
61   Lactantius, *Divinarum Institutionem*, 4. 3. 14–17; SC 377, pp. 49–51. *De ira*, 22. SC 289, pp. 198–203. Both texts trans. in ANF 7, pp. 103; 279.
62   Benko, *Pagan Rome and the early Christians* (Bloomington: Indiana University Press, 1984), p. 68, comments on Gnosticism and ritual sexuality. O'Meara provides a useful synthesis of Manichaean doctrine concerning sexuality in the light of its appeal to Augustine: *Young Augustine*, chapter 4, esp. pp. 74 and 77.
63   *Con.*, 3. 11. *PL* 32. 692, P-C, pp. 68–9.
64   *Con.*, 3. 12. *PL* 32. 692, P-C, p. 69–70.
65   *Con.*, 6. 1. *PL* 32. 719, P-C, p. 111.
66   *Con.*, 6. 13. *PL* 32. 731, P-C, p. 130.
67   Cf. *Con.*, 4. 1; 5. 8; 6. 3. *PL* 32. 693; 712; 721, P-C, pp. 71; 101; 114. Cf. Clarissa Atkinson, ' "Your servant, my mother": the figure of Saint Monica in the ideology of Christian motherhood' in C. W. Atkinson, C. H. Buchanan and M. R. Miles, eds., *Immaculate and powerful: the female in sacred image and social reality* (Boston: Beacon Press, 1985, p. 143), p. 143.
68   *Con.*, 6. 1. *PL* 32. 719, P-C, p. 111.
69   *Con.*, 5. 9. *PL* 32. 714, P-C, p. 102.
70   Cf. *Con.*, 9. 13. *PL* 32. 778, P-C, p. 203. He says that he may have been guilty of too much fleshly affection. What 'too much affection' meant to him we cannot objectively know.
71   His friends also: *Con.*, 9. 9; cf. 9. 12. *PL* 32, 773; 777, P-C, pp. 196; 201.
72   *De beata vita*, 1. 6. *PL* 32. 962, FC 5, p. 49.
73   *Con.*, 9. 12. *PL* 32, 776, P-C, p. 201.
74   *De cura pro mortuis*, 13. 16. *PL* 40. 604, FC 27, p. 373.
75   *Con.*, 9. 12. *PL* 32. 777. P-C, p. 202–3.
76   *Con.*, 8. 12. *PL* 32. 762–3, P-C, pp. 178–9.
77   *Ep.* 243. *PL* 33. 1058, FC 32. p. 225.

78 This narrative is found in *Con.*, 5. 8. *PL* 32. 712–13, P-C, pp. 100–1.

79 *Con.*, 5. 8. *PL* 32. 713, P-C, p. 101.

80 Here I am indebted to Denis Minns for his personal communications on this passage.

81 Tertullian actually uses Dido as a model for Christian widows. She preferred 'to burn' literally, rather than to marry again. *De monogamia*, 17; cf. *Exhortatio castitatis*, 13. 3. *CCL* 2. 1252; 1034, ANF 4, p. 72b.

82 *Con.*, 6. 1. *PL* 32. 719, P-C, p. 111.

83 *Ep.* 243. *PL* 33. 1957, FC 32, p. 225.

84 *Ep.* 243. *PL* 33. 1058, FC 32, pp. 221–5. Augustine here relegates filial duty to its proper place 'where higher duties do not call'.

85 Later he defined a preference for private property as the mark of sin: *De trin.*, 12. 9. 14–12. 11. 16. *PL* 42. 1005–7, WAA 7, pp. 295–7. Cf. Edmund Hill, 'Trinitarian politics or towards an Augustinian Marxism?' in *Prudentia*, 5, 2 (1973), pp. 91–8.

86 *Con.*, 6. 12. *PL* 32. 720, P-C, p. 128.

87 *Con.*, 6. 14. *PL* 32. 731, P-C, p. 131.

88 *De ordine*, 2. 1. 1. *PL* 32. 995, FC 5, p. 273.

89 *De bono con.*, 13–14. *PL* 40. 382–3, PNF 1/3, p. 405ab. However, Rousselle makes clear that some wives were excluded from their husband's lives almost totally: *Porneia*, pp. 40, 73, 95.

90 He never relinquished his desire for a life devoted to study and writing: Possidius, *Vita*, 24. *PL* 32. 53–4, FC 15, p. 101.

91 So Evans, *Augustine on evil*, p. 21; Lawless, *Monastic rule*, p. 20.

92 These assumptions are explicit in the writings of Brown, *AH*, p. 30; Lawless, *Monastic rule*, p. 20; Marrou, *Influence*, p. 24; Sister Marie Aquinas McNamara, *Friends and friendship for Saint Augustine* (New York: Alba House, St Paul Publications, 1957), pp. 31–2; O'Connell, *Odyssey*, pp. 69, 107; O'Meara, *Young Augustine*, p. 128; and Te Selle, 'Augustine as client', p. 92.

93 Dixon, *Roman mother*, p. 5, also pp. 62–3.

94 *De ordine*, 1. 11. 32. *PL* 32. 993–4, FC 5, p. 271.

95 *De ordine*, 2. 16. 44; 2. 8. 25; 1. 11. 32. *PL* 32. 1015; 1006; 993–4, FC 5, pp. 320, 301–2, 271.

96 *De ordine*, 1. 11. 32; 2. 7. 24. *PL* 32. 993–4; 1006, FC 5, p. 271, 301.

97 Representatives of the former group are Robert P. Russell, 'Note on *De ordine*', FC 5, f.n. 5, p. 272; Ludwig Schopp, 'Note on *De beata vita*', FC 5. f.n. 9, p. 75; Mary Inez Bogan, 'Note on *Retractiones*', p. 13; Evans, *Augustine on evil*, p. 9. Representative of the latter group is O'Connell, *Early theory*, p. 227, who judges Augustine's literary treatment of his mother at Cassiciacum as 'pathetic'.

98 *De ordine*, 1. 11. 31. *PL* 32. 992, FC 5, p. 270.

99 *De ordine*, 1. 8. 22–3. *PL* 32. 987–8, FC 5, p. 259.

100 *De beata vita*, 4. 27; *PL* 32. 972, FC 5, p. 75; *De ordine*, 2. 1. 1. *PL* 32. 993, FC 5, p. 273.

101 *De ordine*, 1. 11. 32. *PL* 32. 994, FC 5, p. 271. Cf. F. Van der Meer, *Augustine the bishop: The life work of a father of the church* (London: Sheed and Ward, 1961), p. 433 on Augustine's perception of the *sensus catholicus*.

102 *Con.*, 6. 2–3. *PL* 32. 720, P-C, pp. 112–14.

103 Much later, post 426, he will write to a young man contemplating baptism that although he might know more doctrine than his already

baptised wife, she is more secure in the mystery, and that knowledge without baptism avails nothing for the soul is too weak to achieve virtue unaided. *Letter 2**. 2–5. Divjak, pp. 61–6, FC 81, pp. 19–22.

104 Brown, *AH*, p. 118 (my emphasis).

105 *De ordine*, 2. 20. 52. *PL* 32. 1019, FC 5, p. 329.

106 *De ordine*, 1. 11. 31. *PL* 32. 992–3, FC 5, pp. 270–1.

107 *De ordine*, 2. 17. 45–6; cf. 2. 1. 1. *PL* 32. 1015–16; 993, FC 5, pp. 321–2, 273.

108 O'Connell, *Early theory*, p. 231.

109 *Con.*, 9. 11. *PL* 32. 776, P-C, p. 200. Cf. J. Kevin Coyle, 'In praise of Monica: a note on the Ostia experience of *Con.* IX', *AS*, 13 (1982), p. 92.

110 *De beata vita*, 2. 10. *PL* 32. 965, FC 5, p. 56; *De ordine*, 2. 1. 1. *PL* 32. 993, FC 5, p. 273.

111 *Con.*, 9. 10. *PL* 32. 773–5, P-C, pp. 197–9.

112 Atkinson, 'Your servant', p. 141.

113 *Con.*, 9. 3. *PL* 32. 765, P-C, p. 184.

114 *Con.*, 9. 10. *PL* 32. 775, P-C, pp. 198–9.

115 Ambrose, *De excessu fratris Satyri*, 1. 1, 4–6 and *passim*; 2. 1, 11–13. *PL* 16. 1347–9; PNF 2/10, pp. 161–2ff; 174a; 175b.

116 *Con.*, 9. 12. *PL* 32. 776, P-C, pp. 200–1. Melanie Klein wrote that the source of mother separation anxiety is both fear of loss and the need for reassurance that mother is not the 'bad' attacking mother that they fear. For Augustine it could be restated as the fear of loss and the need to reassure himself that she was not really the embodiment of Eve that he feared. Klein notes elsewhere that the introjected 'bad' mother is often more cruel and stern than the real mother: *Psychoanalysis*, pp. 27, 249.

117 *Con.*, 9. 12. *PL*. 32. 777, P-C, p. 201.

118 *Con.*, 9. 12–13. *PL* 32. 777–9, P-C, pp. 202–4.

119 There is also the probability that his mother's death reactivated the unresolved grief he felt about his father, and his concubine (see following section). Dutton argues that after the vision at Ostia which marked Augustine's spiritual maturity, Monica's work was done – hence her readiness to die. Thus Dutton reads Monica's death as the symbolic end of Augustine's spiritual infancy and his shift from God as mother to God as Father: ' "When I was a child" ', p. 119.

120 *Con.*, 9. 12. *PL* 32. 777–8, P-C, p. 203.

121 If her weeping is not exaggerated it would suggest very strongly that for many years Monica was seriously depressed, and perhaps repressing great anger. This raises tantalising psychological questions that the text does not permit us to answer. On weeping as symptomatic of depression originating in the unawareness of repressed anger, see Scarf, *Unfinished business*, pp. 261, 544.

122 *Con.*, 2. 3. *PL* 32. 678, P-C, p. 46.

123 *Con.*, 9. 13. *PL* 32. 778, P-C, p. 203–4.

124 *Con.*, 3. 11. *PL* 32. 692, P-C, p. 69.

125 *Con.*, 9. 9. *PL* 32. 773, P-C, p. 196.

126 *Contra* Raoul Mortley who argues that Monica tried to model herself on subordinate Eve: *Womanhood: the feminine in ancient Hellenism, Gnosticism, Christianity and Islam* (Sydney: Delacroix Press, 1981), p. 113.

127 The citations for Mary as handmaid are all documented in the following

chapter. For Monica: *Con.*, 2. 3; 3. 11; 9. 8; 9. 9; 9. 12; 9. 13. *PL* 32. 678; 691; 771; 773; 776–8; 780, P-C, pp. 46; 68; 192–3; 195; 202; 203–4.

128 *Con.*, 5. 9; cf. 6. 1. *PL* 32. 714 cf. 719, P-C, p. 103; cf. 112.

129 *Con.*, 5. 9. *PL* 32. 714, P-C, p. 103.

130 *Con.*, 9. 9. *PL* 32. 772–3, P-C, p. 195.

131 *Con.*, 3. 11; 5. 9; cf. 2. 3; 9. 9. *PL* 32. 691; 714; cf. 678; 772, P-C, pp. 69; 102; cf. 45–6; 195.

132 *Con.*, 5. 9. *PL* 32. 714, P-C, p. 102.

133 *Con.*, 9. 8. *PL* 32. 771, P-C, p. 192. Note that Monica fills the church's function, true spiritual birth.

134 *Con.*, 9. 8; 3. 6; 1. 11; cf. 9. 9, 'your good servant in whose womb you created me'. *PL* 32. 771; 687; 669, cf. 773, P-C, pp. 192; 60; 32; cf. 195. Given his belief about concupiscence and original sin, this is not his usual way of speaking about human conception.

135 Van der Meer, *Augustine the bishop*, p. 570; Marrou, *Influence*, p. 64.

136 *De ordine*, 2. 1. 1. *PL* 32. 993, FC 5, p. 273. There is an interesting glimpse of Monica's *gravitas* in *De beata vita*, 3. 21. *PL* 32. 969, FC 5, p. 68.

137 *De beata vita*, 2. 16. *PL* 32. 967, FC 5, p. 64.

138 *De ordine*, 1. 11. 32; *PL* 32. 993–4, FC 5, p. 271. *Con.*, 9. 7; 9. 11; 6. 1. *PL* 32. 756; 760–1; 719, P-C, pp. 191; 199–200; 111.

139 Brown, *AH*, p. 118.

140 *Con.*, 9. 4. *PL* 32. 776, P-C, p. 186.

141 *Ep.* 93. 2, 4, 6 and *passim*. *PL* 33. 322–4, WAA 6, pp. 398–440. So also Atkinson, 'Your servant', p. 140 and J. Patout Burns, 'Response to Peter Brown', *Colloquy* 46 (1983), pp. 15–16.

142 *Con.*, 6. 3. *PL* 32. 720–1, P-C, p. 114. *Ep.* 243. *PL* 33. 1054–9, FC 32, p. 224.

143 *De mor. eccles. cath.*, 1. 30. 62–3. *PL* 32. 1336, PNF 1/4, p. 58ab.

144 *Con.*, 5. 7, 12. *PL* 32. 711; 716, P-C, pp. 99–100; 106.

145 *Con.*, 7. 18; 7. 14; 8. 11. *PL* 32. 745; 742; 761, P-C, pp. 152; 149–50; 176.

146 *Solil.*, 1. 13. 22. *PL* 32. 881, FC 5, p. 373.

147 As did he and Monica at Ostia: *Con.*, 6. 6; 7. 10–11; 7. 14; 7. 17–18; *PL* 32. 724; 742; 744–5, P-C, pp. 119; 146–7; 149–50; 152. *Ep.* 93. 2, 4–5. *PL* 33. 322–4, WAA 6, pp. 398–9.

148 *Con.*, 1. 14; cf. 3. 4. *PL* 32. 671; 685–6, P-C, p. 35; 59.

149 Augustine even compares God to a mother who sprinkles her breasts with gall to force the child to wean itself: *Serm.*, 311. 17. *PL* 38–9. 1419.

Chapter 8

1 An earlier version of this material appeared as '*Sed unam tamen*: Augustine and his concubine', *AS*, 24 (1993), pp. 49–76.

2 van Bavel, *Ever ancient*, pp. 259–75; Brundage, *Law*, pp. 99–100; LaPorte and Weaver, 'Augustine on women', pp. 115–31; Brown, *Body and society*, p. 390. Possidius, Augustine's first biographer, simply erases her from his life.

3 So van Bavel, *Ever ancient*.

4 Elizabeth A. Clark, 'Adam's only companion: Augustine and the early Christian debate on marriage', *Recherches Augustinniene*, XXI (1986), pp. 139–62.

5   So Brundage, *Law*, pp. 99–100. Arguing for love: van Bavel, *Ever ancient*; Roland E. Ramirez, 'Demythologizing Augustine as a great sinner', *AS*, 12 (1981), pp. 61–88, especially p. 75, and McNamara, *Friends*, p. 49. There seems little ground for McNamara's assumption that it was largely through Adeodatus that their relationship was transformed from passion to love.

6   *Con.*, 4. 2; 6. 15. *PL* 32. 693; 752, P-C, pp. 72; 131.

7   Detailed studies on concubinage are John T. Noonan, 'Marital affection in the Canonists', *Studia Gratiana*, 12 (1967), pp. 481–9; Beryl Rawson, 'Roman concubinage and other *de facto* marriages', *TAPA*, 104 (1974), pp. 279–305; Rousselle, *Porneia*, pp. 80–5 and Brundage, *Law*, pp. 35–43, 99–101.

8   In Book 6. 15 Augustine calls her 'the one with whom I was accustomed to sleep'. Both the Loeb and Penguin editions use the word 'mistress'. Scaff, PNF 1/1 retains the literal 'one', and Chadwick, 'a woman . . . the only girl for me' (p. 53).

9   Rawson, 'Roman concubinage', pp. 280–2. Prior to the Christian-influenced *Sententiae Pauli* of the fourth century, Roman men could keep an official concubine even if they were legally married: Rousselle, *Porneia*, p. 96, note 12, and p. 97.

10 See Gardner, *Roman law*, for detailed discussion and sources on Roman marriage and concubinage, pp. 31–65.

11 *Stuprum* included sex relations with a boy, girl or widow of good family, or a 'repudiated woman' who retained the title *materfamilias*. For this reason slave women were sometimes freed to enhance their status as concubines: Rousselle, *Porneia*, pp. 79–81, 97.

12 Cf. Rawson, 'Roman concubinage', p. 286.

13 Brundage, *Law*, p. 43.

14 Noonan, 'Marital affection', esp. pp. 481, 486–7.

15 Rawson, 'Roman family', pp. 20–1.

16 Brundage, *Law*, p. 99; Brown, *Body and society*, p. 390. In the later Empire a concubine's rights were better protected by law, and, in the Christian era, she even had the right to inherit a modest part of her partner's estate. This right was somewhat tenuous, being revoked in 397 and reinstated in 405. Brundage, *Law*, pp. 10; 102.

17 *Serm.*, 288. 5, *PL* 39. 2291 and also *De bono con.*, 5. *PL* 40. 377, PNF, 1/3, p. 401. After Toledo, even opponents of concubinage decided that there were simply too many cases to excommunicate all the Christians living in such relationships. See Leo I, *Ep.* 167. 13. *PL* 54. 1207. On Caesarius of Arles see Brundage, *Law*, pp. 70–104.

18 Canon 17 of the Council, 'Let the man be content with one woman, whether wife or concubine.' Cited in Lawless, *Monastic rule*, p. 18. Cf. Gardner, *Roman law*, p. 53.

19 Brundage, *Law*, p. 98–101.

20 If she had a dowry, a concubine could recover it. If she was dowerless, then she had no means of supporting herself: Rousselle, *Porneia*, pp. 91–105.

21 Jerome, *Ep.* 69. 3, 5–7, cf. *Ep.* 22. 14. *PL* 22. 656–8, cf. 403.

22 Hippolytus, *Apostolic Constitutions*, 16. 23 in Gregory Dix and Henry Chadwick, *The treatise on the Apostolic tradition of St Hippolytus of Rome* (London: The Albion Press, rev. ed. 1992), p. 27.

23 Rousselle, *Porneia*, pp. 104–5.

24 Documentation on Christianity's debates concerning concubinage is available from the second century on. Compare *Apostolic Constitutions*, 16. 23 with 16. 24b, pp. 27, 28, and see Dix, p. xviii; Brundage, *Law*, pp. 70–104, and Rousselle, *Porneia*, pp. 96, 103–6.

25 Most scholars assume that she was a freedwoman, but Brown and Clarke argue that she would be from a lower-class free family. This would be consistent with the necessity of concubinage to avoid the charge of *stuprum*. Brown, *AH*, p. 62; Clark, 'Adam's only companion', p. 158.

26 Rawson, 'Roman concubinage', note 50, p. 293 and *passim*.

27 Although not condoning concubinage as a bishop, Augustine cites the conditions he accepts in *De bono con.*, 5. *PL* 40. 377, PNF 1/3, p. 401a.

28 McNamara, *Friends*, p. 48. Cf. D. Schaps, 'The women least mentioned: etiquette and women's names', *CQ*, n.s. 27 (1977), pp. 323–30.

29 So Lawless, *Monastic rule*, p. 19.

30 Evans, *Augustine on evil*, p. 21.

31 *Con.*, 9. 13. *PL* 32. 780, P-C, p. 204.

32 *Con.*, 4. 4. *PL* 32. 696–7. P-C, pp. 75–6.

33 *Ep.* 27. 4–6; *PL* 33. 109–10, WAA 6, p. 75, 77. Cf. *Con.*, 6. 16; 8. 6. *PL* 32. 752; 754–6, P-C, pp.131–2; 166.

34 O'Meara, *The young Augustine*, p. 55; cf. *Con.*, 3. 3. *PL* 32. 685, P-C, p. 57.

35 *Con.*, 6. 15. *PL* 32. 732, P-C, p. 131. So also Brown, *AH*, pp. 62, 89.

36 See *Con.*, 9. 16. *PL* 32. 769, P-C, p. 190.

37 *Con.*, 4. 2; 9. 6. If Augustine's relationship, was a 'bargain struck for lust', then of necessity, she is a sinner also. Cf. 6. 12; 8. 7; 3. 2. *PL* 32. 693; 769; 730; 757; 684, P-C, pp. 72; 190; 128; 169; 56–7.

38 *Con.*, 3. 11. *PL* 32. 311, P-C, p. 68.

39 *Con.*, 9. 12. *PL* 32. 776, P-C, p. 200.

40 *Con.*, 6. 14. *PL* 32. 698–9; P-C, p. 79. Pine-Coffin's translation changes the sentence construction to avoid precisely this difficulty, and Chadwick's avoids it by a circumlocution.

41 Cf. Brown, *AH*, pp. 89–90 and pp. 62–3.

42 *Con.*, 6. 11; *PL* 32. 729, P-C, p. 127. Cf. *Solil.*, 1. 10. 17. *PL* 32. 878, FC 5, p. 365.

43 Augustine consciously used it for this reason: *De ordine*, 2. 13. 38. *PL* 32. 1013, FC 5, p. 315.

44 *Con.*, 3. 1. *PL* 32. 683, P-C, p. 55. Cf. '*Hoc in turpi et exsecranda laetetia*'; *Con.*, 8. 3. *PL* 32. 750–1, P-C, p. 162.

45 Putrid running sores are a favourite image for worldly desires: *Con.*, 6. 12; 8. 7; cf. 3. 2; *PL* 32. 730; 757; 684, P-C, pp. 128; 169, 57. *Serm.*, 138. 6. *PL* 38. 766, WStA III/8, p. 98.

46 *Con.*, 2. 3; 6. 12; 8. 1. *PL* 32. 678; 730; 749, P-C, p. 46; 128–9; 158. Also 6. 15; 8. 5; 8. 10. *PL* 32. 732; 753; 760, P-C, pp. 131, 164, 175.

47 *Solil.*, 1. 11. 19. *PL* 32. 880, FC 5, p. 369. He admits elsewhere that a wife's dowry was also important, 'so that the expense would be no burden, and this would be the limit of my ambition', (*Con.*, 6. 11. *PL* 32. 729, P-C, p. 127). In the earlier *Soliloquia* he had a much longer 'wish list' a wife would have to meet.

48 *Con.*, 8. 7. *PL* 32. 757, P-C, p. 169.

49 *Con.*, 4. 1. *PL* 32. 693–4, Chadwick, p. 53.

50 Ramirez, 'Demythologizing Augustine', pp. 69, 76; McNamara, *Friends*, p. 49. Cf. Van der Meer, *Augustine the bishop*, p. 180.

51 In *Sermo.*, Mai 20. 1, dated by Hill to 397–8, though possibly later, the wrote that to love and not to have was a torment to the heart. *PLS* 2. 464–5, WStA III/3, 65a, p. 199.

52 *Solil.*, 1. 11. 18. *PL* 32. 879, FC 5, p. 368.

53 See Boyle, 'Garden of Zeus', p. 119.

54 At the time he wrote the *Confessiones*. Even fifteen years after her dismissal, he softens his attitudes to concubines who follow his lady's example: *De bono con.*, 5. *PL* 40. 377, PNF 1/3, p. 401a.

55 *Con.*, 9. 6. *PL* 32. 769, P-C, p. 190.

56 *Con.*, 1. 6. *PL* 32. 663, P-C, p. 25.

57 *Con.*, 9. 12. *PL* 32. 776, P-C, p. 200.

58 As does McNamara, *Friends*, p. 52.

59 On the affective barrenness of many Roman marriages see Rousselle, *Porneia*, pp. 73 and 15, 20, 29, 40ff.

60 *Solil.*, 1. 10. 17. *PL* 42. 878, FC 5, p. 365.

61 Cf. *Con.*, 9. 12. *PL* 32. 776–7, P-C, pp. 200–2.

62 *Con.*, 6. 12; cf. 6. 11. *PL* 32. 730; 729, P-C, p. 129; 127. 'This life too is sweet. It has its own charms. They are not of small account.'

63 *Con.*, 6. 15. *PL* 32. 732. All translators avoid the use of the more biblical 'cleaving' to translate *adhaereo*, which Augustine uses in this sense in *De gen. ad. litt.*, 9. 19. *PL* 34. 408. ACW 42, p. 95.

64 These texts stand in blatant contradiction to *Con.*, 9. 1. *PL* 32. 763, P-C, p. 181.

65 *Adhaerebo* is the same word he uses in *De gen. ad litt. PL* 34. 408. ACW 42, p. 95.

66 Dating from Brown, *AH*, p. 74.

67 *De ordine* 2. 18. 48. *PL* 32. 1017, FC 5, pp. 325–6.

68 So also van Bavel, *Ever ancient*, p. 39.

69 *De bono con.*, 5. *PL* 40. 377, PNF 1/3, p. 401a. Cf. Hippolytus, *Apostolic constitutions*, 16. 23. Dix and Chadwick, p. 27.

70 See also *Serm.*, 392. 2. *PL* 39. 1710.

71 In keeping Adeodatus with him after his mother left, Augustine is treating him like a legitimate son. Significantly, he omits any mention of her feelings at the loss of both partner and son.

72 *Con.*, 4. 1; cf. 3. 6ff. *PL* 32. 693; 687, P-C, pp. 71, 60ff. See Brown, *Body and society*, p. 391.

73 Vern Bullough, 'Introduction: the Christian inheritance', in Vern L. Bullough and James A. Brandage, eds., *Sexual practices and the medieval church* (Buffalo, New York: Prometheus Books, 1982), pp. 1–13.

74 So Brown, *Body and society*, p. 390, and Clark, 'Adam's only companion', p. 147. Given Augustine's assertion that he never wanted children, the name Adeodatus (given by God) is thought-provoking.

75 *Con.*, 3. 1; 4. 2; cf. 6. 15. *PL* 32. 683; 693; 732 P-C, pp. 55; 72; 131.

76 *De bono con.*, 4. *PL* 40. 376, PNF 1/3, pp. 400–1.

77 *Con.*, 8. 6, 11–12; 9. 1–3. *PL* 32. 755–6; 760; 763, P-C, pp. 167; 176–9; 181–4. This tension between sexual activity and godliness was so common in religious and philosophic traditions throughout the ancient world that Augustine had to argue that only 'orthodox' Christian sexual abstinence was praiseworthy: *De nupt. et con.*, 1. 4. 4. *PL* 44. 415, PNF 1/5, p. 264b-5a.

78 Augustine himself was aware that many would see his choice as self-

aggrandisement: *Con.*, 9. 2; 10. 30; cf. 1. 10, 17, 19. *PL* 32. 763; 792–3, cf. 665; 667; 670, P-C, pp. 182; 233; cf. 31; 37; 39–40.

79 *Ep.* 26. 2. *PL* 33. 104, WAA 6, p. 69. This letter is dated 395, but still reverberates with the emotion Augustine felt at the dismissal of his concubine.

80 Monica and Verecundus died in 387 and Adeodatus and Nebridius in 390: *Con.*, 9. 3; 9. 6; 9. 8. *PL* 32. 765; 769; 771, P-C, pp. 184; 190; 192. See also *De nupt. et con.*, 1. 17. 19; *PL* 44. 424–5, PNF 1/5, p. 271b. *De trin.*, 12. 5. 5. *PL* 42. 1000–1, WAA 7, p. 288. James Dittes argues that Augustine rejected human relationships and fixated on God because all his intimate human relationships were failures. 'Augustine: search', pp. 57–63. I would argue that, more subtly, it was the loss of significant and successful human relationships that made him fear grief.

81 Cf. *Ep.* 243. *PL* 33. 1054–9, FC 32, p. 225.

82 *Con.*, 2. 6. *PL* 32. 681, P-C, p. 50.

83 *Solil.*, 1. 11. 18. *PL* 32. 879, FC 5, p. 368. This potential bride is a more flattering portrait of a wife as *adiutor* than the later *De gen. ad litt.*, 9. 3. 5; 9. 5. 9. *PL* 34, 395; 396, ACW 42, pp. 73, 75.

84 Cf. *Con.*, 6. 12. *PL* 32. 730, P-C, pp. 128–9; he interprets his praise of his concubinage to Alypius as tempting him to follow his example.

85 The original model was presented by Elisabeth Kübler-Ross, *On death and dying* (New York: Macmillan Publishing Co., 1969), pp. 38–137.

86 M. H. Marx, *Introduction to psychology* (New York: Macmillan Publishing Co., 1976), pp. 208–11.

87 *Con.*, 7. 7; 8. 5; 8. 8; 8. 10. *PL* 32. 739–40; 753–4; 757; 759, P-C, pp. 143; 164–5; 170; 173 and *passim* in the *Confessiones*.

88 *Con.*, 3. 4. *PL* 32. 685, P-C, p. 58. Cf. *De ordine*, 2. 16. 44; 2. 8. 25; 1. 11. 32. *PL* 32. 1015; 1006; 993–4, FC 5, pp. 320; 301–2; 271. Klein consistently found that boyish competitiveness and a striving for manly achievements arise from strong castration anxiety and the fear of impotence. Some men resolve their consequent ambivalent feelings about feminine role models by identifying their masculinity (fundamentally, pride in the penis) with intellectual achievement. Klein perceived this as the parallel dynamic to penis envy, and found that this displacement caused 'an inimical rivalry towards women', *Psychoanalysis*, pp. 256, 262, 338–9. Augustine was such a lad and sometimes would even cheat to win. Cf. *Con.*, 1. 10; 1. 17; 1. 19. *PL* 32. 668; 673–4. P-C, pp. 31; 37; 39.

89 For the story of Verecundus who felt that if he could not be an ascetic like Ambrose and Augustine, then he could not be a Christian at all, see *Con.*, 9. 3. *PL* 32. 765–6, P-C, pp. 183–5. Note Augustine's self-flagellation because men *without schooling* storm the gates of heaven while he lies grovelling in the world of flesh and blood (my emphasis): *Con.*, 8. 8; cf. 9. 2. *PL* 32. 757; 764, P-C, pp. 170, 182.

90 *Con.*, 7. 7. *PL* 32. 740, P-C, p. 143.

91 *Con.*, 8. 1. *PL* 32. 749, P-C, p. 158.

92 See *Solil.*, 1. 14. 25. *PL* 32. 882, FC 5, p. 376.

93 *Con.*, 4. 4–9. *PL* 32. 696–9, P-C, pp. 75–9. About six times the space he devotes to his concubine.

94 *Con.*, 4. 5; cf. 9. 13 on Monica. *PL* 32. 697; 815, P-C, pp. 76; 203. *Con.*, 9. 6. *PL* 32. 769, P-C, p. 190.

95 Bear in mind that Augustine had experienced all these bereavements by the time he was barely in his mid-thirties.

96 *See Solil.*, 1. 14. 25. *PL.* 32. 882, FC 5, p. 376.

97 *Con.*, 8. 11. *PL* 32. 760, P-C, p. 175.

98 *Con.*, 7. 8. *PL* 32. 740, P-C, p. 144. Cf. *Ep.* 263. 2 to Sapida where he reduces grief simply to force of habit. *PL* 33. 1082, WAA 13, p. 460.

99 *Con.*, 9. 4. *PL* 32. 768, P-C, p. 188.

100 *Con.*, 8. 1. *PL* 32. 749, P-C, p. 158.

101 This aspect of sexuality is one Augustine applied to all women: *Solil.*, 1. 10. 17. *PL* 32. 878, FC 5, p. 365. Cf. *De gen. ad litt.*, 9. 18. 34. *PL* 34. 407, ACW 42, p. 94.

102 'The very toys of toys and vanity of vanities... plucked softly at this fleshly garment' (8. 11. *PL* 32. 760, Watts' translation, p. 459). Cf. *Con.*, 10. 30. *PL* 32. 796, P-C, p. 233.

103 Brown understands Augustine's sexual behaviour as being the result of a failure in his will rather than any sexual dysfunction, but it is rather simplistic to see his sexual need as a lack of self-control. Such an analysis remains within the categories that Augustine has defined and does not challenge them (*Augustine and sexuality*, p. 3). On the use of libido to control anxiety and sexuality see Klein, *Psychoanalysis*, pp. 171, 276–7. Extremely high levels of anxiety and guilt result in compulsive behaviour. If anxiety was a major problem for Augustine one would expect the will to fail until the anxiety can be resolved in some other way. On the 'canker of anxiety' he suffered see *Con.*, 8. 1; 9. 1; cf. 8. 10. *PL* 32. 747–9; 763; 759–60, P-C, pp. 158; 181; cf. 172–5.

104 See Ramirez's discussion, 'Demythologizing Augustine', pp. 72–3. Cf. *Con.*, 6. 13. *PL* 32. 730–1, P-C, pp. 129–30.

105 Brown, *AH*, p. 62.

106 *Solil.*, 1. 9. 16; 1. 12. 20; 2. 13. 23. *PL* 32. 877–8; 880; 896, FC 5, pp. 363; 370; 408. Cf. *Con.*, 6. 11, *PL* 32. 729, P-C, p. 127, for a similar internal debate centred around the fear of death.

107 *Solil.*, 1. 14. 25 is significant because Augustine identifies God with reason. *PL* 32. 882–3, FC 5, p. 376.

108 *Con.*, 10. 28. *PL* 32. 795, P-C, p. 232. Cf. *Solil.*, 1. 9. 16; 1. 1. 6. *PL* 32. 877–8; 872, FC 5, pp. 363; 350. The three things Augustine feared were the loss of those he loved, pain and death.

109 Cf. *Con.*, 8. 3. *PL* 32. 750–1, P-C, pp. 161–2.

110 *Civ. Dei*, 16. 34. *PL* 41. 512, GB 18, pp. 442b-3a. He founders on a literal exegesis and falls back on the standby of 'Mystery'. Also see *Quæst. in hept.*, 1. 90. *PL* 34. 571.

111 *De gen. ad litt.*, 9. 12. 20–1. *PL* 34. 400–1, ACW 42, pp. 83–5.

112 Dated 401. *De gen. ad litt.*, 10. 2; cf. 9. 12. 21. *PL* 34. 409; 401, ACW 42, pp. 97; 84. Cf. Genesis 2. 23–4.

113 Kari Børresen, *Subordination*, p. 118. Elizabeth Clark, following Orestano, 'Adam's only companion', p. 161.

114 *De nupt. et con.*, 1. 10–13. *PL* 44. 419–22, PNF1/5, pp. 268–9. Cf. Ambrose *De institutione virginis*, 6. 41. *OO* 14/2, p. 232. I would understand this text as establishing that Mary and Joseph were married in Ambrose's eyes, *pace* Clark, 'Adam's only companion', p. 151.

115 *De serm. Dom. in monte*, 1. 15. 41. *PL* 34. 1250, WAA 8, p. 33; cf. *De*

nupt. et con., 1. 1; 1. 4; 1. 8. *PL* 44. 413–15; 418–19; PNF 1/5, pp. 263; 265; 267a.

116 *De bono con.*, 3. *PL* 40. 375, PNF 1/3, p. 400b.

117 *De bono con.*, 16. Cf. 6. *PL* 40. 384; 377, PNF 1/3, pp. 406a; 402a; *De nupt. et con.*, 1. 17. 19. *PL* 44. 424–5, PNF 1/5, p. 271. Van Bavel, *Ever ancient*, argues hard for marriage as a good, basing his argument on references to the friendship of marriage in Augustine's sermons, but he does not distinguish between goods for their own sake, and second-order goods which depend on other goods for their justification.

118 *Solil.*, 1. 13. 22. *PL* 32. 881, FC 5, p. 273. Cf. O'Connell, *Colloquy* 46, p. 24.

119 This fellowship includes companionship, but it is tainted by the concupiscence that accompanies physical sexuality. It is not true friendship because the partners are not equal: *De bono con.*, 1. *PL* 40. 373, PNF 1/3, p. 399a. If genuine spiritual companionship is sought it is better found in celibate communities. See *De nupt. et con.*, 1. 9. 8. *PL* 44, 419, PNF 1/5, p. 267a. For a different reading of Augustine's thought see Donald Burt, 'Friendship and subordination in earthly societies', *AS* 22 (1991), pp. 83–123. Burt accepts uncritically Augustine's models of hierarchical leadership and omits Augustine's own rejection of friendships with women, as well as the more controversial texts concerning women. See note 115 above.

120 Marriage itself was characterised by three goods; fidelity, offspring and 'sacrament', i.e. lifelong commitment: *De gen. ad litt.*, 9. 7. 12; *PL* 34. 397, ACW 42, p. 78; *De nupt. et con.*, 1. 10. 11; 1. 21. 23. *PL* 44, 420; 427; PNF 1/5, pp. 268a; 273b.

121 *De bono con.*, 9. *PL* 40. 380, PNF 1/3, p. 403b. There must also be the desire to have the children born again in Christ: *De nupt. et con.*, 1. 9. 8; *PL* 44. 419, PNF 1/5, p. 267a; *De bono con.*, 22; 19; *PL* 40. 388; 386–7, PNF 1/3, pp. 409a; 407b; *Civ. Dei*, 14. 21. *PL* 41. 428–9, GB 18, pp. 392–3.

122 *Con.* 2. 2., *PL* 32. 676, P-C, p. 44. *De gen. ad litt.*, 9. 7. 12; *PL* 34. 397, ACW 42, pp. 77–8; *De bono con.*, *passim*; *PL* 40. 373–96, PNF 1/3, pp. 399–413; *De nupt. et con.*, 1. 16. 18 and *passim*. *PL* 44. 424, PNF 1/ 5, p. 271ab and *passim*.

123 *De bono con.*, 9. *PL* 40. 380, PNF 1/3, p. 403b.

124 On the nature of friendship see *Con.*, 2. 5; 4. 8–9; 6. 14. *PL* 32. 679; 698–9; 731, P-C, p. 48; 79; 130. This nuances the glowing picture of married fellowship presented by van Bavel, Bonner, Burt and McCleese as typical of Augustine, as does the master–slave imagery.

125 Ambrose also holds to this position, *De institutione virginis*, 6. 41. *OO* 14/2, p. 142.

126 This theology is consistent throughout his works although the later writing indicates the possibility of a controlled and ordered desire within paradise: *Contra Iul.*, 2. 7. 20; 3. 14. 28–3. 16. 30; 3. 23. 52; 3. 25. 57. *PL* 44. 687; 716–18; 729–30; 731–2. FC 35, pp. 81; 131–4; 154; 158.

127 Cf. *Con.*, 6. 14. *PL* 32. 731, P-C, p. 130.

128 In *Civ. Dei*, 19. 16–17 Augustine relates civic and domestic peace, with the onus on male authority to ensure it. See *Ep.* 243. *PL* 33. 1054–9, FC 32, p. 225.

129 Although some 'loans' were made that often posed a legal question as

to whether it was a marriage dowry or a gift to a concubine: Brundage, *Law*, p. 102. McLeese argues persuasively that Augustine was trying to close the legal loopholes which permitted men to exploit concubinage to avoid marriage and inheritance laws at the expense of their concubines: *Augustine and sexism*, pp. 35–40.

130 *Serm.*, 9. 11. 12; *CCL* 41. 129–31. *Serm.*, 224. 3. *PL* 38. 1194. Cf. van Bavel, *Ever ancient*, p. 36.

131 *De bono con.*, 6; cf. 5; *PL* 40. 377. PNF 1/3, p. 401b; *De con. adult.*, 1. 1. 1. *PL* 40. 452, FC 27, p. 62; *Serm.*, 9. 3–4, 10, 14; 392. 4; 224. 3. *PL* 38–9. 77–85; 1711–12; 1094. Van der Meer says that Augustine spoke on marital chastity and the double standards of his community so often that it was called his 'hobby horse' (*Augustine the bishop*, p. 180).

132 *Serm.*, 9. 4. *PL* 38. 78b. Cf. van Bavel, *Ever ancient*, p. 38; J. van Oort, 'Augustine on sexual concupiscence and Original Sin', *Studia patristica*, XXII, ed. Elizabeth A. Livingstone (Leuven: Peeters Press, 1989), pp. 382–6. It is notable that he makes no mention of Adeodatus' feelings about his mother's departure

133 *De nupt. et con.*, 1. 13. *PL* 44. 422, PNF 1/5, pp. 269; *En. in pss.*, 53. 10; 55. 16. *PL* 36. 626; 658, PNF 1/8, pp. 208b; 223b.

134 *En. in pss.*, 56. 16. *PL* 36. 656, PNF 1/8, p. 223b.

135 Recent scholarship indicates that there was wider opposition to asceticism than had been thought. See articles of Hunter and Sivan.

136 *De bono con.*, 15. *PL* 40. 384, PNF 1/3, p. 405b. Cf. *Civ. Dei*, 14. 16. *PL* 41. 425, GB 18, p. 390a. Cf. 1 Thess. 4. 4.

137 *Civ. Dei*, 14, especially 12, 15–26. *PL* 41. 420; 422–5, GB 18, pp. 388b–96. Desire/concupiscence/lust are synonyms for each other, and the appetite is seen as the punishment for sin. Cf. *De gen. ad litt.*, 9. 3. 6; 9. 10. 18; 11. 31. 41; *PL* 34. 395; 399; 446, ACW 42, pp. 73; 81; 163–4; *De nupt. et con.*, 1. 23. 25. *PL* 44. 428, PNF 1/5, p. 274; *Retractions*, 1. 15. 2. *PL* 32. 608–9, FC 60, p. 72; *De gen. contra Man.*, 1. 19. 3. *PL* 34. 187. See also Brown, *Augustine and sexuality*, pp. 2, 7; J. Patout Burns, *Colloquy* 46 (1983), p. 15.

138 The Donatists and the Pelagians were among those who accused him of still being a Manichee. In contemporary writing, van Oort, 'Augustine', argues he was a Manichee, it is raised as a possibility by O'Connell in *Colloquy* 46 (1983), p. 24, and by B. P. Prusack, 'Woman: seductive siren and source of sin', in Rosemary Radford Ruether, ed., *Religion and sexism: images of women in the Jewish and Christian tradition* (New York: Simon and Schuster, 1974), p. 106.

139 Van Oort presents an interesting argument to the contrary: 'Augustine', pp. 3–153.

140 *Con.*, 5. 2–3. *PL* 32. 706–8, P-C, p. 91–4. Cf. Power, 'Latin Fathers'. Brown sees this fearful fantasy as paving the way for Christian males' acceptance of continence, *Body and society*, p, 19.

141 *De con. adult.*, 2. 8. 7. *PL* 40. 474–6, FC 27, p. 108. 'Men should be able to control themselves.'

142 *Con.*, 8. 6. *PL* 32. 755–6, P-C, pp. 166–8.

143 A situation with many parallels to that of Augustine is found in *Ep.* 259. *PL* 33. 1073–5, esp. col. 1074, FC 32, pp. 253–7; 254. Augustine excoriates Cornelius for taking several concubines after the death of his wife, Cypriana. Perhaps he had himself in mind, as well as Cornelius.

Chapter 9

1 Possidius, *Vita*, 15; 26. *PL* 32. 46; 55, FC 15, p. 105. Brown, *Body and society*, p. 396, speaks of Augustine's 'monochrome, all-male world'.
2 *Con.*, 8. 12. *PL* 32. 761–3, P-C, pp. 177–8. Cf. *En. in pss.*, 127. 1; *PL* 36. 1677 PNF 1/8, p. 606; *Civ. Dei*, 14. 11. *PL* 41. 417, GB 18, p. 386b.
3 Because of this rumour, Augustine's ordination was repudiated by some including the senior Bishop of Numidia: *Contra litt. Pet.*, 3. 16. 19. *PL* 43. 357, PNF 1/4, p. 604a; *Contra Cresc.*, 3. 80. 92. *PL* 43. 545. Brown suggests that this lady may have been Therasia, wife of Paulinus of Nola, a very close friend of Augustine's: *AH*, pp. 203–4.
4 However, authority over consecrated women was part of the bishop's role.
5 Possidius, *Vita*, 27. *PL* 32. 57, FC 15, p. 105.
6 *Ep.* 211. 1. *PL* 33. 958, WAA 13, p. 392. It is difficult to see why physical proximity would affect his anger. In this context van der Meer quotes him as saying, 'Fly from the bars of a nunnery, otherwise you will only lose time and get nothing for your pains but a lot of talk', *Augustine the bishop*, p. 222 (no source cited).
7 *Letter 20*. 5. 1.* Divjak, pp. 297–8.
8 Augustine's letters will be quoted from WAA 6 and 13. This translation is more literal, and provides the convenience of subsections for those wishing to refer to the letters in other editions. Letters which are omitted from the Dods' collection will be quoted from PNF 1/1 and FC 123; 18; 20; 30; 32.
9 *Ep.* 265. *PL* 33. 1086, FC 12, p. 277.
10 *Ep.* 25. 3. *PL* 33. 102, WAA 6, p. 66. *Ep.* 94 is also written in the first person singular, *PL* 33. 347–51, FC 18, pp. 106–16 but *Ep.* 32 employs the first person plural. *PL* 33. 125–9, FC 12, p. 117.
11 *Ep.* 31. *PL* 33. 121, WAA 6, p. 97; *Ep.* 95. *PL* 33. 351, FC 18, p. 115. Here he addresses both as 'most beloved lords, holy, desirable and venerable brothers, fellow disciples under our Lord Jesus'.
12 See *Ep.* 130; 131; 150; 188; 263; *PL* 33. 494; 507; 645; 848; 1082, WAA 13, pp. 142; 166; 249; 357; 460; *Ep.* 262; 266; 267. *PL* 33. 1077; 1089; 1091, FC 32, pp. 261; 282; 285. Augustine probably felt more comfortable relating to women from the authority and safety of the *paterfamilias* role than he did as a brother. The exception is Therasia who is addressed as 'Brother' in association with her husband Paulinus. See *Ep.* 95. *PL* 33. 351, WAA 13, p. 1. This virile acclamation is lost in the translation of J. Cunningham who uses 'brother and sister'.
13 But note *Ep.* 220. In a letter of chastisement, Augustine addresses the letter to his 'son' rather than his brother. *PL* 33. 992, PNF 1/1, p. 573a–76b.
14 *Ep.* 27. 1; 3. 5. *PL* 33. 107–8; 65–6, WAA 6, pp. 72–3; 8–9.
15 *Ep.* 267. *PL* 33. 1091, FC 32, pp. 285–6.
16 *Ep.* 71. 2. *PL* 33. 242, WAA 6, p. 261.
17 *Ep.* 31. 4. *PL* 33. 122–4, WAA 6, pp. 96–8.
18 *Ep.* 27. 2. *PL* 33. 107–8, WAA 6, pp. 72–3. Augustine wrote that longing for Paulinus tormented the innermost part of his being and pleaded: 'Say not that I do wrong to grieve because of my not yet knowing you, when you have disclosed to me your mind, which is the inner man.'
19 *Ep.* 10. 3. See *Ep.* 9. 1. *PL* 33. 76; 75, WAA 6, pp. 24; 20.
20 *Con.*, 3. 1 implies that Augustine did engage in some homosexual activity

in his youth, prior to his concubinage. 'To love and have my love returned was my heart's desire, and it would be all the sweeter if I could also enjoy the body of the one who loved me. So I muddied the stream of friendship with the filth of lewdness and clouded its clear waters with hell's black river of lust.' Augustine never uses 'friend' to describe his concubine, and the language of *amicitia* implies male friendship. PL 32. 683, P-C, p. 55.

21 On organisations, Claire Burton, 'Masculinity and femininity in the organisation', *The promise and the price* (Allen and Unwin, 1991), pp. 13–24. Bonner suggests that Augustine's character had a stoical element that made him suited to male company such as a military mess or college common room (*sic*). Therefore he found all the companionship he needed in the monastic community: 'Women and *amicitia*', p. 270.

22 *Ep.* 188. 1. 1. Cf. 265; 208. 7. PL 33. 848; 1086; 953, WAA 13, p. 357; FC 32, p. 276; WAA 13, p. 384.

23 Bonner, 'Women and *amicitia*', p. 260, argues that Augustine does not condescend to these women. But these are 'virile' women, and his tone is usually paternalistic.

24 *Ep.* 27. 2. PL 33. 108, WAA 6, p. 74.

25 Cf. *Civ. Dei*, 14. 11. PL 41. 419–20, GB 18, p. 386b. See Brown, *Body and society*, pp. 10–11, on Roman men's fear that they might 'descend' into femininity.

26 *Ep.* 262. PL 33. 1077–82, FC 32, pp. 261–9.

27 Bonner, 'Women and *amicitia*', p. 263.

28 See *Ep.* 220. 12. PL 33. 997, PNF 1/1, pp. 572a-6. He affirms Boniface as a 'wise man' who will appreciate reproof from his pastor.

29 *Ep.* 246. 3. PL 33. 1061–2, WAA 13, p. 454.

30 *Ep.* 35. 1. PL 33. 134, WAA 6, p. 110.

31 *Ep.* 35. 4. PL 33. 135, WAA 6, p. 111. This letter gives some idea of the tensions and danger of violence in the controversy. See *Ep.* 23. 7, dated 392; cf. the conciliatory *Ep.* 33, dated 396. PL 33. 98; 129–31, WAA 6, pp. 63, 101–5.

32 Cf. *Ep.* 93, dated 408. PL 33. 321–47, WAA 6, pp. 395–440 and *Ep.* 105, dated 409. PL 33. 396–404, FC 18, pp. 195–211.

33 *Ep.* 246. 2–3. PL 33. 1061, WAA 13, p. 453. See the articles on corporal punishment and slaves by Richard Saller, 'Corporal punishment, authority and obedience in the Roman household' in B. Rawson (ed.), *Marriage, divorce and children in ancient Rome* (Oxford: Clarendon Press, 1991), pp. 143–63; Emil Eyben, 'Fathers and sons', *ibid.*, pp. 114–43.

34 *Ep.* 243. PL 33. 1055, FC 32, p. 220.

35 *Serm. dom. in monte*, 1. 15. 42. PL 34, 1250, PNF 1/6, p. 18b. Cf. *Ep.* 243. PL 33. 1055, FC 32, p. 220.

36 He mentions visiting Florentina's parents at home: *Ep.* 266. 4. PL 33. 1091, FC 32, p. 285. In *Ep.* 130. 7. 14. he says that the love of neighbour is best expressed in persuading the neighbour to love God. PL 33. 499, WAA 13, p. 152.

37 *Ep.* 130. 2, 4, 6–7, 13–14. PL 33. 499, WAA 13, pp. 151–2.

38 *Ep.* 254. PL 33. 1069–70, WAA 13, pp. 459–60. Full correspondence in *Ep.* 252–5.

39 Synod of Elvira, Canon 15. The Canon mentions the disparity in numbers between Christian girls and youths, but mixed marriages will cause 'adultery of the soul' (Laeuchli, p. 128).

40 *Letter* 3*. 2 and *passim*. Divjak, pp. 98, 94–107, FC 81, pp. 34, 31–7.
41 A full discussion of this letter and the North African context is found in W. H. C. Frend, 'The Divjak letters: new light on St Augustine's problems, 416–428', *JEH*, 34, 4 (October, 1983), pp. 504–9.
42 Frend, 'New light', p. 505.
43 *Letter* 20*. 1; 17. [314]-18. [335]; 33. Divjak, pp. 293; 318–21; 342 and *passim*. FC 81 pp. 131–49.
44 *Letter* 20*. 14; 17. 314–18. [335]. Divjak, pp. 318–21. Cf. Frend, 'New light', p. 508, on the role of local aristocratic landholders in maintaining ecclesiastical unity.
45 Augustine, *Ep.* 124, 125, 126. *PL* 33. 471–83, PNF 1/1, pp. 452a-9b. *Ep.* 125 is to Alypius, to whom he wrote about the dispute. All letters trans. FC 18, pp. 337–56.
46 *Ep.* 124; 126. *PL* 33. 417–73; 477–83, PNF 1/1, pp. 452a; 455a.
47 *Ep.* 126. *PL* 33. 477–83, PNF 1/1, pp. 455a-9b.
48 *Ep.* 125. 1–2. *PL* 33. 474–5, PNF 1/1, p. 453ab.
49 Jerome's description of one of Augustine's letters to him. *Ep.* 72. 2. *PL* 33. 244, WAA 6, p. 265. It is fascinating that Paulinus, with whom Augustine was on such good terms, referred to his letters as honeycomb: *Ep.* 94. *PL* 33. 347–51, FC 18, p. 107.
50 *Ep.* 124. 1. *PL* 33. 471–2, PNF 1/1, p. 452a.
51 *Ep.* 125. 2. *PL* 33. 474–5, PNF 1/1, p. 453b.
52 Cf. Elizabeth Clark, on the incredible wealth of Melania the Younger and Pinianus: 'Piety, propaganda and politics in the life of Melania the Younger', in *Ascetic piety*, pp. 71–2.
53 Cf. *Ep.* 94. *PL* 33. 347–51, FC 18, pp. 108–110.
54 *Ep.* 124. 1. *PL* 33. 471, PNF 1/1, p. 452a.
55 *Ep.* 210. 2. *PL* 33. 957, PNF 1/1, p. 563a.
56 *Ep.* 211. 1. *PL* 33. 958, PNF 1/1, p. 563b.
57 The traditional opinion that *Ep.* 211 retained the original Augustinian rule has been overturned by George Lawless, who demonstrates the temporal priority of the masculine version: *Augustine of Hippo and his monastic rule* (Oxford: Clarendon Press, 1987).
58 *Ep.* 211. 4. *PL* 33. 959, PNF 1/1, p. 564ab.
59 *Ep.* 211. 3. *PL* 33. 959, PNF 1/1, p. 564a. cf. *Ep.* 188. 1. 1. *PL* 33. 848, WAA 13, p. 358.
60 *Ep.* 211. 15; cf. 211. 4. *PL* 33. 964–5; 959, PNF 1/1, p. 568a; 564a. See Lawless, on disorder: *Monastic Rule*, p. 112.
61 *Ep.* 211. 14–15; 211. 4. *PL* 33. 964–5, 959, WAA 13, pp. 403, 394. Cf. Lawless, *Monastic rule*, p. 117.
62 Nevertheless she must ask pardon from God: *Ep.* 211. 14. *PL* 33. 964, PNF 1/1, p. 568a.
63 *Ep.* 211. 4. *PL* 33. 959, PNF 1/1, p. 564b.
64 *Ep.* 211. 16. *PL* 33. 965, PNF 1/1, p. 568a.
65 Ambrose, *Expositio evangelii secundum Lucam*, 2. 7. *CSEL* 14. p. 33.
66 *Ep.* 266. *PL* 33. 1089–91, FC 32, pp. 282–5. Florentina was a young woman of studious bent whose parents asked Augustine to oversee her studies.
67 See *Ep.* 27. 1; 92. 2. *PL* 33. 108; 318, WAA 6, p. 72–3; 391; *Ep.* 130. 2. 4. *PL* 33. 495, WAA 13, p. 143. See also Brown, *Body and society*, pp. 208–26.

68 *Ep.* 26. 2. *PL* 33. 104, WAA 6, p. 69.
69 See Gould, *Transformations*, p. 34.
70 On the order of love see *De doct. Christ.*, 1. 23. 22; cf. 1. 27. 28. *PL* 34. 27; 29, GB 18, p. 630a; 631b.
71 *Ep.* 243. *PL* 33. 1054, FC 32, pp. 219–27; *Con.*, 13. 32. *PL* 32. 866, P-C, p. 344. This order is found consistently in his other writings: *De ordine*, 1. 8. 26; *PL* 32. 989, FC 5, p. 263; *Quæst. in hept.*, 1. 53. *PL* 34. 563; *Civ. Dei*, 22. 24. *PL* 41. 791, GB 18, p. 61a.
72 Suzanne Treggiari, 'Divorce Roman style', p. 32.
73 Plutarch, *Moralia II. Advice to bride and groom*, trans. F. C. Babbit, (Loeb Classical Library, Cambridge: Harvard University Press, 1927), pp. 328, 331–2, 339.
74 Fr George Lawless in a personal communication.
75 Tertullian, *Ad uxorem*, 8. 6–9. *CCL* 1, p. 393–4, ANF 4, p. 48b.
76 Ambrose, *Hexameron*, 5. 7. 18–19. *OO* I, pp. 258–60, FC 42, pp. 172–5.
77 *Con.*, 9. 9, *PL* 32. 772, P-C, p. 195: '*ex quo illas tabulas quae matrimoniales vocantur, recitari audissent, tanquam instrumenta quibus ancillae factae essent*'. Cf. *De bono con.*, 14; *PL* 40. 383, PNF 1/3, p. 405; Shaw, 'The family in late antiquity', p. 28, and f.n. 104.
78 Bridegroom threatens: *Serm.*, 46. 36; *PL* 38. 290, WStA III/2, p. 287; unlawful love as polluting: *Serm.*, Mai 20. 1. *PLS* 2. 464–5, WStA III/3, 65A, p. 198–9.
79 *Deus terret: Serm.*, 19. *PL* 38. 257; the 'crushed heart': 19. 3. *PL* 38. 133, WStA III/1, p. 384; 380.
80 See note 33 above on Saller and Eyben.
81 He justifies Sara beating Hagar to curb her pride: *Ep.* 93. 2. 6. *CCL* 34/2, p. 450, PNF 1/1, p. 384a.
82 Augustine, *Serm.*, 332. 4. *PL* 38–9. 1463.
83 There are 308 uses of *ancilla-ae* on the CETEDOC data base.
84 Seven out of ten uses. *Ep.* 36. 2. 4; 78. 8; 93. 2. 6; 140. 19; 185. 2. 9, 11; 196. 3; 211. 16. *PL* 33. 136; 272; 322; 558; 797; 892; 965, PNF 1/1, p. 266a; 348b; 384a; 568ab; *Ep.* 140. 19. FC 20, p. 97; *Ep.* 185. 2. 9. 11. FC 30, pp. 150, 151.
85 Also in *Ep.* 185. 2. 9. *PL* 33. 796, *En. in pss.*, 119. 7. *PL* 37. 1603, PNF 1/8, [par. 6] p. 590b.
86 *Ep.* 211. 16, and 111. 3. *PL* 33. 965; 423 PNF 1/1, pp. 568ab and 434a.
87 Something of this complexity can be found in *En. in pss.*, 122. 5. *PL* 37. 1633, PNF 1/8, p. 597a. God is both master and mistress and Christians are servants and slave girls; feminine as church, masculine as the people of God.
88 Ambrose, *Hexameron*, 5. 7. 19. *OO* I, pp. 260–2.
89 Saller, 'Corporal punishment', p. 157.
90 Shaw, 'The family in late antiquity', p. 12. On the family as the natural basis of society see *Civ. Dei*, 19. 14. *PL* 41. 643, GB 18, p. 520; *De bono con.*, 1. *PL* 40. 373, PNF 1/3, p. 399a.
91 *De cont.*, 9. 23. *PL* 40. 364, PNF 1/3, pp. 388b–9a.
92 See the passages on God's flagellation of the sinner: *Con.*, 5. 8; *PL* 32. 713, P-C, p. 101; *De trin.*, 13. 5. 8. *PL* 42. 1019, WAA 7, p. 317.
93 *Con.*, 10. 4. *PL* 32. 781, P-C, p. 209: '*fraternus ille qui cum approbat me, gaudet de me; cum autem improbat me, contristatur pro me; quia sive approbet ne sive improbet, diliget me.*' Bonds between Christians took precedence

over filial duties and reversed the status of married parents and continent children: *Ep.* 243. *PL* 33. 1054–9, FC 32, pp. 219–27; *Ep.* 188. 2. 6. *PL* 33. 851, WAA 13, p. 361.

94 Ambrose offers a scathing portrait of a step-mother in *Hexameron*, 5. 3. 7. *OO* 1, pp. 244–6, FC 42, pp. 164–5. Cf. Cicero, *De officiis*, 1. 97. For Roman attitudes to stepmothers, see Dixon, *Roman mother*, pp. 155–9. See further discussion in the context of original sin, Part IV.

95 *De trin.*, 13. 18. 23. *PL* 42. 1032–3, WAA 7, p. 337; *Civ. Dei*, 14. 12, 22–4. *PL* 41. 420; 429–33, GB 18, pp. 387, 392b–5a. *De nupt. et con.*, 1. 8. 9. *PL* 44. 418–19, PNF 1/5, p. 267a; Brown, *Augustine and sexuality*, p. 10; Brown, *Body and society*, pp. 408–23 on the *poena reciproca*.

96 *Solil.*, 1. 10. 17. *PL* 32. 878, FC 5, p. 365. Cf. Tavard, *Woman*, p. 118.

97 *De gen. ad litt.*, 11. 31. 40. *PL* 34. 445–6, ACW 42, p. 162. See also Brown, *Augustine and sexuality*, p. 10. Cf. Ernst Becker, *The denial of death* (New York: Free Press, 1973), pp. 40, 42, 163, on the archetypal psychological association between coitus and death.

98 For Roman attitudes see Rawson, 'Roman family', p. 9. For assimilation of sexual desire and hunger see *De bono con.*, 18. *PL* 40. 385–6, PNF 1/3, p. 407.

99 *Con.*, 6. 12. *PL* 32. 730, P-C, p. 129.

100 Present in canon law today. See Canon 1055.

101 Which, in his earlier writings, Augustine has reduced to the prison of habit, and to the failure of the will.

102 *Ep.* 262 to Ecdicia. *PL* 33. 1077–82, FC 32, pp. 261–9.

103 *De nupt. et con.*, 1. 22. 24. *PL* 44. 427–8, PNF 1/5, pp. 273b–4a; *Civ. Dei*, 14. 16, 18. *PL* 41. 424–6, GB 18, p. 390a, 391b.

104 *De ordine*, 2. 11. 31. *PL* 32. 1009, FC 5, p. 300; *De gen. ad litt.*, 11. 32. 42. *PL* 34. 419, ACW 42, pp. 164–5; *De cont.*, 11; 17. *PL* 40. 355–6; 359–60, PNF 1/3, pp. 383a; 391b; *De nupt. et con.*, 1. 5. 6. *PL* 44. 416–17, PNF 1/5, p. 265a. *De gratia Christi*, 2. 38. 43. *PL* 44. 407, PNF 1/3, p. 253a.

105 van de Meer, *Augustine the bishop*, p. 186. Brown, *AH*, pp. 248–9.

106 Both Mortely, *Womanhood*, pp. 90–1, and Ruether, 'Misogynism and virginal feminism in the fathers of the church' in *Religion and Sexism*, pp. 162–3 argue that Augustine's stance dehumanises people. Mortely applies it equally to men and women; Ruether focuses on the dehumanising aspect of women being perceived as simply the vessel of procreation. Cf. E. Clasby, 'Chaucer and Augustine and the doctrine of use', *AS*, 13 (1982), pp. 81–6.

107 Brown, *Augustine and sexuality*, p. 12.

108 Especially in *De cont.*, 20. 23; cf. 9. 9, and the qualifying passage in 9. 18. 23. *PL* 41. 354–5; 360–1; 364–5, PNF 1/3, pp. 382b; 386a; 388b. See also *Con.*, 2. 2; 6. 12; *PL* 32. 670; 730, P-C, p. 44; 129; *De bono con.*, 5. *PL* 40. 377, PNF 1/3. p. 412b; *Solil.*, 1. 10. 17. *PL* 32. 878, FC 5, p. 365; *Serm.*, 149. 2, 7. *PL* 38. 1529–33; *En. in pss.*, 127. 5. *PL* 37. 1679. Cf. 29. 3–4. *PL* 36. 214, PNF 1/8, p. 67b.

109 *En. in pss.*, 55. 17. *PL* 36. 658, PNF 1/8, p. 233b.

110 *Con.*, 8. 12. *PL* 32. 761–4, P-C, pp. 177–8.

111 Cf. Power, 'Latin Fathers'.

112 *De bono con.*, 1. *PL* 40. 373, PNF 1/3, p. 399a.

113 The fact that upper-class husbands were often called away on civic duty,

warfare or politics would not only have affected their marriages but also their participation in church life. As in other spheres, their wives would often administer their responsibilities in their absence.

114 So also Brown, *AH*, p. 205, and Mortley, *Womanhood*, p. 90, on woman as the pleasure principle.

115 In his avoidance behaviour, Augustine anticipated the second Council of Nicaea which legislated this: Canon 18. PNF 2/14, p. 567.

116 Cf. *Civ. Dei*, 14. 11; cf 15. 7. PL 41. 418–20; 445, CB 18, pp. 385b-7; 402b; *De cont.*, 22. PL 40. 363–4, PNF 1/3, p. 388a.

117 The *Liberalia* was celebrated on March 17. See Brown, *Body and society*, p. 28; Rousselle, *Porneia*, p. 79.

118 Shelton, *Romans*, p. 152, note 154.

119 *Con.*, 2. 3. PL 32. 677, P-C, p. 45.

120 See *Ep.* 262. PL 33. 1081, FC 32, p. 269; *Letter* 20*. Divjak, p. 342.

121 *Serm.*, 392. 4–5; cf. *Serm.*, 92. 8, 11; 332. 4. PL 39. 1711–12; cf. 511. PL 1463.

122 On her death bed Monica says that she cannot remember Augustine speaking a single hard or disrespectful word. One can only speculate on how she remembered his deception of her to travel to Italy. *Con.*, 9. 12; cf. 5. 8. PL 32. 776; 712–3, P-C, pp. 200; 100–1.

123 *Con.*, 1. 6; cf. 3. 11; 6. 7. PL 32. 664; cf. 691–2; 725, P-C, pp. 25; 68–9; 120; *De doct. Christ.*, 1. 31. 34. PL 34. 32, GB 18, p. 633ab. See O'Connell, *Odyssey*, p. 181 on Augustine's metaphysical position.

124 Atkinson, 'Your servant', p. 164; Brown, *AH*, p. 175, and Coyle, 'In praise of Monica', p. 90.

125 O'Connell, *Odyssey*, p. 36, maintains the opinion that all human mothers and mistresses stand as so many 'stammering hints of transcendent beauty'.

Chapter 10

1 An early version of some of this material was published in 'Augustine and the feminine as the image of God' in Mark Garner and John Stanley Martin, eds., *St Augustine: the man who made the West* (Department of Germanic Studies, University of Melbourne, 1990), pp. 22–32.

2 J. O'Faolin, and L. Martines, *Not in God's image*. The title of this book was taken from Augustine's text in *De trinitate*. Rosemary Radford Ruether, 'The liberation of Christology from patriarchy' in *NB* (July/August 1985), p. 236. Cf. 'Mysogynism', pp. 150–83.

3 Lynda Brownsey, 'The eikon of the Holy Spirit: our mother Spirit–Dilley bag theology', *Woman-church*, 13 (Spring 1993), p. 45. Brownsey appears to be following Ruether's argument.

4 Ruether, 'The liberation of Christology', p. 235.

5 *Ibid.*

6 Edmund Hill, 'Response to R. R. R. on women' in *NB* (November 1985), p. 503–4. LaPorte and Weaver, 'Augustine and women', p. 131.

7 WStA 1/5, note 27, p. 339.

8 RSV. The Vulgate has *quoniam imago et gloria Dei est, mulier autem gloria viri est*. Man as the 'glory of God' is even stronger than the modern translation of 'reflection'.

9 Helena was also active in the martyr cult, and built the first Marian shrine in Nazareth in 325. Jo Ann McNamara, *'Matres patriae/Matres*

ecclesiae, women of the Roman empire' in Renate Bridenthal et al., eds., *Becoming visible, women in European history*, 2nd edition (Boston: Houghton Mifflin Company, 1987), p. 121.

10 This argument is developed more fully in my paper, ' "A fortified city . . . a city besieged". Ambrose of Milan's symbolic interpretation of the body in *Hexameron 6*', *NAPS*, Chicago: May, 1994.

11 J. N. Adams, *The Latin sexual vocabulary* (London: Duckworth, [1982] 1990), pp. 31, 72, 180, 192.

12 Sly, *Philo*, pp. 59–70.

13 Philo, *Quaestiones et solutiones in Exodum*, 1. 7–8. Trans. Ralph Manheim, *Philo: Supplement II*, Loeb Classical Library, London: Wm Heinemann Ltd, [1953] 1961. Cf. *De pificio mundi*, 45. 132. Yonge, p. 19a.

14 Philo. *Quaestiones et solutiones in Genesim*, 1. 33; 1. 43; 3. 47. Yonge, pp. 798; 799a–800a; 857.

15 Philo, *De opificio mundi*, 53. 151–2. Yonge, p. 21b.

16 Philo, *Quaestiones et solutiones in Genesim*, 1. 33, 46; 3. 47. Yonge, pp. 798; 800a; 857. See Aspegren's commentary, *Male Woman*, p. 90.

17 Philo, *Quis rerum divinarum heres sit*, 13. 64. Yonge, p. 280a. Through mind's study of philosophy man is made immortal: *De opificio mundi*, 25. 78. Yonge, p. 12a.

18 Aspegren, *Male Woman*, p. 83.

19 Origen, *Hom. Gen.*, 4. 4; 5. 2, 6. *PG* 12. 186ab; 190ab; 193, FC 71, pp. 107; 114; 124; Ambrose, *Ep*. 45. 1. 17. *PL* 16. 1194, FC 26, p. 13; *De paradisio*, 2. 11; 11. 51. *CSEL* 32/1, pp. 271; 308, FC 42, pp. 294; 329; cf. comments by Savage, 'Introduction', FC 42, p. ix–x. Cf. Aristotle on the two aspects of the soul.

20 Origen, *Hom. Gen.*, 5. 4; 11. *PG* 12. 191–2; 220–5, FC 71, pp. 116; 168–9; Ambrose, *De paradisio*, 4. 24; 10. 46–7; cf. 2. 11. *CSEL* 32/1, pp. 280–2; 304; 271, FC 42, pp. 301–2; 325–6 cf. *Ep*. 69 to Irenaeus. *PL* 16. 1285–87, FC 26, pp. 437–47.

21 Ambrose, *Ep*. 45 to Sabinus (*c*. 390), 1. 4–5. *PL* 16. 1191–4, FC 26, pp. 130–1. The Platonic sources of Ambrose's thought are found in *Ep*. 25 *PL* 16. 1083–6, FC 26, pp. 129–34; *De bono mortis* (*c*. 387–391), 5. 19. *CSEL* 32/1, p. 720, FC 65, p. 84; *De Isaac vel anima, passim. CSEL* 32/1, pp. 641–700. Isaac, the type of the ideal soul, is male. On the soul's feminine propensity to sin see *De Isaac vel anima*, 2. 1–4. *CSEL* 32/1, pp. 642–5, FC 65, p. 14. Cf. *De virginitate*, 15. 93. *OO* I, p. 74. The linguistic gender is interpreted to reveal not only the soul's vulnerability to the passions of the body, but also its sweet, gentle reasoning that calms said passions: *Ep*. 31 to Irenaeus. *PL* 16. 1110–14, FC 26, p. 423. Cf. Plato, *Republic*, 442. Plato represents the feminine soul as trying to overturn masculine reason.

22 Ambrose makes this connection himself in *De Cain et Abel*, 2. 1. 5. *CSEL* 32/1, p. 380–1, FC 41, p. 404. Clark, 'The gaze', presents an excellent theorisation of this dynamic in late antiquity.

23 Augustine, *Con.*, 13. 32. *PL* 32. 866, P-C. p. 344; *De trin.*, 12. 3. 3. *PL* 42. 999. WAA 7, p. 286; *De gen. ad litt.*, 3. 22. 34. *PL* 34. 293, ACW 41, pp. 98–9.

24 *De trin.*, 12. 3. 3. *PL* 42. 999. WAA 7, p. 286. Cf. Ambrose, *De paradisio*, 11. 51. *CSEL* 32/1, p. 308, FC 42 pp. 329–30.

25 The preferred translation would be 'knowledge', as Augustine consistently

uses it in this sense in other contexts. Overall a CETEDOC survey indicates 412 uses of the term. In a pejorative sense it is the knowledge that 'puffs up' when detached from love or wisdom.

26 *De trin.*, 12. 12. 17; 12. 14. 22. *PL* 42. 1007; 1009–10; WAA 7, pp. 298; 301.

27 *De trin.*, 12. 13. 21. *PL* 42. 1009, WAA 7, p. 301.

28 *De trin.*, 7. 3. 5. *PL* 42. 938, WAA 7, p. 187.

29 Philo, *Quod deterius potiori insidiari solet*, 54; 115–17; *Legum allegoriarum*, 14. 49. Yonge, pp. 118a; 125a; 43a.

30 A useful discussion on the relationship and parallels between Judaic, Christian and pagan symbols of Wisdom is found in H. C. Kee, 'Myth and miracle: Isis, Wisdom and the Λόγος of John' in Alan M. Olsen, ed., *Myth, symbol and reality* (Notre Dame: University of Notre Dame Press, 1980), pp. 153–61.

31 *De gen. ad litt.*, 3. 22; 34. *PL* 34. 293; ACW 41, p. 98.

32 *De trin.*, 12. 8. 13. *PL* 42. 1005, WAA 7, p. 294.

33 *De trin.*, 12. 5. 5. *PL* 42. 1001, WAA 7, pp. 287–8.

34 *De trin.*, 12. 7. 9. *PL* 42. 1003, WAA 7, p. 291.

35 *De trin.*, 15. 7. 11. *PL* 42. 1065, WAA 7, p. 389.

36 *De opere mon.*, 32. 40. *PL* 40. 579–80, FC 16, p. 392.

37 *De trin.*, 12. 7. 10, 12. *PL* 42. 1003; 1005, WAA 7, pp. 291–2; 293. So also Gregory of Nyssa, *De opificio hominis*, 16. 9. *PG* 44. 182, PNF 2/5, pp. 404–6. The translation unfortunately makes no effort to reflect the inclusion of women.

38 *De trin.*, 12. 7. 12. *PL* 42. 1005, WAA 7, p. 293.

39 *De gen. ad litt.*, 6. 12. 22. *PL* 34. 348, ACW 41, p. 193.

40 *Civ. Dei.*, 14. 11. *PL* 41. 419, GB 18, p. 386a.

41 *De trin.*, 12. 7. 12; cf. 15. 7. 11. *PL* 42. 1005; 1065, WAA 7, pp. 294; 389.

42 *De gen. ad litt.*, 3. 22. 34. *PL* 34. 293–4, ACW 41, p. 99, *De trin.*, 12. 7. 12. *PL* 42. 1005, WAA 7, p. 293.

43 *De trin.*, 12. 7. 10; cf. 12. 3. 3. *PL* 42. 1003; 999, WAA 7, pp. 292; 286.

44 *De trin.*, 12. 12. 1. *PL* 42. 1007, WAA 7, p. 298.

45 *De trin.*, 12. 3. 3; 12. 4. 4. *PL* 42. 999; 1000, WAA 7, p. 286.

46 *De trin.*, 11. 5. 8. *PL* 42. 991, WAA 7, p. 271.

47 *De opere mon.*, 32. 40. *PL* 40. 579–80, FC 16, p. 392.

48 The existence of this model, even though it too ascribed temporal duties to the feminine and eternal roles to the masculine, does indicate that there were other Christians, struggling to explain the manner in which the feminine is image, who privileged Genesis over Paul. What is common to all is that the feminine is subordinate.

49 *De gen. ad litt.*, 3. 22. 34. *PL* 34. 293, ACW 41, p. 98.

50 *De gen ad litt.*, 6. 6. 10; cf. 11. 42. 58 *PL* 34. 343; 452, ACW 41, p. 184; ACW 42, p. 175. For a detailed examination of how the creation of human beings affects their relationship to God and to one another, see Børresen, *Subordination*, pp. 16–17.

51 *De gen. ad litt.*, 11. 42. 58. *PL* 34. 452–3, ACW 42. p. 175.

52 *De gen. ad litt.*, 9. 11. 19. *PL* 34. 399, ACW 42, p. 82.

53 Augustine intimately associated bodily difference with sexual desire. Neither have any place in the *imago Dei*.

54 *De trin.*, 15. 8. 14. *PL* 42. 1068, WAA 7, p. 393.

55 *De trin.*, 14. 7. 10. *PL* 42. 1044, WAA 7, p. 356.

56   *De trin.*, 12. 3. 3. *PL* 42. 999, WAA 7, pp. 285–6.
57   *De trin.*, 12. 7. 10. *PL* 42. 1003, WAA 7, p. 292.
58   *De gen. ad litt.*, 9. 5. 9. *PL* 34. 396, ACW 42, p. 75. As Adam and Eve were the human prototypes, so their relationship is definitive of male/female relationships.
59   Lewis & Short, p. 38. It is interesting that Augustine uses the masculine rather than the feminine *adiutrix*. Possibly it is his way of reinforcing the absence of gender in the mind.
60   *De trin.*, 12. 3. 3; 12. 4. 4. *PL* 42. 999; 1000; WAA 7, pp. 285–6.
61   *De trin.*, 12. 12. 17. *PL* 42. 1007, WAA 7, p. 298.
62   *De trin.*, 12. 7. 10. *PL* 42. 1003–4, WAA 7, p. 292.
63   *De trin.*, 12. 3. 3. *PL* 42. 999, WAA 7, p. 286.
64   *De trin.*, 12. 14. 22. *PL* 42. 1010, WAA 7, p. 302.
65   *De trin.*, 12. 14. 23. *PL* 42. 1010, WAA 7, p. 303.
66   *De trin.*, 14. 12. 15. *PL* 42. 1018, WAA 7, p. 362.
67   *Participatione* in *De trin.*, 14. 12. 15. *PL* 42. 1018, WAA 7, p. 362; cf. *particeps* in 14. 8. 11. *PL* 42. 1044, WAA 7, p. 357.
68   *De trin.*, 14. 8. 11; 11. 5. 8. *PL* 42. 1044–5; 991, WAA 7, p. 356; 271.
69   *De trin.*, 14. 14. 20. *PL* 42. 1051, WAA 7, p. 367. Cf 1 Cor. 6.17.
70   *De trin.*, 14. 12. 15. *PL* 42. 1018, WAA 7, p. 362.
71   *De trin.*, 14. 14. 18; *PL* 42. 1050, WAA 7, p. 365; the defaced is restored at 14. 16. 22; 14. 17. 23. *PL* 42. 1053; 1054, WAA 7, pp. 370; 372; 'defaced' means loss of righteousness and holiness.
72   *Civ. Dei*, 14. 17. *PL* 41. 425, GB 18, p. 390b.
73   *De trin.*, 12. 15. 25. *PL* 42. 1012, WAA 7, pp. 305–6.
74   *De trin.*, 12. 14. 22. *PL* 42. 1010, WAA 7, p. 302.
75   *De trin.*, 14. 8. 11. *PL* 42. 1045, WAA 7, p. 358.
76   *De trin.*, 13. 20. 26. *PL* 42. 1086, WAA 7, p. 342.
77   *De trin.*, 14. 8. 11. *PL* 42. 1045, WAA 7, p. 358. See also 13. 2. 5. *PL* 42. WAA 7, p. 313.
78   In this Augustine seems to differ from Paul in 1 Cor. 13.13, where faith, hope and love remain, but the greatest is love.
79   *De trin.*, 14. 8. 11. *PL* 42. 1045, WAA 7, p. 358. Cf. 1 Cor. 13.9–12. He ignores verse 13.
80   *De trin.*, 14. 2. 4. *PL* 42. 1038, WAA 7, p. 347.
81   The implications of this statement are serious. What follows from this is that only virtue grounded in Christian faith can really merit the name virtue, a statement explicit in *De trin.*, 12. 7. 11. *PL* 42. 1004, WAA 7, p. 293.
82   *De trin.*, 13. 9. 12; 13. 20. 25–6. *PL* 42. 1025; 1034–6, WAA 7, pp. 323; 340–2.
83   *De trin.*, 13. 5. 8; 13. 20. 25. *PL* 42. 1019; 1034, WAA 7, pp. 318; 340.
84   *De trin.*, 13. 8. 11. *PL* 42. 1023, WAA 7. p. 321.
85   *De trin.*, 13. 7. 10. *PL* 42. 1021, WAA 7, p. 320.
86   *De trin.*, 13. 10. 14. *PL* 42. 1024, WAA 7, p. 325.
87   I use the word 'rage' advisedly here, as will become clear in the discussion of the feminine as concupiscence. Cf. *De nupt. et. con.*, 1. 8. 9. *PL* 44. 419, PNF 1/5, p. 267.
88   *De trin.*, 12. 8. 13. *PL* 42. 1006, WAA 7, p. 295.
89   *De opere mon.*, 32. 40. *PL* 40. 580, FC 16, p. 393.
90   *De trin.*, 12. 12. 17. *PL* 40. 1008, WAA 7, p. 298–9.

91 *De opere mon.*, 32. 40. *PL* 40. 580, FC 16, p. 393.
92 *De trin.*, 12. 12. 17. *PL* 42. 1007, WAA 7, p. 298.
93 *De trin.*, 12. 13. 21. *PL* 42. 1009, WAA 7, p. 301.
94 *De trin.*, 12. 8. 13. *PL* 42. 1005–6, WAA 7, p. 295.
95 *De trin.*, 12. 11. 16. *PL* 42. 1007, WAA 7, pp. 296–7. Here Augustine uses *concupiscitur*. Earlier in the same passage, col. 1006, he used *cupiditas*.
96 *De trin.*, 12. 1. 1. *PL* 42. 999, WAA 7, p. 284.
97 *De trin.*, 12. 12. 17. *PL* 42. 1007, WAA 7, p. 298.
98 *De trin.*, 11. 3. 6. *PL* 42. 988, WAA 7, p. 267–8.
99 *De opere mon.*, 32. 40. *PL* 40. 580, FC 16, p. 393; cf. *De nupt. et con.*, 1. 22, 24. *PL* 44. 428, PNF 1/5, p. 273.
100 *Civ. Dei*, 14. 16. *PL* 41. 424–5, GB 18, p. 390 a.
101 *De nupt. et con.*, 1. 1; 4. 5; cf. 6. 7–8. 9. *PL* 44. 414; 415; cf. 417–18, PNF 1/5, pp. 263 a; 264 a; cf. 266 b–267a.
102 *De nupt. et con.*, 23. 25. *PL* 44. 428, PNF 1/5, p. 274 a.
103 *De nupt. et con.*, 1. 8, 9. *PL* 44. 419, PNF 1/5, p. 267.
104 *De trin.*, 12. 12. 17. *PL* 42. 1007, WAA 7, p. 298.
105 *De trin.*, 12. 11. 16. *PL* 42. 1007, WAA 7, p. 297.
106 *De trin.*, 12. 9. 14. *PL* 42. 1006, WAA 7, p. 295.
107 *De trin.*, 12. 9. 14. *PL* 42. 1006, WAA 7, p. 296.
108 *De gen. ad litt.*, 11. 30. 39. *PL* 34. 445, ACW 42, p. 162.
109 *De gen. ad litt.*, 11. 42. 59. *PL* 34. 453, ACW 42, p. 176. 'Men' is not *vir* but *homo*. In the following paragraph he speculates whether the fact that Eve, in fact, did not die after eating the fruit, might have helped tempt Adam to 'a new experience' (11. 42. 60. *PL* 34. 454, ACW 42, p. 176). Elsewhere, he spoke collectively of Adam and Eve offending 'by pride and arrogant love of their own independence', and an eagerness to experience the unknown (11. 32. 42. *PL* 34. 447, ACW 42, p. 164).
110 *De gen. ad litt.*, 11. 42. 59. *PL* 34. 453, ACW 42, p. 176; also *Civ. Dei*, 14. 11. *PL* 41. 418, GB 18, p. 387a.
111 *De trin.*, 12. 12. 17. *PL* 42, 1008, WAA 7, pp. 298–9.
112 *De trin.*, 12. 12. 18. *PL* 42. 1008, WAA 7, p. 299.
113 An unusual twist, because he is quite sure that even in paradise women were subordinate, although the quality of the relationship was different: *De gen. ad litt.*, 11. 37. 50. *PL* 34. 450, ACW 42, p. 171.
114 *De trin.*, 12. 12. 18. *PL* 42. 1008, WAA 7, p. 298.
115 *De trin.*, 12. 10. 15. *PL* 42. 1006, WAA 7, p. 296.
116 As in Monica's sip by sip descent into closet tippling.
117 *De trin.*, 12. 10. 15–11. 16. *PL* 42. 1007, WAA 7, pp. 296–7.
118 *De trin.*, 12. 11. 16. *PL* 42. 1007, WAA 7, p. 297.
119 See *De trin.*, 13. 7. 10; cf. 13. 9. 12. *PL* 42. 1020; 1024, WAA 7, pp. 319; 324. 'God, in whom alone and from whom alone, the blessed can be made partakers in that immortality.' Also *Con.*, 10. 2. *PL* 32. 779, P-C. p. 208.
120 *Ep.* 188. 2. 7–8. *PL* 33. 851, WAA 13, p. 261.
121 *De trin.*, 13. 16. 21. *PL* 42. 1031, WAA 7, p. 335.
122 *De trin.*, 13. 7. 10. *PL* 42. 1020, WAA 7, pp. 318–9; cf. *Ep.*, 95. 2. *PL* 33. 353, WAA 13, p. 3. 'Behold whence it comes that our whole life on earth is a temptation' (Job 7:1 in the Vulgate).
123 *De trin.*, 12. 12. 17. *PL* 42. 1008, WAA 7, p. 298.
124 *De trin.*, 13. 1. 1. *PL* 42. 1013, WAA 7, p. 307.

125   *Ep.*, 188. 1. 3. *PL* 33. 849, WAA 13, p. 257.
126   *De trin.*, 12. 3. 3. *PL* 42. 999, WAA 7, p. 286.
127   Cf. B. Bubascz, 'Augustine's dualism and the inner man', *MS*, 54 (1977), p. 249.
128   Apart from the texts dealt with in the previous chapter, see *De gen. contra Man.*, 2. 11. 15. *PL* 34. 204. Even when he applied a spiritual interpretation to Eve's role she was still Adam's *adiutor* – *pace* Bonner, who concludes that if the relationship had been spiritual, Eve must have been perceived as companion. Bonner cites 1. 9. 30. However, the biological procreative role was simply spiritualised, '*ut copulatione spiri-tuali spirituales fetus ederet id est bona opera divinae laudis*': Bonner, 'Women and *amicitia*', p. 261.
129   *De gen. ad litt.*, 9. 5. 9; cf. 8. 8. 15. *PL* 34. 396; 379, ACW 42, pp. 75; 45, where Augustine explains the delight and pleasure in tilling the soil so that it is not labour.
130   *De gen. ad litt.*, 9. 5. 9; cf. 9. 3. 5. *PL* 34. 396; 395, ACW 42, p. 75; 73.
131   *De gen. ad litt.*, 9. 5. 9. *PL* 34. 396, ACW 42, p. 75. A man created second would also have ranked second to Adam, so there would have been no conflict over leadership.
132   Galen held that women possessed an inferior procreative seed, but his was not the dominant model. See Laqueur, *Making sex*, for a social history of medical models.
133   *De gen. ad litt.*, 9. 3. 5. *PL* 34. 395, ACW 42, p. 73; also *Civ. Dei*, 14. 21. *PL* 41. 428–9, GB 18, p. 392b. The image of woman as seed-bed is a commonplace in classical and patristic literature.
134   *De gen. ad litt.*, 9. 3. 5. *PL* 34. 395, ACW 42, p. 73.
135   *De trin.*, 12. 7. 12. *PL* 42. 1005, WAA 7, p. 294.
136   *De trin.*, 15. 8. 14. *PL* 42. 1068, WAA 7, p. 393.
137   *De trin.*, 12. 7. 10. *PL* 42. 1003–4, WAA 7, p. 292.
138   *De trin.*, 12. 7. 10. *PL* 42. 1003–4, WAA 7, p. 292.
139   *De trin.*, 12. 7. 11. *PL* 42. 1004, WAA 7, p. 293.
140   *De trin.*, 12. 12. 17. *PL* 42. 1007, WAA 7, p. 298.
141   *De trin.*, 12. 8. 13. *PL* 42. 1005–6, WAA 7, p. 294.
142   *De opere mon.*, 32. 40. *PL* 40. 580, FC 16, p. 393. '*Sed corporis sui sexu non eam significant.*'
143   *Con.*, 13. 32. *PL* 32. 866, P-C, p. 344.
144   *De trin.*, 12. 5. 5. *PL* 42. 1001, WAA 7, p. 288.
145   *Civ. Dei*, 14. 15. *PL* 41. 423–4, GB 18, p. 389b. Cf. *De nupt. et con.*, 1. 23. 25. *PL* 44. 428, PNF 1/5, p. 274.
146   *Civ. Dei*, 14. 16. *PL* 41. 424, GB 18, p. 390a. Lust 'usually suggests to the mind the lustful excitement of the organs of generation'. (*libido . . . non fere assolet animo occurrere nisi illa, qua obscenae corporis partes excitantur.*)
147   *De nupt. et con.*, 1. 22. 24. *PL* 44. 428, PNF 1/5, pp. 273–4.
148   *De nupt. et con.*, 1. 24. 27. *PL* 44. 429, PNF 1/5, p. 275.
149   *De nupt. et con.*, 1. 22. 24. *PL* 44. 427–8, PNF 1/5, pp. 273–4.
150   *De gen. ad litt.*, 11. 32. 42. *PL* 34. 447, ACW 42, p. 165.
151   M. French, *Beyond power: on women men and morals* (Glasgow: Collins/ Abacus Books, 1986), p. 95.
152   On asceticism as *vita angelica*, see chapter 12.
153   *De nupt. et con.*, 1. 6. 7. *PL* 44. 418, PNF 1/5, p. 266.

154 The veiled is shameful: *Contra Iul.*, 4. 12. 58; 5. 2. 7. *PL* 44. 766; 786,
     FC 35, pp. 216; 246–7. On seemliness, *Contra Iul.*, 4. 16. 80. *PL* 44.
     779–80, FC 35, p. 237; veiling sex because intrinsically shameful: *De
     nupt. et con.*, 1. 5. 6.-1. 7. 6; 2. 13. 26; 2. 22. 37; 2. 30. 52. *PL* 44. 416–8;
     451; 458; 467, PNF 1/5, pp. 265–6; 298a; 304b. Cf. *Contra duas ep. Pel.*,
     1. 16. 32–3. *PL* 44. 564–5, PNF 1/6, pp. 386b-7a.
155 *De trin.*, 1. 8. 16. *PL* 42. 830–1, PNF 1/3, p. 26; *Serm.*, 19. 3. *PL* 38.
     133, WStA III/1, p. 380.
156 *De trin.*, 15. 8. 14. *PL* 42. 1067–8, PNF 1/3, p. 206. PNF uses 'open
     faces', 'veil' is retained in Hill's translation, WStA 1/5, p. 406.
157 *Serm.*, 19. 3; 46. 36–7; 137. 6. *PL* 38. 133; 290–1; 758, WStA III/1,
     p. 380; /2, p. 287; /4, p. 376. Sermons dated *c.* 409–410, when he was
     writing the end of *De trinitate*.
158 Unlawful loves: *Serm.*, Mai 20. 1. *PLS* 38. 464–5, WStA III/3, 65A
     p. 198. RSV: 'Tell me, you whom my soul loves, where do you pasture
     your flock, where do you made it lie down at noon?' Augustine's version
     differs slightly from the RSV. RSV: 'For why should I come as one
     veiled?' Augustine: 'Lest I come as one veiled.'
159 *Serm.*, 138. 6–7, 8, 10; 146. 2. *PL* 38. 766–9; 798; WStA III/4, pp. 388–9;
     390; 446; *Serm.*, Denis 12. 5. *MA* I, p. 54, WStA III/4, 147A. 5, p. 455.
160 *Serm.*, 138. 6–7, 10. *PL* 38. 766–9, WStA III/4, pp. 388–92; *Serm.*, Morin
     6. 4. *PLS* II. 674, WStA III/3, 62A. 4, p. 172.
161 Bad daughters: *Serm.*, 37. 27; 46. 36–7; bad desire: *Serm.*, 138. 8;
     putrescent: *Serm.*, 138. 6. Cf. Mai 20. *PL* 38. 233; 290–2; 767–8; 766;
     cf. PLS II. 464–6, WStA III/2, p. 198–9; 288; /4, p. 390; 388; cf. III/3,
     65A. p. 199.
162 It was a strong tradition in antiquity that sexual pleasure was essential
     for conception to take place. John Chrysostom, *Homily 'Propter fornic-
     ationes'*, 2. 210. *PG* 51. 217–18. This belief would also seem to be implied
     in Gregory of Nyssa, *De hominis opificio*, 30. 30. *PG* 44. 255, PNF 2/5,
     p. 426b.
163 *De nupt. et con.*, 1. 8. 9. *PL* 44. 418–19, PNF 1/5, p. 267. See Origen on
     sexual desire as 'necessity', *De principiis*, 3. 4. 4. *SC* 268, pp. 211–15,
     ANF 4, p. 340 a.
164 *Contra Iul.*, 4. 12. 58–4. 13. 62. *PL* 44. 766–8, FC 35, pp. 216–19.
165 *Solil.*, 1. 10. 17. *PL* 32. 878, FC 5, p. 365. Cf. *De gen. ad litt.*, 9. 18. 34.
     PL 34. 407, ACW 42, p. 94.
166 *De gen. ad litt.*, 9. 13. 23. *PL* 34. 402, ACW 42, p. 86.
167 *De gen. ad litt.*, 9. 18. 34. *PL* 34. 407, ACW 42, p. 94.
168 *De trin.*, 1. 9. 18. *PL* 42. 832, PNF 1/3, p. 27ab. Consistently he used
     the story of the Magdalene in the garden to distinguish between faith
     in the human Jesus and faith in the post-Resurrection Word. Mary was
     forbidden to touch Jesus because she still believed in him as a human
     being. When he called her by name she believed in him as the Word.
     There is no distinction between Mary and the male disciples in this.
     This context is the only one that I have found where Augustine even
     discusses Mary Magdalene. He considers that she loved Jesus more than
     the men because she was a woman and therefore softer than the 'hard'
     male disciples, but does not suggest that she be taken as a model. Rather
     her desire to 'touch' the humanity of Jesus rather than his divinity is a
     lesson for the faithful. On the other hand, she is not cast in the role of

prostitute or sexual woman by Augustine although sometimes by his translators. On Mary, *Serm.*, 229L. 1–2. *MA* I, 484–5; *Serm.*, 244. 1–3; 245, 1–2; 246. 3–4. *PL* 38. 1147–50; 1154–55, WStA III/6, pp. 312–13; / 7, p. 95–9; 100–1; 104–5. All but the first sermon are dated *c.* 409–413. Cf. *De con. ev.* (dated 400), 3. 24. 69. PNF 1/6, pp. 213–14. Mary loved more ardently than other women. For interpretative trans. see *En. in pss.*, 46. 8; 140. 5. *PL* 36. 528–9; *PL* 37. 1818, PNF 1/8, pp. 248b; 645 a.

169 *Civ. Dei*, 22. 16–17. *PL* 41. 778, GB 18, p. 602b.
170 *Solil.*, 1. 13. 22. *PL* 32. 881, FC 5, p. 373. *Con.*, 8. 11. *PL* 32. 761, P-C, p. 176.
171 There were only three years between the *Confessiones* and the beginning of *De trinitate* in 400, but it was not concluded until 419, although it first appeared in 414 according to Brown, *AH*, Chronological table D. Therefore, Book 12 may present a much later viewpoint.

Chapter 11

1 See T. L. Miethe's discussion, 'St Augustine and sense knowledge', *AS*, 8 (1977), pp. 1–19. Ambrose, *Hexameron*, 6. 9. 61. *OO* I, p. 406, FC 42, p. 273.
2 This will become even clearer in the discussion of human birth and original sin in the following chapter.
3 Klaus Thraede, 'Zwischen Eva und Maria: das Bild der Frauen bei Ambrosius und Augustine auf dem Hintergrund der Zeit' in *Frauen in Spätantike und Frühmittelalter: Lebenbedingungen – Lebensnormen – Lebensformen* (Sigmaringen: Jan Thorbecke Verlag, 1990), pp. 129–39.
4 For sources see the brief discussion of cosmology in chapter 3, p. 24.
5 *De nupt. et con.*, 1. 9. 8. *PL* 44. 418, PNF 1/5, p. 267.
6 See chapter 10, p. 132.
7 *De gen. ad litt.*, 11. 37. 50. *PL* 34. 450, ACW 42, pp. 170–1; *Civ. Dei*, 14. 11. *PL* 41. 419, GB 18, p. 386b. Cf. *De nupt. et con.*, 1. 9. 10. *PL* 44. 419, PNF 1/5, pp. 267–8.
8 An example is *Ep.* 262. *PL* 33. 1077–82, FC 32, pp. 261–9. I am not suggesting that Augustine believed children did not owe a certain obedience to their mothers.
9 *Serm.*, 392. 4. *PL* 38–9. 1711. Cf. Børresen, *Subordination*, p. 104.
10 *Serm.*, 332. 4. *PL* 38–9. 1463.
11 That such a viewpoint existed see Wilson-Kastner, *A lost tradition*, p. xxiii.
12 On classical men and marriage and the lack of mutuality see Rouselle, *Porneia*, pp. 5–20, 40.
13 *Serm.*, 9. 12. *PL* 38. 84. K. Børresen states that Augustine's concern in emphasising this right was to exhort men to Christian standards of morality rather than to assert women's spiritual equivalence: *Subordination*, p. 104.
14 *De trin.*, 11. 5. 80. *PL* 42. 991, WAA 7, p. 271.
15 *De serm. dom. in monte*, 1.15. 41. *PL* 34. 1250, WAA 8, p. 33.
16 Alexander, 'Sex and philosophy', pp. 198–200.
17 Børresen, *Subordination*, p. 24.
18 *De nupt. et con.*, 1. 17. 19. *PL* 44. 424, PNF 1/5, p. 271b, 'the overbearing lust of pleasure'.
19 *De nupt. et con.*, 1. 8. 9. *PL* 44. 418–19, PNF 1/5, p. 267 a.
20 *De mendacio*, 7. 10. *PL* 40–1, 495–6, FC 16, p. 143. Also *De nupt. et con.*,

1. 8. 9. *PL* 44. 418–19, PNF 1/5, p. 267ab; *De bono con.*, 6. *PL* 40. 377, PNF 1/5, p. 401b-2a.
21 *De nupt. et con.*, 1. 24. 27. *PL* 44. 429, PNF 1/5, p. 275.
22 *De mendacio*, 7. 10. *PL* 40–1. 495, FC 16, p. 143.
23 A not uncommon opinion in antiquity: *Contra Iul.*, 2. 7. 20. *PL* 44. 687, FC 35, p. 81.
24 So also Børresen, *Subordination*, p. 117. 'Thus the strivings of a virtuous man against the temptations of concupiscence breed in him a hostility towards woman, who has been created with a sexual function in view.'
25 An example of the manner in which cultural values are internalised by women as well is Proba's *Cento*. Proba was as hard or harder on Eve than Augustine when she wrote in the fifth century. Trans. by Jeremiah Reedy in *A lost tradition*, pp. 45–70. Cf. C. Christ, 'Why women need the goddess' in *Womanspirit rising*, p. 275.
26 Rouselle, *Porneia*, p. 131 argues that 'the pagan experiments with sexual abstinence and the social conditions which prevented women giving free expression to their sexuality prepared the way for Christian asceticism and even in a sense led to its emergence as an alternative to hysteria.'
27 Jerome *Ep.* 117. 7. *PL* 22. 953–60, PNF 2/6, pp. 215–20. Jerome's vitriol is directed at a young celibate woman who is living under the protection of a celibate man. Many early Christians lived in these brother–sister marriages, but they so contravened the mores of society they were regarded with great suspicion and condemnation and forbidden as conducive to sin and scandal. Jerome accuses the virgin of being in a clandestine sexual relationship. On the other hand, Jerome's enemies accused him of making the whole story up to indulge himself. See note, PNF 2/6, p. 215.
28 Augustine believed that marriages where sexual desire is totally controlled by the will so rare as to be non-existent: *Civ. Dei*, 14. 23. *PL* 41. 430–1, GB 18, p. 393b. This is because even procreative intercourse depends on desire to 'set these members in motion': *De nupt. et con.*, 1. 6. 7. *PL* 44. 418, PNF 1/5, p. 266b.
29 Børresen, *Subordination*, p. 118.
30 Benko, *Pagan Rome*, p. 94.
31 *De nupt. et con.*, 1. 11. 12. *PL* 44. 420, PNF 1/5, p. 268b.
32 *De trin.*, 12. 5. 5. *PL* 42. 1001, WAA 7, p. 288; *Serm.*, 215. 3. *PL* 38–9. 1073; *Contra Iul.*, 1. 2. *PL* 44. 641–2, FC 35, p. 6.
33 *Civ. Dei*, 14. 17–18. *PL* 41. 425, GB 18, pp. 390a-1a; *De nupt. et con.*, 1. 22. 24. *PL* 44. 428, PNF 1/5, p. 274.
34 Armstrong, *Gospel*, p. 35.
35 *Civ. Dei*, 14. 17. *PL* 41. 425–6, GB 18, p. 390ab.
36 Cormac Burke, 'St Augustine and conjugal chastity', *Communio*, 17 (Winter 1990), pp. 545–65.
37 Cf. Hunter (following Bonner), 'Augustinian pessimism? a new look at Augustine's teaching on sex, marriage and celibacy', *AS*, 25 (1990), p. 169.
38 My thanks to the anonymous referee for his comments.
39 The male celebration was at puberty when the youth donned the *toga virilis*. The young woman's celebration took place just before her marriage.
40 I have found the work of Robert Markus most helpful in understanding this dynamic in Augustine's thought as it applies to sexual behaviour: *End*, pp. 50–1.

41 *De trin.*, 9. 8. 13. *PL* 42. 968, WAA 7, p. 234.
42 *De trin.*, 10. 10. 13. *PL* 42. 981, WAA 7, p. 256. Latin verbs are *utor et fruor.*
43 Lewis & Short, p. 1947. J. F. Mountford, ed., *'Bradley's Arnold' Latin prose composition*, new edition (London: Longmans, Green and Company, [1938] 1960), # 228, Note. The passive form with the ablative case offers insight into the Latin usage.
44 *De trin.*, 10. 11. 17. *PL* 42. 982–3, WAA 7, p. 258–9.
45 *De gen. ad litt.*, 9. 5. 9. *PL* 34. 396, ACW 42, p. 75.
46 *De trin.*, 12. 7. 12; cf. 10. 7. 9; 11. 5. 8; 12. 15. 25. *PL* 42. 1005; cf. 978; 991; 1012, WAA 7, p. 294; cf. 234; 271–2; 305.
47 *Con.*, 13. 22. *PL* 32. 866, P-C, p. 344.
48 Ambrose even had to defend the fact that women could assist men: *De paradisio*, 10. 48. CSEL 32/1, p. 306, FC 42, p. 327.
49 *De trin.*, 12. 7. 12. *PL* 42. 1005, WAA 7, p. 294. Cf. *De opere mon.*, 32. 40. *PL* 40. 579–80, FC 16, p. 393.
50 *De gen. ad litt.*, 3. 22. 34. *PL* 34. 293, ACW 41, p. 99.
51 Tavard, *Woman*, p. 115. See *De gen. ad litt.*, 11. 30. 39; 11. 35. 48; 11. 42. 58; 11. 42. 60. *PL* 34. 445; 449; 454, ACW 42, pp. 162; 169, 175–6.
52 *De gen. ad litt.*, 9. 5. 9. *PL* 34. 396, ACW 42, p. 75.
53 *Quaest. in Hept.*, 1. 53. *PL* 34. 561, 'the weaker mind should serve the stronger'.
54 *Civ. Dei*, 14. 11. *PL* 41. 419, GB 18, p. 386b. In other texts Augustine comments that men were more inclined to adultery than women: *De con. adult.*, 1. 4. 4; 1. 6. 6. *PL* 40. 453–5, FC 27, pp. 65–7; *Serm.*, 9. 9. 12; 9. 3. 3; 132. 2. *PL* 38, 84; 77; 735.
55 Rader, *Breaking boundaries*, p. 116. M. Farley, 'The dialogue continues' in *Women and Catholic priesthood*, p. 61.
56 *De trin.*, 11. 5. 8. *PL* 42. 991, WAA 7, p. 271.
57 *De trin.*, 12. 15. 25. *PL* 42. 1012, WAA 7, p. 305.
58 *De gen. ad litt.*, 3. 22. 34. *PL* 34. 293, ACW 41, p. 98.
59 Jerome, *Commentarius in epistolam ad Ephesios*, 3. 5 (*PL* 26. 567), trans. Mary Hayter, *The new Eve in Christ: the use and abuse of the Bible in the debate about women in the church* (London: SPCK, 1987), p. 139. Cf. Brown, *Body and society*, pp. 146–59 on the role of the widow.
60 Eleanor C. McLaughlin, 'Equality of souls, inequality of sexes: woman in medieval theology' in *Religion and sexism*, p. 234. Cf. the Collect for martyrs.
61 This will be developed in Part V, chapter 13.
62 A classic study of the gendered interpretation of symbols is found in Caroline Walker Bynum's *Holy feast, holy fast: the religious significance of food to medieval women*, Berkeley and Los Angeles: University of California Press, 1987.
63 On the pornographic elements of some martyr hagiography see Virginia Burrus, 'Word and flesh: the bodies and sexuality of ascetic women in Christian antiquity', *JFSR*, 10, 1 (1994), pp. 27–52. Cf. Elaine Pagels on differing concepts of freedom for men and women, though she overstates the differences. ' "Freedom from necessity": philosophic and personal dimensions of Christian conversion' in Gregory A. Robbins, ed., *Genesis 1—3 in the history of exegesis: intrigue in the garden* (Lewiston, New York: Edwin Mellen Press, 1988), pp. 67–98.

64 David G. Hunter presents Jovinian's teaching as a response to Manichaeism in Rome in the late 380s: 'Resistance to the virginal ideal': see also Hunter, 'Helvidius'.
65 Clement of Alexandria, *Stromateis*, 3. 6. ANF 2, p. 390b. ANF has the Latin text here. Trans. Chadwick, LCC 2, pp. 61–6.
66 Jovinian was circulating his opinions in the late 380s. The Synods met between 390 and 393. Jerome wrote in the same period. Augustine was later, writing *De bono coniugali* in 401. See Hunter, 'Resistance', p. 45, note 2.
67 Callam, 'Clerical continence', pp. 10–12.
68 Hunter, 'Resistance', p. 45; Callam, 'Clerical continence', p. 14.
69 Børresen, *Subordination*, p. 32ff.
70 *De trin.*, 10. 7. 9. PL 42. 978, WAA 7, p. 251.
71 Børressen, *Subordination*, p. 27.

Chapter 12

1 *Serm.*, 51. 11. 18–19. PL 38–9. 343, PNF 1/6, p. 252a *Serm.* 92.2. PL 38–9. 1012, FC 38, pp. 32–3. Sermons will be numbered according to Migne, not according to the renumbered sermons translated in PNF 1/6. The new translation, *The works of St Augustine: a translation for the 21st century*, Part III, vols. 1–8, trans. and annotated by Edmund Hill, ed. John E. Rotelle, New Rochelle, New York: New City Press, 1990–94, would be a preferable reference.
2 Most of what Augustine writes about the continent applies to celibate men as well as celibate women. Yet the concept of 'virgin' has a feminine bias and treatises on virginity were invariably addressed to women. See *En. in pss.*, 147. 10. PL 36–7. 1920, where he explicitly identifies virginity and the feminine. Virgin=soul.
3 H. Graef, *Mary in doctrine and devotion*, Vol. 1 (London: Burns & Oates, 1962), p. 76. One example is John Chrysostom, *Homily on St John*, 21. 2–30. Cf. *Homily* 44 on Matthew 12. 46–9.
4 For Hippolytus, see F. Quasten, *Patrology*, II, p. 201, and for Ambrose, see Power, 'Philosophy'.
5 Tertullian, *De carne*, 4. PL 2. 758–60, ANF 3, p. 524. For discussion see E. Schillebeeckx, *Clerical celibacy under fire: a critical appraisal*, trans. C. A. L. Jarot (London: Sheed and Ward, 1968), p. 50.
6 Michele Pelligrino, 'Mary in the thought of St Augustine' in John Rotelle, ed., *Mary's yes: readings on Mary throughout the ages* (London: Collins Liturgical Publications, 1988), pp. 15, 21–2, 24. George S. Bebis, 'Theotokos', and Eugene La Verdière, 'Mary', both in *EEC*, pp. 895; 585.
7 Treatises with significant Marian content: against Helvidius and Jovinian: Jerome, *De perpetua virginitate B. Mariae adversus Helvidium* and *Adversus Iovinianum* PL 23. 193–352; Ambrose, *Ep.* 42. PL 16. 1172–7, FC 26, pp. 225–30; Augustine, *De fide rerum*, dated 400; *De virg.*, dated 401; against the Pelagians: *De bono viduitatis*, dated 414; *Tract. in Io. ev.*, dated 414–17; *Contra duas ep. Pel.*, c. 420; *Contra Iulianum*, dated 421.
8 Augustine quotes Irenaeus in *Contra Iul.*, 1. 3. 5. PL 44. 643–4, FC 35, p. 7. The doctrine of Irenaeus is in *Adversus haereses*, Bks 1–2. PG 7. 433–1225, ANCL 5 and 9.
9 *The Protoevangelium of James, The Gospel of the nativity of Mary, The Gospel*

of pseudo-Matthew and *The history of Joseph the Carpenter*, are all found in ANF 8.

10 Particularly evident in Ambrose of Milan. One of the clearest examples is *De institutione virginis*.

11 Markus, *End*, p. 41.

12 No treatises by these writers are extant, so there is no unbiased access to their thought. These men were not the only dissidents. Bishop Bonosus concurred with Jovinian as did the Antidicomarians condemned by Epiphanius, *Panarion ad. Antidicom. PG* 42. 699–740, Williams pp. 601–20; Ambrose, *De causa Bonosi. PL* 16. 1222–4.

13 Not simply because women were so attracted to asceticism, but because sexual being was feminised in antiquity as today.

14 Cf. F. Quasten, *Patrology*, III, p. 142; Graef, *Mary*, Vol. 1, pp. 50, 78. B. Witherington, 'The anti-feminist tendencies of the "Western" text in Acts', *JBL*, 103, 1 (March 1983), pp. 82–4; Rosemary Radford Ruether, *Mary the feminine face of the church* (Philadelphia: Westminster Press, 1977), p. 54.

15 Augustine quotes Ambrose in *De nupt. et con.*, 2. 5. 15. *PL* 44. 444–5, PNF 1/5, p. 288b); *Contra Iul.*, 1. 3. 10; 1. 7. 32; 5. 15. 52. *PL* 44. 645; 662–3, 813, FC 35, pp. 10, 38–9; 293. He cites Ambrose and Cyprian in *De doct. Christ.*, 4. 21. 47–50. *PL* 34. 112ff GB 19, p. 691b–3a. Tertullian did support the virginal conception. On Tertullian see Tavard, *Woman*, p. 100.

16 Ambrose, *De institutione virginis*, 5. 35ff, and especially 13. 84–6; 14. 89–92. *OO* 14/2, pp. 136ff; 170; 172–4.

17 *De symb. ad cat.*, 3. 6. *PL* 40. 630, PNF 1/3, p. 371a; *Serm.*, 51. 18; 192. 1–2. *PL* 38–9. 343, 1012, Sermon 51. 18, PNF 1/6, p. 252a; Sermon 192. 2, FC 38, p. 32; *Contra duas ep. Pel.*, 1. 2. 4. *PL* 44. 552, WAA 15, p. 239; *Contra Iul.*, 1. 2. 4. *PL* 44. 643, FC 35, p. 6; *Opus imperf. contra Iul.*, 1. 22. *PL* 45. 1418.

18 *Serm.*, 51. 18; 186. 2; 213. 2; 214. 6. *PL* 38–9, 343; 999; 1061; 1068, FC 38, pp. 11; 122; 136. Cf. Tertullian, *De praescriptione adversus haereticos*, 13. *PL* 1. 26, ANF 3, p. 249; Athanasius, *Expositio fidei*, 1. *PG* 25. 202, PNF 2/4, p. 84a.

19 *Tract. in Jo. ev.*, 8.7. *PL* 35. 1454, PNF 1/7, p. 60a; *Serm.*, 1. *PL* 38–9. 1275–6.

20 *Serm.*, 51. 3. *PL* 35. 335, PNF 1/6, p. 246b; *De fide et symb.*, 4. 9. *PL* 40. 186, FC 27, p. 325; *Serm. (de Script. N.T.)*, 2. 3. *PL* 38–9. 334–5, trans. E. Pryzwara, *An Augustine synthesis* (London: Sheed and Ward, 1936), #280, p. 178.

21 *Tract. in J. ev.*, 8. 9. *PL* 35. 1455, PNF 1/7, p. 60b; *Serm.*, 196. 1. *PL* 38–9. 1019, FC 38, p. 43; *Serm.* 12. 2; 195.3. *PL* 38–9. 1012; 1019, FC 38, pp. 32; 43 *De nupt. et con.*, 1. 11. 12. *PL* 44. 421, PNF 1/5, p. 268.

22 And through Philo to Plato. See Sly, *Philo*, pp. 82–3 for the relevant texts and discussion.

23 *Tract. in Jo. ev.*, 8. 9. *PL* 35. 1456, PNF 1/7, p. 61b, although he does speak of Mary as mother of her Lord in *Serm.* 51. 12. 10. *PL* 38–9. 344, PNF 1/6, 1. 20. p. 252b.

24 *Tract. in Jo. ev.*, 8. 9. *PL* 35. 1455–6, PNF 1/7, p. 61ab.

25 *De fide et symb.*, 4. 9. *PL* 40. 186, FC 27, p. 325; *De doct. Christ.*, 1. 14.

13. *PL* 34. 24; GB 18, p. 628a; *Serm.*, 51. 2. 3. *PL* 38–9. 334–5, Pryzwara, #280, p. 178.

26   *Con.*, 7. 19. *PL* 32. 746, P-C, p. 152.

27   *De fide rerum*, 5. *PL* 40. 171, PNF 1/3, p. 339b; *Ep.* 137. *PL* 33. 519, FC 20, p. 29–30; *Civ. Dei*, 10. 29. *PL* 41. 308, GB 18, p. 317b.

28   *Serm.*, 200. 1. *PL* 38–9. 1029, FC 38, p. 64.

29   *De virg.*, 6. *PL* 40. 399, PNF 1/3, p. 419a.

30   On the likeness of sinful flesh, see *De gen. ad litt.*, 10. 18. 32. *PL* 34. 422, ACW 42, pp. 119–120; *Contra Iul.*, 5. 15. 52. *PL* 44. 813, FC 35, pp. 293–4. On the Incarnation without concupiscence see *De trin.*, 13. 18. 23. *PL* 42. 1032, WAA 7, p. 337–8; *Serm.*, 233. 3–4; 246. 5. *PL* 38–9. 1114; 1156, FC pp. 220; 296; *Contra Iul.*, 2. 4. 8; cf. 2. 6. 15; 5. 15. 54. *PL* 44. 678, 684; 814, FC 35, p. 65, 75; 295.

31   *Contra Iul.*, 5. 15. 54; 6. 19. 62. *PL* 44. 814; 861, FC 35, pp. 295; 374.

32   If the Scriptures had not grounded his belief, he would probably have had to invent the concept. See *Serm.*, 151. 5. *PL* 38–9. 817; *De trin.*, 13. 12. 16; 13. 16. 21. *PL* 42. 1026; 1034, WAA 7, pp. 327; 335; *Ep.* 217.5. 16. *PL* 33. 984, FC 32, p. 86; *De doct. Christ.*, 1. 14. 13. *PL* 34. 24, GB 18, p. 628a; *Contra Iul.*, 5. 15. 52. *PL* 44. 813, FC 35, p. 293.

33   Cf. Ton H. C. van Eijk, 'Marriage and virginity, death and immortality' in J. Fontaine and C. Kannengiesser, eds., *Epektasis: mélanges patristiques offerts au Cardinal Jean Daniélou* (Paris: Beauchesne, 1972), pp. 209–35.

34   *De trin.*, 1. 7. 14; cf. 1. 9. 18. *PL* 42. 828; 832, WStA, 1/5, pp. 74; 78. Jesus' form as servant is never at the expense of his equality to the Father, and it is only as servant that he was born of Mary. This form becomes a hindrance to belief in the incorporeal Word after the Resurrection, and must be removed from human sight. Hence the ascension to the Father.

35   *De nat. et gratia*, 42. 36. *PL* 44. 267, PNF 1/5, p. 135b; *Serm.*, 290. 6; 291. 6. *PL* 38–9. 1315; 1319.

36   Eugene Portalié perceived the doctrine as implicit in Augustine in *A guide to the thought of St Augustine*, trans. J. Bastian (London: Burns and Oates, 1960), p. 175–6. For a dissenting opinion see Pelligrino, 'Mary', p. 33b.

37   One of Ambrose's favourite expressions is that the virgin is free of the 'admixture' of male seed.

38   *Integritas* connotes completeness, innocence, integrity, chastity and purity. It conveys a sense of undiminished, unimpaired, sound, fresh, untainted, blameless, honest and virtuous (Lewis & Short, p. 973). Cf. Børresen, *Subordination*, p. 127, on Augustine's usage.

39   Origen, *Homily on Genesis*, 1. PG 12. 145–60, FC 71, pp. 47–71; Athanasius, *Contra gentes*, 22. 30; 39. 15–20, Thompson, pp. 61; 107–9; Augustine, *De gen. ad litt.*, 1.7.13. *PL* 34.251 ACW 41, p. 26.

40   *De virg.*, 29. *PL* 40. 412, PNF 1/3, p. 427a. Augustine uses '*pereat*'. Cf. *Con.*, 10. 29. *PL* 32. 796, P-C, p. 233; *De trin.* 4. 18. 24. *PL* 42. 905, PNF 1/3, p. 81.

41   *De trin.*, 4. 7. 11–9. 12. *PL* 42. 895–6, PNF 1/3, p. 75b-6a. The alienation between individuals has the same causes as the self-alienation which destroys integrity.

42   *De nupt. et con.*, 2. 5. 14. *PL* 44. 444, PNF 1/5, p. 288b.

43   *Serm.*, 188. 4. *PL* 38–9. 1004–5, FC 38, p. 19. Cf. *De virg.*, 27. *PL* 40. 410, PNF 1/3 p. 426b; *De fide rerum*, 3. 5. *PL* 40. 175, PNF 1/3, p. 339b.

44 *De bono vid.*, 10. 13. *PL* 40. 438, PNF 1/3, p. 446b. Cf. *De fide rerum*, 3. 5. *PL* 40. 175, PNF 1/3, p. 339b.

45 The root of *corruptione, cor-rumpo*, certainly implies injury, spoilage, and can bear the meaning of destruction. See *Con.*, 7. 12. *PL* 32. 743, P-C. p. 148 for a discussion on the corruption of a good. *Aufero* he also uses regularly. Cf *De virg.*, 4. *PL* 40. 398, PNF 1/3, p. 418a; *Serm.* 214. 6; 225. 2. *PL* 38–9. 1068; 1096; *Serm* 214. PNF 1/33, p. 418a; 225. 2. FC 38, p. 190, where Sr Mary Muldowney translates its cognate as 'Joseph was not the *destroyer* of Mary's chastity but its guardian.'

46 Adams, *Latin sexual vocabulary*, pp. 199, n. 1; 219; 223.

47 *Serm.*, 195. 1; 186. 1; 244. 4; 231. 2. *PL* 38–9. 1017; 999; 1150; 1105, FC 38, pp. 42; 9–10; 286; 205.

48 Ambrose, *Secundum Lucam*, 2. 56–7 [760]. *CCL* 14, pp. 54–5; *Cain*, 1. 10. 46. *CSEL* 32/1, p. 37**, FC 42, p. 399.

49 *Serm.*, 247. 2. *PL* 38–9. 1157, FC 38, p. 298; *De fide rerum*, 4. 7; cf. 3. 5. *PL* 40. 176; 174, PNF 1/3 p. 340b.

50 *Serm.*, 213. *PL* 38–9. 1061, FC 38, p. 122; *De symb. ad cat.*, 3. 6. *PL* 40. 630, PNF 1/3, p. 371a; *Contra Iul.*, 6. 19. 62. *PL* 44. 861, FC 35, p. 374.

51 *Tract. in Jo. ev.*, 4. 10. *PL* 35. 1410, PNF 1/7, p. 285.

52 *Serm.*, 195. 1. Cf. 196. 1; 215. 3. *PL* 38–9. 1017–19; 1073, FC 38, pp. 42; 44; 143ff.

53 *Serm.*, 190. 1. *PL* 38–9. 1007, FC 38, p. 29; *Ep.* 137. *PL* 33. 519, FC 20, p. 24. Cf *Tract. in Jo. ev.*, 9. 15. *PL* 35. 1465, PNF 1/7, p. 68.

54 This follows from the teaching that spiritual kinship is preferred to carnal kinship. See *Serm.*, 72A. *PL* 38–9. 408–9, on the 'proper order of charity'. Augustine believed that there was an affective bond between Mary and Jesus. See *Serm.*, 218. 10. *PL* 38–9. 1086, FC 38, p. 167.

55 *De virg.*, 3. *PL* 40. 398, PNF 1/3, p. 418a.

56 *De virg.*, 27: '*illibatae virginitatis in corpore, inviolatae veritatis in corde*'. *PL* 40. 410, PNF 1/3, p. 426b.

57 *Serm.*, 214. 6; 215. 2.4; 233. 3. 4. *PL* 38–9. 1068; 1073; 1114, FC 38, pp. 136; 220.

58 *En. in pss.*, 18. 6. 6. '*Et ipse tamquam sponsus procedens de thalamo suo et ipse procedens de utero virginali ubi Deus naturae humanae tanquam sponsus sponsae copulatus est.*' *PL* 36–7. 155, ACW 19, p. 178. Cf. Ps. 18. *Second en. in ps.* 18. 6. 6. *PL* 36–7. 160–1, PNF 1/6, pp. 54–5. Also *Serm.*, 191. 2, where he refers to '*sponsus infans de thalamo suo*', *PL* 38–9. 1016 and *Serm.*, 195. 3. *PL* 38–9. 1019, FC 38, p. 43. On the word becoming flesh see *Serm.*, 195, 3; 214. 6; 215. 3. *PL* 38–9. 1018; 1068; 1073, FC 38, pp. 43, 136; 143; *Tract. in Jo. ev.*, 10. 3. *PL* 35. 1468, PNF 1/7, p. 70.

59 *De fide et symb.*, 4. 8. *PL* 40. 186, FC 27, p. 325; *Serm.*, 51. 20; 187. 4; 195. 1. *PL* 38–9. 350; 1002–3; 1017–101. 195 in FC 38, p. 42.

60 Adams, *Latin sexual vocabulary*, p. 99. See Galen, *On the usefulness of the parts*, 14. 11. [II. 322–3]; 14. 14. [346]; 15 3. [346], trans. and ed., Margaret Tallmadge May (Ithaca: Cornell University Press, 1968), pp. 645–6; 653; 660. Guilia Sissa discusses the implications of this belief in Greek thought, *Greek virginity* (Cambridge, Mass: Harvard University Press, 1991), pp. 53–66.

61 Ambrose, *De institutione virginis*, 9. 62; 17. 111; *Exhortatio virginitatis*, 6. 35. *OO* 14/2, pp. 158; 190; 226.

62 *De cont., passim., PL* 40. 345–73, PNF 1/3, pp. 379–93. Latin uses *homo interior.*

63 *De trin.,* 4. 5. 9. *PL* 42. 894, FC 45, p. 142.

64 *De trin.,* 4. 18. 24. *PL* 42. 905, PNF 1/3, p. 82b.

65 *Contra Faustum,* 2. 3. *PL* 42. 210, PNF 1/4, p. 15; *Serm.,* 189. 2–3; 191, 2; 196. 2. *PL* 38–9. 1005–6; 1010; 1020. *Serm.,* 185. 2 *PL.* 38–9. 998, FC 38, p. 8.

66 *En. in pss.,* 66. 8. *PL* 36–7, 810, PNF 1/8, p. 284b. Also *De virg.,* 3. *PL* 40. 398, PNF 1/3, p. 418a; *Serm.,* 196. 1; 214. 6; 290. 6; 291. 5. *PL* 38–9. 1019; 1068; 1315; 1318–19.

67 *En. in pss.* (2nd ser.), 34. 3. *PL* 36–7. 335, ACW 30, p. 211; *De nat. et gratia,* 42. 36. *PL* 44. 267, PNF 1/5, p. 135b; *Serm.,* 290. 6; 291.6. *PL* 38–9.1315; 1319.

68 On privilege and merit see *De nat. et gratia,* 42. 36. *PL* 44. 267, PNF 1/5, p. 135b. On spiritual kinship see *De virg.,* 5. *PL* 40. 399, PNF 1/3, p. 418b.

69 *Serm.,* 51. 18. *PL* 38–9. 343, PNF 1/6, p. 252a; *De bono con.,* 35. *PL* 40. 416, PNF 1/3, p. 413; *De virg.* 5. *PL* 40. 399, PNF 1/3, 418b; *Serm.,* 214. 6. *PL* 38–9. 1069 ('*Charitate fervente*'); *De gen. ad litt.,* 10. 18. 32. *PL* 34. 422, ACW 42, p. 120–1.

70 Ambrose, *De institutione virginis,* 13. 81–14. 88. *OO* 14/2, pp. 168–72. Cf. Justin Martyr, who compared Mary's conception of the Word to the conceptions of quasi-divine sons by both Danäe and Leda (*Apology* 1. 21. 22. *PG* 6. 359–63, ANF 1, p. 170ab). M. Esther Harding, *Women's mysteries: ancient and modern* [1955], reprinted, London: Rider, 1982, is still an excellent and accessible study of the moon goddesses and Christianity from the Jungian perspective.

71 *Serm.,* 51. 18; 215. 2; 291. 5–6. *PL* 38–9. 343; 1073; 1318–19. John McQuade, 'Introduction to *De virginitate*', FC 27, p. 139, states that Mary's vow is implicit in Ambrose and Jerome. Graef, *Mary,* p. 96, states that Augustine was the first Latin father to adduce a vow of virginity.

72 *Contra Iul.,* 5. 12. 48. *PL* 44. 811, FC 35, 289; *De virg.,* 4. *PL* 40. 398, PNF 1/3, p. 418.

73 *Serm.,* 51. 18; 215. 2; 291. 5–6. *PL* 38–9. 343; 1073; 1318–19. See also Pelligrino, 'Mary,' p. 17.

74 *De virg.,* 4. *PL* 40. 398, PNF 1/3, p. 418 a-b.

75 Graef, *Mary,* p. 96. Pseudo-Matthew clearly comes from a community where communal living for virgins is well established, and a retired life is prescribed for them.

76 *Tract. in Jo. ev.,* 10. 2–3; 28. 3. *PL* 35. 1467–8; 1623, PNF 1/7, p. 69b.

77 Jerome, *Adversus Helvidium,* 13. *PL* 23. 205–6, PNF 2/6, p. 340a. Dated 383.

78 Jerome, *Adversus Helvidium,* 4. *PL* 23. 195–7, PNF 2/6, p. 336 ab. Jerome's argument hinges on the Greek and Hebrew versions of the Gospel and the prophecy from Isaiah.

79 Ambrose, *De institutione virginis,* 5. 35–6. *OO* 14/2, pp. 136–8; Augustine, *Tract. in Jo. ev.,* 10. 2. *PL* 35. 1467, PNF 1/7, p. 69b; *Serm.,* 51. 11. 18. *PL* 38–9. 343, PNF 1/6, p. 252a.

80 General references to Mary as the new Eve are found in *Serm.,* 51. 3; 184. 2; 190. 2; 289. 2. *PL* 38–9. 334–5; 996; 1008; 1308; *Serm.,* 190. 2, FC 38, p. 30.

81 *Contra Iul.*, 1, 2, 4. *PL* 44. 643, FC 35, p. 5; *De nupt. et con.*, 2. 12. 25. *PL* 44. 450, PNF 1/5, p. 293a. Dated 419–21.

82 *Contra Iul.*, 4. 16. 83. *PL* 44. 781–2, FC 35, p. 394.

83 Purgatory was not invented until the Middle Ages, when Thomas Aquinas saw it as a way of moderating Augustine's severity.

84 *Contra duas ep. Pel.*, 1. 16. 32. *PL* 44. 564–5, WAA 15, p. 262.

85 *Contra duas ep. Pel.*, 1. 5. 10; 1. 17. 34–5. *PL* 44. 555; 565–6, WAA 15, pp. 244; 261–2; *Contra Iul.*, 5. 9. 8. *PL* 44. 807, FC 35, p. 281.

86 *Civ. Dei*, 14. 26. *PL* 41. 434–5, GB 18, p. 396ab. Dated *c.* 418. '*sine libidinis morto... sine ardoris illecebroso... corporis nulla corruptione integretatis...*' *De gratia Christ.*, 2. 41. 36. *PL* 44. 405, PNF 1/5, p. 252.

87 Julian here is arguing from a belief common in antiquity. *Contra duas ep. Pel.*, 1. 15. 30. *PL* 44. 564, WAA 15, p. 259. See Power, 'Philosophy', (forthcoming).

88 *De bono con.*, 3. *PL* 40. 375, PNF 1/3, p. 400b; *Serm.*, 159. 2. *PL* 38. 868, WStA III/5, p. 122.

89 Just how he expected children to be born is not clear, because the Romans, unlike the Greeks, believed that the hymen virtually blocked the vagina.

90 Ambrose, *Exhortatio virginitatis*, 6. 36. *OO* 14/2, p. 226; cf. *Ep.* 42. *PL* 16. 1172–3, FC 26, p. 226. Jerome, *Adversus Lovinianum*, 1. 4. *PL* 23. 225, PNF 2/6, p. 348. Brown, 'Notions', p. 430; on Chrysostom, Ranke-Heinnemann, *Eunuchs*, p. 43.

91 *De gen. ad litt.*, 11. 30. 39; 11. 35. 47. *PL* 34. 445; 448–9, ACW 42, pp. 162; 168–9.

92 *De gen. contra Man.*, 2. 17. 26 – 2. 18. 28. *PL* 34. 209–10; *De gen. ad litt.*, 11. 42, 59. *PL* 34. 453–4; ACW 42, p. 176. Note that Augustine's theft of the pears was motivated by his friendship for the other boys: *Con.*, 2. 4. *PL* 32. 678–9, P-C, pp. 47–8. In *Serm.*, 45. 5, Augustine contradicts his usual position to say that Adam was seduced by woman so that he fell into death. *PL* 38–9. 266; Przywara, # 282, p. 178.

93 *Sermo. dom. in monte* (dated 394), 1. 12. 34. *PL* 34. 1246, PNF 1/6, p. 15b; *De gen. contra Man.* (dated 388–9), 2. 21. 31. *PL* 34. 212.

94 *Contra Iul.*, 4. 16. *PL* 44. 744–5, FC 35, p. 236. He refers here to Ambrose.

95 *Contra Iul.* 4. 12. 59. *PL* 44. 767, FC 35, p. 217.

96 *Civ. Dei*, 14. 17. *PL* 41. 425–6, GB 18. pp. 390a–1a. Cf. *De nupt. et con.*, 1. 15. 17; 1. 21. 24; 2. 12. 25. *PL* 44. 423–4; 427–8; 450, PNF 1/5, pp. 271a; 273b; 292b; *Contra Iul.*, 4. 12. 58–9. *PL* 44. 766–7, FC 35, p. 217; *Contra duas ep. Pel.*, 1. 16. 33. *PL* 44. 565, WAA 15, pp. 260–1.

97 *Contra Iul.*, 4. 13. 62. *PL* 44. 768, FC 35, p. 219.

98 *Contra Iul.*, 1. 7. 32. Cf. 2. 9. 32; 2. 5. 11 and *passim*. *PL* 44. 662–3, cf. 695; 681, FC 35, pp. 38–9; 94; 70; *De nupt. et con.*, 1. 19. 21. *PL* 44. 426, PNF 1/5, p. 272b; *De gen. ad litt.*, 10. 26. 35. *PL* 34. 424, ACW 42, p. 123.

99 *Contra duas ep. Pel.*, 1. 6. 11. *PL* 44. 555, WAA 15, p. 245.

100 *Pace* S. Heine, who argues that Augustine does not hold Eve responsible for sin. She quotes only one text, *Enchiridion*, 48. 14. *PL* 40. 255, FC 2, pp. 410–12: *Women and early Christianity* (London: SCM Press, 1987), p. 19.

101 *Serm.*, 232. 2. *PL* 38–9. 1108, FC 38, p. 210–11. Cf. *De doct. Christ.*, 1.

14. 13. *PL* 34. 24; GB 18, p. 628a; *Serm.*, 45. 5. *PL* 38–9. 266; Przywara, # 292, p. 178.

102 My emphasis. *Serm.*, 298. 2. *PL* 38–9. 1308; Przywara, # 281, p. 178. *Concepit* is the verb used of Eve.

103 *De doct. Christ.*, 1. 14. 11. *PL* 34. 24; GB 18, p. 628. *Serm.*, 213. 7. *PL* 38–9. 1064, FC 38, p. 127.

104 *De cont.*, 2. 5. *PL* 40. 352, PNF 1/3, pp. 379–81.

105 *Contra Iul.*, 2. 6. 15. *PL* 44. 684, FC 35, p. 75–6. The permeation of the very fibre of the child's being by sin is strong in this passage.

106 *De doct. Christ.*, 1. 14. 11. *PL* 34. 24, GB 18, p. 628a.

107 *De gratia Christ*, 2. 43–5. *PL* 44. 406–7, PNF 1/5, pp. 252b–253b. *Contra Iul*, 6. 22. 68. *PL* 44. 864, FC 35, p. 380. Mary, because of her virginal birth-giving, did not need to be purified after the birth like other women. *Quaest. in Hept.* 3. 40. *PL* 34. 694–5.

108 Jerome's translation of the Greek ἐξαπατηθεῖ σαÁ in the Vulgate reads: *mulier autem seducta in praevaricatione fuit*. The Latin *seduco*, lead aside, take apart, sever, took on the meaning of sexual seduction in ecclesiastical Latin. Lewis & Short, p. 1660, *seduco*; cf. *seductio* and *seductor*.

109 Ambrose offers a fascinating metaphor of the viper as sexual pleasure, where his poison is construed as adulterous desire arising from masculine hard-heartedness and lack of gentleness with wives: *Hexameron*, 5. 7. 19. *OO* I, pp. 260–4, FC 42, pp. 174–5.

110 *De nupt. et con.*, 1. 19. 21. *PL* 44. 426, PNF 1/5, p. 272b; cf. *Contra Iul.*, 3. 19. 21. *PL* 44. 722, FC 35, p. 141.

111 *De virg.*, 6. *PL* 40. 39, PNF 1/3, p. 419a.

112 *Contra Iul.*, 3. 26. 59–60. *PL.* 44. 732, FC 35, p. 160.

113 See *Contra Iul.*, 2. 2. 4. *PL* 44. 673–4, FC 35, pp. 58–9.

114 *Contra Iul.*, 3. 26. 59. *PL* 44. 732, FC 35, p. 159. Augustine is here citing his own *De nuptiis et concupiscentia* 1. 1.

115 *Contra Iul.*, 5. 4. 17; 5. 9. 37. *PL* 44. 794; 806, FC 35, pp. 261; 281. Cf. *De virg.*, 37. *PL* 40. 417, PNF 1/3, p. 430b; *De nupt. et con.*, 1. 19. 21. *PL* 44. 426, PNF 1/5, p. 272b. *Contra duas ep. Pel.*, 11. 7. *PL* 44. 555, WAA 15, p. 245. *Contra Iul.*, 2. 2. 4; 2. 10. 33; 6. 7. 17. 20. *PL* 44. 673–4; 696–7; 854; 832–3, FC 35, pp. 58–9; 97. 329–30.

116 *Contra Iul.*, 2. 6. 15; 5. 14. 51. *PL* 44. 684; 812–13, FC 35, pp. 75; 291–2.

117 *Contra Iul.*, 4. 2. 8. *PL* 44. 738–40, FC 35, p. 171.

118 *Contra Iul*, 4. 14. 71, 73. *PL* 44. 773–4; 775, FC 35, pp. 228; 230.

119 *De nupt. et con.*, 2. 4. 12. *PL* 44. 442–3, PNF 1/5, p. 287b; *De gen. contra Man.*, 2. 21. 31. *PL* 34. 212.

120 *De virg.*, 6. *PL* 40. 399, PNF 1/3, p. 419a.

121 Donnelly, *Radical love*, p. 7.

122 Graef, *Mary*, pp. 97–8.

123 *Serm.*, 191. 2; 215. 4. *PL* 38–9. 1016; 1074.

124 *Serm.*, 190. 2. *PL* 38–9. 1007–8, FC 38. pp. 28–9, Cf. *De virg.*, 7. *PL* 40. 400, PNF 1/3, p. 419b. *Serm.*, 192. 2; *PL* 38–9. 1012, FC 38, p. 33; *Serm.*, 188. 4. *PL* 38–9. 1004–5. Przywara, # 408, p. 239. See Pelligrino, 'Mary', p. 29, on this point. He argues that in the person of Christ, the womb of Mary also gave birth to the church.

125 *Tract. in Jo. ev.*, 8. 4. *PL* 35. 1452, PNF 1/7, p. 585.

126 Przywara uses 'body unsullied' to translate. '*corpus intactum*'. 'Intact' is more appropriate. *En. in pss.*, 147.10. *PL* 36–7. 1920, #410, p. 239.

However, such translations do show the mental associations between virginity and purity.

127 *De virg.*, 8. *PL* 40. 400, PNF 1/3, p. 419b.

128 *De bono vid.*, 8. *PL* 40. 434, PNF 1/3, p. 443–4a.

129 Note his prayer to be liberated by grace from nocturnal emissions, the 'unclean acts inspired by sensual images which lead to the *pollution* of the body' (my emphasis): *Con.*, 10. 30, *PL.* 32. 797, P-C; p. 234. *De bono con.*, 3. *PL* 40. 375, PNF 1/3, p. 400a; *De bono vid.*, 8. *PL* 40. 434, PNF 1/3, p. 444a. Texts dates range from 396 to 414.

130 Clement of Alexandria, *Stromateis*, 3. 6. 53. ANF 2, p. 390b. Clement was greatly influenced by the Stoics, and Julian too applied Stoic principles to theology: *Contra Iul.*, 3. 3. 8; 4. 12. 58. *PL* 44. 706; 766, FC 35, p. 112; 216.

131 *Serm.*, 195. 2. *PL* 38–9. 1018, Przywara, # 407, p. 238: '*Est ergo et Ecclesiae, sicut Mariae, perpetua integritas et incorrupta fecunditas.*' Cf. *Serm.*, 213. 7. *PL* 38–9. 1063–64, FC 38, pp. 126–7; *Serm.* 51. 2–3; 291–6. *PL* 38–9. 334; 1319. Brown, *Body and society*, pp. 369–70, discusses the practical fruitfulness of continent women in learning and evangelisation.

132 *Serm.*, 190. 2. *PL* 38–9. 1007–8, FC 38, p. 30.

133 *De virg.*, 2. *PL* 40. 397, PNF 1/3, p. 417b.

134 *Con* 10. 29. *PL* 32. 796, P-C, p. 233.

135 *Serm.*, 192. 1–2. *PL* 38–9. 1012, FC 38, p. 32.

136 *Ep.* 188. 2. 5. *PL* 33. 850, WAA 12, p. 360.

137 *En. in pss.*, 18. 10. *PL* 36–7. 155, PNF 1/8, p. 55.

138 *De fide rerum*, 3. 5–6. *PL* 40. 175, PNF 1/3, p. 339b. Cf. Ps. 44.

139 These are texts which will later be used of Mary in the church's official prayer, and will inspire Christian art on the enthronement of Mary.

140 *De virg.*, 2. *PL* 40. 397, PNF 1/3, p. 417b.

141 *En. in pss.*, 44.3. *PL* 36–7, 494–4, PNF 1/8, p. 146a unites the symbols of Christ as bridegroom of the church and the virginal womb as the bridal chamber of Word and flesh.

142 Plato, *Symposium*, [206–9]. *GB* 7, pp. 165a–6b.

143 Platonic thought entered Christian thought through many channels: as part of the philosophic currency of a classical education, through the writings of Philo, Origen and Methodius, and through the Neoplatonist school which influenced Ambrose and Augustine.

144 *De trin.*, 13. 16. 21. *PL* 42. 1034, WAA 7, p. 335; *Contra Iul.*, 5, 15, 56; 6. 16. 50. *PL* 44. 815; 851, FC 35, p. 296. 359.

145 *De virg.*, 37. *PL* 40. 417, PNF 1/3, p. 430b.

146 *Serm.*, 261. 7. *PL* 38–9. 1080, FC 38, pp. 156–7, in contrast to Jerome and Ambrose who believed that Christian virginity transcended the curse of Eve: Jerome, *Ep.* 22. 21. *PL* 22. 407–8, PNF 2/6, p. 30. Ambrose, *Exhortatio virginitatis*, 7. 42. *OO* 14/2, p. 232.

147 *Serm.*, 151.8. *PL* 38–9. 819; *Serm.*, 261. 8. *PL* 38–9. 1081, FC 38, p. 157–8.

148 *Civ. Dei*, 22. 17. *PL* 41.778–9; GB 18, p. 603a.

149 *Serm.*, 336. 5.5. *PL* 38–9. 1474–5, Przywara, # 409, p. 239. Cf. *Tract. in Jo. ev.*, 120. 2. *PL* 35: 1963, PNF 1/7, p. 434a-5b; *Civ. Dei*, 22. 17. *PL* 41. 778–9, GB 18, p. 603a; *Serm.*, 218. 14. *PL* 38–9. 1087, FC 38, p. 169, on the blood and water; *De nupt. et con.*, 2. 4. 12. *PL* 44. 442–3, PNF 1/5, p. 287a.

150 In Roman culture, *latus* (side), was another euphemism for the genitals or even the womb. Adams, *Latin sexual vocabulary*, for genitals, pp. 49, 90; for womb, p. 108.
151 Cf. Armstrong, *Gospel*, p. 69.
152 *Tract. in Jo. ev.*, 10. 2. *PL* 35. 1467, PNF 1/7, p. 69b. Cf. *De virg.*, 4–5. *PL* 40. 398–9, PNF 1/3, p. 418b; *De bono vid.*, 16. 20. *PL* 40. 442, PNF 1/3, p. 449a; *Serm.*, 194. 4; 343. 4. *PL* 38–9. 1017; 1507–8; *Serm.*, 192.2. *PL* 38–9. 1012, Przywara, # 417, p. 244.
153 *De virg.*, 35; 27. *PL* 40. 416; 410, PNF 1/3, pp. 429b; 426b.
154 *De virg.*, 41–3; *De bono vid.*, 28–9. *PL* 40. 420–2; 450, PNF 1/3, pp. 432a-3ab; 454ab; *Ep.* 188.2. 6. *PL* 33. 850–1, WAA 13, pp. 360–1.
155 *Serm.*, 93. 2. 2. *PL* 38–9. 574, PNF 1/6, p. 402.
156 *De virg.*, 27. *PL* 40. 410, PNF 1/3, p. 426a.
157 *De bono vid.*, 23. 29. *PL* 40. 450, PNF 1/3, p. 454b.
158 *De virg.*, 46. *PL* 40. 423, PNF 1/3, p. 434ab; *De bono vid.*, 3. 4; 6. 9. *PL* 40. 432–3, PNF 1/3, p. 442b; 444a.
159 *De virg.*, 4. *PL* 40. 398, PNF 1/3, p. 418b, on free choice. Cf. *Civ. Dei*, 22. 17. *PL* 41. 779, GB 18, p. 603b, on women being 'given' in marriage. Women did not always choose virginity freely. Cf. McNamara, 'Muffled voices,' pp. 13–15.
160 So McNamara, 'Muffled voices', p. 15. However, *Ep.* 211. *PL* 33. 958–65 mentions peasant and lower-class women in the community.
161 Rader, *Breaking boundaries*, p. 79.
162 *De virg.*, 8. *PL* 40. 400, PNF 1/3, p. 419b.
163 Even Judaism, which is usually perceived as having far more positive attitudes to marital sexuality than Christianity, experienced a tension between Torah and sex, which has been explored by Daniel Boyarin: ' "Behold, Israel according to the flesh": on anthropology and sexuality in late antique Judaisms', *YJC* 5. 2 (Spring 1992), pp. 27–57.
164 *De bono con.*, 13. *PL* 40. 382–3, PNF 1/3, p. 405a.
165 *De virg.*, 16. 16, *PL* 40. 403–4, PNF 1/3, p. 422a.
166 *De virg.*, 16; 56. *PL* 40. 403–4; 428, PNF 1/3, pp. 422a; 437b.
167 *De bono vid.*, 20. 25. *PL* 40. 447, PNF 1/3, p. 452a.
168 Ambrose, *Hexameron*, 5. 7. 18–19. *OO* I, pp. 258–64, FC 42, pp. 173–5. Funeral eulogy *CIL* VI. 1527/*ILS* 8393, L&F # 207, pp. 208–11; cf. L&F, # 223, p. 236. That some men also suffered from these separations as keenly as women is clear from Pliny the Younger's letters to his wife Calpurnia, L&F, # 226, p. 237–9.
169 This is not to imply that asceticism did not liberate men from social expectations. There is an abundance of literature on women and asceticism: the work of Elizabeth A. Clark, Ross S. Kraemer, Jo Ann McNamara, and Rosemary Rader. More recently, see that of Virginia Burrus, Elizabeth Castelli and Karen J. Torjesen.
170 *De virg.*, 5. *PL* 40. 399, PNF 1/3, p. 418b; *Serm.*, 192.2. *PL* 38–9. 1012, FC 38, pp. 32–3.
171 *De virg.*, 11. *PL* 40. 401, PNF 1/3, p. 420b.
172 *De bono vid.*, 14. 18. *PL* 40. 441, PNF 1/3, p. 448a; *Ep.* 188. 1. 1. *PL* 33. 849, WAA, 13, p. 357.
173 *Ep.* 188. 1. 1. *PL* 33. 849, WAA 13, p. 356.
174 *Ep.* 150. *PL* 33. 645, WAA 13, p. 250. Note the dependence on Platonic substitution of spiritual for physical procreation.

175 On the 'spirit of salvation' see *De virg.*, 39. *PL* 40. 418–19, PNF 1/3, p. 431b. On Christ as husband see *De virg.*, 56. *PL* 40. 428, PNF 1/3, p. 437b.

176 *Ep.* 188. 1. 1. *PL* 33. 849, WAA 13, p. 357. Cf. Ps. 44.

177 *Serm.*, 191. 2. 3; 3, 4. *PL* 38–9. 1010–11; Przywara, *Synthesis* # 418, p. 344–5.

178 R. Kraemer, 'The conversion of women to ascetic Christianity', *Signs*, 6, 2 (1980), p. 303; Castelli, 'Virginity', pp. 70–1. Virginia Burrus, 'Word and flesh: the bodies and sexuality of ascetic women in Christian antiquity', *JFSR*, 10, 1, (1994), pp. 27–52. Cf. Jerome, *Ep.* 22; Ambrose, *De virginitate*, 79.

179 *De virg.*, 18, 21. *PL* 40. 404–6, PNF 1/3, 422b; 423b; *De bono vid.*, 4. 6; 5. 7. *PL* 40. 433–4, PNF 1/3 p. 443ab.

180 *De virg.*, 18; 19; 21; 25. *PL* 40. 404–6; 409, PNF 1/3, 422b; 423ab; 425b-6a.

181 *De bono vid.*, 8. 11. *PL* 40. 436, PNF 1/3, p. 445a; *Ep.* 188. 2. 6. *PL* 33. 850–1, WAA 13, p. 361.

182 *De doct. Christ.*, 4. 21. 27. *PL* 34. 112, FC 2, p. 217; *Serm.*, 132. 3. 3. *PL* 38–9. 736, PNF 1/6, p. 505; *De virg.*, 24; 54. *PL* 40. 409; 427, PNF 1/3, p. 425a; 437a. Cf. Gregory of Nyssa, *De virginitate*, 13. *PG* 46, 375–82, PNF 2/5, p. 359. Again the literature is extensive; on Augustine see Brown, *Augustine and sexuality*, p. 6.

183 *De bono vid.*, 6. 8. *PL* 40. 434–5, PNF 1/3, p. 444a.

184 *Ep.* 208. 7. *PL* 33. 953, WAA 13, p. 383.

185 *De virg.*, 45–7. *PL* 40. 422–4, PNF 1/3, p. 434a, 435a.

186 *Ep.* 37.2. *PL* 33.152, WAA 13, p. 110; *Contra duas ep. Pel.*, 3. 14. *PL* 44. 598, WAA 15, p. 312.

187 *De bono vid.*, 21. 26. *PL* 40. 447, PNF 1/3, p. 452a.

188 *De bono con.*, 30. *PL* 40. 393, PNF 1/3, p. 412a: Note that curiosity, female speech, and women taking legal action are defined as sin and disobedience.

189 *De virg.* 1; 33. *PL* 40. 397; 415, PNF 1/3, 417b; 429a. His description is, like St Paul's, 'puffed up'. Mortley, *Womanhood*, p. 83, detects a spiritual pride over achievements in the suppression of sexual instinct.

190 *De virg.*, 45–7. *PL* 40. 422–4, PNF 1/3, p. 434a–5a.

191 Cf. Cyril of Jerusalem, *Catecheses*, 4. 25. *PG* 33. 487, PNF 2/7, p. 25a.

192 *Ep.* 211. 6. *PL* 33. 960, WAA 13, p. 395.

193 *De virg.*, 38. *PL* 40. 417, PNF 1/3, p. 431a.

194 *Serm.*, 51. 11. 18; 215. 2; 291. 5–6. *PL* 38–9. 343; 1073; 1318–19. See also Pelligrino, 'Mary', p. 17.

195 *En. in pss.*, 66. *PL* 36–7. 810, PNF 1/8, p. 284b, *De virg.*, 41. *PL* 40. 420, PNF 1/3, p. 432ab. Jerome feared the same thing. See Brown, *Body and society*, p. 376.

196 Rousselle, *Porneia*, p. 133, offers the timely warning that the real problems faced by celibate women and the solutions they found are not accessible to us. Cf. Castelli, 'Virginity', pp. 84–8.

197 *Ep.* 211. 10. *PL* 33. 961, WAA 13, pp. 397–8; *De virg.*, 34; 54. *PL* 40. 415, 427, PNF 1/3, p. 429b; 437ab.

198 *Ep.* 211. 10. *PL* 33. 961, WAA 13, p. 398. Even to wish to remarry is to 'wax wanton'. See *De gratia et lib.*, 4. 7–8. *PL* 44. 886, PNF 1/5, pp. 446b-

7a. See Rader, *Breaking boundaries*, p. 115, and Brown, *Body and society*, p. 268, on the virile physical deportment prescribed for virgins elsewhere.

199 Also, fasting is necessary now because Adam and Eve did not fast in the garden. *Contra Iul.*, 1. 5. 15; cf. 1. 7. 23. *PL* 44. 652; 656–7, FC 35, pp. 21; 39. There is evidence that stringent and consistent fasting will reduce desire and potency. See Rouselle, *Porneia*, ch. 10, pp. 160ff esp. p. 176, ch. 11, pp. 179ff. Armstrong, *Gospel*, also discusses in detail the connections between food and sex on the psychological level, p. 166, and chapter 4, *passim*.

200 *De gratia et lib.*, 7–9. *PL* 44. 886–7, PNF 1/5, p. 447ab: the inversion of Siricius' instruction that one must be continent to pray. On Siricius see Callam, 'Clerical continence', p. 46.

201 *De bono vid.*, 29. *PL* 40. 450, PNF 1/3, p 454b.

202 *Ep.* 211. 14. *PL* 33. 964, WAA 13, p. 403.

203 *De virg.*, 34. *PL* 40. 415, PNF 1/3, p. 429ab.

204 It may be such women whom the community is exhorted to 'watch and warn' in *Ep.* 211. 11. *PL* 33. 962, WAA 13, pp. 399–400. Rousselle, *Porneia*, p. 133, notes the same differentiation in writing for virgins and widows in the writing of John Chrysostom.

205 *De virg.* 34. *PL* 40. 415, PNF 1/3, p. 429ab.

206 *Ep.* 130. 16, 30. *PL* 33. 506, WAA 13, p. 165. This epistle is full of instruction about the lifestyle appropriate to continent women. McNamara, 'Muffled voices', pp. 18ff, provides a detailed discussion of the domestic lives of the consecrated.

207 *De bono vid.*, 21. 26. *PL* 40. 448, PNF 1/3, p. 452b; *De virg.*, 34. *PL* 40. 415, PNF 1/3, 429b. *Ep.* 211. *PL* 33. 958–65 sets out the basis of the Augustinian rule for women.

208 See the letter to Proba, *Ep.* 130. 1. *PL* 33. 494, WAA 13, p. 145. As Proba was the grandmother of Demetrias, set as an example to continent women in *De bono vid.*, 29, it can be taken that what he says to her is applicable to virgins as well. *PL* 40. 450, PNF 1/3, p. 454b.

209 Jerome, *Ep.* 14; cf. 22.8. *PL* 22. 347–58; 399. Jerome saw Paula's physical decline as a mark of sanctity.

210 *Ep.* 130. 13. 24; 211.8. *PL* 33. 503; 960, WAA 13, pp. 160; 397. *De bono vid.*, 21. 26. *PL* 40. 448, PNF 1/3, p. 452b. Cf. *Ep.* 130. 3. 7. *PL* 33. 496. WAA 13, p. 148, where he gives the alternative view – only take care of the body in so far as is necessary for health. Paula, Eustochium and Melania the elder modelled themselves more on radical eastern practices. See Jerome, *Ep.* 108.21, and Lawless, *Monastic rule*, p. 42. Armstrong, *Gospel*, p. 58, examines some of the more extreme forms of female asceticism which are close to self-mutilation.

211 Ambrose, *De virg.*, 3. 4. 15–16. *OO* 14/2, p. 224, PNF 1/10, p. 383b.

212 Objections to celibacy are enumerated and argued against in *De bono vid.*, 28. *PL* 40. 450, PNF 1/3, p. 453b.

213 *Contra duas ep. Pel.*, 1. 2. 4. *PL* 44. 552, WAA 15, p. 239.

214 *De virg.* 7. *PL* 40. 399–400, PNF 1/3, p. 419a.

215 *De virg.*, 8. *PL* 40. 400, PNF 1/3, p. 419b. See discussion on the patriarchs in chapter 4, pp. 34–5.

216 *De bono vid.*: on lust, 6. 9; on the end times, 20. 25. *PL* 40. 433; 447, PNF 1/3, pp. 444b; 452a. The influence of 1 Cor. 7 is apparent here.

The fall of the empire and the barbarian invasion would have been influential social factors.

217   *De opere mon.*, 4. 5. *PL* 40. 552, PNF 1/3, p. 506a. Augustine followed Jerome in this. Christian texts *circa* 200 regard Paul as married. Also, Jerome's first translation of the Greek text into the Vulgate Latin in 383 used 'wife' (*uxor*) in this text, but in 385 he changed it to the more ambiguous 'woman' (*mulier*). Ranke-Heinemann, *Eunuchs*, pp. 29, 38.

218   See *De gen. ad litt.*, 9. 7. 12. *PL* 34. 397, ACW 42, p. 77. In a circular argument, Augustine asks how else could the great merit and high honour of virginity be explained unless it was that in his era, sexual desire does not demand what is not required for procreation.

219   *De virg.*, 9. *PL* 40. 400, PNF 1/3, p. 419b-20a.

220   *De bono vid.*, 3. 5. *PL* 40. 433, PNF 1/3, p. 442b.

221   *De virg.*, 12. *PL* 40. 401, PNF 1/3, p. 420b.

222   *Serm.*, 192. 2. *PL* 38–9, 1012; FC 38, p. 32–3.

223   *Serm.*, 93. 3. 4. *PL* 38–9. 574, PNF 1/6, p. 402a.

224   *De bono vid.*, 5; 28. *PL* 40. 443; 449, PNF 1/3, pp. 442b; 453b–4a.

225   Ambrose argued similarly: *De institutione virginis*, 6. 41. *OO* 14/2, p. 142.

226   *De nupt. et con.*, 1. 11. 12. *PL* 44. 420, PNF 1/5, p. 268; *Serm.*, 51. 20. 30. *PL* 38–9. 350–1, PNF 1/6, p. 256b.

227   Chapter 8, p. 105.

228   *Contra Faustum*, 23. 8. *PL* 42. 471, PNF 1/4, p. 315b. *Contra Iul.*, 5. 12. 48. *PL* 44. 811, FC 35, p. 289.

229   This notion would not have been so alien to Roman thought. Roman paternity was a juridical construct. No child, however closely related by blood, was deemed child and heir unless acknowledged by the father before witnesses. Children were often adopted to provide an heir for the *familia. Serm.*, 51. 13. 21; 51. 20. 30. *PL* 38–9. 344–5; 350, PNF 1/6, pp. 252b; 257a.

230   *Serm.*, 51. 11–18, esp. 17; 51. 20. 30. *PL* 38–9. 339–43; 350–1, PNF 1/6, pp. 251ff; 265b.

231   *Serm.*, 51. 10. 16. *PL* 38–9. 342, PNF 1/6, p. 251a.

232   *Contra Iul.*, 5. 12. 47. *PL* 44. 810–11.

233   *Serm.*, 51. 11. 18. *PL* 38–9. 343, PNF 1/6, p. 251b. It is significant that both divine and human sons are portrayed as teaching their mothers how to behave appropriately. See *Ep.* 243. *PL* 33. 1054–9, FC 32, pp. 219–27.

234   *Serm.*, 51. 13. 21. *PL* 38–9. 345, PNF 1/6, p. 253a.

235   *De bono vid.*, 6. 8. *PL* 40. 434, PNF 1/3, p. 443b.

236   *Serm.*, 188. 2. 4; 189. 3. 3. *PL* 38–9. 1004–5; 1006, Przywara, # 408, # 419, pp. 238–9; 245. *Serm.*, 191. 4. *PL* 38–9. 1011; *De virg.* 5. *PL* 40. 399, PNF 1/3, p. 418b.

237   *Serm.*, 93. 3. 4. *PL* 38–9. 575, PNF 1/6, p. 402b.

238   *Serm.*, 215. 3. *PL* 38–9. 1073, FC 38, p. 146.

239   *De virg.*, 5. *PL* 40. 399, PNF 1/3, p. 418b.

240   *Serm.*, 189. 3. 3. *PL* 38–9. 1006, FC 38, p. 22.

Chapter 13

1   Ruether, 'Mary', p. 35, argues that the New Testament does not imply support of virginity over marriage, but is rather a statement about the election of Jesus' birth. It is not concerned with Mary but Jesus.

2   Brown, *Augustine and sexuality*, p. 30.

3   Origen attests to this as early as 246–248, and apparently refers to the *Protoevangelium of James*, *Commentarius in Mattaeum*, 17. *SC* 162. p. 215–19, ANF 9, p. 424b.
4   Fiorenza, 'Critical theology,' *passim*. Cf. Tavard, *Woman*, p. 136.
5   The tracts on the dress of women, the veiling of virgins, the letters of Jerome all manifest variations on this theme.
6   Hunter, 'Virgin Bride'.
7   *Contra duas ep. Pel.*, 3. 14. *PL* 44. 598, WAA 15, p. 312. Concerning the hierarchies within the church see D. Winslow, 'Priesthood and sexuality in the post-Nicene Fathers', *St Luke's Journal*, 18 (1975), pp. 352–65.
8   *De virg.* 10. *PL* 40. 401. PNF 1/3, p. 420a. He modifies this stance in *Ep.* 188. 6. *PL* 33. 851, WAA 13, p. 260. 'Though you '[Juliana, mother of Demetrias] are inferior to her, in this you are made equal to her that your marriage was the cause of her birth.' Possibly, the fact that Juliana and her mother Proba were both continent widows from a great Roman house influenced Augustine here.
9   The insistence on virginity *in partu*, as well as the purification of women after childbirth, implies this. A redactional introduction to *The martyrdom of Perpetua* states that she was purified after childbirth by her martyrdom: *A lost tradition*, p. 18.
10 See *Con.*, 7. 12. *PL* 32. 743, P-C, p. 148 for a discussion on the corruption of a good.
11 Augustine uses the rape of the Sabines and its consequences to subvert Roman marriage customs and morality: *Civ. Dei*, 3. 13. *PL* 41. 104, GB 18, pp. 174b-5a.
12 Notably, Rousselle, *Porneia*; Brown, *Body and society*; Brundage, *Law*; Dixon, *Roman mother*; Gardner, *Women*; Rawson, *Marriage* and Laqueur, *Making sex*.
13 *Serm.*, 332. 4. *PL* 38–9. 1463. Cf. Rousselle, *Porneia*, pp. 40, 192–3. See also the preceding chapter.
14 See Anne Yarbrough, 'Christianization in the fourth century: the example of Roman women', CH, 45, 2 (June 1976), pp. 159–60; S. R. Johansson, '"Herstory" as history: a new field or another fad?' in B. Carroll, ed., *Liberating women's history: theoretical and critical essays* (Urbana: University of Indiana Press, 1976), p. 420, on virginity as role revolt. More recently, see Brown, *Body and society*, on different forms of ascetic life.
15 Børresen, *Subordination*, p. 25, states that as woman takes on equivalence she becomes 'defeminised' to the extent that she is free from subordination.
16 Ambrose, *Ep.* 31. *PL* 16. 1113, FC 26, p. 423.
17 The influence of Philo's perception of the virginal can be perceived here.
18 Rosemary Radford Ruether, *Sexism and God-talk: towards a feminist theology* (London: SCM Press, 1983), p. 101.
19 Brown, *Body and society*, p. 407. Tavard, *Woman*, p. 85 agrees with Brown in that he believes that the qualities of spiritual virginity attributed to bodily virginity are only rhetorical.
20 *Civ. Dei*, 14. 26. *PL* 41. 434–5, GB 18, p. 396a.
21 *De bono con.*, 21. *PL* 40. 388, PNF 1/3, p. 408a.
22 Found in Seneca, Clement, Plutarch and even John Paul II. See discussion in Ranke-Heinemann, *Eunuchs*, p. 38. Augustine's position is more moderate than that of Jerome who argued that if to abstain from coitus is to

honour a wife, then not to abstain is to insult her. *Adversus Iovinianum* 1. 7. *PL* 23. 228–9, PNF 2/6, p. 351b.

23   Rousselle, *Porneia*, pp. 192–3, 198.

24   Wilson-Kastner, 'Introduction' to *A lost tradition*, p. xxiii, writes that in some communities women were penalised for leaving the married state for asceticism, but men were not.

25   *Ep.* 262 is a case in point. *PL* 33, 1077–82, FC 32, pp. 261–9. John Chrysostom also held women responsible for their husband's adultery if due to wifely withdrawal of conjugal rights: *Homily XIX on 1 Corinthians*, [3] verse 5. *PG* 61. 154–6, PNF 1/12, p. 106a.

26   *Ep.* 220. 12 offers a clear indication of Augustine's stand. *PL* 33. 997, PNF 1/1, p. 576a.

27   See Fuchs, *Sexual desire and love*, p. 97, on shame, intimacy and attitudes to sexuality.

28   Fiorenza, *In memory*, p. 278.

29   Castelli offers a thoughtful discussion of this form of asceticism, 'Virginity and its meaning for women's sexuality in early Christianity', *JFSR*, 2. 1 (Spring 1986), pp. 80–1. Cf. Brown, *Body and society*, pp. 267–88 for a most helpful analysis of Basil of Ancyra.

30   *Serm.*, 205, 2; 208. 1; 210. 6. 9. *PL* 38–9. 1039; 1044–5; 1052; FC 38, pp. 85; 93; 105; *Serm.*, 292(a). *PL* 38–9. 2298.

31   Ranke-Heinemann, *Eunuchs*, pp. 120–1.

32   M. Klein was convinced that the 'more remote and unreal the personal feminine is, the more intense the male's yearning for a projection of an eternal feminine onto social institutions that assume a maternal character in embracing, protecting, nourishing and approving the individual' (*Psychoanalysis*, p. 201). Cf. M.-L. von Franz on the disadvantage of worship of anima figures, 'The process of individuation', in C. G. Jung, ed., *Man and his symbols* (London: Aldus/Jupiter Books, [1964] 1979), p. 188.

33   Harding, arguing from a Jungian perspective, states that the relation of a man to his anima determines the nature of his relationship to women and to his own inner self: *Women's Mysteries*, p. 30. There can be little doubt that in either orthodox spiritual terms or Jungian terms, Mary is an anima figure.

34   *Contra Iul.*, 5. 15. 53; 3. 19. 37. *PL* 44. 813–4; 722–3, FC 35, p. 294–5; 141; *Ep.* 166. 6. 16. *PL* 33. 727–8, WAA 13, pp. 308–9; *Contra duas ep. Pel.*, 2. 8. *PL* 44. 576, WAA 15, p. 278; *Ep.* 217. 5. 16. *PL* 33. 984, FC 32, p. 86. Cf. *De trin.*, 13. 12. 16. *PL* 42. 1026, WAA 7, p. 327. See Brown, *AH*, p. 391ff.

35   Cf. John Selby Spong, *Born of a woman: a bishop rethinks the birth of Jesus* (HarperSanFrancisco, 1992), p. 206.

36   Tony Kelly, 'Restoring the feminine in our image of God: liberation from the half human', *National outlook* (July 1983), p. 10.

37   Fiorenza, 'Critical theology', p. 623.

38   N. Foley, 'Celibacy in the men's church' in *Concilium*, 134, 4, p. 33. Also John Rowan, 'Psychic celibacy' in Oonagh Hartnett, Gill Boden and Mary Fuller, eds., *Sex role stereotyping* (London: Tavistock Publishers, 1979), p. 59.

39   See Rawson, 'The Roman family', p. 9.

40   Brundage, *Law*, p. 65, also f.n. 74; Schillebeeckx, *Clerical celibacy*, p. 47, on

the Christianisation of pagan ideals of sexual abstinence, pp. 16–43. The ideal of continence was held up for all, and certainly, as detailed above, even sexually active marriages were expected to practise periodic continence. Kraemer, 'The conversion of women', p. 303, notes that in both the culture and the church, the choices for women were between sexuality and death, although the conflict between the cultural and religious ideals meant that the choice was rewarded differently in each sphere. The world was quite capable of savagely punishing young women who refused marriage. The church demeaned women who accepted the sexual role by typing her as the symbol of sin and death. *The Life of St Cyprian*, Bk 2, p. 167, and *The martyrdom of Perpetua*, pp. 19–32 *passim*, illustrate the social pressures brought to bear on ascetic young women, and the connections between sexuality and death.

41 Harding, *Women's mysteries*; Neumann, *The great mother*, also a Jungian-based study. Other studies of Mary are Marina Warner, *Alone of all her sex: the myth and cult of the Virgin Mary*, New York: Pocket Books, 1976; Andrew Greeley, *The Mary myth*, Washington: Seabury, 1976; Raymond E. Brown et al, eds., *Mary in the New Testament*, Philadelphia: Fortress Press, 1978, and more recently Spong, *Born*.

42 The triadic face of women was presented in the Graces, the Fates, the Norns, the Eumenides. Nor Hall, *The moon and the virgin: reflections on the archetypal feminine* (New York: Harper and Row, 1980), p. 190. I am indebted to Hall in the following discussion especially pp. 11, 110, 127.

43 Neumann, *Great mother*, p. 336.

44 Neumann, *Great mother*, p. 317.

45 Plato, *Republic*, 2. [381] b-c. GB 7, p. 323a. God is perfect, so any change would make him less than perfect: therefore change is incompatible with godliness. This view was balanced in classical culture by the goddess symbol.

46 Cf. van Eijk's comparison of Christian and classical attitudes in 'Marriage and virginity', pp. 209–35.

47 It is clear from the work of Sissa that there exist intriguing parallels between the symbolism surrounding the virgin priestess at Delphi and that used of Mary in early patristic texts, especially those by Ambrose. See *Greek virginity, passim*.

48 Beard, 'Vestal virgins', p. 15.

49 Gordon Laing, 'Roman religious survivals in Christianity', pp. 80–1.

50 Harding, *Mysteries*, p. 128–30.

51 Shelton, *Romans*, p. 383. The feast was instituted by Pope Gelasius as early as 494.

52 Laing, 'Roman survivals', p. 83; Harding asserts that in Syria the feasts were originally celebrated on the same day: *Mysteries*, p. 110.

53 Hall, *The moon*, p. 11, for the former; for the Vestal virgins as the latter, Helen M. Luke, *Woman; earth and spirit. The feminine in symbol and myth* (New York: Crossroad Publishing Co., 1984), pp. 47–9.

54 Harding, *Mysteries*, p. 103.

55 Rahner, *Mary, mother of the Lord* (London: Nelson, 1953), p. 69.

56 Ambrose, on the virgin: *De virginibus*, 2. 6. 43. *OO* 14/1, p. 202, Shiels, p. 59; *De virginitate*, 12. 73. *OO* 14/2, pp. 62; 226, Shiels, p. 103; on Mary: *De institutione virginis*, 7. 46; 14. 88. *OO* 14/2, pp. 144; 172.

57 Independent male ascetics were also suspect as disorderly, but women

even more so by virtue of their inferiority. Women were not to make themselves conspicuous, even in virtue. See McNamara, 'Muffled voices', p. 27; see Fiorenza, 'Critical theology', p. 623, for a comment on the increasing importance of ecclesial authority over communities of nuns.

58 Sissa, *Greek Virginity*, pp. 21–3.
59 Neumann, *Great mother*, p. 324.
60 Geoffrey Ashe, *The virgin* (London: Routledge & Kegan Paul, 1976), p. 32.
61 See Neumann, *Great mother*, p. 33; Ruether, *Mary*, p. 15.
62 Neumann, *Great mother*, p. 136.
63 Neumann, *Great mother*, pp. 307, 332. Neumann postulates the pagan triad as Demeter–Kore–divine son; he presents the Christian model as Anne–Mary–Jesus, an unusual triad. I would suggest that in the ultimate model, Mary assumes both the Demeter/Kore roles at a more primitive level of the archetype. Cf. Neumann, *Great mother*, p. 21, 309, 317.
64 Neumann, *Great mother*, pp. 329, 331.
65 Neumann, *Great mother*, p. 61.
66 Laing, 'Roman survivals', p. 82.
67 For example, Augustine regularly uses 'vessel' as a symbol for woman. The vessel was the symbol *par excellence* for the transformational power of the feminine; the vessel as blossom was the symbol of Sophia wisdom, and the Vestal virgins, as symbols of the positive characteristics of the Great Mother, were keepers of the sacred vessels. Neumann, *Great mother*, pp. 127, 133, 325–6.
68 Neumann, *Great mother*, p. 58; *Ep.* 243, *passim. PL* 33. 1054–9, FC 32, pp. 221–3, cf. 225.
69 Carol P. Christ following Adrienne Rich, 'Why women need the goddess', in *The laughter of Aphrodite: reflections on a journey to the Goddess* (San Francisco: Harper and Row, 1987), p. 129.
70 The Easter vigil, blessing of the water in the font, *St John's Missal for everyday* (New York: Brepols' Catholic Press, 1955), p. 469. Neumann drew this ritual to my attention: *Great mother*, pp. 311–12.
71 Cf. Harding, *Mysteries*, pp. 192–4.
72 Neumann, *Great mother*, p. 81, discusses how the crone aspect of the archetype attracts the negative feelings attached to the 'bad' mother who will not indulge the child, or who frustrates/rejects her/him. For studies on the wise woman see Barbara G. Walker, *The crone: woman of age, wisdom and power*, San Francisco: Harper and Row, 1985; Hall, *The moon*, chs. 8 and 9. On the theological flight from the death crone see Ruether, *Sexism and God-talk*, p. 144.
73 Cf. Walker, *The crone*, pp. 83, 89 and *passim*; Andrew Greeley, *The Mary myth*, pp. 185–96 on the feminine as *pieta*. On Eve see Prusak, 'Woman: seductive siren', p. 97.
74 One caveat here: Ambrose saw death as a post-lapsarian mercy which reunited the individual with God. See *De bono mortis. OO* 13, FC 65.
75 I am utilising the work of Dinnerstein and Klein, here, applying their categories to the virgin-mother symbolism. See Dinnerstein, *Cradle*, and Klein, *Psychoanalysis*.
76 Cf. *Ep.* 211. 10–11. *PL* 691–2, PNF 1/1, p. 566a for the instruction that the nuns were to keep watch on one another for sexual infringement

of the rule and report to the superior. If one's peers do not see one, then God will.

77   Klein, *Psychoanalysis*, p. 364. Klein states that the pure and untouched woman symbolised the Good Mother, unsullied by the father's penis, or not destroyed by it. She can therefore give her lover [children] good healing and pure substances out of her own body. The overlap between Klein's language and Augustine's is remarkable.

78   Jungian anthropologists and theorists have argued that the ideal of virginity is the result of the incest taboo. In the idealised virgin, the son regains his mother in a love divested of sexual implications. John Layard, 'The incest taboo and the virgin archetypes', *Images of the Untouched*, eds., Joanne Stroud and Gail Thomas (Dallas, Texas: Spring Publications Inc., 1982), pp. 145–84. But the androcentrism of the theory remains. Only male feelings, 'instincts' and needs are addressed by Layard. Women exist to meet these as either physical mother or abstract vision.

79   J. Rowan, 'Psychic celibacy', p. 58. Cf. Meeks, 'The image of the androgyne', p. 207.

80   Fuchs, *Sexual desire and love*, pp. 113–14.

81   *De fide et symb.*, 4. 9. *PL* 40. 186, FC 27, p. 325. Cf. Cyril of Jerusalem, who pronounced that if the Virgin could boast because the Christ lay nine months in her womb, then how much more men can glory because Christ was for 33 years a man. Possibly reflecting a feminine argument in his community? *Catecheses*, 12. 33. *PG* 33. 767, PNF 2/7, p. 81.

82   Børresen, *Subordination*, p. 24, sees Augustine's concern to give balance and wholeness to the work of redemption as laudable. His position is more ambiguous than Børresen concedes.

83   *Inter Insigniores*, p. 179ff.

84   Cf. *De trin.*, 4. 18. 24. *PL* 42. 905, WAA 7, p. 133–4.

Chapter 14

1   That Augustine subscribed to this belief is apparent in *Serm.*, 9. 12. *PL* 38. 84, WStA III/1 pp. 269–70.

2   Augustine, *De gen. ad litt.*, 5. 13. 29–5. 14. 31. *PL* 34. 331–2, ACW 41, pp. 164–5.

3   Cf. *Letter* 6.* 6. Divjak, p. 134, FC 81, p. 56. P. Brown concludes that the social landscape of Augustine's paradise reflects the ideal Roman *domus*, and that it was easily recognisable as such in fourth-century Africa: *Body and society*, p. 400.

4   *De cont.*, 8. 19. *PL* 40. 3614, PNF 1/3, p. 387a.

5   If 'true being' never changes, then the radical alterations accompanying the resurrection of women's bodies reinforce the implication of the *ordo amoris* that women are further removed from such true being than men are. *Con.*, 7. 11. *PL* 32. 742, P-C, p. 147. Cf. *Civ. Dei*, 22. 17; 11. 16. *PL* 41. 778–9; 331, GB 18, pp. 603a; 331a.

6   The devaluation of transformation typifies patriarchal cultures: Neumann, *Great mother*, pp. 3, 53–9.

7   *De doct. Christ.*, 1. 23. 22; cf. 1. 27. 28. *PL* 34. 27; 29, GB 18, p. 630a; 631b. Beings further away from God are less like God. *Con.*, 7. 16. *PL* 32. 744, P-C, p. 150. The permutations of this order are played out in *Serm.*, 21. 3; 37; 100. 2. *PL* 38. 143–4; 221–35; 603–4, WStA III/2, pp. 31;

197; III/4 p. 64, *Serm.*; Mai 20, *passim. PLS* II. 672–4, WStA III/3, 65A, pp. 199–209.

8   *Civ. Dei*, 15. 7. *PL* 41. 443–5, GB 18, p. 402b.

9   Cf. *Serm.*, Mai 20. 4. *PLS* II. 605, WStA III/3, 65A, p. 200.

10 *De doct. Christ.*, 31. 34. *PL* 34. 32, PNF 1/2, p. 531b.

11 *De doct. Christ.*, 25. 26. *PL* 34. 29, PNF 1/2, p. 529b. *De cont., passim. PL* 40. 345–72.

12 *De cont.*, 8. 19. *PL* 40. 361–2, PNF 1/3, p. 387a. *Ep.* 140. 2. *PL* 33. 538–9, FC 20, pp. 59–60; cf. *De nupt. et con.*, 1. 31. 35. *PL* 44. 433, PNF 1/5, p. 277b–8a.

13 *De cont.*, 8. *PL* 40. 354, PNF 1/3, p. 382ab.

14 See also Carole Pateman, 'The disorder of women: women, love and the sense of justice' in *Ethics*, 91. 1 (October 1980), pp. 20–34.

15 *De trin.*, 12. 9. 14. 42. *PL* 1005–6, WAA 7, p. 295. See full discussion in chapter 14.

16 Brown, *Body and society*, p. 6.

17 Ambrose, *Hexameron*, 5. 7. 19. *OO* I, pp. 260–2, FC 42, p. 174.

18 Earlier scholarship, particularly that influenced by Freud's concept of polymorphous perversity, would have seen women's sexuality as less immediately genital – a factor that Freud constructed as less mature. However, in feminist scholarship the experience of women's sexuality unmediated by androcentric perceptions of women is still a matter for debate. See discussion by Judith Butler in *Gender trouble: feminism and the subversion of identity* (New York: Routledge, 1990), pp. 25–34; Janet Sayers offers a critique of psychoanalytic essentialism in *Sexual contradictions: psychology, psychoanalysis and feminism* (London: Tavistock Publications, 1986), pp. 35–48.

19 Julian appears to have noted the androcentrism in Augustine's argument: *Contra Iul.*, 4. 13. 62. *PL* 44. 768, FC 35, p. 219.

20 *Letter* 6.* 5, 8. Divjak, pp. 132, 142, FC 81, pp. 56, 59.

21 The bodiliness of the *poena reciproca* is underestimated by Hunter, 'Augustinian pessimism?'

22 Hunter following Bonner accepts the concept of the 'flawed instinct', 'Augustinian pessimism?' p. 169.

23 Clement of Alexandria, *Quis dives*, 37. *PG* 9. 642, ANF 2, p. 601b.

24 Ambrose, *De patriarchis*, 11. 51. *CSEL* 32/2, p. 153, FC 65, p. 269.

25 *En. in pss.*, 444. 4. *PL* 36. 496, PNF 1/8, p. 146b. My emphasis.

26 Cf. *De trin.*, 9. 8. 13. *PL* 42. 968, WAA 7, p. 234.

27 Mircea Eliade, *Images and symbols* and *The myth of the eternal return*, trans. Willard Trask, New York: Random House, 1954.

28 On Monica and the ideology of Christian motherhood, see Atkinson, 'Your servant, my mother', pp. 164–5.

29 R. R. Ruether, 'Misogynism and virginal feminism in the Fathers of the church' in *Religion and sexism*, p. 165.

30 John Layard, 'The incest taboo', p. 167. For the recent work in Freudian thought I am indebted to the Seminar, *Reengendering the parental figure*, David Cunningham, Mary Ellen Jordan and James Tait, University of St Thomas, Minnesota, 1994.

31 Hunter, 'Augustinian pessimism?', p. 169. Hunter is not asserting the Augustinian view of gender relations here, simply offering an excellent

definition of pride in Augustine's thought, which I am applying to gender relations.

32 Dinnerstein, *The rocking of the cradle.* Cf. Ambrose who actually calls the church 'the breast that never fails': *De virginibus*, 1. 5. 22. *OO* 14/1, p. 12, PNF 2/10, p. 366.

33 Neumann, *Great Mother*, p. 58.

34 Neumann, *Great Mother*, p. 331.

35 Brown, *AH*, p. 393.

36 As in the Aeschylus version of the Orestes myth.

37 *Con.*, 4. 1; 7. 14. *PL* 32. 693; 744, P-C, pp. 71; 149–50.

38 Yet experience is the primordial matter of religion. By totally denying the feminine presence he had experienced he was unfaithful to God and to himself.

39 For the influence of parent–child relationships on an individual's image of God see Ana-Maria Rizzuto. If Rizzuto is correct, Augustine's representation of a mothering God also informs us about the quality of his early experience with Monica. *The birth of the living God: a psychoanalytic study* (Chicago: University of Chicago Press, 1979), pp. 180–210, esp. 187 and 196.

40 *Con.*, 13. 22. Cf. 10. 4. *PL* 32. 858; 782, P-C, pp. 332; 210. Dutton's study, 'When I was a child', accepts Augustine's hierarchy of experience without critique.

41 Dutton ignores this aspect of Augustine's stages of spiritual growth, 'When I was a child'.

42 The difference in age between husband and wives meant that in real life, it was more likely that young men would be independent and possibly *paterfamilias* themselves. If Augustine was the eldest child, he would have been *paterfamilias* at sixteen.

43 As Antti Arjava has previously noted, he was at pains to explain that his moral stance should be accepted because such moral positions had been accepted by all men. See 'Women in the Christian empire: ideological change and social reality' in Elizabeth Livingstone, ed., *Studia Patristica* (Leuven: Peeters Press, 1993), p. 6, for discussion and references.

44 Implicit in the powerful social roles of the Vestal virgins.

45 Even Jerome's friends rejected his treatise *Adversus Iovinianum* as far too extreme, withdrawing it from circulation. See Brown's discussion, *Body and society*, p. 377.

46 A. Armstrong, 'Neoplatonic evaluations of nature, body and intellect', *AS*, 3 (1972), pp. 35–59, esp. pp. 38–9.

47 Alexander, 'Sex and philosophy', pp. 199–206.

48 I do not include here his condemnation of the sexual double standard of morality, because that was firmly entrenched in Christian culture from the apostolic period and was a true Christian innovation that never really caught on.

49 Stephen J. Duffy, 'Original sin: our hearts of darkness revisited', *TS*, 49, 4 (1988), p. 605, presents a nuanced discussion on concupiscence as natural desire.

Chapter 15

1 Hunter, 'Augustinian pessimism?' p. 162.

2 Ranke-Heinnemann, *Eunuchs*, p. 242.

3 *De con. adult.*, 1. 6. 6. *PL* 40. 454–5, FC 27, p. 67.
4 One can hardly say harmony.
5 Bearing in mind that slaves were always beaten. On the marriage contract being a vital influence on twentieth-century women who remain in violent relationships, see Del Martin, *Battered wives* (San Francisco: Glide Publications, 1976), p. 36.
6 Hunter, 'Augustinian pessimism?' p. 170. Cf. Part 5 for a full discussion of the sexual imagery surrounding Eve's sin.
7 Carole Pateman, 'The disorder of women', pp. 20–34. Pateman's identification of women with love, especially familial love, in opposition to the abstract justice of the state, has relevance for this study.
8 Cf. *Contra Iul.*, 4. 5. 35, and 4. 12. 58; 5. 2. 7. *PL* 44. 756 and 766; 786, FC 35, pp. 199 and 216; 246–7. For detailed discussion of the discourse of the veil see chapter 10.
9 Ambrose, *De virginibus*, 3. 33–6. *OO* 14/1. pp. 236–40, Shiel, pp. 74–5. *De virginitate*, 5. 24. *OO* 14/2, p. 28, Callam, p. 26. Augustine, *Civ. Dei*, 1. 17, 19. *PL* 41. 30–4, GB 18, p. 140a.
10 *Civ. Dei*, 1. 19. *PL* 41. 32–4, GB 18, pp. 141a-2b.
11 The corruption of the virgin in her first sexual encounter therefore presumes sexual desire on her part. See chapter 12 on *cor-rumpo*, n.45, p. 291.
12 *Civ. Dei*, 1. 16. *PL* 41. 30, GB 18, p. 139 b.
13 *Contra mend.*, 9. 20. *PL* 40. 531, FC 16, p. 148.
14 *De mend.*, 7. 10; *Contra mend.*, 7. 18. *PL* 40. 496; 528, FC 16, pp. 69; 148.
15 *De mend.*, 6–7. 10; 20. 41; *Contra mend.*, 19. 38, cf. 20. 40; *PL* 40. 494–6; 515; 545–6, 547, FC 16, pp. 67–70; 106; 174; 176; *Civ. Dei*, 1. 18. *PL* 41. 31, GB 18, p. 140ab.
16 *De mend.*, 7. 10. *PL* 40. 496, FC 16, p. 70.
17 *Contra mend.*, 9. 21. *PL* 40. 532, FC 16, p. 148.
18 *Civ. Dei*, 1. 16. *PL* 41. 30, GB 18, p. 139b.
19 Clark, *Ascetic piety*, p. 40.
20 On hyperbole see *Tract. in Ioh. ev.*, 124. 8. *PL* 35. 1976, PNF 1/7, p. 452b.
21 I am specifically speaking of relationships between adults here. Adult/child relationships are not relationships of equality, yet the goal should be the child's full development into autonomous adulthood.
22 Even though the men and women are far more likely to be age and work peers in modern society. See S. Moore's exposition of sexual relationships structured by Hegel's master–slave paradigm: *The fire and the rose are one* (London: Darton, Longman & Todd, 1980), p. 47–8.
23 *De fide rerum*, 3. 6; 7. 10. *PL* 40. 175–6; 179–80, PNF 1/3, pp. 340; 343. *De opere mon.*, 28. 36. *PL* 40. 575, PNF 1/3, p. 521.
24 *Serm.*, 138. 6. *PL* 38. 766, WStA III/4, pp. 388–9.
25 G. Bonner suggests that *caritas coniugalis*, as described in *De gen. ad litt.*, 3. 21. 33, should be placed on a level with *amicitia*: 'Women and *amicitia*', p. 274. As Augustine uses it here to distinguish between affection and sexual desire, it would be a Platonic marital friendship untainted by desire. *Tract. in Ioh. ev.*, 8. 4 offers a fruitful exposition of the love of Jesus the bridegroom. *PL* 35. 1452, PNF 1/7, p. 58b.
26 Ambrose, *Exhortatio virginitatis*, 12. 82. *OO* 14/2, p. 262.
27 Jerome, *Ep.* 22. 2. *PL* 22. 395, PNF 2/6, p. 23a. Cf. Ambrose, *De virginibus*, 1. 65. *OO* 14/1, p. 160. It is a constant theme in Augustine's sermons.

Examples are *Sermo* Mai 20 *passim*. *PLS* II. 464–7. WStA III/ 3, 65A, pp. 200–9. Cf. *Serm*. 100 *passim*. *PL* 38. 602–5, WStA III/4, pp. 60–3.

28 Clark, following Demant and Brummer, has argued that Serena, wife of Stilicho, was executed for helping Melania and Pinianus liquidate their assets for ascetic purposes: 'Piety', p. 71. Paternal opposition to freedom of choice is expressed violently in some of the Apocryphal *Acts* and vehemently in Milan. Ambrose, *De virginitate*, 6. 32–3; 7. 36. *OO* 14/2, pp. 34–6; 38, Callam, pp. 20–2.

29 Augustine seems to indicate that this is a real marriage, not simply a hypothetical one: *Tract. in Ioh. ev.*, 9. 2. *PL* 35. 1458–9, PNF 1/7, p. 63b. It is taken so also by John Bugge, *Virginitas: an essay in the history of a medieval ideal* (The Hague: Martinus Nijhoff, 1975), p. 78.

30 *De pecc. mer. et rem.*, 3. 13. 22. *PL* 44. 499, PNF 1/5, p. 78 a. Possibly because fathers retained control of their children in any divorce; so stepfathers would be rarer than stepmothers.

31 *Ep.* 211. 12. *PL* 33. 962–3, PNF 1/1, p. 566b-7a. The nuns are to have one storeroom, one wardrobe. No one is to make anything for personal use, no gifts are to be kept by individuals, but everything belongs to the common stock.

32 Markus, *End*, pp. 78, followed by Hunter, 'Augustinian pessimism?', p. 169.

33 For prior cases see chapter 9.

34 In *Sermo* Mai 20. 6 he says that Christ even snubbed his mother for the sake of finishing a sermon on the Kingdom. *PLS* II. 46, WStA III/3, p. 201.

35 In a far broader context, Thunberg argues that because the church is always communal, ecclesiology is always anthropology: 'The human person as the image of God: I. Eastern Christianity' in B. McGinn et al., eds., *Christian spirituality I: origins to the twelfth century* (New York: Crossroad, 1986), pp. 291–311.

36 Ambrose, *Hexameron*, 6. 9. 57. *OO* I, p. 402, FC 42, p. 270.

37 This birth-giving aspect of the church's role was taken so literally in one ancient church in North Africa that the baptistry there is built in the shape of a woman's labia. Robin Jensen, 'Archaeology and North African baptism: the ambiguity of material remains', *NAPS*, Plenary Address, Chicago: May 1994.

38 Note the parallels to Monica's role in Augustine's conversion. Cf. *Ep.* 150. *PL* 33. 645. FC 2, p. 266–8. Virginal fertility is of the mind not the womb, motherhood is not the fruitful breast but the ardent heart and virgins give birth not to earth in travail but to heaven in prayer.

39 Augustine refers to himself as 'master' (*dominus*) of the church in Hippo: *Ep.* 126. *PL* 33. 480, FC 18, p. 350.

40 See chapter 13's discussion.

41 Brown, *AH*, p. 389.

42 *Sic.* Devereux, 'Psychology', p. 253.

ABBREVIATIONS

Primary sources

Latin and Greek texts:

CCL	*Corpus Christianorum, Series Latina* (Turnout-Paris 1953–)
CSEL	*Corpus Scriptorum Ecclesiasticorum Latinorum* (Vienna 1866–)
MA	*Miscellanea Agostiniana* (Rome 1930–31)
OO	*Opera Omnia di Sant'Ambrogio* (Milano, 1979–)
PG	*Patrologia Graeca*, ed. J. P. Migne (Paris 1857–1866)
PL	*Patrologia Latina*, ed. J. P. Migne (Paris, 1878–1890)
PLS	*Patrologiae Latinea, Supplementum*, ed. A. Harmann (Paris, 1957–)
SC	*Sources Chrétiennes* (Paris, 1940)

Translations:

ACW	*Ancient Christian Writers.*
A lost tradition	P. Wilson-Kastner et al., *A lost tradition.*
ANCL	*Ante-Nicene Christian Library.*
ANE	J. Stevenson, editor, *A new Eusebius: documents illustrative of the history of the church to A.D. 337.*
ANF	Ante-Nicene Fathers.
Bright	Pamela Bright, translator, Ambrose's *De virginibus.*
Callam	Daniel Callam, translator, Ambrose's *De virginitate.*
CCC	J. Stevenson, editor, *Creeds, councils and controversies.*
Chadwick	*Saint Augustine, Confessions.*
Divjak	*Lettres 1*-20*.*
GB	*Great books of the Western world.*

FC	*Fathers of the church.*
L&F	Mary R. Lefkowitz and Maureen B. Fant, editors, *Women's life in Greece and Rome: a source book in translation.* First edition.
Laeuchli	Canons of the Synod of Elvira. Appendix, *Power and sexuality: the emergence of canon law at the Synod of Elvira.*
LCC	*Library of Christian Classics.*
Hunter	David G. Hunter, editor, *Marriage in the early church.*
Maenads	Ross S. Kraemer, editor, *Mænads, martyrs, matrons and monastics: a sourcebook on women's religions in the Greco-Roman world.*
P-C	R. S. Pine-Coffin, translator, *St Augustine: Confessions.*
PNF	*Nicene and post-Nicene Fathers.*
Przywara	E. Przywara, translator, *Sermons,* Section III, *An Augustine synthesis.*
Shelton	Jo-Ann Shelton, editor, *As the Romans did: a sourcebook in Roman social history.*
Shiel	James Shiel, translator, Ambrose's *De virginibus,* Books I-III; *De virginitate.*
Thompson	Robert Thompson, ed. Gk text and translator, Athanasius's *Contra gentes* and *De incarnatione.*
WAA	*The works of Aurelius Augustine, Bishop of Hippo.*
Watts	W. Watts, translator, *St Augustine's Confessions.*
WSt.A	The works of St Augustine: *a translation for the 21st century.*
Yonge	C. D. Yonge, translator, *The Works of Philo.*

Secondary sources

Dictionary

Lewis & Short	Lewis and Short, *A Latin dictionary*

Journals:

AAR	*American Academy of Religion.*
ACPAP	*American Catholic Philosophical Association Proceedings.*
AHR	*American Historical Review.*
AP	*Australian Psychologist.*
ARCTOS	*Arctos: Acta Philologica Fennica.*
AS	*Augustinian Studies.*
BTB	*Biblical Theology Bulletin.*
CBQ	*Catholic Biblical Quarterly.*

CH	*Church History.*
CQ	*Classical Quarterly.*
Colloquy	*Protocols of the Colloquy of the Center for hermeneutical studies in Hellenistic and modern culture at Berkeley.*
Concilium	*Concilium: women in a men's church.*
FS	*Feminist Studies.*
GRBS	*Greek, Roman and Byzantine studies.*
HR	*History of Religions.*
HTR	*Harvard Theological Review.*
IJP	*International Journal of Psychoanalysis.*
JAAR	*Journal of the American Academy of Religion.*
JBL	*Journal of Biblical Literature.*
JECS	*Journal of Early Christian Studies.*
JEH	*Journal of Ecclesiastical History.*
JFSR	*Journal of Feminist Studies in Religion.*
JRH	*Journal of Religion and Health.*
JRS	*Journal of Roman Studies.*
JSSR	*Journal for the Scientific Study of Religion.*
JTS	*Journal of Theological Studies.*
MS	*Modern Schoolman.*
NAPS	*North American Patristic Society.*
NB	*New Blackfriars.*
NBPS	*Newsletter of the British Psychological Society.*
RHR	*Radical History Review.*
RTAM	*Recherches de théologie ancienne et medievale.*
SBL	*Society of Biblical Literature.*
Signs	*Signs: Journal of Women in Culture and Society.*
TAPA	*Transcripts of the American Philological Association.*
TD	*Theology Digest.*
TS	*Theological Studies.*
YJC	*Yale Journal of Criticism.*

Select bibliography

Source books

Coleman-Norton, P. R., ed. *Roman state and Christian church: a collection of legal documents to A.D. 535*, Vols. 1–3. London: SPCK, 1966.

Hunter, David G., ed. and trans. *Marriage in the early church.* Sources in early Christian thought. Minneapolis: Fortress Press, 1992.

Kraemer, Ross S., ed. *Maenads, martyrs, matrons and monastics: a sourcebook on women's religions in the Greco-Roman world.* Philadelphia: Fortress Press, 1988.

Lefkowitz, Mary R. and Maureen B. Fant, eds. *Women's life in Greece and Rome: a source book in translation.* Baltimore: Johns Hopkins University Press, 1982.

Shelton, Jo-Ann, ed. *As the Romans did: a source book in Roman social history,* New York: Oxford University Press, 1988.

Stevenson, J., ed. *A new Eusebius.* London: SPCK, 1957, 1980.

Stevenson, J., ed. *Creeds, councils and controversies.* London: SPCK, 1966, 1972, 1981.

Suggestions for further reading

Alexander, W. 'Sex and philosophy in St. Augustine.' *Augustinian studies* 5 (1974), pp. 197–208.

Aspegren, Kerstin. *The male woman: a feminine ideal in the early church.* Ed. René Kieffer. Stockholm: Almquist & Wiksell, 1990.

Atkinson, Clarissa W., C. H. Buchanan and M. R. Miles, eds. *Immaculate and powerful: the female in sacred image and social reality.* Harvard women's studies in religion series. Boston: Beacon Press, 1985, pp. 139–72.

Aubert, Jean-Jacques. 'Threatened wombs: aspects of ancient uterine magic.' *Greek, Roman and Byzantine studies,* 30, 3 (Autumn 1989), pp. 421–49.

Augustinus magister. Congrès international Augustinien. Paris: Études Augustiniennes, 1955.

Beard, Mary. 'The sexual status of the Vestal virgins.' *Journal of Roman studies* (1980–81), pp. 12–27.

Benko, S. *Pagan Rome and the early Christians.* Bloomington: Indiana University Press, 1984.

Bonner, G. 'Augustine's attitude to women and *"amicitia".' Homo spiritalis.* Festgabe für Luc Verheijin. Eds. Cornelius Mayer and Karl H. Chelius. Würzburg: Augustinus Verlag, 1987, pp. 259–75.

Børresen, Kari Elisabeth. 'In defence of Augustine: how *femina* is *homo.' Collectanea Augustiniana: mélanges T. J. Bavel.* Eds. B. Brunning, M. Lambergits and J. Van Houtem. Bibliotheca Ephemeridum Theologicarum Lovaniensium. Leuven: Leuven University Press, 1990, pp. 411–27.

Børresen, Kari Elisabeth. *Subordination and equivalence: the nature and role of women in Augustine and Thomas Aquinas.* Washington: University Press of America, 1981.

Børresen, Kari Elisabeth. 'Women's studies of the Christian tradition.' *Contemporary philosophy.* Ed. Guttorm Fløistad. Dordrecht: Kluwer Academic Publishers, 1991, pp. 901–1001.

Boyarin, Daniel. ' "Behold, Israel according to the flesh": on anthropology and sexuality in late antique Judaisms.' *Yale Journal of Criticism*, 5, 2 (Spring 1992), pp. 27–57.

Brooten, Bernadette J. 'Early Christian women and their cultural context: issues of method in historical reconstruction.' *Feminist perspectives on biblical scholarship.* Ed. Adela Yarbro Collins. Chico, California: Scholar's Press, 1985, pp. 65–91.

Brown, Peter R. L. *Augustine of Hippo: a biography.* Berkeley: University of California Press, 1969.

Brown, Peter R. L. *The body and society: men, women and sexual renunciation in early Christianity.* Lectures on the history of religions, new series, 13. New York: Columbia University Press, 1988.

Brown, Peter R. L. *The cult of the saints: its rise and function in Latin Christianity.* London: SCM Press, 1981.

Brown, Peter R. L. 'Sexuality and society in the fifth century AD: Augustine and Julian of Eclanum.' *Tria cordia: Scritti in onore di Arnaldo Momigliano.* Ed. E. Gabba. Como: New Press, 1983, pp. 49–70.

Brown, Peter R.L. *Society and the holy in late antiquity.* London: Faber and Faber, 1982.

Brundage, James A. *Law, sex and Christian society in medieval Europe.* Chicago: University of Chicago Press, 1987.

Bullough, Vern and James A. Brundage, eds. *Sexual practices and the medieval church*. Buffalo, New York: Prometheus Books, 1982.

Burke, Cormac. 'St. Augustine and conjugal chastity.' *Communio* 17 (Winter 1990), pp. 545–65.

Burns, J. Patout. 'Variations on a dualist theme: Augustine on body and soul.' *Interpreting tradition: the act of theological reflection*. Ed. Jane Kopas. Progts. 29. Chico, California: Scholar's Press, 1984, pp. 13–26.

Burrus, Virginia. *Chastity as autonomy: women in the stories of apocryphal acts*. Studies in women and religion 23. Lewiston: Queenstown: Edwin Mellen Press, 1987.

Burrus, Virginia. 'The heretical woman as symbol in Alexander, Athanasius, Epiphanius and Jerome.' *Harvard theology review*, 84, 3 (1991), pp. 229–48.

Burrus, Virginia. 'Word and flesh: the bodies and sexuality of ascetic women in Christian antiquity.' *Journal of feminist studies in religion*, 10. 1 (1994), pp. 27–52.

Callam, Daniel. 'Clerical continence in the fourth century: three papal decretals.' *Theological studies*. 41, (March 1980), pp. 3–50.

Cameron, Averil, ed. *History as text: the writing of ancient history*. Chapel Hill and London: University of North Carolina Press, 1989.

Caplan, Patricia, ed. *The cultural construction of sexuality*. London and New York: Tavistock Press, 1987.

Capps, Donald E., ed. 'Symposium on St. Augustine's Confessions.' *Journal for the scientific study of religion*. 25. 1 (March 1986), pp. 56–115.

Castelli, Elizabeth. 'Virginity and its meaning for women's sexuality in early Christianity.' *Journal of Feminist Studies in Religion* 2, 1, (Spring 1986), pp. 61–88.

Christ, Carol. 'Why women need the goddess.' Reprinted in *The laughter of Aphrodite: reflections on a journey to the Goddess*. San Francisco: Harper and Row, 1987, pp. 117–34.

Christ, Carol P. and Judith Plaskow, eds. *Womanspirit rising: a feminist reader in religion*. San Francisco: Harper and Row, 1979.

Clark, Elizabeth A. 'Adam's only companion: Augustine and the early Christian debate on marriage' *Recherches Augustiniennes*, XXI (1986), pp. 139–62.

Clark, Elizabeth A. 'Ideology, history, and the construction of "woman" in late ancient Christianity.' *Journal of Early Christian Studies*, 2, 2 (1994), pp. 155–184.

Clark, Elizabeth A. *Jerome, Chrysostom and friends*. Studies in women and religion 2. Lewiston, Queenstown: Edwin Mellen Press, 1979.

Clark, Elizabeth A. 'New perspectives on the Origenist controversy:

human embodiment and ascetic strategies.' *Church history*, 59 (June 1990), pp. 145–62.

Clark, Elizabeth A. 'Sex, shame and rhetoric: en-gendering early Christian ethics.' *Journal of the American Academy of Religion*, LIX, 2 (1990), pp. 221–45.

Clark, Elizabeth A. 'Theory and practice in late antique asceticism: Jerome, Chrysostom and Augustine.' *Journal of Feminist Studies in Religion*, 5, 2(1989), pp. 25–46.

Clark, Elizabeth A., ed. *Ascetic piety and women's faith; essays on late ancient Christianity*. Studies in women and religion 20. Lewiston, Queenstown: Edwin Mellen Press, 1986.

Clark, Stephen B. *Man and woman in Christ: an examination of the roles of men and women in light of scripture and the social sciences*. Ann Arbor, Michigan: Servant Books, 1980.

Cooper, John C. 'The basic philosophical and theological notions of St. Augustine.' *Augustinian studies*, 15 (1984), pp. 93–113.

Coriden, James, ed. *Sexism and church law: equal rights and affirmative action*. New York: Paulist Press, 1977.

Courcelle, Pierre. *Les Confessions de St. Augustin dans le tradition littéraire*. Paris: Etudes Augustiniennes, 1963.

Courcelle, Pierre. *Recherches sur les confessions de St. Augustin*. Paris: De Boccard Press, 1950.

Coyle, J. Kevin. 'In praise of Monica: a note on the Ostia experience of Confessions IX.' *Augustinian studies*, 13 (1982), pp. 87–96.

Davies, Bronwyn. 'Lived and imaginary narratives and their place in taking oneself up as a gendered being.' *Australian Psychologist*, 25, 3(1990), pp. 318–32.

Davies, J. G. *The early Christian church*. London: Weidenfeld and Nicholson, 1965.

Davies, Stevan. *The revolt of the widows: the social world of the apocryphal Acts*. Carbondale, Illinois: Southern Illinois University Press, 1980.

Devereux, George. 'The psychology of feminine genital bleeding: an analysis of Mohave Indian puberty and menstrual rites.' *International Journal of Psychoanalysis*, 21(1950), pp. 237–57.

Dinnerstein, Dorothy. '*The rocking of the cradle and the ruling of the world*.' London: Souvenir Press, 1978.

Dittes, James, E. 'Augustine: search for a fail-safe God to trust.' *Journal for the scientific study of religion* 25, 1 (March 1986), pp. 57–63.

Dixon, Suzanne. *The Roman mother*. London and Sydney: Croom Helm Ltd, 1988.

Donaldson, James, *Woman: her position and influence in ancient Greece and Rome, and among the early Christians*. Frankfurt/Main: Minerva Verlag GMBH, [1907] 1984.

Douglas, Mary. *Natural symbols: explorations in cosmology.* Middlesex: Penguin education, 1970, 1973.

Douglas, Mary. *Purity and danger: an analysis of concepts of pollution and taboo.* London: Routledge & Kegan Paul, 1966.

Douglas, Mary. *Risk and blame: Essays in cultural theory.* London and New York: Routledge, 1992.

Duffy, Stephen S. 'Our hearts of darkness: original sin revisited.' *Theological studies,* 49, 4 (December 1988), pp. 597–622.

Dutton, Marsha L. ' "When I was a child": spiritual infancy and God's maternity in Augustine's *Confessiones.' Collectanea Augustiniana: Augustine: 'Second founder of the faith'.* Eds. Joseph C. Schnaubelt and Frederick Van Fleteren. New York: Peter Lang, 1990, pp. 113–40.

Elizondo, Virgil and Norbet Greinacher, eds. *Concilium: women in a men's church,* 134, 4. Edinburgh: T. & T. Clark, 1980.

Evans, G. R. *Augustine on evil.* Cambridge: Cambridge University Press, 1982.

Fenn, Richard. 'Magic in language and ritual: notes on Augustine's Confessions.' *Journal for the scientific study of religion,* 25, 1 (March 1986), pp. 77–91.

Ferguson, Everett, ed. *Encyclopedia of early Christianity.* Garland reference library of the humanities, Vol. 846. New York: Garland Publishing, 1990.

Ferrari, Leo C. 'The boyhood beatings of St. Augustine.' *Augustinian studies,* 5(1974), pp. 1–14.

Ferrari, Leo C. 'The dreams of Monica in St. Augustine's Confessions.' *Augustinian studies,* 10 (1979), pp. 3–18.

Finley, M. I. 'The silent women of Rome.' *Horizon,* 5(1965), pp. 57–64.

Fiorenza, Elisabeth Schüssler. *In memory of her: a feminist reconstruction of Christian origins.* London: SCM Press, 1983.

Foucault, Michel. *The history of sexuality,* Vols. 1–3. Trans. Robert Hurley. New York: Vintage Books, [French edn 1984] 1990.

Fredrickson, P. 'Augustine and his analysts: the possibility of a psychohistory.' *Sounds,* 61(Summer 1978), pp. 206–77.

Fredriksen, Paula. 'Paul and Augustine: conversion narratives, orthodox traditions, and the retrospective self.' *Journal of theological studies,* NS, 37, Pt. 1 (April 1986), pp. 3–34.

French, Marilyn. *Beyond power: on women men and morals.* Glasgow: Collins/Abacus Books, 1986.

Frend, W. H. C. 'The Divjak letters: new light on Augustine's problems 416–428.' *Journal of ecclesiastical history.* 34 (October 1983), pp. 497–512.

Fuchs, Eric. *Sexual desire and love: origins and history of the Christian ethic of sexuality and marriage*. Trans. Marsha Daigle. Cambridge: James Clark & Co., 1983.

Gardner, Jane F. *Women in Roman law and society*. London/Sydney: Croom Helm Ltd., 1986.

Garnsey, P. and R. Saller. *The Roman empire: economy, society and culture*. Berkeley and Los Angeles: Duckworth and Son Inc., 1987.

Gay, Volney. 'Augustine: the reader as selfobject.' *Journal for the scientific study of religion*, 25, 1 (March 1986), pp. 64–75.

Goldenberg, Naomi. 'Archetypal theory and the separation of mind and body: reason enough to turn to Freud.' *Journal of feminist studies in religion*. 1, 1 (Spring 1985), pp. 55–72.

Gould, Roger L. *Transformations: growth and change in adult life*. New York: Simon and Schuster, 1978.

Grubbs, Judith Evans. 'Constantine and the imperial legislation on the family.' *The Theodosian Code: studies in the imperial law of late antiquity*. Eds. Jill Harries and Ian Wood. London: Duckworth, 1993, pp. 120–42.

Gryson, Roger. *The ministry of women in the early church*. Trans. Jean Laporte, and Mary Louise Hall. Minnesota: The Liturgical Press, 1976.

Hall, Nor, *The moon and the virgin: reflections on the archetypal feminine*. New York: Harper and Row Publishers/Harper Colophon Books, 1980.

Hamilton, A. 'The Confessions: autobiographical theology.' *Colloquium*. 17, 1 (October 1984), pp. 33–42.

Harding, M. Esther. *Women's mysteries: ancient and modern*. [1955] Reprinted, London: Rider, 1982.

Hayter, Mary. *The new Eve in Christ: the use and abuse of the Bible in the debate about women in the church*. London: SPCK, 1987.

Heine, Susan. *Women and early Christianity*. Trans. John Bowden. London: SCM Press, 1987.

Hess, Beth B. and Myra Marx Ferree, eds. *Analyzing gender: a handbook of social science research*. Newbury Park: Sage Publications, 1987.

Hill, Edmund. 'Comment: St. Augustine's two vocations.' *New Blackfriars*. 67, 793/794 (July/August 1986), pp. 302–5.

Hill, Edmund. 'Response: St. Augustine and R.R.R. on women.' *New Blackfriars* 66, 785 (November 1985), pp. 503–4.

Hill, Edmund. 'Trinitarian politics or towards an Augustinian Marxism?' *Prudentia*, 5, 2 (1973), pp. 91–98.

Holte, Ragnar. '*Logos spermatikos*: Christian and ancient philosophies according to St. Justin's Apologies' Trans. Tina Pierce. *Studia theologica*. XII (1958), pp. 109–168.

Hunter, David G. 'Augustinian pessimism? A new look at Augustine's teaching on sex, marriage and celibacy.' *Augustinian studies*, 25 (1994), 153–177.

Hunter, David G. 'Helvidius, Jovinian, and the virginity of Mary in late fourth century Rome.' *Journal of early Christianity*, 1, 1 (1993), pp. 47–71.

Hunter, David G. 'Resistance to the virginal idea of late fourth century Rome: the case of Jovinian.' *Theological studies*, 48, 1 (March 1987), pp. 45–64.

Hunter, David G. 'On the sin of Adam and Eve: a little known defence of marriage and childrearing by Ambrosiaster.' *Harvard Theological Review*, 82 (1989), pp. 283–99.

Hunter, David G. 'The paradise of patriarchy: Ambrosiaster on woman as (not) God's image.' *Journal of theological studies*, n.s. 43, 2 (1992), pp. 447–69.

Irvine, Dorothy, 'The ministry of women in the early church: the archeological evidence.' *Duke Divinity School review*, 45, 2 (1980), pp. 76–86.

Jensen, Robin. 'Archaeology and North African baptism: the ambiguity of material remains.' *NAPS*, Plenary Address, Chicago: May, 1994.

Jewett, Paul K. *Man as male and female: a study in sexual relationships from a theological point of view*. Grand Rapids, Michigan: Wm. B. Eerdmans, 1975.

Kaufman, Peter Iver. 'Augustine, martyrs and misery.' *Church history*, 63, 1 (March 1994), pp. 1–14.

Klein, Melanie. *The psychoanalysis of children*. Trans. Alix Strachey. Ed. Ernest Jones. International psycho-analytical library 22. London: Hogarth Press, 1932, 1950.

Kliever, Lonnie D. 'Confessions of unbelief: in quest of the vital life.' *Journal for the scientific study of religion*, 25, 1 (March 1986), pp. 102–115.

Kraemer, Ross S. 'The conversion of women to ascetic Christianity.' *Signs*, 6, 2 (1980), pp. 298–307.

Kraemer, Ross S. *Her share of the blessings: women's religions among pagans, Jews and Christians in the Greco-Roman world*. New York: Oxford University Press, 1992.

Laeuchli, Samuel. *Power and sexuality: the emergence of canon law at the Synod of Elvira*. Philadelphia: Temple University Press, 1972.

Laing, Gordon. 'Roman religious survivals in Christianity.' *Environmental factors in Christian history*. Eds. John Thomas McNeill, Matthew Spink, Harold R. Willoughby. Port Washington NY: Kenuckat Press, 1970, pp. 72–90.

La Porte, Jean and F. Ellen Weaver. 'Augustine on women: relationships and teachings.' *Augustinian studies*, 12 (1981), pp. 115–31.

Laqueur, Thomas. *Making sex: body and gender from the Greeks to Freud.* Cambridge: Harvard University Press, 1990.

Laqueur, Thomas. 'Orgasm, generation and the politics of reproductive biology.' *Representations*, 14 (1986), pp. 1–41.

Lawless, George. *Augustine of Hippo and his monastic rule.* Oxford: Clarendon Press, 1987.

Loewenstein, Sophie. 'A feminist perspective.' *Handbook of clinical social work.* Eds. A. Rosenblatt and D. Waldfogel. San Francisco: Jossey-Bass Publishers, 1983, pp. 518–48.

Luke, Helen M. *Woman: earth and spirit: the feminine in symbol and myth.* New York: Crossroad Press, 1984.

Lynch, John E. 'Marriage and celibacy of the clergy, the discipline of the western church: an historico-canonical synopsis.' *The Jurist*, 32 (1972), Part I, pp. 214–38, Part II, pp. 189–212.

MacMullen, Ramsey. 'Woman in public in the Roman empire.' *Historia*, 29 (1980), 208–18.

MacMullen, Ramsay. *Christianizing the Roman Empire (AD 100–400).* Newhaven/London: Yale University Press, 1984.

Markus, R. A. *Christianity in the Roman world.* New York: Scribner's Sons, 1974.

Markus, R. A. *The end of ancient Christianity.* Cambridge: Cambridge University Press, [1990] 1993.

Marshall, A. J. 'Roman women and the provinces.' *Ancient society*, 6 (1975), pp. 109–27.

McLeese, C. E. *Augustine and sexism: interpretation and evaluation of* The good of marriage *and* Holy virginity. Unpublished thesis: Université de Montréal, 1994.

McNamara, Jo Ann. '*Matres patriae/Matres ecclesiae*, women of the Roman empire.' *Becoming visible: women in European history*, 2nd edition. Eds. Renate Bridenthal, Claudia Koonz and Susan Stuard. Boston: Houghton Mifflin Company, 1987, pp. 107–29.

McNamara, Jo Anne, 'Muffled voices: the lives of consecrated women in the fourth century.' *Medieval religious women. Vol. 1. Distant echoes.* Eds. John A. Nichols and Lillian Thomas Shank. Cistercian studies series 71. Kalamazoo: Cistercian Publications Inc., 1984, pp. 11–30.

McNamara, Sr Marie Aquinas. *Friends and friendship for Saint Augustine.* New York: Alba House, 1964.

Meier, John P. 'On the veiling of hermeneutics (1 Cor. 11. 2–16).' *Catholic Biblical Quarterly*, 40 (1978), pp. 202–26.

Meeks, Wayne. 'The image of the androgyne: some uses of a symbol in earliest Christianity.' *History of religions.* 13 (1973), 165–208.

Meyer, Ben E., and E. P. Sanders eds. *Jewish and Christian self-definition. Vol. 3. Self definition in the craeco-Roman world.* London: SCM Press, 1980.

Miethe, T. L. 'St. Augustine and sense knowledge.' *Augustinian studies*, 8 (1977), pp. 1–19.

Miles, M. R. *Augustine on the body*. Missoula: Scholar's Press, 1979.

Miles, M. R. 'The evidence of our eyes: patristic studies and popular Christianity in the fourth century.' *Studia patristica*, XVIII. Vol. 1. Ed. Elizabeth A. Livingstone. Kalamazoo: Cistercian Publications, 1985, pp. 59–63.

Miller, Patricia Cox. 'The blazing body: ascetic desire in Jerome's letter to Eustochium,' *Journal of early Christian studies*, 1. 1 (Spring 1993), pp. 21–45.

Neuer, Werner. *The great mother: an analysis of the archetype*. Trans. Ralph Manheim. Princeton, New Jersey: Princeton University Press, 1963.

Neumann E. *Man and woman in Christian perspective* London: Hodder and Stoughton, 1990.

Noonan, John T. 'Marital affection in the Canonists.' *Studia Gratiana*, 12 (1967), pp. 481–9.

O'Connell, R. J. 'Isaiah's mothering God in Augustine's Confessions.' *Thought* 58 (June 1983), pp. 188–206.

O'Connell, R. J. 'The God of St Augustine's imagination.' *Thought*, 57 (March 1982), pp. 30–40.

O'Meara, J. J. 'The works of St Augustine and a bibliographic Guide' Adapted in *St Augustine and his influence throughout the ages*, by H. Marrou. Trans. by Patrick Hepburn Scott. New York: Harper and Bros., 1957, pp. 182–86.

O'Meara, J. J. 'Virgil and St Augustine: the Roman background to Christian sexuality.' *Augustinus*, 13 (1968), pp. 307–26.

Oddie, William. *What will happen to God? feminism and the reconstruction of Christian belief*. London: SPCK, 1984.

Ortner, Sherry, and Harriet Whitehead, eds. *Sexual meanings: the cultural construction of gender and sexuality*. Cambridge: Cambridge University Press, 1981.

Pagels, Elaine. ' "Freedom from necessity": philosophic and personal dimensions of Christian conversion.' *Genesis 1—3 in the history of exegesis: intrigue in the garden*. Ed. Gregory A. Robbins. Lewiston, New York: Edwin Mellen Press, 1988, pp. 67–98.

Padgug, Robert A. 'Sexual matters: on conceptualizing sexuality in history.' *Radical History Review*, 20 (Spring/Summer 1979), pp. 3–23.

Pateman, Carole. ' "The disorder of women": women, love and the sense of justice.' *Ethics: an international journal of social, political and legal philosophy*, 91, 1 (1980), pp. 20–34.

Pincherle, Alberto. 'The Confessions of St Augustine: a reappraisal.' *Augustinian studies*. 7 (1976), pp. 119–133.

Plaskow, J. *Sex, sin and grace: women's experience and the theologies of*

Reinhold Niebuhr and Paul Tillich. Washington: University Press of America, 1980.

Plaskow, Judith and Joan Arnold, eds. *Women and religion.* Rev. edn, Montana: Scholars Press for the American Academy of Religion, 1974.

Power, Kim E. 'Philosophy, medicine and sexual gender in Ambrose of Milan.' *Proceedings: Ancient history in a modern university: a tribute to Edwin Judge.* Eds. Alanna Nobbs, Ted Nixon, Rosalin de Kearsley and Tom Hillard. Sydney, Primavera Press, 1995 (forthcoming).

Power, Kim E. 'The rehabilitation of Eve in Ambrose of Milan's *De institutione virginis.' Proceedings: Religion in the ancient world.* Ed. M. Dillon. Amsterdam: Adolf Hakkert, 1995 (forthcoming).

Rader, Rosemary. *Breaking boundaries: male/female friendship in early Christian communities.* New York: Paulist Press, 1983.

Ramirez, J. Roland E. 'Demythologizing Augustine as a great sinner.' *Augustinian studies.* 12 (1981), pp. 61–88.

Ranke-Heinemann, Uta. *Eunuchs for heaven: the Catholic church and sexuality.* Trans. John Brownjohn. London: Andre Deutsch, 1990.

Rawson, Beryl, ed. *Marriage, divorce and children in ancient Rome.* Oxford: Clarendon Press, 1991.

Rawson, Beryl. 'Roman concubinage and other de facto marriages.' *Transactions of the American Philological Association,* 104 (1974), pp. 279–305.

Rawson, Beryl, ed. *The family in ancient Rome: new perspectives.* London & Sydney: Croom Helm Ltd., 1986.

Ricouer, Paul. 'Freudianism and Augustine's Confessions.' *Journal of the American academy of religion,* 53, (March 1985), pp. 93–114.

Rizzuto, Ana-Maria. *The birth of the living God: a psychoanalytic study.* Chicago: University of Chicago Press, 1979.

Rossi, Mary Ann. 'Priesthood, precedent, and prejudice: on recovering the women priests of early Christianity. Containing a translation from the Italian of "Notes on the female priesthood in antiquity" by Georgio Otranto,' *Journal of feminist studies in religion,* 7, 1 (Spring 1991), pp. 73–94.

Rousselle, Aline, *Porneia: on desire and the body in antiquity.* Trans. Felicia Pheasant. Oxford: Basil Blackwell, 1988.

Rowan, John. 'Psychic celibacy.' *Sex role stereotyping.* Eds. Oonagh Hartnett, Gill Boden and Mary Fuller. London: Tavistock Publications, 1979, pp. 57–68.

Ruether, Rosemary Radford, ed. *Religion and sexism: images of women in the Jewish and Christian traditions.* New York: Simon and Schuster, 1974.

Ruether, Rosemary Radford. 'The liberation of Christology from patriarchy.' *New Blackfriars* (July-August 1985), pp. 324–35.

Ruether, Rosemary Radford. *Womanguides: readings towards a feminist theology.* Boston: Beacon Press, 1985.

Salisbury, Joyce. *Church Fathers, independent virgins.* London: Verso, 1991.

Sayers, Janet. *Sexual contradictions: psychology, psychoanalysis and feminism.* London: Tavistock Publications, 1986.

Schaps, D. 'The women least mentioned: etiquette and women's names.' *Classical Quarterly,* n.s. 27 (1977), pp. 323–30.

Scott, Joan W. 'Gender: a useful category of historical analysis.' *American History Review* (1986), pp. 1053–75.

Seidenberg, Robert. 'Is anatomy destiny?' *Psychoanalysis and women.* Ed. Jean Baker Miller. Harmondsworth, Middlesex: Penguin Books, 1978, pp. 306–9.

Shapiro, Judith. 'Anthropology and the study of gender.' *Soundings,* 64, 4 (1981), pp. 445–65.

Shaw, Brent. 'The family in late antiquity: the experience of Augustine.' *Past and present,* 115 (May 1987), pp. 3–51.

Sissa, Guilia *Greek virginity.* Cambridge, Mass: Harvard University Press, 1991.

Sly, Dorothy. *Philo's perceptions of woman.* Atlanta: Scholars Press, 1990.

Spelman, Elizabeth. 'Woman as body: ancient and contemporary views.' *Feminist studies,* 8, 1 (Spring 1982), pp. 109–131.

Spong, John Selby. *Born of a woman: a bishop rethinks the birth of Jesus.* HarperSanFrancisco, 1992.

Tavard, George H. *Women in the Christian tradition.* London: University of Notre Dame Press, 1973.

Te Selle, Eugene. 'Augustine as client and theorist.' *Journal for the scientific study of religion,* 25, 1 (March 1986), 92–101.

Tilley, Maureen A. 'The ascetic body and the (un)making of the martyr.' JAAR, LIX, 3 (1991), pp. 467–79.

Torjesen, Karen Jo. *When women were priests: women's leadership in the early church and the scandal of their subordination in the rise of Christianity.* HarperSanFrancisco, 1993.

van Bavel, Tarcisius. *Ever ancient . . . ever new . . . Augustine's view on women.* Villanova: Augustinian Press, 1990.

van der Meer, F. *Augustine the bishop: the life work of a father of the church.* Trans. B. Battershaw and G. R. Lamb. London: Sheed and Ward, 1961.

van Eijk, Ton H. C. 'Marriage and virginity, death and immortality.' *Epektasis: mélanges patristiques offerts au Cardinal Jean Daniélou.* Eds. Jacques Fontaine et Charles Kannengiesser. Paris: Beauchesne, 1972, pp. 209–35.

van Oort, J. 'Augustine on sexual concupiscence and original sin.,'

Studia patristica XXII. Ed. Elizabeth A. Livingstone. Leuven: Peeters Press, 1989, pp. 382–386.

Vesey, Mark. 'St Augustine: *Confessions.*' *Augustinian studies*, 24, (1993), pp. 163–81.

Walton, Heather. 'Theology of desire.' *Theology and sexuality*, 1, 1. (Spring 1994), p. 41.

Warner, Marina. *Alone of all her sex: the myth and cult of the Virgin Mary*. New York: Pocket Books, 1976.

Wuellner, W., ed. *Colloquies 14, 17, 34, 35, 46 of the Center for hermeneutical studies in Hellenistic and modern culture*. Berkeley. The Center for hermeneutical studies in Hellenistic and modern culture, 1975, 1975, 1980, 1980, 1983.

Yarbrough, Anne. 'Christianization in the fourth century; the example of Roman women.' *Church history*, 45, 2 (June 1976), pp. 149–63.

INDEX

ALSO PUBLISHED BY CONTINUUM

Marla J. Selvidge
Notorious Voices
Feminist Biblical Interpretation, 1500–1920

An examination of the prefeminist writings of women and men who reinterpreted the Bible from a woman-centered perspective.

Edward Peter Nolan
Cry Out and Write
A Feminine Poetics of Revelation

An analysis of the writings of Hildegard of Bingen, Vibia Perpetua, and Julian of Norwich. "A powerful contribution to the theory of interpretation."
— *R.J. Schoeck*

Andrew Kadel
Matrology
A Bibliography of Writings by Christian Women from the First to the Fifteen Centuries

Includes original and English-language editions, along with brief notes on the particular author and her work. "Accessible and thorough....One could not ask for a more conscientious bibliography."
— *Choice*

Bernard McGinn, Editor
Meister Eckhart and the Beguine Mystics
Hadewijch of Brabant, Mechthild of Magdeburg,
and Marguerite Porete

"The essays are all excellent....Taken as a whole,
this book about later medieval 'vernacular
theology' (McGinn's apt phrase) is superbly
researched, suitably nuanced, challenging, and
above all illuminating. Highly recommended."
—*Booklist*

Karen Green
The Woman of Reason
Feminism, Humanism, and Political Thought

"An original and important contribution to the
history of feminist theory."
—*Josephine Donovan*